The Kennedys and Cuba

THE KENNEDYS AND CUBA

*The Declassified
Documentary History*

EDITED WITH COMMENTARY BY

Mark J. White

Ivan R. Dee

CHICAGO 1999

THE KENNEDYS AND CUBA. Copyright © 1999 by Mark J. White. All rights
reserved, including the right to reproduce this book or portions thereof in any form. For
information, address: Ivan R. Dee, Publisher, 1332 North Halsted Street, Chicago
60622. Manufactured in the United States of America and printed on acid-free paper.

Library of Congress Cataloging-in-Publication Data:
The Kennedys and Cuba : the declassified documentary history / edited with
    commentary by Mark J. White.
        p.   cm.
    Includes bibliographical references and index.
    ISBN 1-56663-265-X (acid-free paper)
        1. United States—Foreign relations—Cuba Sources.   2. Cuba—Foreign
relations—United States Sources.   3. United States—Foreign relations—1961–1963
Sources.   4. Kennedy, John F. (John Fitzgerald), 1917–1963.   5. Kennedy, Robert
F., 1925–1968.   I. White, Mark J.
E183.8.C9K46   1999
327.7307291'09'046—dc21   99-28417

For Barry Riccio —
gifted historian, inspirational friend

I wish to thank Ivan Dee, Lloyd Gardner, Reginald Horsman, and Barry Riccio for encouraging me to take on this project.

Contents

Leading Figures Mentioned in the Text

DEAN G. ACHESON, ad hoc adviser to President Kennedy and former secretary of state

KONRAD ADENAUER, chancellor of West Germany

ALEXANDER A. AKALOVSKY, interpreter for President Kennedy

ADMIRAL GEORGE W. ANDERSON, chief of naval operations between August 1961 and August 1963

WILLIAM ATTWOOD, U.S. delegate to the United Nations

GEORGE W. BALL, under secretary of state for economic affairs, February–December 1961; thereafter under secretary of state

TRACY BARNES, assistant deputy director (plans) for covert action, Central Intelligence Agency

FULGENCIO BATISTA, dictator of Cuba before Fidel Castro's revolution in 1959

DAVID BELL, budget director

ADOLF A. BERLE, chairman of the Department of State Task Force on Latin America

RICHARD M. BISSELL, JR., deputy director for plans, CIA, until February 1962

CHARLES E. BOHLEN, ambassador to France from September 1962

GEORGI BOLSHAKOV, KGB officer

CHESTER BOWLES, under secretary of state, January–December 1961; thereafter special representative and adviser on African, Asian, and Latin American affairs

IGOR D. BUBNOV, third secretary at the Soviet embassy in Washington

MCGEORGE BUNDY, special assistant to the president for National Security Affairs

WILLIAM P. BUNDY, deputy assistant secretary of defense for international security affairs

ADMIRAL ARLEIGH A. BURKE, chief of naval operations until August 1961

HOWARD L. BURRIS, military aide to Vice-President Lyndon B. Johnson

GENERAL CHARLES P. CABELL, deputy director, CIA, until January 1962

JOSEPH A. CALIFANO, secretary of the army's special assistant

HOMER E. CAPEHART, senator from Indiana (Republican)

LIEUTENANT GENERAL MARSHALL S. CARTER, deputy director, CIA, from April 1962

FIDEL CASTRO, prime minister of Cuba

RAUL CASTRO, minister of the armed forces of Cuba

GORDON CHASE, National Security Council staff member

CLARK CLIFFORD, informal adviser to President Kennedy

BRIGADIER GENERAL CHESTER V. CLIFTON, military aide to President Kennedy

WYMBERLEY DeR. COERR, deputy assistant secretary of state for inter-American affairs

ANDREW CORDIER, dean of Columbia University's School of International Relations

STERLING J. COTTRELL, deputy assistant secretary, Bureau of Inter-American Affairs, and coordinator of Cuban affairs, Department of State, after January 1963

BRIGADIER GENERAL WILLIAM H. CRAIG, Department of Defense project officer for Operation Mongoose until June 1962

PATRICK H. DEAN, British representative at the United Nations

GENERAL CHARLES DE GAULLE, president of France

ADMIRAL ROBERT L. DENNISON, commander-in-chief, Atlantic

C. DOUGLAS DILLON, secretary of the treasury

ANATOLY F. DOBRYNIN, Soviet ambassador to the United States after March 1962

JAMES B. DONOVAN, New York attorney involved in negotiations for the release of prisoners captured at the Bay of Pigs

ALLEN W. DULLES, director, CIA, until November 1961

J. S. EARMAN, executive assistant to the CIA director until April 1962

DWIGHT D. EISENHOWER, president of the United States until January 1961

WALTER ELDER, executive assistant to the CIA director from April 1962

ALEXSANDR FEKLISOV, KGB officer

THOMAS K. FINLETTER, U.S. ambassador to the North Atlantic Treaty Organization (NATO)

DESMOND FITZGERALD, director of plans, CIA

ARTURO FRONDIZI, president of Argentina

J. WILLIAM FULBRIGHT, senator from Arkansas (Democrat)

ROSWELL L. GILPATRIC, deputy secretary of defense

ARTHUR GOLDBERG, secretary of labor

BARRY M. GOLDWATER, senator from Arizona (Republican)

RICHARD N. GOODWIN, assistant special counsel to the president until November 1961; thereafter deputy assistant secretary of state for inter-American affairs

JOÃO GOULART, president of Brazil

MAJOR GENERAL DAVID W. GRAY, chief of the Subsidiary Activities Division, Plans and Policy, Joint Staff, Joint Chiefs of Staff

ANDREI A. GROMYKO, Soviet minister of foreign affairs

ERNESTO (CHE) GUEVARA, president of the Cuban National Bank

CHARLES HALLECK, minority leader in the House of Representatives (Republican, Indiana)

RAYMOND HARE, U.S. ambassador to Turkey

W. AVERELL HARRIMAN, under secretary of state for political affairs from April 1963

BRIGADIER GENERAL BENJAMIN T. HARRIS, Department of Defense project officer for Operation Mongoose from June 1962

WILLIAM K. HARVEY, chief of Task Force W, Directorate for Plans, CIA; project officer for Operation Mongoose

COLONEL JACK HAWKINS, chief of Paramilitary Operations, Branch 4, Western Hemisphere Division, Directorate for Plans, CIA

WALTER HELLER, chairman of the President's Council of Economic Advisers

RICHARD M. HELMS, chief of operations, Directorate for Plans, CIA, until February 1962; thereafter deputy director for plans

ROGER HILSMAN, director of the Bureau of Intelligence and Research, Department of State, from February 1961

LISA HOWARD, correspondent for the American Broadcasting Company

ROBERT A. HURWITCH, officer, Bureau of Inter-American Affairs, Department of State; project officer for Operation Mongoose

LYNDON B. JOHNSON, vice-president of the United States

U. ALEXIS JOHNSON, deputy under secretary of state for political affairs from April 1961

KENNETH B. KEATING, senator from New York (Republican)

JOHN F. KENNEDY, president of the United States

ROBERT F. KENNEDY, attorney general

SHERMAN KENT, chairman of the CIA's Board of National Estimates

NIKITA S. KHRUSHCHEV, chairman of the Council of Ministers of the USSR

COLONEL J. C. KING, chief, Western Hemisphere Division, Directorate for Plans, CIA

WILLIAM E. KNOX, U.S. businessman

VASILY V. KUZNETSOV, Soviet first deputy minister of foreign affairs

BRIGADIER GENERAL EDWARD G. LANSDALE, deputy assistant for special operations to the secretary of defense until May 1961; thereafter assistant for special operations; also chief of operations for Operation Mongoose after November 1961

CARLOS LECHUGA HEVIA, Cuban delegate to the United Nations

GENERAL CURTIS E. LEMAY, chief of staff, U.S. Air Force

GENERAL LYMAN L. LEMNITZER, chairman of the Joint Chiefs of Staff until October 1, 1962

WALTER LIPPMANN, distinguished newspaper columnist

HAROLD MACMILLAN, British prime minister

THOMAS C. MANN, assistant secretary of state for inter-American affairs until April 1961

EDWIN M. MARTIN, assistant secretary of state for economic affairs until May 1962; thereafter assistant secretary of state for inter-American affairs

JOHN J. MCCLOY, presidential adviser and chairman of the Coordinating Committee for U.S.-Soviet Negotiations over Cuba at the United Nations

JOHN A. MCCONE, director, CIA, from November 1961

ROBERT S. MCNAMARA, secretary of defense

LEONARD C. MEEKER, State Department's deputy legal adviser

ANASTAS I. MIKOYAN, Soviet first deputy chairman of the Council of Ministers

JOSÉ MIRÓ CARDONA, president of the Cuban Revolutionary Council (a leading Cuban exile organization)

EDWARD R. MURROW, director of the U.S. Information Agency

PAUL H. NITZE, assistant secretary of defense for international security affairs

RICHARD M. NIXON, Republican presidential candidate in 1960; vice-president of the United States until January 1961; candidate for the governorship of California in 1962

GENERAL LAURIS NORSTAD, supreme commander of Allied Forces in Europe

THOMAS A. PARROTT, assistant to the president's military representative

JAMES RESTON, *New York Times* correspondent

WALT W. ROSTOW, deputy special assistant to the president for national security affairs until December 1961; thereafter counselor of the Department of State and chairman of the Policy Planning Council

DEAN RUSK, secretary of state

BERTRAND RUSSELL, British philosopher

RICHARD B. RUSSELL, senator from Georgia (Democrat)

PIERRE SALINGER, press secretary for President Kennedy

LEVERETT SALTONSTALL, senator from Massachusetts (Republican)

JOHN SCALI, correspondent for the American Broadcasting Company

ARTHUR M. SCHLESINGER, JR., special assistant to the president

HERBERT SCOVILLE, JR., deputy director for research, CIA

VLADIMIR S. SEMENOV, Soviet deputy foreign minister

BROMLEY SMITH, acting executive secretary of the National Security Council until August 1961; thereafter executive secretary

THEODORE C. SORENSEN, special counsel to the president

ADLAI E. STEVENSON, U.S. permanent representative at the United Nations

VICTOR M. SUKHODREV, interpreter for Soviet premier Khrushchev

WALTER C. SWEENEY, commander-in-chief, Tactical Air Command

GENERAL MAXWELL D. TAYLOR, chairman of the Cuba Study Group, April–June 1961; president's military representative from July 1961 until October 1962; thereafter chairman of the Joint Chiefs of Staff

U THANT, secretary general of the United Nations

LLEWELLYN E. THOMPSON, U.S. ambassador to the Soviet Union, and then ambassador-at-large, Department of State, from October 1962

WILLIAM R. TYLER, assistant secretary of state for European affairs

STEWART UDALL, secretary of the interior

RENE VALLEJO ORTIZ, personal aide to Castro

CYRUS R. VANCE, secretary of the army

CARL VINSON, member of the House of Representatives (Democrat, Georgia); chairman of the House Armed Services Committee

LIEUTENANT GENERAL EARLE G. WHEELER, director of the Joint Staff, Joint Chiefs of Staff

JEROME B. WIESNER, science adviser to President Kennedy

DONALD M. WILSON, deputy director, U.S. Information Agency

ROBERT F. WOODWARD, assistant secretary of state for inter-American affairs, July 1961–March 1962

Abbreviations Used in the Text

AFB, air force base
AG, attorney general
ARA, Bureau of Inter-American Affairs, Department of State
CEF, Cuban Expeditionary Force
CIA, Central Intelligence Agency
CINCLANT, commander-in-chief, Atlantic
CINCSTRIKE, commander-in-chief, Strike command
COMNAVBASE, GTMO, commander, naval base, Guantanamo
CRAF, Cuban Revolutionary Air Force
CRC, Consejo Revolucionario Cubano, Cuban Revolutionary Council
DCI, director, Central Intelligence Agency
DDCI, deputy director, Central Intelligence Agency
DOD, Department of Defense
DRE, Directorio Revolucionario Estudiantil, Student Revolutionary Directorate
ExComm, Executive Committee (of the National Security Council)
FBI, Federal Bureau of Investigation
FBIS, Foreign Broadcast Information Service
GCI, Ground Control Intercept
GMO, G'Mo, Guantánamo, U.S. naval base in Cuba
HEW, Department of Health, Education and Welfare
ICRC, International Committee of the Red Cross
IL–28, Soviet light bomber
INS, Immigration and Naturalization Service, Department of Justice
IRBM, intermediate-range ballistic missile
ISA, Office of International Security Affairs, Department of Defense
JCS, Joint Chiefs of Staff
KLM, Royal Dutch Airlines
LA, Latin America
LST, landing ship, tank
MEB, Marine Expeditionary Brigade
MIG, Soviet-made fighter aircraft
MRBM, medium-range ballistic missile
NATO, North Atlantic Treaty Organization

NIE, National Intelligence Estimate

NORAD, North American Air Defense Command

NRO, National Reconnaissance Office

NSAM, National Security Action Memorandum

NSC, National Security Council

NSC 5412 Committee, National Security Council committee overseeing covert operations; also known as the Special Group

NY, New York

OAS, Organization of American States

OD, operating directive

OP, operations

OPLAN, operations plan

OSD, Office of the Secretary of Defense

PAA, Pan American Airways

PNG, persona non grata

POL, petroleum, oil, and lubricants

PT, motor torpedo boat

SA-2, Soviet surface-to-air missile

SAC, Strategic Air Command

SAM, surface-to-air missile

SCCS, Special Consultative Committee on Security (OAS)

SGA, Special Group (Augmented)

SNIE, Special National Intelligence Estimate

SS-4, Soviet medium-range ballistic missile

SSM, surface-to-surface missile

SYG, secretary general of the United Nations

TAC, Tactical Air Command

TASS, Telegraphnoye Agentstvo Sovyetskogo Soyuza (Telegraph Agency of the Soviet Union)

U–2, U.S. high-altitude reconnaissance aircraft

UDT, Underwater Demolition Team

UN, United Nations

USAF, United States Air Force

USG, United States government

USIA, United States Information Agency

USIB, United States Intelligence Board

USSR, Union of Soviet Socialist Republics

USUN, United States Mission to the United Nations

VOA, Voice of America

WH, Western Hemisphere

The Kennedys and Cuba

Introduction

IT IS NO EXAGGERATION to say that the political career of John F. Kennedy is centrally important to modern American history. For one thing, Kennedy was the first president in the twentieth century who was compelled to deal in a direct, concerted fashion with what has always been a fundamental issue in American society, namely race. For another, JFK had a cultural significance beyond any other modern American president. A cluster of factors—his youth, good looks, charisma, effective exploitation of the television medium, and his premature and violent death—made Kennedy an icon in American popular culture, akin to James Dean or Marilyn Monroe. As David Halberstam once put it, Kennedy was able to present himself "not just as leader, but as star." Finally, it was on Kennedy's watch that the most dangerous episode in the entire cold war epoch took place, the Cuban missile crisis, triggered in mid-October 1962 when JFK learned that Soviet Premier Nikita S. Khrushchev had deployed nuclear weapons in Cuba.[1]

The Kennedy legacy is a product not only of John Kennedy's political record and image but of the Kennedys' impact as a dynasty. The strivings of the patriarch, Joseph P. Kennedy, and brothers Robert F. Kennedy and Edward M. Kennedy, have also been important. Robert Kennedy's role was especially significant. His own tragic death in the midst of his bid for the 1968 Democratic presidential nomination enlarged the sense of myth and tragedy that had come to envelop Americans' memory of the Kennedys. In a more concrete sense, his position as attorney general and closest adviser to John Kennedy in the years from 1961 to 1963 shaped JFK's presidency in various ways. For example, Robert succeeded in persuading his brother to commit more strongly to civil rights reform in the wake of the Birmingham, Alabama, crisis in the spring of 1963, and, specifically, to introduce in Congress a bill to end segregation. The Cuban missile crisis was another crucial episode during which Robert strongly influenced JFK.[2]

---

[1] David Halberstam, "Introduction," in *The Kennedy Presidential Press Conferences* (New York, 1978), p. iii.

[2] The standard work on Robert Kennedy is Arthur M. Schlesinger, Jr., *Robert Kennedy and His Times* (Boston, 1978).

Understanding the missile crisis therefore is requisite for an appreciation of the overall legacy of John and Robert Kennedy. This involves more than examining the events of October 1962, for what historians have come to mean by the Kennedy record in the missile crisis has changed. In recent years historians have become more interested in the origins and to some degree the consequences of the October 1962 confrontation. How the Kennedys managed the missile crisis is clearly an important historical question. But so is the issue of whether their policies helped bring on the crisis in the first place, and exploring that question requires an analysis of the Kennedys' handling of Cuba in 1961–1962. A wide-ranging examination of the crisis also demands evaluation of its aftermath. During the final year of "Camelot," John and Robert Kennedy had to consider how best to handle Cuban leader Fidel Castro in the context of a crisis that had brought the United States and the Soviet Union to the brink of nuclear war, but had been resolved.[3]

Kennedy inherited the problem of Cuba from the Republican administration of President Dwight D. Eisenhower. A left-wing revolution had brought Castro to power in Cuba in 1959, after which relations between his government and Eisenhower's administration rapidly deteriorated. Castro seized control of American oil refineries and ordered a good many diplomats at the U.S. embassy in Havana to leave the country. Eisenhower, for his part, imposed economic sanctions, approved planning for a scheme to use Cuban exiles in an invasion of Cuba, and, shortly before leaving office, broke off diplomatic ties with Cuba.[4]

Given the fear that Castro generated in the United States of a Communist foothold in America's backyard, it was no surprise that Cuba became a major issue in the 1960 presidential campaign between the Democratic nominee John Kennedy and Richard M. Nixon, Eisenhower's vice-president. Candidate Kennedy used Cuba to attack Nixon. The Eisenhower-Nixon administration had been "soft" on Castro, Kennedy claimed, adding that he would take vigorous action to oust the Cuban leader. That JFK ran on an anti-Castro platform in the 1960 campaign explains in part the inimical policies toward Cuba that he would carry out as president.[5]

After defeating Nixon by the narrowest of margins, Kennedy's first decision regarding Cuba was whether to implement the CIA plan to utilize Cuban emigrés in a planned invasion—what would become the Bay of Pigs operation. He authorized revisions to the plan to make America's involvement less apparent, changes that made the operation less militarily feasible, and then gave the go-ahead for a landing at the Bay of Pigs. It turned out to be a disaster. Castro's forces easily routed the exile army. To Kennedy's embarrassment, U.S. backing for the

---

[3]An example of work on Kennedy and Cuba that dwells on the question of whether JFK's policies caused Khrushchev to put missiles in Cuba is Thomas G. Paterson, "Fixation with Cuba: The Bay of Pigs, Missile Crisis, and Covert War Against Fidel Castro," in Paterson, ed., *Kennedy's Quest for Victory: American Foreign Policy, 1961–1963* (New York, 1989).

[4]A fine study of Eisenhower's foreign policy and indeed his presidency in general is Stephen E. Ambrose, *Eisenhower: The President* (New York, 1984).

[5]Mark J. White, *The Cuban Missile Crisis* (New York, 1996), pp. 8–13.

invasion became known to the American public and the international community.[6]

The question JFK faced in the wake of the Bay of Pigs calamity was how to handle Castro given that the invasion attempt had failed. The answer that Kennedy and his advisers produced in November 1961 was Operation Mongoose, designed to provoke an anti-Castro uprising by carrying out such actions as sabotage against Cuba. Robert Kennedy was given a central role in this enterprise. In addition, in early 1962 the Kennedy administration secured Cuba's removal from the Organization of American States and thus its diplomatic isolation, imposed an economic embargo on the island, and carried out intimidating military maneuvers in the Caribbean which Castro and Khrushchev may have interpreted as rehearsals for an actual invasion of Cuba.[7]

It was in this period, the spring of 1962, that Khrushchev made the fateful decision to deploy nuclear missiles in Cuba. He seems to have been motivated by a number of concerns. Most likely he believed that JFK's consistently hostile approach toward Cuba portended an invasion of the island that had to be deterred, and that the vast lead in nuclear weapons enjoyed by the United States over the Soviet Union at the time had to be reduced. Khrushchev viewed missiles in Cuba as a solution to both these problems. Other factors, such as his need to respond to criticism from Communist China that Moscow was failing to support revolutions in the Third World, may also have prompted Khrushchev's missile gambit. With Castro's consent, a Russian military buildup on the island of Cuba, involving the delivery of troops and conventional weapons as well as nuclear missiles, began in the summer of 1962.[8]

By autumn the pressure on Kennedy to take action over Cuba had mounted. The Russian buildup, though initially assumed by most not to include nuclear weapons, was being reported in the press. The Republican party, with an eye on the November 1962 congressional elections, had no hesitation in using this issue to attack the president. He was accused of underestimating the Soviet buildup in Cuba and urged to take forceful action. In September Kennedy issued public statements seeking to allay public concerns over the situation in the Caribbean, to counter the Republican assault, and to warn Khrushchev against pushing too far in Cuba. At the covert level he intensified Operation Mongoose and accelerated the contingency planning for military action against Cuba that had been developed along with Mongoose.[9]

The Cuban missile crisis began when JFK was informed on October 16, 1962, that an American U–2 flight had identified Russian nuclear weapons in Cuba. The stakes could not have been higher, for here was a situation that threatened an apocalyptic closure to the cold war and perhaps to civilization it-

---

[6]The two standard accounts of the Bay of Pigs episode are Trumbull Higgins, *The Perfect Failure: Kennedy, Eisenhower, and the CIA at the Bay of Pigs* (New York, 1989), and Peter Wyden, *Bay of Pigs: The Untold Story* (New York, 1979).

[7]James G. Hershberg, "Before 'The Missiles of October': Did Kennedy Plan a Military Strike Against Cuba?" *Diplomatic History* 14 (Spring 1990), 163–198.

[8]Mark J. White, *Missiles in Cuba: Kennedy, Khrushchev, Castro and the 1962 Crisis* (Chicago, 1997), pp. 30–55.

[9]Ibid., pp. 56–78.

self. The Soviet-American contest had reached its zenith. Kennedy dealt with this drastic situation by concealing from the American public, his Western allies, and the Russians his knowledge of the missiles in Cuba. Instead he held a series of secret meetings with senior advisers on how to handle the crisis. After being offered a range of plans that included an air strike on the missile sites, Kennedy decided to establish a naval blockade around Cuba, an option that Robert Kennedy and other U.S. officials urged him to select. JFK announced the blockade of Cuba in a dramatic address to the nation on the evening of October 22. This, he calculated, would show Khrushchev that he meant business. But unlike a military strike on Cuba, it would provide breathing space for the superpowers to cut a deal.[10]

During the second week of the crisis, from JFK's October 22 address to the achievement of a settlement six days later, Kennedy and Khrushchev initially fired off messages to each other, defending their own positions and assailing their adversary's. But a series of developments from October 26 to 28 suddenly brought the crisis to an end. Khrushchev's messages to JFK on October 26 and 27 proposed two different settlements: the first was an American pledge not to invade Cuba in return for withdrawal of Russian missiles from the island; the second called for an additional concession from Kennedy, the removal from the Soviet border of America's Jupiter missiles in Turkey. JFK managed to formulate a response to these offers that Khrushchev found acceptable: a public promise not to invade Cuba, and a private commitment to withdraw the Jupiters. The most dangerous episode of the entire cold war era ended, only twelve days after it had begun.[11]

In the aftermath of the crisis, JFK and Khrushchev in their correspondence, Robert Kennedy in the role of diplomatic intermediary, and U.S. and Soviet officials at the United Nations sought to implement the settlement reached at the end of the crisis. Whether the U.S. no-invasion pledge should be codified in a UN document, and whether the Russians should remove their IL–28 bombers as well as the nuclear missiles from Cuba, were among the questions that dominated the Soviet-American dialogue in the final weeks of 1962. In 1963, what would turn out to be the final year of the Kennedy presidency, JFK's Cuban policies diverged. On the one hand he continued to exert pressure at the covert level, especially by resuming sabotage activities against Cuba in the summer of 1963. On the other hand he endorsed a clandestine initiative in the autumn aimed at developing a dialogue with Castro. What would have become the dominant motif of his policy toward Cuba had he lived—accommodation or confrontation—is only one of a series of fascinating but ultimately unanswerable questions raised by John Kennedy's assassination in Dallas on November 22, 1963.[12]

---

[10]There are a number of good accounts of the missile crisis, such as the one in Michael R. Beschloss, *The Crisis Years: Kennedy and Khrushchev, 1960–63* (New York, 1991).

[11]Ibid.

[12]Schlesinger, *Robert Kennedy and His Times* (1979 Ballantine edition), pp. 574–602, provides a detailed account of the post-missile-crisis period.

The Kennedys' handling of Castro, from inauguration to assassination, has generated a broad spectrum of opinion among historians. To a large extent the debate has mirrored the general discourse on the Kennedy presidency. In the years immediately following JFK's assassination, a decidedly positive view of his presidency prevailed. Kennedy aides Theodore C. Sorensen and Arthur M. Schlesinger, Jr., published elegant, laudatory, and popular books on JFK in 1965, and these works served to define what became known as the Camelot school. Civil rights reform, the Nuclear Test Ban Treaty, and the resolution of crises in Berlin in 1961 and in Cuba in 1962 were among the many accomplishments highlighted by Camelot writers.[13]

Starting in the 1970s perceptions changed. The Vietnam War had been a disaster for which JFK seemed to bear some responsibility, as he had escalated U.S. involvement in that conflict. Juicy revelations about Kennedy's personal life—his philandering and his use of drugs—suggested that there had been a sordid underside to Camelot. The result of these and other developments was the emergence of a revisionist or counter-Camelot school, which contested the extravagant claims of Sorensen, Schlesinger, *et al*. In doing so, these scholars developed a cluster of arguments which were no less extreme than those they were seeking to refute. They depicted JFK as a belligerent cold warrior, a hesitant supporter of civil rights reform, and—on a personal level—a reprobate. Thomas Reeves went as far as to assert that Kennedy had no moral center, that he lacked a basic understanding of the difference between right and wrong.[14]

In the 1980s and 1990s a more evenhanded view has gradually emerged. Historians such as Herbert Parmet and James Giglio have integrated Camelot and counter-Camelot perspectives to produce a more nuanced interpretation. They see the Kennedy record as a mix of success and failure. It is not clear at present whether this eclectic analysis will become generally accepted, as some scholars continue to endorse the arguments of either the Camelot or counter-Camelot school.[15]

The debate on Cuba resembles the general discussion on the Kennedy presidency. Initially John Kennedy's handling of the missile crisis was thought to be outstanding. Robert Kennedy too was given high marks for his role in ending the confrontation, especially for the passion with which he argued for a blockade and against a military strike on Cuba. The Bay of Pigs invasion was acknowledged as a mistake, but the issue of whether JFK played any significant role in causing the missile crisis was not even broached. It seemed obvious that the root

---

[13]Theodore C. Sorensen, *Kennedy* (New York, 1965); Arthur M. Schlesinger, Jr., *A Thousand Days: John F. Kennedy in the White House* (Boston, 1965).

[14]Two important counter-Camelot works are Garry Wills, *The Kennedy Imprisonment: A Meditation on Power* (Boston, 1982), and Thomas C. Reeves, *A Question of Character: A Life of John F. Kennedy* (New York, 1991).

[15]Herbert S. Parmet, *JFK: The Presidency of John F. Kennedy* (New York, 1983); James N. Giglio, *The Presidency of John F. Kennedy* (Lawrence, 1991). See also Mark J. White, ed., *Kennedy: The New Frontier Revisited* (New York, 1998). Recent examples of Camelot and counter-Camelot works are, respectively, Irving Bernstein, *Promises Kept: John F. Kennedy's New Frontier* (New York, 1991), and Seymour M. Hersh, *The Dark Side of Camelot* (Boston, 1997).

of the crisis was Khrushchev's aggressive and misguided decision to send nuclear weapons to Cuba.[16]

Only a few criticisms of Kennedy's handling of Cuba were voiced in the 1960s. But numerous reservations about JFK's management of the missile crisis soon appeared. Some historians wondered why the president chose a public confrontation (with his October 22, 1962, television address on the missiles in Cuba) rather than private diplomacy. Perhaps most important, Kennedy's role in the coming of the missile crisis was carefully examined. No longer assuming Khrushchev's culpability, historians stressed JFK's unremitting hostility toward Castro in 1961–1962, as demonstrated by the Bay of Pigs invasion, Operation Mongoose, and U.S. economic sanctions against Cuba. These policies, some historians claimed, were misguided. They had the effect of convincing Khrushchev that a U.S. attack on Cuba was probable, and that missiles needed to be installed on the island in order to deter such an assault. Research on U.S. contingency planning for military action against Cuba indicates that just before the missile crisis, JFK and his advisers considered carrying out these plans.[17]

As in the general debate on Kennedy, there have been recent attempts to provide a more balanced analysis of the Cuban issue. In my own work I have castigated Kennedy for the excessive belligerence of his Cuban policies before the missile crisis while praising him for his generally adroit management of the crisis itself. It may well have been the case that Khrushchev would not have put missiles in Cuba (and hence there would have been no missile crisis) had Kennedy not attempted to oust Castro and authorized a vast U.S. military buildup. During the crisis, however, he displayed a moderation lacking in his earlier policies. By the end of the October 1962 confrontation he seemed determined to resolve it through diplomacy, not by force.[18]

The documents in this volume have been selected so as to enable readers to develop their own interpretation of the Kennedys and Cuba. Some of the documents originate from the John F. Kennedy Library in Boston. Many are from the volumes on Cuba for 1961–1963 in the U.S. Department of State *Foreign Relations of the United States* series, others from the volumes on JFK in the *Public Papers of the Presidents of the United States*, which records all public statements made by chief executives. Some are translations of documents recently unearthed in Russian archives. Also included are materials released under the aus-

---

[16]Elie Abel, *The Missile Crisis* (Philadelphia, 1966), was an important early account. The classic work written in the decade after the crisis was Graham T. Allison, *Essence of Decision: Explaining the Cuban Missile Crisis* (Boston, 1971).

[17]See, inter alia, David Detzer, *The Brink: Cuban Missile Crisis, 1962* (New York, 1979); Paterson, "Fixation with Cuba"; Robert Smith Thompson, *The Missiles of October: The Declassified Story of John F. Kennedy and the Cuban Missile Crisis* (New York, 1992); Hershberg, "Before 'The Missiles of October.'"

[18]White, *Cuban Missile Crisis* and *Missiles in Cuba*. Other recent works include Aleksandr Fursenko and Timothy Naftali, *"One Hell of a Gamble": Khrushchev, Castro, and Kennedy, 1958–1964* (New York, 1997); Philip Nash, *The Other Missiles of October: Eisenhower, Kennedy, and the Jupiters, 1957–1963* (Chapel Hill, 1997).

pices of the Assassination Records Review Board, established during the presidencies of George Bush and Bill Clinton, and charged with overseeing the expeditious declassification of documents relating to the assassination of John Kennedy. A small number of documents come from other sources: the *Congressional Record*, the Public Record Office (in Kew, England), which houses British government documents, and a collection of Central Intelligence Agency documents on the missile crisis.

In selecting these documents I have tried to strike a balance between recently declassified materials, which are important and would be fresh even to a seasoned missile-crisis scholar, and documents that have long been available but are of clear importance, such as JFK's public statements on September 4 and 13, 1962, his address to the American people on October 22, 1962, and his correspondence with Khrushchev during the missile crisis. The intention is for these documents, collectively, to tell the story of the Kennedys and Cuba, to present to the reader the basic narrative of events.

To help achieve this objective I have as much as possible chosen documents that are interrelated—so, for example, a letter from Khrushchev to Kennedy, and JFK's reply; or a CIA plan of action and Kennedy's decision on whether to implement it; or a request by Kennedy to Secretary of Defense Robert S. McNamara to develop contingency plans for an attack on Cuba, and McNamara's response. This sort of linkage should make the collection of documents more cohesive and comprehensible.

The documents that follow shed most light on the roles of John and Robert Kennedy, but inevitably they illuminate the part played by others. In some instances JFK delegated the implementation of policy to officials other than Robert Kennedy. Covert operations expert Edward G. Lansdale, for instance, was the key figure in Operation Mongoose. Hence the Kennedys' handling of Castro from late 1961 through the fall of 1962 cannot be understood without reference to Lansdale. In addition, JFK's policy decisions can only be properly appreciated in the context of the options provided by his advisers. Some of these documents thus show the perspective of a dissenter, such as UN Ambassador Adlai E. Stevenson, who during the missile crisis wanted a diplomatic proposal to the Russians to accompany the establishment of the blockade, or the various officials who in early 1961 opposed the Bay of Pigs invasion.

While John and Robert Kennedy are the central characters in the unfolding drama presented in these documents, then, other figures are conspicuous too, especially Lansdale, Secretary of Defense McNamara, Secretary of State Dean Rusk, John A. McCone, who in late 1961 replaced the long-serving Allen W. Dulles as director of the CIA, and Special Assistant for National Security Affairs McGeorge Bundy. Nikita Khrushchev also figures prominently in the documents. The focus of this volume is the American dimension of the controversy surrounding Cuba during the Kennedy years, but to an extent U.S. policy was responding to initiatives from Moscow and also Havana. Hence a record of a meeting between JFK and Khrushchev at the Vienna summit in 1961, and correspondence from Khrushchev to Kennedy before, during, and after the missile crisis are included. The documents in this volume reflect too on the roles of other Soviet officials, especially Ambassador to the United States Anatoly F. Dobrynin and Foreign Minister Andrei A. Gromyko.

In analyzing all of these documents, readers should consider a number of issues. One is the need to distinguish between the private and public planes of American policy. The administration's Cuban policies were generated in private discussions between the president and his advisers, the records of which are in many cases presented in this collection. But those policies often had to be "sold" to the American public. Statements by Kennedy in the wake of the Bay of Pigs invasion, in September 1962 at the time of the Soviet military buildup in Cuba, and in the midst of the missile crisis have thus been included as prominent examples of the rhetoric that adorned JFK's Cuban policies.

As these statements were intended for public consumption, they were not always as candid as comments by Kennedy (and others) behind closed doors. His public statements in September, for example, were designed in part to convince the American people that the Russian military buildup in Cuba was not significant, and in this way to undercut Republicans who were trying to alert the public to the Soviet activity. Publicly Kennedy was recommending a moderate response to the Soviet military escalation in Cuba (on the grounds that the buildup did not involve nuclear missiles and therefore did not threaten the United States). But this did not represent his authentic feelings, for at the covert level at this time Kennedy intensified Operation Mongoose as well as contingency planning for military action against Cuba. In other words, the nature of Kennedy's audience—be it an adviser in a private meeting or the American people in a public statement—influenced his degree of candor; and this needs to be borne in mind when analyzing some of the documents.

The issue of motivation should be considered too. While Kennedy's policies toward Cuba are clearly described in these documents, the motivations behind them are less easy to discern. But a number of factors behind Kennedy's evident desire to oust Castro can be identified, including the belief that the Cuban leader was providing the Russians with a base in the Western Hemisphere, that Castro was intent on fomenting revolution in Latin America, that a hard-line U.S. approach toward Cuba (and the Soviet Union) was appropriate given the lesson of the 1930s that totalitarian dictators should be confronted not appeased, and—though it was not something Kennedy would necessarily acknowledge—that any accommodation of Havana would be lambasted by Republican critics. Readers should consider which of these and other possible factors were the most influential, whether certain factors influenced the Kennedy team more at particular junctures than at others, whether different officials had different motivations, whether American thinking on Cuba changed in the midst of the missile crisis, and if the missile-crisis experience itself altered the views of the administration after October 1962.

In the end, one needs to reach an overall assessment of the Kennedy record on Cuba. While I find much to admire in the way JFK, Robert Kennedy, and other American officials managed the missile crisis, and while I recognize some promising signs in the administration's handling of Cuba in 1963, I am unimpressed by U.S. policy before the missile crisis. Particularly disappointing is the myopia of the Kennedy team, their almost total inability to consider how their anti-Castro policies would be interpreted by Havana and Moscow, and how those governments might respond. Having examined these documents, readers might well reach different conclusions.

PART 1

The Bay of Pigs

THE DOCUMENTS in this chapter can be separated into two categories: those preceding and those following the CIA-organized invasion of Cuban exiles at the Bay of Pigs in mid-April 1961. The documents that predate that event show a president interested in implementing the plan he had inherited from the Eisenhower administration to use Cuban emigrés to oust Castro—but determined to conceal United States involvement in the venture. As a verdant Kennedy instructed his subordinates to limit America's role in the operation, he reduced the likelihood that the invasion would succeed. JFK is also seen ignoring the advice of several individuals who opposed the Bay of Pigs invasion.

The documents relating to the actual time of the Bay of Pigs operation and its immediate aftermath reveal American officials in a state of communal shock. Robert Kennedy, almost invisible on foreign policy matters before the Bay of Pigs, emerged as a force in discussions on Cuba during this period. The salient issue for JFK and his advisers at this juncture was how to shape policy toward Castro given that the Bay of Pigs operation had failed to remove him. The answer to that question—a multifaceted drive to weaken and ultimately overthrow the Cuban leader, including almost every anti-Castro device imaginable apart from a direct attack by U.S. forces—was arrived at by May 5. Two important components of the administration's approach in the late spring and summer of 1961 were the development of contingency plans for U.S. military action against Cuba and the fashioning of a covert program to pressure Castro—forerunners of Operation Mongoose, launched in November 1961. Another feature of Kennedy's policies during this period was an apparent refusal to reciprocate a clandestine Cuban proposal (advanced by Castro adviser Che Guevara) aimed at improving relations between Havana and Washington.

Nikita Khrushchev, who was to have a more dramatic impact on Cuban-American relations in 1962, figures prominently in these early documents. In discussions with American officials, including with Kennedy himself at the Vienna summit, and in correspondence, he made clear his sympathy for the Cuban revolution and his determination to help deter American efforts at ousting Castro.

1. Records of a White House Meeting on January 19, 1961, Between President Dwight D. Eisenhower, President-elect John F. Kennedy, and Their Chief Advisers

The day before his inauguration, JFK receives some hard-line advice from Eisenhower.

According to a memorandum produced by veteran Democrat Clark Clifford . . . "President Eisenhower said with reference to guerrilla forces which are opposed to Castro that it was the policy of this government to help such forces to the utmost. At the present time, we are helping train anti-Castro forces in Guatemala. It was his recommendation that this effort be continued and accelerated."

[According to a memorandum on the same meeting produced by the man who would serve as Kennedy's secretary of defense, Robert S. McNamara:] "President Eisenhower stated in the long run the United States cannot allow the Castro Government to continue to exist in Cuba."

2. Memorandum of Discussion on Cuba

Views of senior officials on Cuba are aired a week into the new administration.

Washington, January 28, 1961.

PRESENT

The President, the Vice President [Johnson], the Secretary of State [Rusk], the Secretary of Defense [McNamara], the Director of Central Intelligence [Dulles], the Chairman of the Joint Chiefs of Staff [Lemnitzer], Assistant Secretary Mann, Assistant Secretary Nitze, Mr. Tracy Barnes, Mr. McGeorge Bundy

The meeting began with a description of the present situation in Cuba by the Director of Central Intelligence. The judgment expressed without dissent was that Cuba is now for practical purposes a Communist-controlled state. The two basic elements in the present situation are a rapid and continuing build-up of Castro's military power, and a great increase also in popular opposition to his regime.

The United States has undertaken a number of covert measures against Castro, including propaganda, sabotage, political action, and direct assistance to anti-Castro Cubans in military training. A particularly urgent question is the use to be made of a group of such Cubans now in training in Guatemala, who cannot remain indefinitely where they are.

The present estimate of the Department of Defense is that no course of action currently authorized by the United States Government will be effective in reaching the agreed national goal of overthrowing the Castro regime. Meanwhile, the Department of State sees grave political dangers to our position throughout the Western hemisphere in any overt military action not authorized and supported by the Organization of American States.

After considerable discussion,[1] the following proceedings were authorized by the President:

1. A continuation and accentuation of current activities of the Central Intelligence Agency, including increased propaganda, increased political action and increased sabotage. Continued overflights for these purposes were specifically authorized.

2. The Defense Department, with CIA, will review proposals for the active deployment of anti-Castro Cuban forces on Cuban territory, and the results of this analysis will be promptly reported to the President.

3. The Department of State will prepare a concrete proposal for action with

---

[1]According to a May 5 memorandum by Naval Intelligence, Lemnitzer provided a description of this meeting shortly after its conclusion indicating that the discussion went as follows:

"The President wanted to know how the JCS felt about the prospects for success of a landing in Cuba by the forces being trained in Guatemala. It was indicated that they wanted a JCS study and evaluation of CIA's plan and the JCS opinion of its chances for success. The Chairman offered a personal opinion that in view of the strong forces Castro now had that the Cubans would have very little chance of success. As opposed to this, CIA took a very optimistic view of the force's ability to land and hold a beach head. The Chairman also pointed out that whereas they might be able to take a small beach head that after a relatively short time Castro would be able to mount heavy forces against them. The problem would then be one of who would come to their assistance."

other Latin American countries to isolate the Castro regime and to bring against it the judgment of the Organization of American States. . . .

Finally, it was agreed that the United States must make entirely clear that its position with respect to the Cuban Government is currently governed by its firm opposition to Communist penetration of the American Republics, and not by any hostility to democratic social revolution and economic reform. The President intends to deal with this matter himself in the State of the Union Address.[2]

The President particularly desires that no hint of these discussions reach any personnel beyond those most immediately concerned within the Executive Branch.[3]

3. Memorandum from the Joint Chiefs of Staff to Secretary of Defense Robert S. McNamara

The Joint Chiefs provide a generally positive assessment of the CIA plan to use Cuban exiles to overthrow Castro.

Washington, February 3, 1961.

SUBJECT

Military Evaluation of the Cuban Plan

Attached hereto is the Military Evaluation of the Central Intelligence Agency Para-Military Plan, Cuba. Subject to your concurrence,[1] the Joint Chiefs of Staff propose to forward copies of their assessment of the plan to the Director for Central Intelligence with the proposal that they meet with the Director for Central Intelligence and members of his staff for further discussion of this project.

For the Joint Chiefs of Staff:
L. L. Lemnitzer
Chairman
Joint Chiefs of Staff

Attachment

MEMORANDUM FOR THE SECRETARY OF DEFENSE

SUBJECT

Military Evaluation of the CIA Para-Military Plan, Cuba

[2]Delivered on January 30.
[3]McGeorge Bundy prepared this memorandum.
[1]McNamara agreed that this assessment should be passed on to the CIA.

1. The Joint Chiefs of Staff have evaluated the feasibility of the military portion of the CIA plan for action to effect the overthrow of the Castro regime and arrived at the following conclusions:

a. Since the success of this operation is dependent on the degree of local Cuban support, this factor should be a matter of continuous evaluation until a decision to execute the operation is made. . . .

e. If surprise is achieved and the estimates of Castro's air defense capabilities are correct, the plan of air operations is within the capability of the Air units and should be successful.

f. Since it is highly improbable that the airborne assault would be opposed, it should be successful.

g. The amphibious assault should be successful even if lightly opposed; however the personnel and plans for logistic support are marginal at best. Against moderate, determined resistance logistic support as presently planned will be inadequate.

h. The scheme of maneuver to secure the beachhead area is basically sound. . . .

l. Since the Cuban Army is without experience in coordinated offensive action, the invasion force should be able to successfully resist the initial attacks.

m.   Even if the task force is expanded by local volunteers, it is estimated that, lacking a popular uprising or substantial follow-on forces, the Cuban Army could eventually reduce the beachhead, but no estimate of the time this would require is possible.

n. This operation as presently envisaged would not necessarily require overt U.S. intervention. . . .

p. In summary, evaluation of the current plan results in a favorable assessment, modified by the specific conclusions set forth above, of the likelihood of achieving initial military success. It is obvious that ultimate success will depend upon political factors; i.e., a sizeable popular uprising or substantial follow-on forces. It should be noted that assessment of the combat worth of assault forces is based upon second and third hand reports, and certain logistic aspects of the plan are highly complex and critical to initial success. . . .

q. Despite the shortcomings pointed out in the assessment, the Joint Chiefs of Staff consider that timely execution of this plan has a fair chance of ultimate success and, even if it does not achieve immediately the full results desired, could contribute to the eventual overthrow of the Castro regime.

2. It is recommended that the enclosed study be forwarded to the Director, Central Intelligence Agency, for information and consideration. . . .

4. Memorandum of Meeting with President Kennedy

State Department officials raise objections to the CIA plan to topple Castro.

Washington, February 8, 1961.

PRESENT

> Messrs. Rusk, Berle, Mann, Bohlen, McNamara, Nitze, Barnes, W. P. Bundy, Haydn Williams, Dulles, Bissell, McG. Bundy

The meeting opened with an account by Mr. Bissell of the current plan for launching the troops from Guatemala.[1] He reported that the JCS, after careful study, believed that this plan had a fair chance of success—"success" meaning ability to survive, hold ground, and attract growing support from Cubans. At the worst, the invaders should be able to fight their way to the Escambray[2] and go into guerrilla action. If the troops are to land in top form, the operation should not be delayed, at the longest, beyond March 31, and the decision to land for it must be made before D minus 21.[3]

Secretary Rusk stated that without careful—and successful—diplomatic preparation such an operation could have grave effects upon the U.S. position in Latin America and at the U.N. Mr. Berle said that it would be impossible, as things stand now, to avoid being cast in the role of aggressor. Both Mr. Rusk and Mr. Berle believed that no present decision on the proposed invasion was necessary, but both made clear their conviction that U.S. policy should not be driven to drastic and irrevocable choice by the urgencies, however real, of a single battalion of men.

The President pressed for alternatives to a full-fledged "invasion," supported by U.S. planes, ships and supplies. While CIA doubted that other really satisfactory uses of the troops in Guatemala could be found, it was agreed that the matter should be carefully studied. Could not such a force be landed gradually and quietly and make its first major military efforts from the mountains—then taking shape as a Cuban force within Cuba, not as an invasion force sent by the Yankees?

The State Department envisioned a long and complex effort to win support and understanding—from other American States for a strong line against Castro. . . . Mr. Berle believed that the President's own authority and leadership would be needed in making the U.S. view understood both at home and abroad. The President asked that the State Department prepare a clear statement of the course it would recommend, and meanwhile he urged all concerned to seek for

[1]Guatemala was the host country for the Cuban exiles being trained by the CIA for an invasion of Cuba.

[2]A mountain range in Cuba.

[3]In other words, at least twenty-one days before the start of the invasion.

ways in which the Administration would make it clear to Latin Americans that it stands squarely for reform and progress in the Americas.

The only new action authorized at the meeting was the organization of a small junta of anti-Castro Cuban leaders, to be supported by a larger Revolutionary Council. This junta will have a strong left-of-center balance, and it will be a response to the urgent demands of the troops in Guatemala for a sense of political direction and purpose. Its members will be selected for their ability, among other things, to join the landing force.[4]

5. Notes on a White House Meeting

JFK calls for the plan to use Cuban exiles to be changed in order more effectively to conceal U.S. involvement.

March 11, 1961.

Present at the meeting were JFK, Vice President Johnson, McNamara, Rusk, Mann, Berle, Dulles, McGeorge Bundy, William Bundy, Gray, Colonel B. W. Tarwater, and (although not mentioned in the President's Appointment Book) presumably Bissell.

According to notes prepared by Major General David W. Gray on May 9, 1961:

"At a meeting with the President, CIA presented a paper which summarized preparations to date for the Trinidad operation.[1] After full discussion, the President stated that he was willing to take the chance of going ahead; that he could not endorse a plan that put us in so openly, in view of the world situation. He directed the development of a plan where US assistance would be less obvious and would like to meet again within the next few days."

6. Notes on a White House Meeting

Following JFK's instructions, the CIA modified the plan so that Cuban exiles would be landed not at Trinidad but at the more sparsely populated, less

[4]McGeorge Bundy prepared this memorandum.
[1]The original CIA plan was to land the Cuban exiles at Trinidad, on Cuba's south coast.

prominent Bay of Pigs (next to the Zapata peninsula). But here JFK imposes further restrictions on the operation.

March 15, 1961.

Present at the meeting were JFK, Vice President Johnson, McNamara, Rusk, Mann, Berle, Dulles, Bissell, McGeorge Bundy, William Bundy, Gray, and (although not mentioned in the President's Appointment Book) probably General Lemnitzer or Admiral Burke of the JCS.

According to notes prepared by Gray on May 9:

"At this meeting the Zapata plan was presented to the President and a full-length discussion of it followed. The President expressed the belief that uprisings all along the island would be better than to concentrate and strike. The President asked how soon it was intended to break out from this area and Mr. Bissell stated that not before about D+10. The President was also concerned about ability to extricate the forces. The President did not like the idea of the dawn landing and felt that in order to make this appear as an inside guerrilla-type operation, the ships should be clear of the area by dawn. He directed that this planning be reviewed and another meeting be held the following morning."

7. Notes on a White House Meeting

CIA officials explain the further revisions they have made to the Cuban operation in response to JFK's instructions the previous day.

March 16, 1961.

Present at the meeting were JFK, Vice President Johnson, McNamara, Rusk, Mann, Berle, Dulles, Bissell, McGeorge Bundy, William Bundy, Gray, and Admiral Burke.

According to notes prepared by Gray on May 9:

"At meeting with the President, CIA presented revised concepts for the landing at Zapata wherein there would be air drops at first light with the landing at night and all of the ships away from the objective area by dawn. The President decided to go ahead with the Zapata planning; to see what we could do about increasing support to the guerrillas inside the country; to interrogate one member of the force to determine what he knows; and he reserved the right to call off the plan even up to 24 hours prior to the landing."

8. Memorandum from Under Secretary of State Chester Bowles to Secretary of State Dean Rusk

The Bay of Pigs plan did not receive unanimous support from American officials. Here Chester Bowles articulates his objections, which Rusk passed on to JFK.

Washington, March 31, 1961.

On Tuesday, April 4th, a meeting will be held at the White House at which a decision will be reached on the Cuban adventure.

During your absence I have had an opportunity to become better acquainted with the proposal, and I find it profoundly disturbing.

Let me frankly say, however, that I am not a wholly objective judge of the practical aspects.

In considerable degree, my concern stems from a deep personal conviction that our national interests are poorly served by a covert operation of this kind at a time when our new President is effectively appealing to world opinion on the basis of high principle.

Even in our imperfect world, the differences which distinguish us from the Russians are of vital importance. This is true not only in a moral sense but in the practical effect of these differences on our capacity to rally the non-Communist world in behalf of our traditional democratic objectives.

In saying this, I do not overlook the ruthless nature of the struggle in which we are involved, nor do I ignore the need on occasion for action which is expedient and distasteful. Yet I cannot persuade myself that means can be *wholly* divorced from ends—even within the context of the Cold War.

Against this background, let me suggest several points which I earnestly hope will be fully taken into account in reaching the final decision.

1. In sponsoring the Cuban operation, for instance, we would be deliberately violating the fundamental obligations we assumed in the Act of Bogota establishing the Organization of American States. The Act provides:

"No State or group of States has the right to intervene, directly or indirectly, for any reason whatever, in the internal or external affairs of any other State. The foregoing principle prohibits not only armed force but also any other form of interference or attempted threat against the personality of the State or against its political, economic and cultural elements.

"No State may use or encourage the use of coercive measures of an economic or political character in order to force the sovereign will of another State and obtain from it advantages of any kind.

"The territory of a State is inviolable; it may not be the object, even temporarily, of military occupation or of other measures of force taken by another State, directly or indirectly, on any grounds whatever. . . ."

I think it fair to say that these articles, signalling an end of U.S. unilateralism, comprise the central features of the OAS from the point of view of the Latin American countries.

To act deliberately in defiance of these obligations would deal a blow to the Inter-American System from which I doubt it would soon recover. The suggestion that Cuba has somehow "removed itself" from the System is a transparent rationalization for the exercise of our own will.

More generally, the United States is the leading force in and substantial beneficiary of a network of treaties and alliances stretching around the world. That these treaty obligations should be recognized as binding in law and conscience is the condition not only of a lawful and orderly world, but of the mobilization of our own power.

We cannot expect the benefits of this regime of treaties if we are unwilling to accept the limitations it imposes upon our freedom to act.

2. Those most familiar with the Cuban operation seem to agree that as the venture is now planned, the chances of success are not greater than one out of three. This makes it a highly risky operation. If it fails, Castro's prestige and strength will be greatly enhanced.

The one way we can reduce the risk is by a sharply increased commitment of direct American support. In talking to Bob McNamara and Ros Gilpatric . . . at the Pentagon, I gathered that this is precisely what the military people feel we should do.

3. Under the very best of circumstances, I believe this operation will have a much more adverse effect on world opinion than most people contemplate. It is admitted that there will be riots and a new wave of anti-Americanism throughout Latin America. It is also assumed that there will be many who quietly wish us well and, if the operation succeeds, will heave a sigh of relief.

Moreover, even if the reaction in Latin America is less damaging than we expect, I believe that in Europe, Asia, and Africa, the reaction against the United States will be angry and the fresh, favorable image of the Kennedy Administration will be correspondingly dimmed. It would be a grave mistake for us to minimize this factor and its impact on our capacity to operate effectively in cooperation with other nations in other parts of the world.

4. If the operation appears to be a failure in its early stages, the pressure on us to scrap our self-imposed restriction on direct American involvement will be difficult to resist, and our own responsibility correspondingly increased. . . .

Since January 20th our position has been dramatically improved in the eyes of the world vis-à-vis the Soviet Union.

The Kennedy Administration has been doing particularly well in Africa and Latin America, and with a little luck in Laos and more affirmative policies, we may soon be able to improve our position in East Asia, South Asia, and the Middle East. Within the next few months we can also begin to strengthen our relations with Western Europe.

I believe it would be a grave mistake for us to jeopardize the favorable position we have steadily developed in most of the non-Communist world by the responsible and restrained policies which are now associated with the President by embarking on a major covert adventure with such very heavy built-in risks.

I realize that this operation has been put together over a period of months. A great deal of time and money has been put into it, and many able and dedicated people have become emotionally involved in its success. We should not, however, proceed with this adventure simply because we are wound up and cannot stop. . . .

If you agree after careful thought that this operation would be a mistake, I suggest that you personally and privately communicate your views to the President. It is my guess that your voice will be decisive.

9. Telegram from U.S. Ambassador to the Soviet Union Llewellyn E. Thompson to the Department of State

The American ambassador to the Soviet Union provides Washington with an account of a meeting between himself and Nikita S. Khrushchev in which the Russian leader reveals his awareness of Kennedy's interest in using Cuban exiles to oust Castro.

Moscow, April 1, 1961.

. . . Turning to Cuba he [Khrushchev] could not agree with our policy there. Each country should be free to choose its social system. They did not agree, for example, with Yugoslav internal policies but this did not prevent them from having good relations with that country. He said President had indicated that financial aid would be given to aid in overthrow of present Cuban Govt. Bands of émigrés had been formed and threats made against Cuban Govt. He said Soviet Govt would openly support Cuban Govt and would give them economic aid. He pointed out Soviet Union had no base in Cuba and only base there belonged to US [Guantanamo]. He then went on to question our policy of having bases all around Soviet Union. . . .

Reverting again to Cuba he asked why we did not establish diplomatic relations with that country and try to resolve our problems with it peacefully. He made clear Cubans had not put him up to this but he was merely speaking his own mind. . . .

I went on to say that I thought what bothered us particularly about Cuba was its use as a base for attempts on overthrow of other Latin American govts. When he disputed this I said I had heard Cuban pilots were being trained in Czechoslovakia in flying jet planes. Cuba would never be able [to] attack US and therefore these presumably were designed for use against other Latin American countries. I said we had been most patient with Castro. In first place we had cut off supply of arms to Batista[1] and although there had been differences of opinion in US about Castro we had been fully prepared [to] accept his govt. However he had made most violent statements against us and had confiscated our assets there without compensation and finally had insisted on reducing our Embassy to handful of people.[2] We had tried to be patient but he had given us no choice. Khrushchev replied Castro said we were using Embassy to harbor spies and Castro was not Communist. He said he had not heard of any training of jet pilots but if he were Castro he would buy jet planes since these were necessary to prevent arms being dropped to counter-revolutionaries from planes flying from US. He thought that in one case we had even admitted this. I said we had taken strict steps to prevent such activities although there had I believed been one case in which a plane had gotten through. In concluding Khrushchev said we should continue to be patient and should try to improve our relations with Cuba. . . .

10. Notes on a Meeting Between President Kennedy and Advisers

Senator Fulbright and Rusk dissent.

April 4, 1961.

[Senator J. William Fulbright of Arkansas was invited to participate.]

According to notes prepared by Gray on May 9:
"This meeting was held in the State Department and Senator Fulbright was also present. Senator Fulbright spoke out against the plan. The President again indicated his preference for an operation which would infiltrate the force in units of 200–250 and then develop them through a build up. Colonel Hawkins from CIA expressed the belief that landing small groups would merely serve to alert Castro and they would be eliminated one by one. He indicated that a group of 200 was below the critical number able to defend themselves. Mr. Rusk expressed opposition to the plan but Mr. Berle and Mr. Mann expressed general approval. Mr. McNamara also expressed approval of the general concept. The President indicated that he still wished to make the operation appear as an internal uprising and wished to consider the matter further the next morning."

[1]Fulgencio Batista was the dictator who had ruled Cuba prior to Castro's revolution in 1959.
[2]Castro had ordered the removal of American officials at the start of 1961, after which the Eisenhower administration cut off diplomatic relations.

11. Notes on a White House Meeting

In a discussion with his advisers, Kennedy again shows his desire both to topple Castro and to mask his administration's involvement in the operation designed to achieve that objective.

April 6, 1961

Present at the meeting were JFK, Rusk, McNamara, Dulles, Berle, Mann, Coerr, Bissell, Gray, and probably Lemnitzer, Burke, and Cabell as well.

According to notes prepared by Gray on May 9:

"Mr. Bissell gave an outline of the planned defection of a pilot on D–3,[1] coupled with air strikes and a D–2 guerrilla landing [at the Bay of Pigs]. This would then be followed by a guerrilla uprising on D+5 in Pinar Del Rio. The President indicated that the council[2] should not be informed ahead of time. Mr. Rusk, when queried by the President, stated that he felt that this plan was as good as could be devised, but that we should now take a look at other questions that might arise. One would be what would the US do in the event there was a serious call for help? Second, what might the Soviets do? The President indicated that Mr. Macmillan[3] had been informed of the prospect. The President questioned whether or not a preliminary strike wasn't an alarm bell. The President also asked as to the last date on which he could delay or cancel the operation, and he was told 16 April. He wanted to know what he could do if the operation was called off and was told by Mr. Bissell that the plan was to divert the [Cuban exile] force to Vieques.[4] At the end of the meeting the President gave the following guidance: continue planning, spread the convoy, provide additional air protection for the Miami area, increase press conferences for Cardona,[5] limit air strikes to essential targets, and diversionary landing was OK. In summary, the President indicated a desire to use the force but he wanted to do everything possible to make it appear to be a Cuban operation partly from within Cuba but supported from without Cuba, the objective being to make it more plausible for US denial of association with the operation although recognizing that we would be accused."

---

[1]In other words, three days before the start of the planned invasion.
[2]The Cuban Revolutionary Council comprised exiled Cuban politicians.
[3]British Prime Minister Harold Macmillan.
[4]An island in the Caribbean.
[5]José Miró Cardona was the leading political figure among Cuban exiles.

12. Telegram from Chairman of the Joint Chiefs of Staff General Lyman L. Lemnitzer to Commander-in-Chief (Atlantic) Robert L. Dennison

The chairman of the Joint Chiefs explains changes in the Bay of Pigs plan— and their implications. In retrospect it can be seen how these modifications made the operation less militarily viable.

Washington, April 13, 1961, 6:30 p.m.

1. Original concept for U.S. naval support of Bumpy Road[1] was to ensure that when once embarked this operation must not fail. This concept modified by the later plan which provides that cancellation possible until landing phase actually starts. Concept further modified by provision in rules of engagement that if intervention by U.S. military element is required and actually takes place while CEF en route to transport area then operation must abort.

2. In view above a change of emphasis is now required. That is, it [is] now important that premature U.S. intervention not occur which would be the cause for cancellation of this highly important and desirable operation.

3. To this end it is important to success of operation that commanders of all sea and air units of your forces engaged in protection of expedition clearly understand and apply rules of engagement along following lines:

A. It is desired to minimize the need to abort the operation because of U.S. engagement of Castro ships or aircraft in conduct of protective mission assigned to you.

B. Actual engagement of Castro ships or aircraft should be withheld until last possible moment and action taken only after it becomes clear that otherwise total destruction of friendly ship or ships may be imminent. For example, nonengagement in event of initial strafing or bomb run by Castro aircraft on friendly ship is acceptable rather than too hasty U.S. intervention with resultant need to abort the whole operation. Same applies importantly to intervention by U.S. surface ships. Initial firing on friendly ship by Castro surface ship is acceptable and U.S. engagement of Castro ship should await evidence that Castro ship is boring in for a kill or capture.

C. Preliminary maneuvering of U.S. aircraft or ships should take into account the above. Effort should be made to minimize blowing the operation by overly active intervention.

4. In the event actual U.S. engagement of Castro craft takes place, immediate report should be passed to Washington together with salient facts involved. Particularly desired are any facts which would support argument that it could be plausibly denied that U.S. intervention was in direct support of CEF.

[1] Bumpy Road was the code name for the naval dimension of the invasion plan.

5. In summary, hope is that over-all operation will not need to be aborted because of U.S. military intervention and to this end CEF prepared to take substantial risks.

13. Memorandum from Deputy Director of the CIA Charles P. Cabell to General Maxwell D. Taylor

Once Kennedy gave the go-ahead for a landing at the Bay of Pigs, an initial air strike on Castro's main airfields was carried out. But as a CIA official recalls here, the president and his advisers rescinded a second strike, set for the morning of the Cuban exile invasion—a decision that diminished the chances for a successful operation.

Washington, May 9, 1961.

1. At about 9:30 p.m. on 16 April (D–1) I was called in the CIA headquarters for the Cuban operation by the Special Assistant to the President, Mr. McGeorge Bundy. He notified me that we would not be permitted to launch air strikes the next morning until they could be conducted from a strip within the beachhead. Any further consultation regarding this matter should be with the Secretary of State [Rusk].

2. I called the Secretary and asked him if I could come immediately to his office and discuss this decision. Mr. Bissell joined me at the Secretary's office where we both arrived at about 10:15 p.m.

3. The Secretary informed us that there were political considerations preventing the planned air strikes before the beachhead airfield was in our hands and usable. The air strikes on D–2 had been allowed because of military considerations. Political requirements at the present time were overriding. The main consideration involved the situation at the United Nations. The Secretary described Ambassador Stevenson's attitude in some detail. Ambassador Stevenson had insisted essentially that the air strikes would make it absolutely impossible for the U.S. position to be sustained. The Secretary stated that such a result was unacceptable.

4. In the light of this he asked that we describe the implications of the decision. We told him that the time was such (now almost 11:00 p.m.) that it was now physically impossible to stop the over-all landing operation, as the convoy was at that time just about beginning to put the first boat ashore, and that failure to make air strikes in the immediate beachhead area the first thing in the morning (D-Day) would clearly be disastrous. I informed him that there would be four effects of the cancellation order as it applied to strikes against Cuban airfields.

a. There would be a great risk of loss of one or more of the ships as they withdrew from the beach. This would be serious but not catastrophic, *provided* that the unloading had proceeded as scheduled and all planned unloading had occurred by daylight. In view of the fact that this was a night landing and close timing was required, it was pointed out that the probability of smooth performance here was doubtful. (As it turned out, the unloading was not accomplished in the time planned.)

b. The disembarked forces in the beachhead would be subjected to a heavier scale of air attack than would otherwise have been the case. In view of the fact that the Cuban Air Force was inadequate for massive air attacks, the attacks to be expected under the new circumstances would be damaging to these forces but not decisive.

c. Failure essentially to neutralize the Cuban Air Force very early on D-Day would have its most serious effect on the use of the Expeditionary Air Force's B–26s to isolate the battlefield. The B–26s were being counted upon to attack approaching Cuban ground and Naval elements and close-in artillery and tanks. No fighter cover was being provided for the B–26s and they would thus face the prospect of serious attrition during these battlefield operations. The beachhead could then be overwhelmed by the superior surface attack which could be brought against it.

d. Loss of efficiency would result from this late change of orders.

5. After considering the foregoing, the Secretary of State agreed that strikes could be made in the immediate beachhead area but confirmed that the planned air strikes against Cuban airfields, a harbor, and a radio broadcasting station, could not be permitted and the decision to cancel would stand. He asked if I should like to speak to the President. Mr. Bissell and I were impressed with the extremely delicate situation with Ambassador Stevenson and the United Nations and the risk to the entire political position of the United States, and the firm position of the Secretary. We saw no point in my speaking personally to the President and so informed the Secretary.

6. Our immediate problem then was quickly to dispatch the necessary order to the Air Base in Puerto Cabezas[1] carrying out the instructions to stop the planned air strike and to require re-planning and re-briefing of crews. (This was barely accomplished as the order to cancel caught the crews in their cockpits.)

7. Our next task was to try and compensate for the loss of effective air strikes. In order to protect the shipping as it withdrew from the beachhead, I arranged with the Navy to stand by pending authority to give fighter cover. At 4:30 a.m., 17 April (D-Day), I called on the Secretary of State at his home and reiterated the need to protect the shipping. The Secretary telephoned the President and put me on the phone. After I made the request the President asked that the Secretary be put back on. After conversation with the President, the Secretary informed me that the request for air cover was disapproved.

---

[1] Puerto Cabezas is located in Nicaragua.

14. Memorandum for the Record Prepared by Chief of Naval Operations Admiral Arleigh A. Burke

After the Bay of Pigs invasion failed, Kennedy established a Cuba Study Group to review the episode. Here he recalls for that group his thinking and decisions regarding the operation.

Washington, May 16, 1961.

SUBJECT

Debrief of Luncheon conversation with the President, 16 May 1961

1. I attended a luncheon with the President, in company with General Taylor, Mr. Allen Dulles and Mr. Robert Kennedy. . . .

3. The President's answers to the questions in general were as follows:

a. Question 1. Was there any doubt about the necessity of some such military action against Castro?

He had some doubt about the necessity for military action against Castro and so did some people in State, but there were pressures such as what to do with the forces being trained, the rainy season coming up and the conduct of covert actions in the atmosphere at the time, that led the President to believe that Castro should be overthrown. It was much better, for example, to put the guerrillas on the beach in Cuba and let them fight for Cuba than bring them back to the United States and have them state that the United States would not support their activities. The end result might have been much worse had we done this than it actually was.

b. Question 2. What was the estimate of the probability of success of Zapata before D-Day?

It was thought that the possibility of some success of the Zapata Plan was fairly good, since if they could not establish a beachhead and hold it, they could go into guerrillas. This was probably the biggest error, as it turned out, but it was thought that they could hold the beachhead for some time and that a Cuban Government could be established on the beachhead which perhaps could be recognized later. He realized that not knocking out the Cuban air [force] precluded this as it turned out.

c. Question 3. What was the feeling of likelihood of a popular uprising following the landing? How essential was such an uprising regarded for the success of the operation? How rapid a reaction was expected by Castro?

He felt that there was a good chance for a popular uprising following the landing but that the beachhead was not held long enough to permit a popular uprising. Although an uprising would be necessary for the overthrow of Castro, if there was no general uprising the members in the landing party could become guerrillas and they would do more good as guerrillas than they would outside of

Cuba. This also answered question 4 which was "What was expected to happen if the landing force effected a successful lodgment but there was no uprising?"

d. Question 5. What was the understanding of the position of the JCS as to Zapata? Was it appreciated that they favored Trinidad over Zapata? What did the President expect from the Chiefs?

The President understood that the JCS preferred the Trinidad Plan to the Zapata Plan from the military point of view. However, policy implications were overriding in that it would be quite evident in the Trinidad operation that it was a United States operation since control of the air would be required, which could be accomplished only with the assistance of the United States. He thought that the Chiefs could very well have stated that if the Zapata Plan was adopted and there was not absolute control of the air, that it would fail. He felt that this could have been more forcibly said than it was.

e. Question 6. Was it understood that control of the air was considered essential to the success of the landing?

He did understand that control of the air was important but he did not believe it to be absolutely essential. If he had, then he would have launched the D-Day strikes.

f. Question 7. What were the circumstances surrounding the cancellation of the D-Day air strikes? How serious was the decision viewed? What was the understanding about pre-landing strikes?

Mr. Rusk had talked with the President in regard to the D-Day strikes and in connection with the activities in the United Nations and the strong recommendations of Mr. Stevenson. He felt, in retrospect, that the decision to cancel the strikes should probably not have been made, but he felt that the case for making the strikes was perhaps not recommended forcibly enough, although he understood why General Cabell would not want to dispute the Secretary of State after the President had made a tentative decision. He was very open minded on this and very fair.

g. Question 8. What was the understanding as to the ability of the landing force to pass to a guerrilla status in an emergency? To what extent did this factor influence approval of the operations?

He certainly had understood that the landing force could pass to guerrilla status and it greatly influenced his thinking of the whole operation.

h. Question 9. What was the understanding of the ammunition situation by the end of April 18?

He realized that there was a shortage of ammunition on the 18th of April, but just how acute it was, of course, he did not know. He realized that there was a long delay in communications and that the situation was never clear here as to exactly what was happening. . . .

i. Question 10. What degree of non-attribution was sought and why? Were the operational disadvantages arising from some of the restrictions imposed by the efforts to achieve non-attribution clearly presented and understood?

Before the operation there was every effort made to keep the situation covert, with no attribution being possible for United States forces. The second part of the question I don't think he answered. . . .

15. Letter from Chairman Khrushchev to President Kennedy

With the Cuban exile force close to surrender at the Bay of Pigs, the Soviet leader fires off a frank message to JFK.

Moscow, April 18, 1961.

Mr. President, I send you this message in an hour of alarm, fraught with danger for the peace of the whole world. Armed aggression has begun against Cuba. It is a secret to no one that the armed bands invading this country were trained, equipped and armed in the United States of America. The planes which are bombing Cuban cities belong to the United States of America, the bombs they are dropping are being supplied by the American Government.

All of this evokes here in the Soviet Union an understandable feeling of indignation on the part of the Soviet Government and the Soviet people.

Only recently, in exchanging opinions through our respective representatives, we talked with you about the mutual desire of both sides to put forward joint efforts directed toward improving relations between our countries and eliminating the danger of war. Your statement a few days ago that the USA would not participate in military activities against Cuba[1] created the impression that the top leaders of the United States were taking into account the consequences for general peace and for the USA itself which aggression against Cuba could have. How can what is being done by the United States in reality be understood, when an attack on Cuba has now become a fact?

It is still not [too] late to avoid the irreparable. The Government of the USA still has the possibility of not allowing the flame of war ignited by interventions in Cuba to grow into an incomparable conflagration. I approach you, Mr. President, with an urgent call to put an end to aggression against the Republic of Cuba. Military armament and the world political situation are such at this time that any so-called "little war" can touch off a chain reaction in all parts of the globe.

As far as the Soviet Union is concerned, there should be no mistake about our position: We will render the Cuban people and their government all necessary help to repel armed attack on Cuba. We are sincerely interested in a relaxation of international tension, but if others proceed toward sharpening, we will answer them in full measure. And in general it is hardly possible so to conduct matters that the situation is settled in one area and conflagration extinguished, while a new conflagration is ignited in another area.

I hope that the Government of the USA will consider our views dictated by the sole concern not to allow steps which could lead the world to military catastrophe.

[1]Kennedy made this statement at a White House press conference on April 12.

16. Memorandum of Chief of Naval Operations Burke's Conversation with Commander Wilhide

A discussion between Arleigh Burke and his aide conveys the sense of bewilderment permeating the administration at this time.

Washington, April 18, 1961.

ADMIRAL BURKE'S CONVERSATION WITH CDR WILHIDE, 18 APRIL 1961

Adm Burke . . . We got over there in the Cabinet Room.[1] The President was talking with CIA people, State Department people and Rostow and a lot of other people. They were talking about Cuba. Real big mess.

Nobody knew what to do nor did the CIA who were running the operation and who were wholly responsible for the operation know what to do or what was happening. A lot of things have happened and they have caused to happen and we the JCS don't know anything whatever about. We have been kept pretty ignorant of this and have just been told partial truths. They are in a real bad hole because they had the hell cut out of them. They were reporting, devising and talking and I kept quiet because I didn't know the general score. Once in a while I did make a little remark like "balls." It wasn't very often. It was a serious meeting. They didn't know what the President should do. . . . When it came out as to what could the United States do—it was all Navy. The upshot of it was that the President moved into his room—his office with Rusk, McNamara, Dulles, Lemnitzer and me. We talked a little bit in there about what could we do, Rusk not being in favor of doing very much. Then we came out. I was sent for again and I was asked could we find out what the score really was, by landing people in helicopters or something like that. That was all right. I wrote some dispatches and did some things. Over there. And I came back.

Then Bobby Kennedy called me up and said the President is going to rely upon you to advise him on this situation. I said it is late! He needs advice. He said the rest of the people in the room weren't helpful. (Call from the President)[2] . . .

---

[1]This meeting started at noon on April 18.

[2]The memorandum seems to have been prepared by Wilhide using a tape recording of this conversation with Burke.

17. Letter from President Kennedy to Chairman Khrushchev

JFK replies quickly and unflinchingly to Khrushchev's message (Document 15).

Washington, April 18, 1961.

MR. CHAIRMAN: You are under a serious misapprehension in regard to events in Cuba. For months there has been evident and growing resistance to the Castro dictatorship. More than 100,000 refugees have recently fled from Cuba into neighboring countries. Their urgent hope is naturally to assist their fellow Cubans in their struggle for freedom. Many of these refugees fought along side Dr. Castro against the Batista dictatorship; among them are prominent leaders of his own original movement and government.

These are unmistakable signs that Cubans find intolerable the denial of democratic liberties and the subversion of the 26th of July Movement[1] by an alien-dominated regime. It cannot be surprising that, as resistance within Cuba grows, refugees have been using whatever means are available to return and support their countrymen in the continuing struggle for freedom. Where people are denied the right of choice, recourse to such struggle is the only means of achieving their liberties.

I have previously stated, and I repeat now, that the United States intends no military intervention in Cuba. In the event of any military intervention by outside force we will immediately honor our obligations under the inter-American system to protect this hemisphere against external aggression. While refraining from military intervention in Cuba, the people of the United States do not conceal their admiration for Cuban patriots who wish to see a democratic system in an independent Cuba. The United States Government can take no action to stifle the spirit of liberty.

I have taken careful note of your statement that the events in Cuba might affect peace in all parts of the world. I trust that this does not mean that the Soviet Government, using the situation in Cuba as a pretext, is planning to inflame other areas of the world. I would like to think that your government has too great a sense of responsibility to embark upon any enterprise so dangerous to general peace.

I agree with you as to the desirability of steps to improve the international atmosphere. I continue to hope that you will cooperate in opportunities now available to this end. A prompt cease-fire and peaceful settlement of the dangerous situation in Laos, cooperation with the United Nations in the Congo and a speedy conclusion of an acceptable treaty for the banning of nuclear tests would be constructive steps in this direction. The regime in Cuba could make a similar contribution by permitting the Cuban people freely to determine their own

---

[1]A reference to the Cuban revolutionary movement.

future by democratic processes and freely to cooperate with their Latin American neighbors.

I believe, Mr. Chairman, that you should recognize that free peoples in all parts of the world do not accept the claim of historical inevitability for Communist revolution. What your government believes is its own business; what it does in the world is the world's business. The great revolution in the history of man, past, present and future, is the revolution of those determined to be free.

18. Memorandum from Attorney General Robert F. Kennedy to President Kennedy

Robert Kennedy, assigned a prominent role in Cuban matters by the president after the Bay of Pigs fiasco, gives JFK some advice. His last sentence is strikingly prescient.

Washington, April 19, 1961.

The present situation in Cuba was precipitated by the deterioration of events inside that state. The news that 100 Cuban pilots were being trained in Czechoslovakia, the information that MIGs and other jet planes had already been shipped to Cuba and that these shipments were expected to continue, that thousands of tons of military equipment had arrived each month in Havana, were all matters of consternation. Cuba it was realized was swiftly becoming a major military arsenal for all of the activities of the Communist Bloc in the Western Hemisphere. For these arms were sent to Cuba not only to keep Castro in power but to provide the necessary tools for Communist agitators in other South American and Central American countries to overthrow their governments. A hundred jet fighters based in Havana and roaming the skies around Florida and Central America will have major repercussions. The psychological effect, let alone the military result of this show of power could conceivably be catastrophic.

The alternative to the steps that were taken this past week would have been to sit and wait and hope that in the future some fortuitous event would occur to change the situation. This, it was decided, should not be done. The immediate failure of the rebels' activities in Cuba does not permit us, it seems to me, to return to the status quo with our policy toward Cuba being one of waiting and hoping for good luck. The events in the last few days makes [sic] this inconceivable.

Therefore, equally important to working out a plan to extricate ourselves gracefully from the situation in Cuba is developing a policy in light of what we expect we will be facing a year or two years from now![1] Castro will be even more bom-

[1]The emphasis here is Robert Kennedy's own.

bastic, will be more and more closely tied to Communism, will be better armed, and will be operating an even more tightly held state than if these events had not transpired.

Our long-range foreign policy objectives in Cuba are tied to survival far more than what is happening in Laos or the Congo or any other place in the world. Because of the proximity of that island our objective must be at the very least to prevent that island from becoming Mr. Khrushchev's arsenal. In our concern over the present situation, we must not lose sight of our objective.

There are three ways that that can be accomplished: Number (1) to send American troops into Cuba; Number (2) to place a strict military blockade around the island of Cuba; Number (3) to call upon the nations of Central and South America to take steps to insure that all arms from outside forces (both American and Russian) are kept out of Cuba.

You have rejected Number (1) for good and sufficient reasons (although this might have to be reconsidered). Number (2) has the same inherent problems as Number (1) although possibly not as acute. On the other hand, it is a drawn-out affair which would lead to a good deal of worldwide bitterness over an extended period of time.

The only way to carry it out successfully would be to be able to demonstrate to the governments of Central and South America that because of the MIG fighters, the tanks and equipment provided by the Communist bloc, that the whole hemisphere is in danger. From my limited knowledge of the situation I suppose it would be most difficult to get them to agree to concerted action.

As for Number 3 and to some extent, Number 2, if it was reported that one or two of Castro's MIGs attacked Guantanamo Bay and the United States made noises like this was an act of war and that we might very well have to take armed action ourselves, would it be possible to get the countries of Central and South America through OAS to take some action to prohibit the shipment of arms or ammunition from any outside force into Cuba? At the same time they could guarantee the territorial integrity of Cuba so that the Cuban government could not say that they would be at the mercy of the United States.

It seems to me that something along these lines is absolutely essential. Maybe this is not the way to carry it out but something forceful and determined must be done. Furthermore, serious attention must be given to this problem immediately and not wait for the situation in Cuba to revert back to a time of relative peace and calm with the U.S. having been beaten off with her tail between her legs.

What has been going on in Cuba in the last few days must also be a tremendous strain on Castro. It seems to me that this is the time to decide what our long-term policies are going to be and what will be the results of those policies. The time has come for a showdown for in a year or two years the situation will be vastly worse. If we don't want Russia to set up missile bases in Cuba, we had better decide now what we are willing to do to stop it.

19. Under Secretary of State Bowles's Notes on Cabinet Meeting

Anger over failure at the Bay of Pigs results in a stormy discussion between JFK and his advisers.

Washington, April 20, 1961.

Cabinet Meeting on Thursday, April 20th, the first day immediately after the collapse of the Cuban expedition became known.

I attended the Cabinet meeting in Rusk's absence and it was about as grim as any meeting I can remember in all my experience in government, which is saying a good deal.

The President was really quite shattered, and understandably so. Almost without exception, his public career had been a long series of successes, without any noteworthy set backs. Those disappointments which had come his way, such as his failure to get the nomination for Vice President in 1956 were clearly attributable to religion.

Here for the first time he faced a situation where his judgment had been mistaken, in spite of the fact that week after week of conferences had taken place before he gave the green light.

It was not a pleasant experience. Reactions around the table were almost savage, as everyone appeared to be jumping on everyone else. The only really coherent statement was by Arthur Goldberg, who said that while it was doubtful that the expedition was wise in the first place, the Administration should not have undertaken it unless it was prepared to see it through with United States troops if necessary.

At least his remarks had an inherent logic to them, although I could not agree under any circumstances to sending troops into Cuba—violating every treaty obligation we have.

The most angry response of all came from Bob Kennedy and also, strangely enough, from Dave Bell, who I had always assumed was a very reasonable individual.

The discussion simply rambled in circles with no real coherent thought. Finally after three-quarters of an hour the President got up and walked toward his office. I was so distressed at what I felt was a dangerous mood that I walked after him, stopped him, and told him I would like an opportunity to come into his office and talk the whole thing out.

Lyndon Johnson, Bob McNamara, and Bob Kennedy joined us. Bobby [Kennedy] continued his tough, savage comments, most of them directed against the Department of State for reasons which are difficult for me to understand.

When I took exception to some of the more extreme things he said by suggesting that the way to get out of our present jam was not to simply double up on everything we had done, he turned on me savagely.

What worries me is that two of the most powerful people in this administration—Lyndon Johnson and Bob Kennedy—have no experience in foreign affairs, and they both realize that this is the central question of this period and are determined to be experts at it.

The problems of foreign affairs are complex, involving politics, economics and social questions that require both understanding of history and various world cultures.

When a newcomer enters the field and finds himself confronted by the nuances of international questions, he becomes an easy target for the military-CIA-paramilitary type answers which are often in specific logistical terms which can be added, subtracted, multiplied, or divided.

This kind of thinking was almost dominant in the conference and I found it most alarming. The President appeared the most calm, yet it was clear to see that he had been suffering an acute shock and it was an open question in my mind as to what his reaction would be.

All through the meeting which took place in the President's office and which lasted almost a half hour, there was an almost frantic reaction for an action program which people would grab onto.[1]

20. Memorandum from Secretary of Defense McNamara to Chairman of the Joint Chiefs of Staff Lemnitzer

JFK instructs the Pentagon to prepare a plan for the possible use of force against Cuba. This sort of contingency planning would be intensified in coming months.

Washington, April 20, 1961.

The President has asked that the Defense Department develop a plan for the overthrow of the Castro government by the application of U.S. military force. The plan should include:

1. An appraisal of the strength of the Cuban military forces.

2. An appraisal of the probable behavior of the Cuban civilian population during the period of military action.

[1]Bowles wrote these notes in May 1961.

April 20, 1961.

[Delivered at the Statler Hilton Hotel in Washington, D.C.]

The President of a great democracy such as ours, and the editors of great newspapers such as yours, owe a common obligation to the people: an obligation to present the facts, to present them with candor, and to present them in perspective. It is with that obligation in mind that I have decided in the last 24 hours to discuss briefly at this time the recent events in Cuba.

On that unhappy island, as in so many other arenas of the contest for freedom, the news has grown worse instead of better. I have emphasized before that this was a struggle of Cuban patriots against a Cuban dictator. While we could not be expected to hide our sympathies, we made it repeatedly clear that the armed forces of this country would not intervene in any way.

Any unilateral American intervention, in the absence of an external attack upon ourselves or an ally, would have been contrary to our traditions and to our international obligations. But let the record show that our restraint is not inexhaustible. Should it ever appear that the inter-American doctrine of noninterference merely conceals or excuses a policy of nonaction—if the nations of this Hemisphere should fail to meet their commitments against outside Communist penetration—then I want it clearly understood that this Government will not hesitate in meeting its primary obligations which are to the security of our Nation.

Should that time ever come, we do not intend to be lectured on "intervention" by those whose character was stamped for all time on the bloody streets of Budapest.[1] Nor would we expect or accept the same outcome which this small band of gallant Cuban refugees must have known that they were chancing, determined as they were against heavy odds to pursue their courageous attempts to regain their Island's freedom. . . .

We will not accept Mr. Castro's attempts to blame this nation for the hatred with which his onetime supporters now regard his repression. But there are from this sobering episode useful lessons for us all to learn. Some may be still obscure, and await further information. Some are clear today.

First, it is clear that the forces of communism are not to be underestimated, in Cuba or anywhere else in the world. The advantages of a police state—its use of mass terror and arrests to prevent the spread of free dissent—cannot be overlooked by those who expect the fall of every fanatic tyrant. If the self-discipline of the free cannot match the iron discipline of the mailed fist—in economic, political, scientific and all the other kinds of struggles as well as the military—then the peril to freedom will continue to rise.

Secondly, it is clear that this Nation, in concert with all the free nations of this hemisphere, must take an ever closer and more realistic look at the menace of external Communist intervention and domination in Cuba. The American

---

[1]This was a reference to the Soviet Union's ruthless suppression of the 1956 Hungarian uprising.

people are not complacent about Iron Curtain tanks and planes less than 90 miles from their shore. But a nation of Cuba's size is less a threat to our survival than it is a base for subverting the survival of other free nations throughout the hemisphere. It is not primarily our interest or our security but theirs which is now, today, in the greater peril. It is for their sake as well as our own that we must show our will.

The evidence is clear—and the hour is late. We and our Latin friends will have to face the fact that we cannot postpone any longer the real issue of survival of freedom in this hemisphere itself. On that issue, unlike perhaps some others, there can be no middle ground. Together we must build a hemisphere where freedom can flourish; and where any free nation under outside attack of any kind can be assured that all of our resources stand ready to respond to any request for assistance.

Third, and finally, it is clearer than ever that we face a relentless struggle in every corner of the globe that goes far beyond the clash of armies or even nuclear armaments. The armies are there, and in large number. The nuclear armaments are there. But they serve primarily as the shield behind which subversion, infiltration, and a host of other tactics steadily advance, picking off vulnerable areas one by one in situations which do not permit our own armed intervention.

Power is the hallmark of this offensive—power and discipline and deceit. The legitimate discontent of yearning people is exploited. The legitimate trappings of self-determination are employed. But once in power, all talk of discontent is repressed, all self-determination disappears, and the promise of a revolution of hope is betrayed, as in Cuba, into a reign of terror. Those who on instruction staged automatic "riots" in the streets of free nations over the efforts of a small group of young Cubans to regain their freedom should recall the long roll call of refugees who cannot now go back—to Hungary, to North Korea, to North Viet-Nam, to East Germany, or to Poland, or to any of the other lands from which a steady stream of refugees pours forth, in eloquent testimony to the cruel oppression now holding sway in their homeland.

We dare not fail to see the insidious nature of this new and deeper struggle. We dare not fail to grasp the new concepts, the new tools, the new sense of urgency we will need to combat it—whether in Cuba or South Viet-Nam. And we dare not fail to realize that this struggle is taking place every day, without fanfare, in thousands of villages and markets—day and night—and in classrooms all over the globe.

The message of Cuba, of Laos, of the rising din of Communist voices in Asia and Latin America—these messages are all the same. The complacent, the self-indulgent, the soft societies are about to be swept away with the debris of history. Only the strong, only the industrious, only the determined, only the courageous, only the visionary who determine the real nature of our struggle can possibly survive.

No greater task faces this country or this administration. No other challenge is more deserving of our every effort and energy. Too long we have fixed our eyes on traditional military needs, on armies prepared to cross borders, on missiles poised for flight. Now it should be clear that this is no longer enough—that our security may be lost piece by piece, country by country, without the firing of a single missile or the crossing of a single border.

We intend to profit from this lesson. We intend to reexamine and reorient our forces of all kinds—our tactics and our institutions here in this community. We intend to intensify our efforts for a struggle in many ways more difficult than war, where disappointment will often accompany us.

For I am convinced that we in this country and in the free world possess the necessary resource, and the skill, and the added strength that comes from a belief in the freedom of man. And I am equally convinced that history will record the fact that this bitter struggle reached its climax in the late 1950's and the early 1960's. Let me then make clear as the President of the United States that I am determined upon our system's survival and success, regardless of the cost and regardless of the peril.

23. Under Secretary of State Bowles's Notes on National Security Council Meeting

In private, as well as in public, hard-line sentiments were expressed, notably by Robert Kennedy.

Washington, April 22, 1961.

There were some thirty-five people at the NSC meeting on Cuba. Again Bob Kennedy was present, and took the lead as at the previous meeting, slamming into anyone who suggested that we go slowly and try to move calmly and not repeat previous mistakes.

The atmosphere was almost as emotional as the Cabinet meeting two days earlier, the difference being that on this occasion the emphasis was on specific proposals to harass Castro.

On two or three occasions I suggested that the greatest mistake we could make would be to pit the United States with its 180 million people in a contest against a Cuban dictator on an island of 6 million people. I stressed that while we are already in a bad situation, it would be a mistake for us to assume that it could not disintegrate further and an almost sure way to lose ground was to reach out in ways that would almost surely be ineffective and which would tend to create additional sympathy for Castro in his David and Goliath struggle against the United States.

These comments were brushed aside brutally and abruptly by the various fire eaters who were present. I did think, however, that the faces of a few people around the table reflected some understanding of the views I was trying to present, notably Dick Goodwin, Ted Sorensen (which is surprising), Arthur Schlesinger, and above all Jerry Wiesner.

The President limited himself largely to asking questions—questions, however, which led in one direction.

I left the meeting with a feeling of intense alarm, tempered somewhat with the hope that this represented largely an emotional reaction of a group of people who were not used to setbacks or defeats and whose pride and confidence had been deeply wounded.

However, I felt again the great lack of moral integrity which I believe is the central guide in dealing with tense and difficult questions, particularly when the individuals involved are tired, frustrated, and personally humiliated.

If every question in the world becomes an intellectual exercise on a totally pragmatic basis, with no reference to moral considerations, it may be that we can escape disaster, but it will certainly be putting the minds of the White House group to a test when it becomes necessary to add up the components, large and small on the plus or minus side of a ledger, and when the minds that are attempting to do this are tired, uneasy, and unsure, the values and the arithmetic are unlikely to reflect wise courses.[1]

24. Memorandum from the Joint Chiefs of Staff to Secretary of Defense McNamara

The Joint Chiefs provide McNamara with the plan for military action against Cuba that he had requested.

Washington, April 26, 1961.

1. Reference is made to your memorandum to the Chairman, Joint Chiefs of Staff, dated 20 April 1961.[1] This memorandum with Appendices is responsive to questions posed by you in reference memorandum.

2. Appendix A contains an analysis of courses of action. Appendix D contains a brief outline plan based upon CINCLANT Operation Plan 312–61 which will provide for the overthrow of the Castro government by the application of US military force, the course of action considered best suited to accomplishment of the objective.

3. This plan, with appropriate additional instructions to CINCLANT as to timing and manner of execution, is responsive to the requirement for a military plan to accomplish the desired objective. The plan is well conceived, has been

[1]Bowles wrote these notes in May 1961.
[1]See Document 20.

reviewed by the Joint Chiefs of Staff, and will insure quick overthrow of the Castro government.

4. There is a need for a well conceived political program to insure rapid turnover of control of government to designated Cuban authorities and permit the rapid withdrawal of US forces. It is recommended that the Secretary of State be requested to develop guidance in support of this operation.

For the Joint Chiefs of Staff:
Earle G. Wheeler

Appendix A

ANALYSIS OF COURSES OF ACTION

1. The objective as stated by the Secretary of Defense is to overthrow the Castro regime by the application of military force.

2. The analysis which follows has taken into consideration the world reaction to the abortive invasion of Cuba [at the Bay of Pigs]. Most nations apparently believe that the United States was wrong to give any support to this operation, particularly since there was no resultant uprising by the Cuban people. In the United Nations the prestige of the United States has deteriorated, and there are indications that the Latin American nations have lost some confidence in the United States. Within Cuba the incident has probably had the effect of strengthening the control held by the Castro government, instilling confidence and loyalty in the militia and other forces, and demoralizing the dissident elements which remain.

3. Any military effort undertaken by the United States against Cuba will engender strong criticism by most of the world. If a military action or series of actions take appreciable time to accomplish the overthrow of the Castro government, this time can be used to the advantage of the Sino-Soviet Bloc and Castro in strengthening his defenses. More important, world Communism can use this period of time to advantage in building up a massive, world-wide, anti-US propaganda effort against the United States course of action, including introduction of a resolution to the UN. If the United States were to embark on such a course, and then, through the pressure of world opinion be forced to abandon its action, the result would be a severe blow to the prestige, the objectives, and the national interests of the United States. Achieving world-wide surprise in an undertaking like this is extremely important. It seems apparent, therefore, that any military operation undertaken to accomplish the above objective should be swift, sharp, and overwhelming and should present the remainder of the world with a fait accompli.

4. The following alternative programs have been considered:

a. *Naval and Air Blockade.* A blockade could be instituted immediately and could be effective. It would stop the influx of [Communist] Bloc military equipment and personnel, and would do much to halt the export of Communism from Cuba to Latin America. The Cuban economy, in particular the oil industry, is especially vulnerable to blockade, and it is believed that a blockade, by itself, could reduce the Cuban economy to chaos. However, a blockade would force great hardships on the Cuban people regardless of political belief, and it is likely that their plight would generate strong resentment in all of Latin America. Since a blockade must be time-consuming, world resistance could be skillfully built up by the Bloc, as pointed out previously, and the blockade might have to be abandoned. Since use of blockade would not, by itself, assure the objective it is not recommended as the only course of action. However, blockade should be utilized to complement a military invasion and, if such an invasion is to be delayed for an appreciable period of time, a limited blockade against military supplies and equipment should be instituted to prevent build-up of Cuban military strength.

b. *Overt Support of Cuban Dissident Forces.* This course of action would strengthen the dissident elements both materially and psychologically. The recent defeat of the invading dissident elements has undoubtedly had a demoralizing effect on them, and has probably weakened them in numbers and organization. Reorganizing these groups, and attracting additional numbers in face of current repressive measures taken by Castro will be extremely difficult. Even if sufficient numbers could be organized, their training would take much time, and it seems evident that their quality could never come up to US standards. These factors all seem to indicate that this course of action by itself would give little assurance of accomplishing the objective, and it is therefore not recommended. While support to dissident elements should not be chosen as the main course of action, it should not be abandoned. These elements can be of great assistance in intelligence collection, serve as focal points for uprisings, and assist in military operations and continual harassment of the Castro regime. Some form of support in Cuba is necessary to give encouragement to resistance movements in Cuba and other countries and to impress them with the fact that the United States will not abandon them. The success of a military operation against Cuba, however, should not be made dependent upon the actions of any dissident elements.

c. *Military Intervention by the Organization of American States.* . . . OAS military actions would be unlikely unless a majority of the states were convinced that they were faced with a clearly discernible external threat. Communist tactics, however, are subtle and cleverly screened. Although there is a growing awareness among the Latin American nations that the totalitarian Castro government is becoming a threat to their security, they do not yet consider it a clear and present danger. For these reasons OAS military action against Cuba is unlikely for the present.

d. *Overt US Actions Supported by Latin American Volunteers.* Participation by volunteers from Latin America in direct US military action against Cuba would soften the impression that the United States would be taking unilateral action contrary to the spirit of the UN and the OAS. In order to be convincing, it would have to be evident that there was a large number of volunteers coming from a variety of Latin American nations. The assembly and organization of these volunteers would be time-consuming, and all security of the operation would be lost. The success of this course of action seems unlikely and it is not recommended in any form.

e. *Unilateral US Action*

(1) Unilateral military action by the United States offers the advantages that there need be no compromise in pursuing US objectives, and that a reasonable degree of surprise can be achieved. Disadvantages are that strong criticism will be voiced by many nations of all political beliefs, and that the Latin American nations may become particularly distrustful of the United States.

(2) If the United States could overthrow the Castro government through a swift and decisive action, it is believed that all nations would, even while criticizing, accept a fait accompli, especially since they recognize the inherent danger to the basic security of a nation posed by a hostile regime located in close proximity. There is also a good possibility that a decisive action taken by the United States against Communism would renew the confidence of many in the Free World whose faith in our leadership has been faltering.

(3) An overt US action, if taken, must be assured of success. Physical capture and control of the Cuban government and key facilities is the only means of insuring that the objective of overthrowing the Castro government is achieved. CINCLANT Operation Plan 312–61 (Cuba), which has previously been reviewed and approved by the Joint Chiefs of Staff, provides the means of achieving this objective. Implementation of the plan should be in such a manner as to achieve surprise, both worldwide and tactical, and to accomplish the objective in the shortest time possible.

(4) Concurrent supporting actions should be taken as required, to assist in the accomplishment of the objective and to insure the establishment in Cuba of a situation satisfactory to the United States following the overthrow of the Castro government. Appropriate agencies of the Federal government should participate in this planning. One action that is recommended is the creation of an incident which will provide justification for the overthrow of the Castro government by the United States. Such an incident must be carefully planned and handled, to insure that it is plausible and that it occurs prior to any indication that the United States has decided to take military action against Cuba. Premature exposure of the fact that the incident was created by the United States could cause a shift in sentiment by the Cuban people against the United States.

5. *More deliberate action*

a. Another alternative to be examined is that of following a more deliberate course, characterized by extensive preparations both military and political. The military forces to be used in the operation could be brought to peak effectiveness at the time desired, and logistic arrangements could be thorough and complete. If the military posture in Cuba continued to improve, requiring additional assault forces to invade Cuba, these forces could be obtained through a selective increase of forces. . . . The time of assault could be chosen during a period when world tensions are low, minimizing the risk of having to conduct military operations in more than one place. The chances of achieving tactical surprise might be enhanced by planning the invasion for a time which coincided with routine training exercises. . . .

b. While a more deliberate course of action offers some advantages, past history seems to indicate that time is on the side of Castro. An invasion should not be conducted during the hurricane season, which lasts from August through November. The Castro regime could use this time to strengthen itself militarily and internally to the point that it would require a large-scale effort to overthrow him. Since this course of action would probably require large military effort, and shows little assurance of achieving the implicit political objectives, it is not recommended.

6. From a military point of view, it is recommended that the course of action proposed in paragraph 4 e above, in conjunction with the courses of action discussed in paragraphs 4 a and 4 b, be adopted if it is decided to accomplish the stated objective. . . .

Appendix D

OUTLINE OPLAN

. . . 2. *Mission*

Commander in Chief Atlantic will, when directed, conduct military operations in Cuba in order to accomplish the following: Defend the Naval Base at Guantanamo Bay; restore and maintain order; support or reestablish the authority of a Cuban Government friendly to the United States, and support the national policy of the United States.

3. *Execution*

a. In the event that military operations are directed, any or all of the following courses of action may be undertaken by CINCLANT:

(1) Reinforce and actively defend the Naval Base, Guantanamo Bay.

(2) Interdict Cuban lines of communication.

(3) Neutralize Cuban offensive capability by overt attack against military installations.

(4) Conduct Naval and air blockade of Cuba.

(5) Conduct assault operations to accomplish the mission.

b. *Concept of Operations*

(1) *Western Cuba.* When directed, operations in Western Cuba will be conducted by Army Airborne, Naval Amphibious, and Air Force and Naval Air Forces with the objective of seizing the Havana port and airfield complex, communications and government facilities in order to establish a base for further operations. Thereafter, operations will be expanded as required in order to accomplish the over-all mission.

(2) *Eastern Cuba.* Naval and Marine Forces under command of COMNAVBASE GTMO, will conduct operations to (a) defend the Naval Base at Guantanamo, (b) protect and/or evacuate United States and other designated nationals, (c) maintain a base for further operations.

(3) It is essential that operations be conducted with rapidity and decisiveness by a concurrent amphibious and airborne assault in Western Cuba. This will require that the amphibious elements be mounted and sail prior to deployment of airborne elements to the objective area. The combined airborne-amphibious assault and link-up of forces will ensure early availability of medium tanks and artillery in support of the airborne forces. The army seaborne echelon must be loaded out and sail so as to be available to commence off-loading on D-day.

(4) Amphibious forces in Western Cuba will be relieved and withdrawn as soon as practicable for further operations in the Eastern Cuban area.

(5) By 60–90 days after the initial landing of combat forces it is expected that conditions will permit the utilization of other forces as occupation troops.

(6) The "objective areas" are initially the Western Cuba area for Army–Naval–Air Force operations and the Guantanamo area for Naval operations. Other objectives such as the Isle of Pines, specific cities, industrial plants or transportation facilities will be designated, dependent upon conditions prevailing at the time.

c. *Phasing*

(1) *Phase 1*

(a) Activation of operating headquarters.

(b) Reinforcement and defense of Naval Base at Guantanamo.

(2) *Phase II*

(a) Naval Task Force deploys to objective areas.

(b) Army Task Force deploys combat and service units to staging bases, prepared for airborne assault operations; deploys to objective area on order.

(c) Air Force Task Force deploys tactical elements to advanced operating airfields as required and air lifts elements of the Army Task Force to staging bases.

(3) *Phase III*

Commander Joint Task Force conducts concurrent airborne and amphibious assault operations in the Havana area and supports defensive operations in the Guantanamo area.

(4) *Phase IV*

(a) Commander Joint Task Force conducts amphibious assault and other operations in the Eastern Cuban area to seize Santiago and other objectives as required.

(b) Offensive land operations will be subsequently conducted to link up Army Forces, Western Cuba and Marine Forces, Eastern Cuba, if required. . . .

25. Under Secretary of State Bowles's Notes on National Security Council Meeting

Chester Bowles notices a mellowing of mood among his colleagues.

Washington, April 27, 1961.

The climate is getting considerably better, and the emotional attitudes are falling back into line. If anyone had not attended the previous meetings, he would have thought the NSC meeting this morning had its share of fire and fury. However, it was in far lower key.

Ted Sorensen called me aside to say that he was glad I had said what I did, and Dick Goodwin called me to say I had shown great courage in the last few meetings and he was grateful for it.

At this stage plans continue for all kinds of harassment to punish Castro for the humiliation he has brought to our door. However, the general feeling is that all this should be handled carefully, that there should not be too much publicity, that attitudes of others should be taken into account. . . .

26. Memorandum from Secretary of Defense McNamara to the Joint Chiefs of Staff

JFK reviews his contingency planning for military action against Cuba, and instructions are issued for this planning to be advanced.

Washington, May 1, 1961.

SUBJ

Cuban Contingency Plans

On Saturday, 29 April, Admiral Burke and I reviewed with the President Contingency Plan 1[1] for the invasion of Cuba by U.S. troops. As you will recall, the Plan was designed to minimize U.S. and Cuban casualties, minimize the time required for subjugation of Cuba, and maximize the assurance of a successful operation. The Plan provided for the use of approximately 60,000 troops, excluding naval and air units, and required 25 days between the date of decision and D-Day. It was estimated that complete control of the island could be obtained within 8 days, although it was recognized that guerrilla forces would continue to operate beyond the 8th day in the Escambray Mountains and Oriente Province. The land, sea, and air forces required for the invasion were to be secured from existing forces—no additions to existing forces, with the possible exception of a few merchant ships, would be required prior to D-Day.

The President concurred in the general outline of the Plan.

Please assign to the Joint Staff and CINCLANT the responsibility for preparing the detailed instructions necessary to implement the Plan.

These instructions should be designed to minimize the lead time required, and maximize security during the period between the decision and the invasion.

I want to repeat again that work on these plans should not be interpreted as an indication that U.S. military action against Cuba is probable.

---

[1]This appears to have been a revision of the plan sent by the Joint Chiefs to McNamara on April 26. See Document 24.

27. Notes on National Security Council Meeting

JFK and his advisers define their post–Bay of Pigs approach toward Cuba at this meeting.

Washington, May 5, 1961.

The President asked Mr. Nitze for a report on the Cuban situation. Nitze replied that the Navy could blockade the island but results would not be immediate but rather long-range, and in the course thereof unfavorable world reaction would probably accrue. Admiral Burke pointed out that only complete interception of all ships approaching Cuba would achieve eventual success, and the job could be done with 24 ships. Mr. Rusk interrupted Admiral Burke to point out that such action would be an act of war and was wholly impracticable.

The President asked about a reported letter from Senator Goldwater in which the statement is made that the Air Force could resolve the Cuban situation. Admiral Burke replied that there had in fact been an Air Force proposal with which other services had disagreed, especially the Marines. In any case, the Air Force had made the suggestion that the Cuban problem be resolved through rather heavy and perhaps indiscriminate bombardment. The President immediately rejected such an idea, and added further that there would be no Navy blockade. He emphasized the importance of more effective watch committee action on Cuba. He also asked Mr. Dulles what new information was available on foreign equipment going into Cuba. Mr. Dulles replied that we know practically everything about the equipment, but offered no specifics. The President directed that close surveillance be continued including overflight with an American pilot. The President approved flights of a frequency of every two or three days, but suggested extreme caution.

The President suggested that all Americans be urged to leave Cuba and asked Secretary Johnson[1] to study ways and means of exit and transit visas. . . .

The President asked what specific courses of action we should take to prevent the crippling influence of the Cuban fiasco, assuming that no military action by the U.S. will be taken. At the same time the President asked what circumstances would have to exist before the United States could move unilaterally against Cuba. Rusk stated that action could be taken under Article 51 of the Rio Treaty.[2] In this connection the President asked if the U.S. could recognize the Cuban Government in Exile and what might be expected of this group. Rusk replied that such recognition was not possible because of the absence of certain essential elements of a governmental organization, identity and territory. . . .

---

[1] A reference to Deputy Under Secretary of State U. Alexis Johnson.
[2] Rusk seems to be referring to either Article 51 of the UN Charter or/and Article 6 of the Rio Treaty (a military alliance between countries in the Western Hemisphere).

Record of Actions[3] for this NSC meeting:

a. Agreed that U.S. policy toward Cuba should aim at the downfall of Castro, and that since the measures agreed below are not likely to achieve this end, the matter should be reviewed at intervals with a view to further action.

b. Agreed that the United States should not undertake military intervention in Cuba now, but should do nothing that would foreclose the possibility of military intervention in the future.

c. Agreed that the United States should not impose a naval blockade or attempt an air war against Cuba; it was noted that neither course had the support of the Department of Defense or the Joint Chiefs of Staff.

d. Noted the importance the President attaches to obtaining timely and adequate intelligence as to Cuban military capabilities, especially the enhancement of such capabilities by Sino-Soviet Bloc military assistance, so that U.S. capabilities for possible intervention may be maintained at an adequate level.

e. Noted the importance the President attaches to publication in the Free World press of the terroristic actions of the Castro regime, and to possible political action to end the current terror.

f. Noted the President's direction that the Central Intelligence Agency, with other departments, should make a detailed study of possible weaknesses and vulnerabilities in the elements which exert control in Cuba today.

g. Agreed that relations with the Revolutionary Council [of anti-Castro Cubans] should be improved and made more open, and while it cannot be recognized as a government-in-exile, support should be given to it insofar as it continues to represent substantial Cuban sentiment.

h. Agreed that no separate Cuban military force should be organized in the United States, but that Cuban nationals would be encouraged to enlist in the U.S. armed forces under plans to be developed by the Secretary of Defense.

i. Agreed that Cuban nationals now holding U.S. visitors' visas will be given refugee status and assisted, under a program to be developed and directed by the Secretary of Health, Education and Welfare, in carrying on their former occupations. Refugees now in Miami will be encouraged to locate in other areas. Cuban nationals entering the United States will be given refugee status. All refugees will be eligible to apply for travel privileges, and it was understood that they would also be eligible for citizenship.

j. Agreed not to impose an immediate trade embargo on Cuba. The Secretary of State agreed to send to the President an analysis of the effects of a U.S. embargo on trade with Cuba in relation to the Battle Act.[4] It was agreed that when an embargo is imposed, it should be as complete as possible, with certain exceptions for Canada and with Red Cross distribution of drugs.

k. Agreed that the United States should at once initiate negotiation to enlarge the willingness of other American states to join in bilateral, multilateral and OAS arrangements against Castro, such as (1) breaking diplomatic relations with

[3]JFK endorsed this record of action on May 16.
[4]This legislation, from the Truman years, sought to restrict trade with the Soviet Union and its satellite states.

Cuba; (2) controlling subversive activities of Cuban agents; (3) preventing arms shipments to Castro; (4) limiting economic relations with Cuba; (5) creating a Caribbean security force; (6) initiating a naval patrol to prevent Cuban invasion of other states in the Caribbean; and (7) denunciation of Castro as an agent of international communism by all nations of this hemisphere.

l. Agreed that the Alliance for Progress should be strengthened by such measures as (1) rapid implementation of selected social development projects; (2) acceleration of the implementation of other Latin American aid; and (3) provision of additional resources for Latin American economic and social development, including consideration of a supplemental appropriation for development loans of the order of $200–$400 million.

m. Agreed that the U.S. Information Agency would expand its existing program in Latin America, but not initiate electronic warfare against the Castro regime; means of propaganda should be made available to non-U.S. groups.

n. Agreed that U.S. military officers, under general guidance to be prepared by the Department of State, would discuss the Castro threat to all Latin America with Latin American officers.

o. Agreed that the Secretary of State should prepare a report on a possible new juridical basis for effective anti-communist action.

p. Agreed that pending appointment of an Assistant Secretary of State for Latin American Affairs, the Task Force on Cuba should be continued under the chairmanship of Richard N. Goodwin, Assistant to the Special Counsel to the President.[5]

28. Telegram from the Joint Chiefs of Staff to Commander-in-Chief (Atlantic) Dennison

The Joint Chiefs transmit the order received on May 1 (Document 26) to flesh out the military planning for Cuba.

Washington, May 9.

Exclusive for Adm Dennison, Gen Powell, Gen Everest. Subject is Guidance for Development of Operations Plan on Cuba.

1. Submit to the JCS for approval a plan for military assault of Cuba. The plan must:

a. Assure overthrow of the Castro government in minimum time.

---

[5]For the Task Force, see Document 35, footnote 1. Harold L. Burris, Vice-President Lyndon Johnson's military aide, prepared the notes for this NSC meeting.

b. Assure necessary control of Cuba following overthrow of Castro government.

c. Assure continuous control of the US base at Guantanamo.

d. Provide the capability of initiating the assault without prior warning and within five days after the order to execute.

e. Be capable of execution at any time during a prolonged period after required forces and equipment are positioned.

2. Forces and equipment will be tailored as necessary to accomplish the plan, and may be repositioned as required. . . .

4. Submit initially, on a priority basis, an outline plan and a concept of operations. Include estimate of time required to accomplish 1 a and b above. Concurrently submit requirements for:

a. Total forces and equipment.

b. Repositioning and/or prepositioning of forces and equipment necessary to obtain required state of readiness. Include estimate of time required to accomplish these actions.

5. Any recommendation you may have as to an alternate solution which will enhance the feasibility of the plan together with its impact on reaction time and total forces required is invited.

6. This guidance should not be interpreted as an indication that US military action against Cuba is probable.

29. Memorandum for the Record of a CIA Meeting

This discussion showed that the Bay of Pigs episode had not dampened the enthusiasm of CIA officials for covert action against Cuba.

Washington, May 9, 1961.

PARTICIPANTS

Mr. Richard M. Bissell, Jr.
Mr. C. Tracy Barnes
Col. J. C. King
[*name not declassified*]
Mr. G. Droller
[*name not declassified*]

. . . 2. Mr. Bissell then stated that there has been a round of policymaking sessions—externally with NSC and Mr. Goodwin of the White House—and internally. He said that there is an urgent need to decide what we are going to do next [about Cuba]—what people and facilities we are going to use. He asked if there was general agreement (there was) that we start building up our internal assets; plus planning and carrying out sabotage operations which would call for the use of a minimum number of people; that we should start commo training promptly; also think of training programs for resistance and underground types. . . . Mr. Bissell commissioned [*less than 1 line of source text not declassified*], with the assistance of Mr. Reichhardt, to come up within a week's time, if possible, with an outline proposal for covert action. [*less than 1 line of source text not declassified*] suggested that the best place to start would be with the old operational plan[1] which could be reviewed, updated and "sprinkled with the experience" which we have gained to date. Mr. Barnes promised to provide a copy of a paper which was recently prepared on this subject. Mr. Barnes, in response to a statement by Mr. Droller that he understood from Dr. Miro that the President was opposed to sabotage operations, said that the White House is expecting a paper from us as to what we propose to do—recommendations for action, unilateral or otherwise, and on the basis of this we could expect to get some policy approval. That sabotage is still open whenever it seems appropriate. Mr. Bissell said we will want to take the paper to the President and also to State and Defense. We will also need the operational outline for our own internal purposes. He asked if there was general agreement to this approach and Col. King said he would like to see included in the plan the use of B–26 aircraft against refineries and other targets but that we could leave the timing open.[2]

30. CIA Paper, "Program of Covert Action Aimed at Weakening the Castro Regime"

This paper displayed the sort of thinking that would later result in the establishment of Operation Mongoose.

Washington, May 19, 1961.

I. Introduction

1. The proposals submitted in this recommended program of covert action directed against the Castro regime are based on a realistic appraisal of existing assets, both in and out of Cuba; on potential assets, both inside and outside of Cuba which are capable of development within acceptable time limits; and on certain assumptions with respect to United States policy.

2. For the purpose of this paper it is assumed that United States policy:

---

[1]This is possibly a reference to the Bay of Pigs plan.
[2]This memorandum was produced in the CIA.

A. Will not contemplate the use of its armed forces to intervene directly or unilaterally in the absence of an aggressive military action on the part of Cuba directed against the United States or another country of this hemisphere.

B. Will not permit the organizing and training of a Cuban exile military force for further action against Cuba.

C. Will permit United States covert support of Cuban clandestine activities and the carrying out of covert unilateral operations as described herein, including the use of maritime and air facilities within the United States as the bases for the staging of sabotage, in-exfiltration, supply, raider and propaganda (including leaflet dropping) operations. . . .

II. Objective

To plan, implement and sustain a program of covert action designed to exploit the economic, political and psychological vulnerabilities of the Castro regime. It is neither expected nor argued that the successful execution of this covert program will in itself result in the overthrow of the Castro regime. This plan should be viewed only as the covert contribution to an overall national program designed to accelerate the moral and physical disintegration of the Castro government and to hasten the day when a combination of actions and circumstances will make possible its replacement by a democratic government responsive to the needs, the aspirations and the will of the Cuban people.

III. Tasks

1. To achieve these objectives a series of short-term and long-term tasks will be undertaken. Wherever feasible and possible, these activities will be carried out under the aegis of the Cuban Revolutionary Council. However, since this will not always be practicable or desirable, for a variety of reasons, unilateral Agency operations and independent operations by acceptable groups and elements outside the framework of the Council will also be undertaken.

Short Term Tasks

A. *Operational Intelligence Collection:* Every effort will be made to improve and expand our capabilities for the collection of operational intelligence on Castro's plans, intentions and capabilities; on specific industrial, military and communications targets; on candidates for defection; on the morale of the civil population and the extent of its support of and discontent with the Castro regime. This will call for the strengthening of existing internal agent nets; the recruitment of legal travelers; the recruitment, training and infiltration of new agents; liaison with Cuban exile groups and individuals with independent access to targets, and the continuation and intensification of existing special intelligence efforts.

B. *Sabotage Operations Against Selected Targets:* Sabotage operations will be planned and executed against such targets as refineries, power plants, micro wave stations, radio and TV installations, strategic highway bridges and railroad facilities, military and naval installations and equipment, certain industrial plants and sugar refineries. This will first require building up present capabilities through recruitment, training and infiltration of sabotage teams.

C. *Operations in Support of Guerrilla Activities:* Operations will be planned and executed in support of guerrilla bands which exist or may emerge in the hills of Cuba utilizing both air and maritime operations for the delivery of arms and supplies and for the infiltration and exfiltration of personnel. Since we believe that there is little likelihood of significant accomplishments by guerrilla activities for some time to come, we will discourage offensive guerrilla activities at this time in order that the strength of such forces may be preserved for a more propitious moment. Depending on success in building solid, reasonably dependable and reasonably compartmented assets, in establishing communication with them, and equipping them, the scale of sabotage and guerrilla activities will be stepped up. Our first concern is the rebuilding of our internal nets and of our capability for mounting significant operations.

D. *Operations Directed at Defection of Castro Officials:* Operations directed at defection, wherever possible in place, of well-placed officials of the Castro government and armed forces will be planned and executed. The objective is twofold:

(1) in the cases of defections in place, to gain an insight into the intentions, plans and capabilities of the regime, and

(2) in the cases of open and publicized defections, to cause embarrassment and loss of prestige for the regime, especially in the rest of Latin America.

E. *Operations Directed at Destroying the Popular Image of Castro:* In the field of psychological warfare, operations will be planned and executed aimed at destroying the image of Castro as a true revolutionary interested in the welfare of his people and the replacement of that image with one of a ruthless dictator who, under the false banners of revolutionary reform, has deprived his people of their basic liberties and turned their country into a Soviet satellite. This will require expansion of existing covert press, radio and other media assets outside of Cuba and the strengthening of clandestine propaganda mechanisms inside of Cuba, including underground printed propaganda, clandestine radio broadcasting stations, radio and TV intrusion operations. . . .

F. *Operations Aimed at Strengthening the Prestige and Acceptability of the Revolutionary Council:* Through all available propaganda warfare assets and mechanisms an effort will be made to strengthen the prestige of the Revolutionary Council and its programs, as well as the prestige of its individual members, in order to assure its acceptability as a provisional successor to the Castro regime. Through adoption of a program of political action an effort will be made (a) to maintain close and cordial contact with the Revolutionary Council for the purpose of providing unobtrusive guidance and material support for its organizational structure and its clandestine activities; (b) to improve the position of the Council by encouraging support of the Council by acceptable political groups and personalities who are now opposed to or do not recognize the Council as leadership of the opposition; (c) to encourage the Council to adopt a conciliatory attitude towards all acceptable political groups; and (d) to broaden its base to make it more representative of all political thought (with exclusion of extreme left and extreme right) and important social and economic sectors (church, labor, military, students, intellectuals, etc.).

Long Term Tasks

A. *Political Action:* Develop friendly and close contact with leaders of the Revolutionary Council, and leaders (and/or potential leaders) of all political parties and social and economic sectors (church, labor, military, students, intellectuals, et al) in order to assure friendly and helpful contacts and attitudes towards the United States throughout the entire political and social spectrum during the post-Castro era.

B. *Intelligence:* From existing and potential assets in Cuba and abroad develop and train unilateral agent networks in all walks of life in order to assure the Agency a flow of reliable and significant intelligence during the confused and chaotic period which will exist during the post-Castro era.

C. *Counter Intelligence:* In coordination and cooperation with the Revolutionary Council create, train and support a highly motivated and professionally competent apolitical and career security service which will be dedicated to the preservation of the democratic form of government. Assign carefully selected and qualified Agency personnel to work with the service during the current and post-Castro eras.

D. *Psychological:* Maintain and strengthen the excellent contacts and relations which now exist with exile press and radio entities and personalities in order to assure friendly and helpful contacts and attitudes within mass media circles during the post-Castro era. . . .

V. Recommendation

It is recommended that the above described program of covert action, designed to exploit any economic, political and psychological vulnerabilities of the Castro regime, be approved.[1]

31. Memorandum of Conversation Between President Kennedy and Chairman Khrushchev

For the only time during his presidency, Kennedy meets Khrushchev — at the Vienna summit. The two leaders clashed, famously, over Berlin, but they also exchanged views on Cuba.

[1]It is not clear which official drafted this paper. Copies of it were sent to a number of officials, including CIA Director Allen W. Dulles.

June 3, 1961
3:00 P.M.

[Residence of the American Ambassador, Vienna]

	US	USSR
PARTICIPANTS:	The President	Chairman Khrushchev
	Alexander A. Akalovsky,	Victor M. Sukhodrev,
	interpreter	interpreter

. . . The President referred to the conversation before lunch and said that some of the problems faced by the two countries had been discussed. Now he wanted to come back to the general thesis. While Laos was one problem now under discussion, others might come up in the future. Thus, it would be useful to discuss the general problem underlying the situation and consider the specifics perhaps later. . . . The President then recalled Mr. Khrushchev's earlier reference to the death of feudalism. He said he understood this to mean that capitalism was to be succeeded by Communism. This was a disturbing situation because the French Revolution, as the Chairman well knew, had caused great disturbances and upheavals throughout Europe. . . . Thus it is obvious that when systems are in transition we should be careful, particularly today when modern weapons are at hand. Whatever the result of the present competition—and no one can be sure what it will be—both sides should act in such a way as to prevent them from coming into direct contact and thus prejudicing the establishment of lasting peace, which, the President said, was his ambition.

Mr. Khrushchev interjected that he fully understood this.

Even the Russian Revolution had produced convulsions, even intervention by other countries, the President continued. He then said that he wanted to explain what he meant by "miscalculation". In Washington, he has to attempt to make judgments of events, judgments which may be accurate or not; he made a misjudgment with regard to the Cuban situation. He has to attempt to make judgments as to what the USSR will do next, just as he is sure that Mr. Khrushchev has to make judgments as to the moves of the US. The President emphasized that the purpose of this meeting was to introduce greater precision in these judgments so that our two countries could survive this period of competition without endangering their national security.

Mr. Khrushchev responded by saying that this was a good idea and that this was what he called demonstration of patience and understanding. However, judging by some of the President's statements, the Soviet Union understood the situation differently. The US believes that when people want to improve their lot, this is a machination by others. . . . He [JFK] believes that when people rise against tyrants, that is a result of Moscow's activities. This is not so. Failure by the US to understand this generates danger. The USSR does not foment revolution but the United States always looks for outside forces whenever certain upheavals occur. . . . The Soviet Union does not sympathize with dictators or tyranny. This is the crux of the matter. No agreement seems to be possible on this point, but this fact should be taken into account. . . . Another example of this situation is

Cuba. A mere handful of people, headed by Fidel Castro, overthrew the Batista regime because of its oppressive nature. During Castro's fight against Batista, US capitalist circles, as they are called in the USSR, supported Batista and this is why the anger of the Cuban people turned against the United States. The President's decision to launch a landing in Cuba only strengthened the revolutionary forces and Castro's own position, because the people of Cuba were afraid that they would get another Batista and lose the achievements of the revolution. Castro is not a Communist but US policy can make him one. US policy is grist on the mill of Communists, because US actions prove that Communists are right. Mr. Khrushchev said that he himself had not been born a Communist and that it was capitalists who had made him a Communist. He continued by saying that the President's concept was a dangerous one. The President had said that the US had attacked Cuba because it was a threat to American security. Can six million people really be a threat to the mighty US? The United States has stated that it is free to act, but what about Turkey and Iran? These two countries are US followers, they march in its wake, and they have US bases and rockets. If the US believes that it is free to act, then what should the USSR do? The US has set a precedent for intervention in internal affairs of other countries. The USSR is stronger than Turkey and Iran, just as the US is stronger than Cuba. This situation may cause miscalculation, to use the President's term. Both sides should agree to rule out miscalculation. This is why, Mr. Khrushchev said, he was happy that the President had said that Cuba was a mistake.

The President said that he agreed with Mr. Khrushchev. . . . The second point he wanted to make, the President said, was that he held no brief for Batista. The disagreement between the United States and Castro is not over monopolies; this question could be subject to discussion. The main point is that Castro has announced his intention to act in that general area, using Cuba as a base. This could eventually create a peril to the United States. A further point is, the President said, that the United States recognizes that it has bases in Turkey and Iran. However, these two countries are so weak that they could be no threat to the USSR, no more than Cuba to the US. The President reminded Mr. Khrushchev of the announced policy of the USSR that it would not tolerate governments hostile to it in areas which it regards as being of national interest to it. He inquired what the USSR's reaction would be if a government associated with the West were established in Poland. The United States stands for the right of free choice for all people and if Castro had acted in that spirit, he might have obtained endorsement. . . . The President concluded by saying that it was critical to have the changes occurring in the world and affecting the balance of power take place in a way that would not involve the prestige or the treaty commitments of our two countries. The changes should be peaceful. Finally, the President said, if certain governments should fail to produce better living for their people, if they failed to give better education, higher standard of living, etc., to their people, and if they worked in the interest of only a small group, their days would be doomed. But in all these developments, the President reiterated, we should avoid direct contact between our two countries so as not to prejudice the interests of their national security.

Mr. Khrushchev said he agreed with the President's conclusion. Likewise, there were some points of agreement between him and the President with regard to Cuba, although there was still considerable disagreement. For instance, Mr. Khrushchev said, he agreed that the right of free choice should be ensured to all peoples but the question of choice should be solely up to the people themselves. If Castro has not held any elections, this is an internal affair and it grants no one the right to intervene. If Castro fails to give freedom to his people he will detach himself from them and he will be removed just as Batista was. It would be a different situation if our two countries took it upon themselves to decide this question. Mr. Khrushchev then said that he had noted some inconsistency in US policy. He specified that he did not mean the policy of the President personally, because he had been in the White House only since quite recently, but rather US policy in general. He said that the United States places great emphasis on democracy. . . . The United States [however] supports the most reactionary regimes and this is how the people see US policy. This weakens US policy. The United States knows that Soviet policy is more popular than US policy in many areas where there is no Communism today. The USSR supports the aspirations of the people but it believes that the main thing is to be tolerant and not to interfere. People should be left to decide for themselves which form of government they desire. As to Fidel Castro, he was no Communist but when the US put pressure on him and applied sanctions against him, the USSR came to his assistance, in the form of trade and technical support. Under the influence of this aid he may turn Communist but, Mr. Khrushchev said, he as a Communist could not see which way Castro would go. Mr. Khrushchev then expressed the hope that the relations between the US and Cuba would improve in such fields as trade, etc. Such a statement, Mr. Khrushchev observed, might sound strange to the United States, but the USSR believes that such a development would improve relations not only in the Western Hemisphere, but also throughout the world.[1]

32. Memorandum for the Record Prepared by Chief of Naval Operations Burke

Still mulling over his post–Bay of Pigs options, JFK discusses military intervention in Cuba with his chief of naval operations.

Washington, July 26, 1961.

SUBJ

Mtg at White House with the President on 26 Jul 61

[1]Akalovsky drafted this memorandum.

The President talked about Cuba. He asked me if I thought we would have to go into Cuba. I said yes. He asked would Castro get stronger. I said yes. Castro would increase his power over his people. He asked whether we could take Cuba easily. I said yes, but it was getting more and more difficult. He asked what did I think would happen if we attacked. I said all hell would break loose but that some day we would have to do it. The danger would be that Castro would flee and go to some other country—Russia or Brazil.

33. CIA Paper on Covert Actions Against Cuba

By August 4, 1961, JFK had approved this covert program. It was given a budget of $5,360,000 for a period of six months.

Washington, undated
(but probably drafted in
early August 1961).

Recommendation

It is recommended that the Special Group[1] approve the following covert action program against Cuba:

a) Intelligence and Counterintelligence

Collection of intelligence on the internal Cuban situation and the attitude of the Cuban people, particularly with regard to opposition elements. Improved and expanded collection of operational intelligence on Castro's plans, intentions and capabilities. Penetration of Cuban security services and protection of Agency [CIA] operations against action by these services.

b) Political Action

Foster support for U.S. national policies with respect to Cuba, throughout Latin America. Combat Castro's subversive efforts in that area. Assist in strengthening unified opposition to Castro among Cubans, inside and outside of Cuba. Identify and support, if found, any such groups or leaders with real potential for overthrowing and replacing the Castro government.

c) Propaganda

Continue to support propaganda assets, including magazines, newspapers, news letters and radio. Conduct continual review of the effectiveness of these media. Attempt to destroy the popular image of Castro in Cuba, and combat his propaganda efforts throughout Latin America.

---

[1]The Special Group, also known as the NSC 5412 Committee, was charged with overseeing covert operations. For Operation Mongoose, established in Novermber 1961, this body was enlarged so as to include—most notably—Robert Kennedy, and was referred to as the Special Group (Augmented) or SGA.

d) Paramilitary

Expand present personnel and support aspects inside and outside of Cuba, for use in working with or through Cuban groups in developing an underground organization or organizations. Once such a secure organization is established, engage in infiltration and exfiltration of personnel, supplies and matériel, in intelligence collection and propaganda, and in a low key sabotage and resistance program. Large scale sabotage activities may be planned for, but will not be mounted until approved by the Special Group. Provide modest support, as approved by the Special Group, to those guerrilla elements that might arise in Cuba and which are believed worthy of support. Maintain a limited air capability largely through pilot training.

e) Support

Maintain necessary personnel, forward-operating base on U.S. territory, maritime base, operational or training sites and communications facilities. . . .

34. Memorandum from Assistant Special Counsel Richard N. Goodwin to President Kennedy

At the close of the Punta del Este conference in Uruguay, a Castro aide met with Kennedy adviser Richard Goodwin at a party and proposed an arrangement for mitigating Cuban-American tensions. Here Goodwin reports the conversation to JFK.

Washington, August 22, 1961.

SUBJECT

Conversation with Commandante Ernesto [Che] Guevara of Cuba

The conversation took place the evening of August 17 at 2 A.M. . . .

Che was wearing green fatigues, and his usual overgrown and scraggly beard. Behind the beard his features are quite soft, almost feminine, and his manner is intense. He has a good sense of humor, and there was considerable joking back and forth during the meeting. He seemed very ill at ease when we began to talk, but soon became relaxed and spoke freely. Although he left no doubt of his personal and intense devotion to communism, his conversation was free of propaganda and bombast. He spoke calmly, in a straightforward manner, and with the appearance of detachment and objectivity. He left no doubt, at any time, that he felt completely free to speak for his government and rarely distinguished between his personal observations and the official position of the Cuban government. I had the definite impression that he had thought out his remarks very carefully — they were extremely well organized. I told him at the outset that I had no authority to negotiate my country's problems, but would report what he said to interested officials of our government. He said "good" and began.

Guevara began by saying that I must understand the Cuban revolution. They intend to build a socialist state, and the revolution which they have begun is irreversible. They are also now out of the U.S. sphere of influence, and that too is irreversible. They will establish a single-party system with Fidel as Secretary-General of the party. Their ties with the East stem from natural sympathies, and common beliefs in the proper structure of the social order. They feel that they have the support of the masses for their revolution, and that that support will grow as time passes. . . .

He began to discuss the difficulties of the Alliance for Progress.[1] He asked me if I had heard his speech at the closing of the [Punta del Este] conference. I said I had listened to it closely. He said that it explained his viewpoint on the Alliance for Progress. (In this speech he said the idea of the Alianza was fine, but it would fail. He spoke also of the play of historical forces working on behalf of communism, etc.—that there would be either leftist revolutions or rightist coups leading to leftist takeovers, and there was also a strong chance that the commies would get in through popular election.) He then said he wished to add that there was an intrinsic contradiction in the Alianza—by encouraging the forces of change and the desires of the masses we might set loose forces which were beyond our control, ending in a Cuba style revolution. Never once did he indicate that Cuba might play a more direct role in the march of history.

He then said, now that he had discussed our difficulties he would like to discuss his own problems—and he would like to do so very frankly. There were in Cuba, he said, several basic problems.

1. There was disturbing revolutionary sentiment, armed men and sabotage.

2. The small bourgeoisie were hostile to the revolution or, at best, were lukewarm.

3. The Catholic Church (here he shook his head in dismay).

4. Their factories looked naturally to the U.S. for resources, especially spare parts and at times the shortages of these resources made things very critical.

5. They had accelerated the process of development too rapidly and their hard currency reserves were very low. Thus they were unable to import consumer goods and meet basic needs of the people.

He then said that they didn't want an understanding with the U.S., because they know that was impossible. They would like a modus vivendi—at least an interim modus vivendi. Of course, he said, it was difficult to put forth a practical formula for such a modus vivendi—he knew because he had spent a lot of time thinking about it. He thought we should put forth such a formula because we had public opinion to worry about whereas he could accept anything without worrying about public opinion.

I said nothing, and he waited and then said that, in any event, there were some things he had in mind.

---

[1]Kennedy's aid program for Latin America.

1. That they would not give back the expropriated [American] properties [in Cuba]—the factories and banks—but they could pay for them in trade.

2. They could agree not to make any political alliance with the East—although this would not affect their natural sympathies.

3. They would have free elections—but only after a period of institutionalizing the revolution had been completed. In response to my question he said that this included the establishment of a one-party system.

4. Of course, they would not attack Guantanamo. (At this point he laughed as if at the absurdly self-evident nature of such a statement.)

5. He indicated, very obliquely, and with evident reluctance because of the company in which we were talking, that they could also discuss the activities of the Cuban revolution in other countries.

He then went on to say that he wanted to thank us very much for the [Bay of Pigs] invasion—that it had been a great political victory for them—enabled them to consolidate—and transformed them from an aggrieved little country to an equal.

Guevara said he knew it was difficult to negotiate these things but we could open up some of these issues by beginning to discuss subordinate issues. . . .

He said they could discuss no formula that would mean giving up the type of society to which they were dedicated.

At close he said that he would tell no one of the substance of this conversation except Fidel. I said I would not publicize it either.

After the conversation was terminated I left to record notes on what had been said. He stayed at the party.

35. Memorandum from Assistant Special Counsel Goodwin to President Kennedy

Further anti-Castro policies, including covert activities, are planned by the Kennedy team.

Washington, September 1, 1961.

The Cuban Task Force[1] met at the White House on Thursday, August 31. Present were Under Secretary Ball, Assistant Secretary Woodward, two members of the ARA Bureau, Dick Bissell, Tracy Barnes and myself.

The following decisions were made:

1. We would proceed immediately to discuss with other Caribbean govern-

---

[1]Kennedy established this group after the Bay of Pigs affair. Chaired initially by Defense Department official Paul H. Nitze and then Goodwin, its objectives were to diminish Castro's influence in Latin America and to oust the Castro government.

ments the possibility of organizing a Caribbean Security Force. . . . Such a Caribbean Security Force would have at least four major aspects:

(1) Advance commitment to come to the aid of other signatories threatened by Castro revolutions and, perhaps the designation of specific units for participation in necessary multilateral actions.

(2) The establishment of a pool of intelligence information concerning subversive activities with provision for exchange of such information.

(3) The establishment of a Caribbean air and sea patrol to watch for suspected infiltration of Castro arms or agents.

(4) A training program in combatting subversive tactics, police organization and procedure, etc.

It was conceded that the substantive aspects of this arrangement could, if necessary, be achieved informally. However, the decision to seek a more formal arrangement was primarily arrived at on the basis of internal political considerations in the United States.

2. It was decided that our public posture toward Cuba should be as quiet as possible—trying to ignore Castro and his island.

3. Our covert activities would now be directed toward the destruction of targets important to the economy, e.g., refineries, plants using U.S. equipment, etc. This would be done within the general framework of covert operations—which is based on the principle that para-military activities ought to be carried out through Cuban revolutionary groups which have a potential for establishing an effective political opposition to Castro within Cuba. Within that principle we will do all we can to identify and suggest targets whose destruction will have the maximum economic impact.

4. We will intensify our surveillance of Cuban trade with other countries and especially U.S. subsidiaries in other countries; and then employ informal methods to attempt to divert this trade—depriving Cuba of markets and sources of supply. I understand that we have already had a few successes in this effort.

5. We will establish next week—in the State Department—a psychological warfare group. This will be a full-time group of three or four people charged with the responsibility of assembling all available information on the Sovietization of Cuba, repression of human rights, failure of the Cuban economy, etc.—much of which has been hitherto classified—putting this information into readable, popularized form, and developing methods of disseminating it through Latin America. Such dissemination would not be primarily through USIA channels but would include feeding it to Latin papers for "exclusive" stories, helping to prepare scripts for Latin American broadcasts, perhaps a direct mailing list of intellectuals and government officials to be handled by a front group, etc. The basic idea is to get this stuff into channels of Latin American communication, instead of treating it as official U.S. propaganda.

6. The CIA was asked to come up—within the week—with a precise, covert procedure for continuing the below-ground dialogue with the Cuban government. The object of this dialogue—to explore the possibility of a split within the

governmental hierarchy of Cuba and to encourage such a split—was fully detailed in my last memorandum to you.[2] This is an effort to find an operational technique.[3]

36. Memorandum of Conversation Between President Kennedy and President Arturo Frondizi of Argentina

In a conversation with the Argentine president, JFK lays the groundwork for the subsequent diplomatic isolation of Cuba from the rest of Latin America. The two leaders were in New York for the opening session of the United Nations General Assembly.

New York, September 26, 1961, 9 a.m.

Referring to the Cuban problem, President Kennedy said that it was important that it be understood that it was not a question of the United States versus Cuba, or of Castro versus Kennedy, because a debate of this kind would only enhance Castro's prestige. He said that it was necessary to isolate Cuba and increase its economic problems, which were already serious. He said that it was important not to leave the impression of the United States, great imperialist power from the North, attacking poor, brave Cuba, which is the impression Castro wants to give.

President Frondizi said that he believed that the basic action to be undertaken with regard to Cuba was to accelerate the launching of the Alliance for Progress, and that he did not believe that another invasion of Cuba should be attempted. He said that it was necessary to show that with democratic methods, with American support for the Latin American people, it was possible to achieve the conditions Castro was seeking in his own country.

President Kennedy said that there were Cubans in all of these countries trying to influence liberals, leftists, and labor movements, and that it was important to take action to discredit the Cuban revolution, identifying it as foreign, alien, and anti-Christian, and not permitting it to be considered as a revolution that was trying to improve the living conditions of the Cuban people. He said that it was

[2]Sent on August 22. (Not, however, the memorandum presented here as Document 34.)
[3]Goodwin told State Department official George W. Ball in a telephone conversation on September 7 that JFK had read the memorandum prepared by Goodwin on the Cuban Task Force meeting, and had approved of the group's decisions.

necessary to show that Castro and company were subversives in the hemisphere, and that it was not a problem of the United States against Cuba.

President Kennedy asked whether President Frondizi saw any merit in the Colombian proposal to try to call a meeting of Foreign Ministers, in order to declare that Cuba is a Soviet satellite and that therefore, according to the terms of the Rio Treaty,[1] can no longer be considered a member of the American family. . . .

President Frondizi said that the solution to the problem must be found within the framework of the OAS. On the basis of his conversations with other Latin American Presidents, he believed that it was indispensable to proceed vigorously with the Alliance for Progress, and on this platform later take decisions within the OAS. Then a meeting of the OAS might be called, in which the Colombian proposal would be a good working tool.

President Kennedy said that some time would be required to get the Alliance for Progress organized, and asked as to the possible date for such a meeting of consultation.

President Frondizi said that it might be the beginning of 1962.

President Kennedy said that with regard to this problem he was somewhat concerned about the position of Brazil, Chile, and Mexico, and to a certain degree, Ecuador. As to Brazil, certain doubts existed as to the position to be taken by President Goulart. He said that in his opinion, Mexico, Brazil, and Argentina were the key countries, and from the American viewpoint, nothing could be done without Argentina.

President Kennedy said that it was necessary to do something so that Castro, as a Communist, should not be appealing to the Latin American people, and that it was necessary to isolate Cuba, pointing it out as a stranger in the house, so that it would not be so appealing to non-Communist leftists. . . .

37. Memorandum for the Record Prepared by Assistant to the President's Military Representative Thomas A. Parrott

This memorandum by the assistant to the president's military representative can be interpreted as implicitly demonstrating the interest of the administration, including the president, in assassinating Castro. Certainly CIA plotting to kill Castro, initiated in Eisenhower's presidency, continued during the Kennedy years.

---

[1]The Rio Pact was a defensive military alliance for countries in the Western Hemisphere, established in 1947.

Washington, October 5, 1961.

SUBJECT

Cuba

In accordance with General Taylor's instructions, I talked to Assistant Secretary Woodward yesterday about the requirement for the preparation of a contingency plan. He told me on the telephone he would be leaving for two weeks and, therefore, his Deputy, Wymberley Coerr, would have to take this project on.

I then met with Mr. Coerr and outlined the requirement to him. I said that what was wanted was a plan against the contingency that Castro would in some way or other be removed from the Cuban scene. I said that my understanding was the terms of reference governing this plan should be quite broad; we agreed, for example, that the presence and positions of Raul and Che Guevara must be taken into account. We agreed that this was an exercise that should be under the direction of State with participation by Defense and CIA. I also pointed out to Mr. Coerr that Mr. Goodwin had been aware of this requirement.

Mr. Coerr said he would get his people started on this right away. As to timing, I said that I did not understand that this was a crash program but that it should proceed with reasonable speed. He then set Monday as a target date for a first draft.

I had mentioned to Mr. Woodward the President's interest in this matter, before General Taylor had told me he preferred this not be done. Therefore, I felt it necessary to tell Mr. Coerr, on the assumption that Mr. Woodward would have already told him. I asked that this aspect be kept completely out of the picture. He understood this fully and volunteered that it could be presented as an exercise emanating from his own office. I said I would leave this up to him but it was perfectly all right to attribute it to General Taylor.

On the covert side, I talked to Tracy Barnes in CIA and asked that an up-to-date report be furnished as soon as possible on what is going on and what is being planned. . . .

PART 2

Operation Mongoose

SCRAMBLING for ways to keep the pressure on Castro after the Bay of Pigs invasion, John and Robert Kennedy came to pin their hopes on Operation Mongoose, the centerpiece of American policy toward Cuba from late 1961 until the onset of the 1962 missile crisis. Despite the fact that the Bay of Pigs turned out to be a catastrophe, the similarities between that operation and Mongoose were striking. Both were meant to be clandestine. (Mongoose actually was; U.S. involvement in the Bay of Pigs had become public knowledge at the time of the event.) Both were based on the belief that a potentially large opposition to Castro's leadership existed in Cuba and could be exploited to America's advantage. And the ultimate objective of both operations was the overthrow of Castro. What Mongoose came to be, in practice, was an attempt to harass the Cuban government, through such means as economic sabotage, and to plan for the use of direct American military force in the event an anti-Castro uprising in Cuba could be triggered. The key figure in this effort was Edward G. Lansdale, a covert-operations wizard who had run anti-Communist campaigns in Vietnam and the Philippines.

The documents in this chapter describe the launching of Mongoose in November 1961, the preliminary conceptions of the operation developed by Lansdale during the next three months, the formal inception of Mongoose's first phase in March 1962, and the review of that initial phase and the consideration of the operation's second phase in July 1962. A number of these documents relate to the military planning that accompanied Mongoose. In these months U.S. military officials developed a cluster of exotic schemes to discredit Castro, considered pretexts that could be used to justify an assault on Cuba, and, in April 1962, actually recommended an immediate U.S. attack on the Caribbean island.

These documents expose Mongoose's internal contradictions. Intelligence reports in both November 1961 and March 1962 made clear that an anti-Castro uprising was not in the cards, yet the likelihood of such a rebellion was a key predicate of the operation. Nor did this sort of problem escape the attention of all administration officials. Both CIA Director John McCone and State Department official Roger Hilsman, in early 1962, identified weaknesses in the operation. Hence administration support for Mongoose was not unanimous.

The zeal with which Robert Kennedy wished to move forward with Operation Mongoose is also evident from these documents. Angry at the humiliation suffered by his brother at the Bay of Pigs, he was determined to exact revenge on Castro, and he saw Mongoose as the best way to do that.

1. Memorandum from Assistant Special Counsel Goodwin to President Kennedy

Richard Goodwin makes the case to JFK that the post–Bay of Pigs effort to put covert pressure on Castro should be expanded. He also proposes that Robert Kennedy play a central role in this endeavor.

Washington, November 1, 1961.

I believe that the concept of a "command operation" for Cuba, as discussed with you by the Attorney General, is the only effective way to handle an all-out attack on the Cuban problem. Since I understand you are favorably disposed toward the idea I will not discuss why the present disorganized and uncoordinated operation cannot do the job effectively.

The beauty of such an operation over the next few months is that we cannot lose. If the best happens we will unseat Castro. If not, then at least we will emerge with a stronger underground, better propaganda and a far clearer idea of the dimensions of the problems which affect us.

The question then is who should head this operation. I know of no one currently in Cuban affairs at the State Department who can do it. Nor is it a very good idea to get the State Department involved in depth in such covert activities. I do not think it should be centered in the CIA. Even if the CIA can find someone of sufficient force and stature, one of the major problems will be to revamp CIA operations and thinking—and this will be very hard to do from the inside.

I believe that the Attorney General would be the most effective commander of such an operation. Either I or someone else should be assigned to him as Deputy for this activity, since he obviously will not be able to devote full time to it. The one danger here is that he might become too closely identified with what might not be a successful operation. Indeed, chances of success are very speculative. There are a few answers to this:

(1) Everyone knowledgeable in these affairs—in and out of government—is aware that the United States is already helping the underground. The precise manner of aid may be unknown but the fact of aid is common knowledge. We

will be blamed for not winning Cuba back whether or not we have a "command operation" and whether or not the Attorney General heads it.

(2) His role should be told to only a few people at the very top with most of the contact work in carrying out his decisions being left to his deputy. If that deputy is someone already closely identified with the conduct of Cuban affairs then it would appear as if normal channels are being followed except that decisive attention would be given to the decisions which came through those channels. There are probably three or four people who could fulfill this criterion.

This still leaves a substantial danger of identifying the Attorney General as the fellow in charge. This danger must be weighed against the increased effectiveness of an operation under his command.

2. Attorney General Kennedy's Notes on a White House Meeting

Two days later, JFK authorizes a new program for covert action against Cuba, Operation Mongoose.

November 3, 1961.

. . . McNamara, Dick Bissell, Alexis Johnson, Paul Nitze, Lansdale (the Ugly American).[1] McN said he would make latter available for me—I assigned him to make survey of situation in Cuba—the problem and our assets. My idea is to stir things up on island with espionage, sabotage, general disorder, run & operated by Cubans themselves with every group but Batistaites[2] & Communists. Do not know if we will be successful in overthrowing Castro but we have nothing to lose in my estimate.

---

[1] Expert in covert operations Edward G. Lansdale was the inspiration for the main character in a novel by Eugene Burdick and William Lederer, *The Ugly American.*
[2] These Cubans were followers of Batista, the dictator who ruled the island before Castro.

3. Memorandum from Chairman of the Board of National Estimates Sherman Kent to CIA Director Allen W. Dulles

As JFK tells his advisers that Mongoose is to be initiated, the CIA concludes that a key assumption of this operation—that there is potentially decisive opposition to Castro in Cuba—is false.

Washington, November 3, 1961.

SUBJECT

The Situation and Prospects in Cuba

Summary

1. The Castro regime has sufficient popular support and repressive capabilities to cope with any internal threat likely to develop within the foreseeable future. The regime faces serious, but not insurmountable, economic difficulties. The contrast between its roseate promises and the grim actuality is producing disillusionment and apathy. Some specially motivated elements have recently dared to demonstrate their disapproval. The bulk of the population, however still accepts the Castro regime, or is at least resigned to it, and substantial numbers still support it with enthusiasm. At the same time, the regime's capabilities for repression are increasing more rapidly than are the potentialities for active resistance. . . .

4. CIA Paper, "Types of Covert Action Against the Castro Regime"

The CIA reviews existing anti-Castro programs on which Operation Mongoose would build.

Washington, November 8, 1961.

1. *Non-Sensitive Activities:* A variety of non-sensitive political warfare and propaganda activities are being conducted outside Cuba. These include: (a) working with the Cuban Revolutionary Council and the number of other Cuban groups in Miami in an effort to improve their competence to undertake action on their own and also to minimize the effects of disunity among the Cubans;

(b) efforts to induce the defection of prominent Cubans from the Castro regime; (c) black operations with the objective of having Castro's diplomats declared PNG or having additional countries break diplomatic relations with Cuba; (d) speaking tours by teachers, student, labor, jurists and women's groups through-out the hemisphere; (e) support of publications and distribution of pamphlets; (f) the support of anti-Castro radio programs on some 60 Latin America stations and 3 stations in Florida; (g) the operation of Radio Swan;[1] (h) the use of a broad-casting ship for intruding radio broadcasts on Cuba t.v. channels. There is believed to be little risk that these activities will give rise to political embarrass-ment, except for that resulting from the jealousy of various Cuban groups and criticism by one of alleged support to another. The following paragraphs consti-tute a list of politically more sensitive types of activities in progress or contem-plated.

2. *Agent Training:* There are currently some . . . Cubans already trained or now in training as activists who can be infiltrated to organize the resistance and to develop sabotage activities. In addition there are some . . . Cuban students in training for infiltration to conduct Agit/Prop[2] activities. For the most part the training is being done in Florida. The men are trained in compartmented small groups. . . . The candidates are of course volunteers and are from a number of the political groups with which we are in contact.

3. *Infiltration/Exfiltration:* We maintain and employ for training and opera-tional purposes a fleet of some 7 craft. They are used primarily for the infiltration and exfiltration of individuals and, if and when feasible, of arms. Currently, in-filtrations are apt to involve no more than 3 to 5 individuals at a time but larger groups (up to 15 or 20) may be infiltrated in the future if and when this becomes feasible. No Americans are allowed on any craft that is going within the 12-mile limit around Cuba. Many infiltration/exfiltration operations involve a meet-at-sea with a Cuban fisherman or a Cuban craft.

4. *Building an Intelligence and Resistance Organization:* Contact is still maintained . . . with . . . agents in Cuba. Their present function is restricted to the furnishing of intelligence and in some cases the maintenance of communi-cation with internal resistance leaders. Every effort will be made to infiltrate ad-ditional trained agents and communicators as rapidly as possible for the purpose of building an internal resistance organization and establishing effective secure communication with internal resistance leaders. The objective will be to de-velop one or more nets of dependable sympathizers and the means of commu-nication both among themselves and to the outside. In the first instance such internal assets, to the extent to which they are subject to control from outside, will be used for intelligence collection, further clandestine recruiting, assisting in infil/exfiltration operations, and mounting low risk sabotage operations. They will be deliberately restrained in this phase from exposing themselves by opera-tions involving high risk or the assembly in one operation of any sizeable num-ber of the resistance.

---

[1]Radio Swan had made clandestine broadcasts in support of the Cuban exiles at the time of the Bay of Pigs invasion.
[2]A reference to Agitation/Propaganda activities presumably.

5. *Accelerated Resistance Activities:* In parallel with the necessarily time consuming effort to build a secure underground organization, it is now planned to support in the next few months larger scale infiltrations of men and arms for sabotage and perhaps ultimately guerrilla activities when well-conceived operations are proposed by reputable opposition leaders now outside the country or are requested by the resistance leadership from within. In most cases the sponsorship and ultimate responsibility for such operations will rest with Cubans and the Agency's role will be that of furnishing support in the form of funds, training, equipment, communications, frequently the facilities to conduct the actual infiltration itself, and resupply following infiltration if required and feasible. These will necessarily be higher risk operations in which some casualties must be anticipated. It will be impossible to conceal U.S. geographical origin but every effort will be made not only possibly to forestall identification of U.S. Government support but also to avoid any appearance of U.S. Government control or ultimate responsibility. What will be impossible to disprove is that the Cubans responsible obtain help in the U.S.

6. *Air Operations:* If the internal resistance grows, it will be desirable at some point to undertake air resupply missions. These would be conducted by Cuban crews using common types of commercial aircraft. They will be night missions and would be undertaken only if reception parties had been identified and were in possession of agent radio sets and, hopefully, beacons so that resupply could be carried out with reasonable efficiency. Aside from such air activity, proposals have been received for both leaflet drops and bombing raids. One successful leaflet mission was recently conducted by Cubans from Florida entirely on their own after Agency support had been refused. Such operations rather infrequently carried out may have a useful morale effect. Up to the present time it has been felt that air bombing, quite aside from international repercussions, would be contraproductive in its effect on the Cubans.

5. Memorandum for the Record Prepared by John A. McCone[1]

The Kennedy brothers express eagerness to move forward with Mongoose.

Washington, November 22, 1961.

Monday, November 20, 1961, 7:00 pm, President Kennedy called personally and asked that I meet with him and Attorney General Robert Kennedy at 4:30 pm the following day.

[1]JFK had decided that McCone would replace Allen Dulles as director of the CIA.

The meeting was held for the purpose of discussing all possible courses of action in Cuba. Present were:

> The President
> Robert Kennedy
> General Lansdale
> Mr. Goodwin of the White House Staff.

The President explained that General Lansdale had been engaging in a study of possible action in Cuba, acting under the direction of the Attorney General, and he, the President, desired an immediate plan of action which could be submitted to him within two weeks.

The Attorney General expressed grave concern over Cuba, the necessity for immediate dynamic action, indicating that such action would embody a variety of covert operations, propaganda, all possible actions that would create dissensions within Cuba and would discredit the Castro regime, and political action with members of the OAS in support of the action. He proposed that the Lansdale committee be made up of representatives of CIA, State, USIA and DOD (Lansdale) and that it be organized so that this committee could "cut across" organization channels within the agencies.

McCone's views were solicited and he stated:

a) That he observed that the Agency and indeed the Administration appeared to be in a condition of "shock" as a result of the happenings in Cuba and, therefore, were doing very little. He supported dynamic action but emphasized that action should not be reckless. . . .

The above points seemed to be generally agreed, and it was decided that Robert Kennedy would attend the "5412" committee on Wednesday, November 22nd, to discuss the plan. . . .

6. Memorandum from General Edward G. Lansdale to Attorney General Kennedy

Lansdale encourages Bobby Kennedy to dismiss the recent intelligence evaluation (Document 3) that could be interpreted as casting doubt on the viability of Mongoose.

Washington, November 30, 1961.

Friday[1] is apparently the "day of decision" for your special project. General Taylor's group[2] has it scheduled as the main item for discussion.

---

[1]December 1.
[2]Seems to be a reference to the meeting described in Document 8.

A special Intelligence Estimate[3] seems to be the major evidence to be used to oppose your project. Copies have just been made available this afternoon. . . . I have underlined key conclusions.

I suggest two points:

1. The intelligence which supports conclusions about the internal situation is far from adequate.

2. The conclusion . . . concerning the possibility of an uprising being fomented is a "conclusion of fact" quite outside the area of intelligence. The key factor in such a conclusion must be our own ability to take action. It is the heart of our proposal that we *can* take effective action, if proper management is provided.

7. Memorandum from President Kennedy

JFK formally launches Mongoose, with Lansdale as head of the operation.

Washington, November 30, 1961.

MEMORANDUM TO

The Secretary of State
The Secretary of Defense
The Director of CIA
The Attorney General
General Taylor
General Lansdale
Richard Goodwin

The following is a summary of the major decisions which have been made in regard to the Cuba Operation.

1. We will use our available assets to go ahead with the discussed project in order to help Cuba overthrow the communist regime.

2. This program will be conducted under the general guidance of General Lansdale, acting as Chief of Operations. It will be conducted by him through the appropriate regular organizations and Departments of the government.

3. The program will be reviewed in two weeks in order to determine whether General Lansdale will continue as Chief of Operations.

4. The NSC 5412 group will be kept closely informed of activities and be available for advice and recommendation.

5. The Secretary of State and the Secretary of Defense and the Director of

[3]See Document 3.

the Central Intelligence Agency will appoint senior officers of their department as personal representatives to assist the Chief of Operations as required. These senior officers should be able to exercise—either themselves or through the Secretaries and Director—effective operational control over all aspects of their Department's operations dealing with Cuba.

6. Knowledge of the existence of this operation should be restricted to the recipients of this memorandum, members of the 5412 group and the representatives appointed by the Secretaries and the Director. Any further dissemination of this knowledge will be only with the authority of the Secretaries of State or Defense or the Chief of Operations.

8. Draft Memorandum for the Record

Lansdale and Robert Kennedy dominate the first meeting of Mongoose planners.

Washington, December 1, 1961.

Cuba

The Attorney General told the Group about a series of meetings which had been held recently with higher authority.[1] Out of these had come a decision that higher priority should be given to Cuba. General Lansdale had been designated as "Chief of Operations," with authority to call on all appropriate Government agencies for assistance, including the assignment of senior representatives from State, Defense and CIA. General Lansdale is to keep the Special Group informed of his progress, but is authorized to take actions now which are clearly desirable to strengthen operations and facilities now in being. . . .

After some discussion, it was agreed that General Lansdale should develop a long-range program which would be reviewed by the Special Group and then presented for approval to higher authority [JFK]. At that time, formal language would be proposed to record the decision to pursue a new or revised Cuba policy. General Lansdale will meet with the Special Group next week to report progress and actions required.

General Lansdale then gave his appreciation of the situation. He said that, bearing in mind the objective of fomenting eventual revolution within Cuba, he had surveyed all resources available. He had concluded that there are a sizeable number of latent as well as active resources, but that there is a very difficult job ahead. He stressed also the necessity of coming to an agreement at some early date as to the future of Cuba after the Castro government is overthrown, so that

[1]Namely, JFK.

appeals to potential resistance elements can be geared to a positive long-range program. General Lansdale also thought it important to obtain cooperation and assistance from selected Latin American countries, preferably those not previously involved with U.S. anti-Castro activities.

General Lansdale then said that he has looked at the proposed operation designed to sabotage a power plant. He had concluded that the conception and planning of this project has been very well done by CIA; on the other hand, he feels that it would be unwise to mount the operation in the immediate future because it would tend to increase Cuban security measures and thereby make it more difficult to get on with building up resistance elements. The Group agreed that, considering all these circumstances, the sabotage operation should be postponed. . . .[2]

9. Memorandum from Chief of Operations (Mongoose) Lansdale

Lansdale develops a preliminary conception of Mongoose.

Washington, December 7, 1961.

MEMORANDUM FOR

General Taylor
Mr. [Alexis] Johnson
Mr. Gilpatric
Mr. McCone

This is to inform you, as the NSC 5412 group, of activities to date on the Cuba project, within the strict security requirements of the project directed by the President.

Policy. The President's memorandum of 30 November 1961,[1] which was read to the Special Group at its last meeting, stated that it had been decided that the United States will use all available assets in a project to help Cuba overthrow the Communist regime.

Concept. The decision stated above was made after consideration of a concept of how to help the Cubans overthrow the Communist regime. The regime is to be overthrown by a popular movement of Cubans from *within* Cuba. The movement is to have the end objective of establishing a free Cuba, of, by, and for Cubans, with the overthrow of the Communist regime a necessary step to-

[2]This memorandum was probably drafted by Thomas Parrott.
[1]See Document 7.

wards this end. The U.S. will help establish a Cuban nucleus within Cuba, which will work for activating a genuine popular movement to overthrow the regime, and the U.S. will help generate supporting actions for the growth of the movement, particularly in encouraging other nations of the Western Hemisphere to do likewise.

Actions. A working group has been formed by the project's Chief of Operations, with the personal representatives of the Secretary of State, the Secretary of Defense, and the Director of Central Intelligence, as well as a selected staff. The Chief of Operations is representing the Secretary of Defense, pro tem. It is planned to employ personal representatives of the Directors of the FBI and USIA, when required. The initial work of the group has been to sharply re-orient the U.S. effort, from being simply an unintegrated series of harassment activities to become a program designed to help Cubans build a popular movement within Cuba, which can (with outside help) take effective actions deposing the Communist regime.

CIA. CIA was found to have important contacts and operational capabilities for use in achieving the policy goal set by the President. It is noted, also, that there is an impressive potential for increasing the CIA's capability. The orientation of planning and programming, however, was definitely out of phase with the objective of establishing a popular movement from within Cuba to overthrow Castro and the Communist regime. In the main, CIA thinking has been to apply militant force covertly (such as action teams for "smash and grab" raids on up to armed resistance groups), in the hope that a popular uprising would possibly harass the regime. The early task, then, has been to re-orient this 180°, with militant (sabotage, etc.) actions to be considered as part of the support of the popular movement we are generating. The basic strategy of building our action upon a genuine internal popular movement is underlined; this will apply the major lesson to be learned from earlier operations in Indonesia and Cuba.

The tasks assigned to the representative of the Director of Central Intelligence are:

a. The CIA organization directed towards Cuba is to be tightened and re-oriented with a hard look at operational effectiveness, especially the management and programs of the field station in Florida.

b. A nucleus for a popular Cuban movement will be formed and positioned within Cuba. This will include the development of a team from Cubans in the U.S., and the development of similar teams under local auspices from Caribbean countries.

c. A program for this Cuban nucleus to use will be developed. Basic intelligence concerning several initial operational points has been requested. There will be a sharp definition of incentives and of a platform for political polarization, for use with the Cuban nucleus. Further, ideas will be developed for local actions that will help generate the national movement required to force the regime out.

d. Special support projects will be readied for use on call. These projects (such as operations to scuttle shipping and otherwise hamper the regime) will be timed to support actions by the movement and to permit the movement to take credit for them. Support in terms of psychological warfare matériel (such as clandestine broadcast transmitters inside Cuba) are to be brought to a practical stand-by capability.

At the same time, the special project team is working on bold new actions to help the popular movement for CIA executive follow through. These include:

1. Enlisting the cooperation of the Church to bring the women of Cuba into actions which will undermine the Communist control system, harass the regime's economic program, and encourage a wave of non-cooperation in all segments of the population.

2. Exploiting the potential of the underworld in Cuban cities to harass and bleed the Communist control apparatus. This effort may, on a very sensitive basis, enlist the assistance of American links to the Cuban underworld. While this would be a CIA project, close cooperation of the FBI is imperative.

3. Labor, students, and other special groups are being considered for practical operational capabilities. . . . This effort is to come mainly from activities in other OAS countries, and suitable Latin American case officers to undertake such positive actions are being considered on a priority basis.

4. Powerful Cuban personalities, with existing capabilities for action within Cuba and who propose a military-type of overthrow, are being assessed for a role in actions which would help generate the popular, anti-regime movement.

State. The Department of State's actions have been essentially at the formal diplomatic level, and thus quite passive or reactive. State must develop and use its dynamic possibilities in political and economic warfare which will be crucial for the success of a popular movement within Cuba.

The representative of the Secretary of State[2] has been tasked with:

a. The possibilities for strong and effective OAS encouragement of the Cuban people in a popular movement will be exploited, particularly noting the President's forthcoming visit to Latin America and the Secretary of State's actions with the OAS in January.[3]

b. State will help with the nucleus for a popular Cuban movement, particularly in the development of a political platform and in the continuing development and public support of leadership (noting necessary consideration of existing Cuban émigré groups and their future cooperation with the internal Cuban movement).

c. Certain supporting actions will be undertaken by State, notably:

1). Appropriately enlisting the initiative of Latin American countries separately in action programs which encourage the popular movement within Cuba. This is being closely coordinated with a similar task assigned to CIA.

2). Making available the names of American returnees from Cuba, for screening in conjunction with CIA for possible leads to operational contacts.

d. Develop, in consultation with top State officials, a practical plan for economic warfare which fully applies the U.S. capability to frustrate the Communist economic program for Cuba. Definite and decisive actions by other U.S.

---

[2] A reference to Alexis Johnson.

[3] OAS foreign ministers were to meet at Punta del Este, Uruguay, in January 1962 to take action against Cuba.

organizations (including Treasury, Commerce, and Agriculture) are to be enlisted under the direction of the Department of State.

Defense. The main Department of Defense role is indicated as one of contingency support in later phases of the popular movement's development. To this end, improved arrangements for training, personnel, and military hardware support of covert operations is under active study. However, immediate support of State and CIA actions is being activated, particularly in the field of intelligence and in consideration of maritime and air needs in readiness for the time when CIA operations require such support. Planning for overt U.S. military operations is not envisioned under this policy.

USIA. The U.S. Information Agency's role in providing open support for developing the popular movement within Cuba is an important one, but must be correctly timed with the actual commencement of the movement. The U.S. will be identified as being in sympathy with the just and true aspirations of the Cuban people, aspirations which are being killed by a Communist dictatorship. Discussion with a designated USIA representative is being scheduled.

Justice. Support from the Department of Justice, particularly the security and investigative capabilities of the FBI and the INS, is being planned through a special representative of the Attorney General.

HEW,[4] *Other U.S. Agencies.* The support capabilities of other U.S. organizations are being considered and will be brought into the project as appears most practical.

10. Memorandum for the Record

Lansdale presents this program to his colleagues.

Washington, December 8, 1961.

SUBJECT

Minutes of Special Group Meeting, 8 December 1961

PRESENT

General Taylor, Mr. [Alexis] Johnson, Mr. Gilpatric, General Cabell
General Lansdale attended the early part of this meeting

General Lansdale presented the outline of a program[1] designed to overthrow the Castro government. This program is centered around the selection and even-

---

[4]The Department of Health, Education and Welfare.
[1]See Document 9.

tual introduction into Cuba of a nucleus of anti-Castro Cubans; once they are in the country and in a position to operate, then a number of collateral supporting actions would be undertaken.

It was agreed that the immediate requirement was for the selection of a suitable group which could agree on a platform for an eventual new government, and which is willing and capable of carrying out the proposed tasks inside the country. When a selection has been made the program will be discussed further with higher authority [JFK].

It was noted that General Lansdale would report periodically to the Special Group on progress he is making.[2]

11. Memorandum for the Record

Lansdale reports on the early progress of Operation Mongoose.

Washington, December 21, 1961.

SUBJECT

Minutes of Special Group Meeting, 21 December 1961

PRESENT

General Taylor; Mr. [Alexis] Johnson; Mr. Gilpatric and General Lemnitzer; Mr. McCone and Mr. Bissell

General Lansdale gave a brief progress report [on Cuba]. He stressed the fact that the proposed operation is primarily a political one, and that economic and paramilitary aspects are secondary to the political. Steps have been taken to increase intelligence coverage and to begin preparations for economic warfare.

General Lansdale felt that by perhaps the first week in January he would be in a position to present certain proposals to the Special Group for policy decision, or for transmission to higher authority. It was noted that if the necessity for quick policy decisions should arise before the next meeting, arrangements could be made to secure concurrence of members of the Group individually.[1]

---

[2]Parrott prepared this memorandum.
[1]Parrott drafted this memorandum.

12. Memorandum for the Record

Lansdale delivers another progress report and is instructed to produce a detailed plan of action.

Washington, January 11, 1962.

SUBJECT

Minutes of Special Group Meeting, 11 January 1962

PRESENT

General Taylor; Mr. [Alexis] Johnson; Mr. McCone and Mr. Bissell
The Attorney General
Mr. Richard Helms
General E. G. Lansdale

Progress Report on Cuba

General Lansdale summarized progress to date, identifying four major broad programs. He emphasized that the current bottleneck is the procurement of suitable Cubans to accomplish the initial task of infiltration. He also touched on other activities which are being undertaken while this problem is being solved, including such things as covert propaganda actions in connection with the OAS meeting of 22 January and selective harassment of the Cuban Government in the form of limited sabotage, etc.

Several members of the Group noted the difficulty of the task ahead, with Mr. McCone calling attention to the fact that the prevailing spirit within Cuba appears to be one of apathy rather than resistance, and that a fanatical pro-Castro minority exists along with an efficient police mechanism.

It was noted that the prevailing policy on sabotage is still in effect, i.e., that no actions which would be dangerous to the population will be undertaken, nor will major demolitions be done at this stage. It was agreed that whenever this policy appears to require change, the matter will be discussed with the Special Group.

It was noted that CIA is proceeding to set up an interrogation center for Cuban refugees in the Miami area and that this will be carefully examined to insure that it will be adequately staffed to produce the optimum amount of intelligence on conditions inside Cuba.

The Group agreed that maritime capabilities for infiltration should be clearly sufficient for any foreseeable tasks of this nature. The need for isolated and uncontaminated real estate was also brought out.

General Lansdale was asked to produce for next week's meeting a consolidated summary of progress to date and an overall plan showing departmental tasks and responsibilities, along with timing of implementation. This plan would then be shown to higher authority.[1]

13. Memorandum for the Record

CIA Director McCone provides Robert Kennedy with a sober evaluation of Operation Mongoose's prospects.

Washington, January 12, 1962.

The Director met with the Attorney General on 11 January 1962 and discussed the following subjects: . . .

3. *Cuban operation*

The Attorney General asked the Director for his frank and personal opinion of General Lansdale and the Cuban effort. The Director pointed out that (a) an operation of this type, as presently planned, has never been attempted before, (b) it will be extremely difficult to accomplish, (c) the CIA and the U.S. Government are short on assets to carry out the proposed program, and (d) the [Central Intelligence] Agency, however, is lending every effort and all-out support.[1]

14. Comments by President Kennedy at a National Security Council Meeting

In a discussion with foreign policy advisers, the president implies that the future use of force against Cuba is an option that cannot be discounted.

January 18, 1962.

. . . We hope that Castro can be effectively isolated at the coming [OAS] meeting at Punta del Este, but we expect this to continue to be a very large problem on which further action might be necessary. The time has not yet come when we must force a solution to the Cuban problem. . . .

[1]Parrott drafted this memorandum.
[1]Prepared by J. S. Earman, executive assistant to the CIA director.

15. Review of Operation Mongoose by Chief of Operations Lansdale

Lansdale provides the detailed plan of action for Mongoose requested a week earlier (see Document 12).

Washington, January 18, 1962.

THE CUBA PROJECT[1]

I. Objective

The U.S. objective is to help the Cubans overthrow the Communist regime from within Cuba and institute a new government with which the United States can live in peace.

II. Concept of Operation

Basically, the operation is to bring about the revolt of the Cuban people. The revolt will overthrow the Communist regime and institute a new government with which the United States can live in peace.

The revolt requires a strongly motivated political action movement established within Cuba, to generate the revolt, to give it direction towards the object, and to capitalize on the climactic moment. The political actions will be assisted by economic warfare to induce failure of the Communist regime to supply Cuba's economic needs, psychological operations to turn the peoples' resentment increasingly against the regime, and military-type groups to give the popular movement an action arm for sabotage and armed resistance in support of political objectives.

The failure of the U.S.-sponsored operation in April 1961 so shook the faith of Cuban patriots in U.S. competence and intentions in supporting a revolt against Castro that a new effort to generate a revolt against the regime in Cuba must have active support from key Latin American countries. Further, the *foreignness* (Soviet Union and Bloc) of the tyranny imposed on the Cuban people must be made clear to the people of the Western Hemisphere to the point of their deep anger and open actions to defend the Western Hemisphere against such foreign invasion. Such an anger will be generated, in part, by appeals from the popular movement within Cuba to other Latin Americans especially.

The preparation phase must result in a political action organization in being in key localities inside Cuba, with its own means for internal communications, its own voice for psychological operations, and its own action arm (small guerrilla bands, sabotage squads, etc.). It must have the sympathetic support of the majority of the Cuban people, and make this fact known to the outside world. (It

---

[1]Copies of this review were sent to John and Robert Kennedy, and nine other officials.

is reported that the majority of Cubans are not *for* the present regime, but are growing apathetic towards what appears to be a hopeless future or the futility of their status.)

The climactic moment of revolt will come from an angry reaction of the people to a government action (sparked by an incident), or from a fracturing of the leadership cadre within the regime, or both. (A major goal of the Project must be to bring this about.) The popular movement will capitalize on this climactic moment by initiating an open revolt. Areas will be taken and held. If necessary, the popular movement will appeal for help to the free nations of the Western Hemisphere. The United States, if possible in concert with other Western Hemisphere nations, will then give open support to the Cuban peoples' revolt. Such support will include military force, as necessary.

III. Estimate of the Situation

Our planning requires sound intelligence estimates of the situation re Cuba. The latest National Estimate (SNIE 85–61) of 28 November 1961[2] contains operational conclusions not based on hard fact, in addition to its intelligence conclusions; this is a repetition of an error in the planning for the unsuccessful operation of last April.

The planning indicated herein will be revised, as necessary, based on the hard intelligence estimate of the situation by the U.S. Intelligence community. A new National Intelligence Estimate (NIE 85–62 on Cuba), due on 23 January, apparently has been postponed until 7 February.[3]

It is recognized that one result of the Project, so far, has been to start the collection of Intelligence on Cuba in depth, to provide facts on which to base firm estimates and operations.

IV. Initial Phase (30 Nov 61–81 [sic] Jan 62)

A. *Establish a U.S. mechanism for the project*
Status: The President's directive of 30 November 1961[4] was implemented by creating a U.S. operations team, with Brig. Gen. Lansdale as Chief of Operations, and with tasks promptly assigned. His immediate staff are Mr. Hand and Major Patchell. Representatives of Secretaries and Agency Directors are:

> State—Woodward (Goodwin, Hurwitch)
> CIA—Helms
> Defense—Brig. Gen. Craig
> USIA—Wilson

B. *Intelligence Support*
Status: CIA made a special survey of U.S. capabilities to interrogate Cuban refugees in the USA (1,700–2,000 arriving per month) and on 16 January approved a program increasing the staff at the Opa Locka Interrogation Center in

---

[2]This was a somewhat expanded version of the intelligence estimate presented in Document 3.
[3]Not completed until March 21. See Document 27.
[4]See Document 7.

Florida from the present 2 people to 34. CIA will build up agent assets (positive intelligence assets inside Cuba are very limited and it has no counter-intelligence assets inside). Special intelligence assets will be exploited more fully. The Cuba Project needs far more hard intelligence in depth than is presently available. CIA will require further assistance from Defense and other U.S. organizations in this intelligence effort, and is submitting specific qualifications for personnel on 19 January.

C. *Political platform for peoples' movement inside Cuba.*

Status: State has sketched in a broad outline. CIA is to produce the firm platform statement of aims for which the Cubans who will operate inside Cuba are willing to risk their lives, and upon which popular support can be generated.

D. *Nucleus for popular movement*

Status: To date, CIA has been unable to produce the necessary political action agents for this purpose. Upon re-evaluation of its capabilities, CIA now hopes to complete spotting and assessing eight to ten Cuban political action agents by 15 February, from among Cubans available in the United States. The minimum need for the Project to be effective is 30 such political action Cubans and CIA is tasked to make a priority search for them among Cubans in the U.S. and Caribbean area.

E. *Deployment of nucleus*

Status: CIA is tasked to select 20 localities within Cuba where political action groups can be established. Initial selection and plans for establishing these action groups are now due 1 February. Havana, and localities in the provinces of Camaguey and Las Villas will receive priority consideration, according to present intelligence. Planning on this must be adjusted as firmer intelligence is acquired.

F. *Diplomatic actions*

Status: State is concentrating on the OAS Meeting of Foreign Ministers, which opens 22 January, hoping to get wide Western Hemisphere support for OAS resolutions condemning Cuba and isolating it from the rest of the Hemisphere. A companion resolution, to offer OAS relief directly to the suffering Cuban people (similar to U.S. relief to Russia, 1919–20) is being considered, as a means to reach the Cuban people sympathetically without going through their Communist government. The OAS meeting is to be supported by public demonstrations in Latin America, generated by CIA, and a psychological campaign assisted by USIA.

The major task for our diplomatic capability is to encourage Latin American leaders to develop independent operations similar to this Project, seeking an internal revolt of the Cuban people against the Communist regime. This is yet to be initiated by State and must be vigorously pressed.

G. *Economic warfare*

Status: This critical key to our political action Project is still in the planning stage under State leadership. State is basing future economic actions, including plans for an embargo on Cuban trade, on the outcome of the forthcoming OAS meeting. Meanwhile, State has chaired an Economic action group, which agreed on developing 13 actions. 15 February is set for a report on implementing plans, so that actions can be initiated. CIA was unable to undertake action to sabotage the sugar harvest, which commences about 15 January, and upon which Cuba's one-crop sugar economy depends. (Sabotage of transport, mills, sugar sacking and cane fields was explored.)

H. *TV intrusion*
Status: Equipment to enable TV intrusion of Havana TV broadcasts has been reactivated on a small vessel under CIA control. CIA plans to attempt intrusion on 22 January during Castro's forthcoming speech and parade demonstrations.

I. *Special sabotage support*
Status: State has explored, with negative results, the feasibility of pre-emptive action with respect to tanker charters (most [Communist] Bloc shipments to Cuba are carried in Western bottoms). CIA has initiated action to contaminate POL[5] supplies for Cuba, although visible results (stoppage of some Cuban transport) are not expected until mid-1962.

J. *Military actions*
Status: Defense has been tasked with preparing a contingency plan for U.S. military action, in case the Cuban people request U.S. help when their revolt starts making headway. This contingency plan will permit obtaining a policy decision on the major point of U.S. intentions, and is looked upon as a positive political-psychological factor in a peoples' revolt, even more than as a possible military action. Defense also has been tasked with fully assisting State and CIA, as commitments of Defense men, money, and matériel are required.

K. *Major elements of the population*
Status: Both State and CIA are continuing to explore their capabilities (with results largely negative to date) for mounting special group operations inside Cuba focused upon dynamic elements of the population, particularly [*1 line of source text not declassified*] through Labor contacts to reach the workers. Other elements include enlistment of the youth and professional groupings. Special consideration is to be given to doing this through Latin American operational contacts. This is vital to the success of our political action nucleus when CIA can put it into place.

L. *Outlook*
Status: As reported to the Special Group last week, there has been a period of a realistic second look at CIA capabilities to mount the required clandestine operations against Cuba, and a subsequent start in "tooling up." After this second look, CIA has concluded that its realistic role should be to create at least the illusion of a popular movement, to win external support for it, to improve CIA op-

---

[5]Petroleum, oil, and lubricants.

erational capability, and to help create a climate which will permit provocative actions in support of a shift to overt action. This outlook, although arrived at thoughtfully within CIA, is far short of the Cuba Project's goals. CIA must take yet another hard look at its potential capabilities, in the light of the following tasking, to determine if it cannot make the greater effort required.

V. Target Schedule

A. *Intelligence*

Task 1: NIE[6] 85–62 on Cuba due 7 February (CIA).

Task 2: By 15 February, Opa Locka Interrogation Center to be made an effective operation for collection and processing of intelligence (CIA with support of Defense, State, I&NS, FBI).

Task 3: Intelligence collection from Cuban refugees elsewhere than Miami area. CIA to survey other refugee points . . . and on a priority basis to ensure maximum coverage of all such source points. 15 February target date.

Task 4: CIA to continue its re-examination of intelligence assets, with priority on agents inside Cuba, and report on capability by 15 February. Also included is coverage of intelligence through third country sources, particularly those having diplomatic relations with Cuba.

B. *Political*

Task 5: CIA to submit plan by 1 February for defection of top Cuban government officials, to fracture the regime from within. The effort must be imaginative and bold enough to consider a "name" defector to be worth at least a million U.S. dollars. This can be the *key* to our political action goal and must be mounted without delay as a major CIA project.

Task 6: CIA to complete plans by 1 February for Cover and Deception actions, to help fracture the Communist regime in Cuba. Defense, State and FBI are to collaborate on this.

Task 7: By 1 February, CIA to submit operations schedule for initiating popular movement within Cuba. This must include localities selected inside Cuba, assessment of selected Cubans, their infiltration, activity assignments, and political platform. One section must deal with the "underground," assess its true status and plans to use it.

Task 8: State to follow up the OAS meeting by having U.S. Embassies in Latin America exploit all opportunities to enlist local sympathy for the Cuban people and to increase hostility towards the Communist regime in Cuba. State to submit report on results of this assignment by 13 February, so further planning can be programmed.

Task 9: By 15 February, State to submit an inventory of operational assets in the Caribbean area, including capabilities of local governments or groups to mount operations on their own, to help achieve the Project's goals. Plans for early use of such capabilities are due by 19 February.

Task 10: CIA to submit operational schedule for using assets in the Carib-

[6]National Intelligence Estimate.

bean area to achieve the Project's political action goals. The objective of working on dynamic elements of the Cuban population (such as workers, farmers) is underscored. Due 19 February.

C. *Economic*

Task 11: State to prepare recommendations to the President on U.S. trade with Cuba, as follow-up to OAS meeting. (If the minimum result of the meeting is an agreement to condemn Cuba as an accomplice of the Sino-Soviet Bloc and adoption of a general statement that Cuba presents a threat to the peace and security of the Hemisphere, State is prepared to recommend to the President that remaining trade between the U.S. and Cuba be barred.)

Task 12: State to plan, with Commerce and other U.S. agencies, on how to halt the *diversion* of *vital* items in the Cuban trade. Due date 15 February. Cooperation of other OAS nations, particularly Canada and Mexico, is to be explored by State.

Task 13: State with Commerce and others involved, to plan on how to make "positive list" items to Latin America be subject to the same licensing procedures as applied to such shipments to other parts of the free world. Due 15 February.

Task 14: State to obtain from Commerce proposal to amend present export controls of technical data (petrochemical, communications equipment) so that Cuba is treated the same as the Sino-Soviet Bloc. Due 15 February.

Task 15: State by 15 February to submit recommendations on issuance of transportation order (T–3) under authority of the Defense Production Act of 1950 forbidding U.S.-owned vessels to engage in trade with Cuba.

Task 16: State plan due 15 February on feasible extension of U.S. port treatment now given to Bloc and Cuban vessels to *charter* vessels of Bloc and Cuba (Treasury to advise on this).

Task 17: State to report by 15 February on feasibility of harassing Bloc shipping by refusing entry into U.S. ports (statedly for security reasons), if vessels have called or will call at Cuban ports.

Task 18: [*2-1/2 lines of source text not declassified*]

Task 19: State to report by 15 February on possibilities for obtaining the discreet cooperation of the National Foreign Trade Council to urge U.S. shippers to refuse to ship on vessels which call at Cuban ports. (Commerce to assist on this.)

Task 20: State to report by 15 February on possibilities to obtain the discreet cooperation of the U.S. Chamber of Commerce and the National Association of Manufacturers to influence U.S. firms having subsidiaries abroad to adhere to the spirit of U.S. economic sanctions. (Commerce to assist on this.)

Task 21: CIA to submit plan by 15 February for inducing failures in food crops in Cuba.

Task 22: State to report by 15 February on status of plans to gain cooperation of NATO allies (bilaterally and in the NATO forum, as appropriate). Objective is to persuade these nations to take steps to isolate Cuba from the West.

Task 23: State to report by 15 February on status of actions undertaken with Japan, which has comparatively significant trade with Cuba, along lines similar to those with NATO nations.

Task 24: CIA to submit plan by February on disruption of the supply of Cuban nickel to the Soviet Union.

D. Psychological

Task 25: USIA to submit plan by 15 February for the most effective psychological exploitation of actions undertaken in the Project, towards the end result of awakening world sympathy for the Cuban people (as a David) battling against the Communist regime (as a Goliath) and towards stimulating Cubans inside Cuba to join "the cause."

Task 26: CIA to submit by 15 February its operational schedule for a psychological campaign to provoke a relaxing of police state control within Cuba. This is to include effective means of publicly indicting "peoples' criminals" for justice after liberation of Cuba. . . .

Task 27: CIA and USIA will report on progress as of 15 February in developing identification of the popular movement inside Cuba, as with songs, symbols, propaganda themes.

Task 28: By 15 February CIA will report on plans and actions for propaganda support of the popular movement inside Cuba. Included will be exactly what is planned for use by the movement inside Cuba, and feasibility of using smuggled food packets (such as the "I Shall Return" cigarette packets to Philippine guerrillas in World War II) as morale boosters in generating the popular movement.

E. Military Action

Task 29: Defense to submit contingency plan for use of U.S. military force to support the Cuban popular movement, including a statement of conditions under which Defense believes such action would be required to win the Project's goal and believes such action would not necessarily lead to general war. Due 28 February.

Task 30: CIA to submit by 15 February its operational schedule for sabotage actions inside Cuba, including timing proposed for the actions and how they affect the generation and support of a popular movement, to achieve the Project goals.

Task 31: CIA to submit specific requests to Defense for required support by Defense as early as possible after its plans firm up. Requests for all major needs are expected by 23 February.

Task 32: Defense will submit plan for "special operations" use of Cubans enlisted in the U.S. armed forces. Due 28 February.[7]

VI. Future Plans

By 20 February, it is expected that sufficient realistic plans for individual tasks will have been received, and initial actions started, to permit a firm time-table to be constructed. Since the President directed that the Chief of Operations[8] conduct the Project through the appropriate organizations and Departments of the Government, and since these U.S. organizations are mainly in the initial inven-

[7]Lansdale added a thirty-third task the next day.
[8]Lansdale.

tory and development of capabilities phase concerning assigned tasks, a precise operations time-table as of today would be too speculative to be useful.

CIA has alerted Defense that it will require considerable military support (including two submarines, PT boats, Coast Guard type cutters, Special Forces trainers, C–54 aircraft, F–86 aircraft, amphibian aircraft, helio-couriers, Army leaflet battalion, and Guantanamo as a base for submarine operations). Also, CIA apparently believes that its role should be to create and expand a popular movement, illusory and actual, which will create a political climate which can provide a framework of plausible excuse for armed intervention. This is not in conformity with the Presidential directive now governing Project tasking. Actually, the role of creating the political climate and plausible excuse for armed intervention would be more properly that of State and Defense, *if such an objective becomes desirable.*

16. Memorandum from CIA Chief of Operations (Directorate for Plans) Richard M. Helms to CIA Director McCone

Robert Kennedy declares that ousting Castro via Operation Mongoose is the administration's main priority.

Washington, January 19, 1962.

SUBJECT

Meeting with the Attorney General of the United States Concerning Cuba

1. I attended a meeting on Cuba at 11:00 A.M. today chaired by the Attorney General. Others present were:

Brig. General E. G. Lansdale (OSD)
Major James Patchell (OSD)
Brig. General William H. Craig (JCS)
Mr. [*name not declassified*] (CIA)
Mr. George McManus (CIA)

(The Department of State was *not* represented although invited.)

2. The Attorney General outlined to us "How it all started," findings as they developed, and the general framework within which the United States Government should now attack the Cuban problem. Briefly, these were the main points:

(a) After failure of the invasion, the United States Government became less active on the theory "better to lay low."

(b) Over the months the complexion of the refugee flow changed (i.e. upper classes out first, then middle classes—dropping to lower middle class, etc.) which, he stated, indicated a strong feeling of opposition to Castro within Cuba.

(c) Progress in Cuba toward a police and Communist state was more rapid during this period than that made by any country in Eastern Europe in an equivalent period of time. Because of the rapidity of advance, immediate action on the part of the United States Government was necessary.

(d) With these factors in mind, the Attorney General had a discussion at the White House during the autumn of 1961 with the President, the Secretary of Defense, and General Lansdale. The Secretary of Defense assigned General Lansdale to survey the Cuban problem, and he (Lansdale) reported to the President, the Secretary of Defense, and the Attorney General (in late November) concluding:

(1) Overthrow of Castro regime was possible

(2) Sugar crop should be attacked at once

(3) Action to be taken to keep Castro so busy with internal problems (economic, political and social) that Castro would have no time for meddling abroad especially in Latin America.

Detail: United States Government was precluded from destroying the current sugar crop (1) we were late and overly optimistic and (b) "the assets of the United States Government were not as great as we were led to believe."

(e) Accordingly, a solution to the Cuban problem today carries "The top priority in the United States Government—all else is secondary—no time, money, effort, or manpower is to be spared. There can be no misunderstanding on the involvement of the agencies concerned nor on their responsibility to carry out this job. The agency heads understand that you are to have full backing on what you need."

(f) Yesterday (18 January 1962), the President indicated to the Attorney General that "the final chapter on Cuba has not been written"—it's got to be done and will be done.

(g) Therefore, the Attorney General directed those in attendance at the meeting to address themselves to the "32 tasks" unfailingly (see program review—The Cuba Project dated 18 January 1962[1]). He said, "It is not only General Lansdale's job to put the tasks, but yours to carry out with every resource at your command."

3. The Attorney General inquired about the progress in establishing a refugee interrogation center at Miami and was informed that this would be in operation by 15 February 1962—the target date. With respect to interrogating the back-log of Cubans in the U.S.A., we agreed that we would attack this problem by getting at the more recent arrivals first. The Attorney General was informed that one could not relate, in time, the establishment of an interrogation facility with the placing of agents in Cuba—in other words, a body of information would have to be developed by intensive interrogation of many sources over a period of time.

4. It was General Lansdale's view that there were several tasks among the "32" outlined upon which action could be taken without awaiting this detailed

[1]See Document 15.

intelligence information. He noted, for example, the defection of top Cubans as being within the immediate capabilities of the CIA.

17. Memorandum from Chief of Operations Lansdale to the Members of the Caribbean Survey Group[1]

In a note to Mongoose officials, Lansdale gives a pep talk.

Washington, January 20, 1962.

At yesterday's meeting,[2] the Attorney General underscored with emphasis that it is your responsibility to develop and apply the maximum effort of your Department (Agency) to win the goal of the Cuba Project.

As he so adequately tasked us, there will be no acceptable alibi. If the capability must be developed, then we must acquire it on a priority basis. It seems clear that the matter of funds and authority offers absolutely no defense for losing time or for doing less than the very best possible effort in your tasks.

In reviewing our program, I appreciate the difficult problems inherent in getting bureaucratic procedures and personnel aroused to do the dynamic thinking and actions demanded by this project. However, I also am very clear about the unreserved requirement laid upon us. You should be equally clear about this. As the Attorney General said, it is untenable to say that the United States is unable to achieve its vital national security and foreign policy goal re Cuba. Castro and his Communist henchmen have many difficult problems to meet in maintaining even a status quo, and we have all the men, money, material, and spiritual assets of this most powerful nation on earth.

It is our job to put the American genius to work on this project, quickly and effectively. This demands a change from business-as-usual and a hard facing of the fact that we are in a combat situation—where we have been given full command.

It is my firm intention to avoid impeding your thinking and actions, except where coordination and constructive direction in the overall interest are involved. In turn, it is your responsibility to keep me informed adequately of your plans and progress. As the Attorney General made plain, you are to call on me, as the Chief of Operations for the Project, at any time for advice and help. He offered the same for himself.

---

[1]The Caribbean Survey Group consisted of the project officers from the Departments of Defense and State, USIA, and CIA who were responsible for the day-to-day running of Mongoose, under the supervision of agency leaders represented on the Special Group (Augmented).

[2]See Document 16.

In the meantime, we must believe that you are getting fully into action on your assigned tasks, and are working towards additional tasks you can come up with to win the Project goal. You were given dead-line dates in the tasks listed in my 18 January paper[3] to the President. I trust that you are not merely attempting to just meet those dates, but are making your own time-table and making it with shorter dead-lines. The urgency and importance of our Project must be reflected in the thinking and actions of the U.S. government people who are to help us win—and that is up to you.

18. Memorandum for the Record

McCone, as he had two weeks earlier (see Document 13), plays the role of skeptic in a meeting on Mongoose.

Washington, January 25, 1962.

SUBJECT

Minutes of Special Group Meeting, 25 January 1962

PRESENT

General Taylor; Mr. [Alexis] Johnson; Mr. Gilpatric, General Lemnitzer; Mr. McCone and Mr. Bissell

Mr. Kennedy, Mr. Helms and General Lansdale were present for Item 1

1. *Cuba*

The Group considered General Lansdale's paper "Cuba Project," 19 January 1962,[1] his paper "Task 33," 19 January 1962; and the CIA paper "Cuba Project," 24 January 1962.[2] In addition General Lansdale circulated, but retained, copies of a paper on actions taken to gain popular support for the U.S. position in connection with the OAS meeting, and another outlining actions taken on the spot, in Punta del Este.

After a lengthy discussion, all agencies currently involved (State, Defense, Joint Staff, CIA) agreed that they accept the tasks assigned to them. In the case of State, this is subject to concurrence by the Secretary upon his return.[3] February 20th is recognized as a target date to take a searching look at progress up to that point and to recommend new lines of policy if appropriate.

General Lansdale commented that it appears that some clarification might

---

[3]See Document 15.
[1]See Document 15. This memorandum was actually dated January 18.
[2]These January 19 and 24 documents have not been included.
[3]Rusk was attending the Punta del Este conference.

be in order as to exactly what is intended in the planning papers. He emphasized that there is agreement that external support of internal operations should be provided for and that it is recognized there might be an internal revolt which could lead to a Cuban group's requesting U.S. intervention. He also said he had met with the JCS and that the latter had responded strongly to the idea of preparing for external action. Additionally, he had met with the intelligence estimators and it had been noted there will be some delay in the NIE[4] because of the need to acquire more intelligence and to digest a sizeable input from the State Department.

Mr. Johnson then pointed out that before the establishment of the Lansdale group, higher authority had directed State and Defense to prepare a plan for military intervention in the event of the removal of Castro from the Cuban scene. He said a great deal of work has been done along these lines and that this should now be directed into the channel of an integrated politico-military plan to cover any contingency.

Mr. McCone made several points: (a) The NIE of November 28,[5] which was commented on in General Lansdale's paper, was based on all available intelligence and dealt with certain operational aspects. The latter had been done at Mr. McCone's direction. (b) Clandestine operations are not susceptible to rigid scheduling and must be approached on a step-by-step basis. Therefore, schedules will have to be reexamined periodically. (c) Sabotage, sanctions and economic warfare can all be attributed to the United States. The Special Group should recognize this as a possible consequence. (d) A popular uprising within Cuba could be brutally suppressed in the manner of [the 1956 uprising in] Hungary. In such an event, unless the U.S. is prepared to give overt assistance, future opportunities to unseat the Castro government would be lost.

In commenting on Mr. McCone's last point, General Taylor noted that the CIA paper of the 24th appears to question the feasibility of the basic objective of overthrowing the Castro regime without overt U.S. military intervention, and that it suggests the need to accept in advance of implementing the Project the definite possibility of having to use U.S. forces. He said that in his view more than contingency plans are required and that, so far as possible, authority should be obtained in advance to undertake major moves which might be required as circumstances develop. He conceded that it may be impossible to get such a firm determination very far in advance. The Group agreed, however, that every effort should be made to line up various situations that might arise, and to formulate recommended policy to capitalize on these situations at the proper time. It was agreed that no action should be taken before February 20th which could have possibilities of involving the U.S. in charges of overt aggression.

General Lemnitzer noted that military contingency plans now in being provide enough American strength to accomplish the job without internal help. He said that while these plans are up-to-date, it will be necessary to build up a number of them based on varying assumptions. He also warned that planning for op-

[4]A probable reference to the March 21, 1962, estimate. See Document 27.
[5]See Document 3 for an earlier version of this intelligence estimate that concluded Castro's political position was solid.

erations of this kind should not involve a firm commitment to a time schedule, as was the case in the earlier unsuccessful [Bay of Pigs] operation.[6]

19. Memorandum from Chief of Operations Lansdale

Lansdale asks his colleagues to consider the issue of whether Mongoose would necessitate American military intervention in Cuba.

Washington, January 26, 1962.

MEMORANDUM FOR

Mr. Hurwitch, State
General Craig, Defense

It is desired that there be an early determination of U.S. policy about the possible use of U.S. military force in the Cuba project. The policy determination will require a clear presentation of the factors to be considered. State and Defense are tasked with making the required presentation, under my guidance. Deputy Secretary Gilpatric of Defense and Deputy Under Secretary Johnson of State have agreed that each of the addressees will represent his Department for this purpose.

The presentation of factors to be considered will include a clear statement of the situations under which U.S. military force would be needed and a clear statement of the proposed use of U.S. military force to meet the needs of each situation. . . .

20. Memorandum from Department of Defense Project Officer for Operation Mongoose William H. Craig to Chief of Operations Lansdale

By this time Dean Rusk had engineered the ejection of Cuba from the OAS at the Punta del Este conference. Meanwhile the Kennedy administration continued its plans to intensify covert pressure on Cuba. Here the Pentagon

[6]Parrott drafted this memorandum.

proposes a cluster of exotic schemes designed to discredit and ultimately to overthrow Castro.

February 2, 1962.

SUBJECT: Ideas in Support of Project

The enclosed ideas are submitted for your consideration and possible use in furtherance of the objectives of the Cuba Project. I think some of them have promise and should you desire our group to develop any of them in more detail, we will do so. . . .

Operation TRUE BLUE

1. *Objective:* To degrade Castro and his government in the eyes of the Cuban people by communications intrusion.

Concept of Operations:

2. By utilizing high powered transmitters in the vicinity of Cuba (Florida, Inagwa, Jamaica, aboard Naval ship) which have the capability of overriding commercial Cuban radio and TV stations, periodically degrade Castro and other government figures in the minds of the Cuban people.

3. The technique of communications intrusion could be exploited by pretaping or live broadcasts of anti-communist and anti-Castro propaganda at station breaks, Castro speeches, etc. This idea envisions the use of a Cuban refugee to make such broadcasts and naturally would require close monitoring of stations to be worked. Any number of thoughts could be injected such as:

a. "Cuba Si, Russia No."

b. Communism exploits the masses.

c. Communism is ruthless totalitarianism.

d. Castro and henchmen feast off the land while we are rationed.

e. Castro and his reign of terror.

f. Castro is a lunatic and should be put away.

g. Castro is the cause of all our troubles.

h. Rise up against the pig Castro, etc. etc.

4. If approved this operation could become a continuous project, perhaps under control of USIA.

Operation "HORN SWOGGLE"

Objective:

1. To crash or force down Cuban MIG aircraft with an all weather intercept capability by communications intrusion.

Concept of Operations:

2. Closely monitor MIG air/ground communications for the purpose of determining frequency and terminology usage for practice or real GCI operations.

3. By use of overriding transmitters and either a decoy aircraft or solid weather conditions, override Cuban controller and have Cuban refugee pilot issue instructions which run MIG out of fuel or towards Florida, Puerto Rico, Jamaica, a carrier, etc.

Operation "NO LOVE LOST"

1. *Objective:* To confuse and harrass [sic] Castro Cuban Pilots by use of radio conversations.

2. *Concept of Operations:* Fly Cuban refugee pilot in sterile aircraft in proximity of Cuba at periodic intervals while communication monitoring Cuban air/ground frequencies utilized for airdrome control. Cuban refugee pilot in sterile aircraft would personally know many of the pilots still flying for Castro. Refugee pilot would get into argument with Castro pilots over radio thus distracting confusing, etc. Would be real trouble for Castro pilots in actual weather conditions. Argument could go, "I'll get you you Red son-of-a-gun," and call by name if appropriate.

POSSIBLE ACTIONS TO PROVOKE, HARRASS, OR DISRUPT CUBA

1. *Operation SMASHER*

a. *Objective:* The objective is to disrupt/disable military and commercial communications facilities in Cuba.

b. *Concept:* This to be accomplished by the clandestine introduction of a "special" vacuum tube into selected communications equipment. The tube, which is available, is virtually undetectable inasmuch as its effectiveness is due to the insertion of a chemical compound in the base of the tube. The chemical, when heated becomes a conductor, when cool a non-conductor.

2. *Operation FREE RIDE:*

a. *Objective:* The objective is to create unrest and dissension amongst the Cuban people.

b. *Concept:* This to be accomplished by airdropping valid Pan American or KLM one-way airline tickets good for passage to Mexico City, Caracas, etc. (none to the U.S.). Tickets could be intermixed with other leaflets planned to be dropped. . . .

3. *Operation TURN ABOUT:*

a. *Objective:* The objective is to create indications to Fidel Castro that his value to the revolutionary cause has diminished to the point where plans are being made for his "removal."

b. *Concept:* This to be accomplished by the use of intelligence means the crecendo increasing until it culminates in Castro's discovery of the mechanism or hardware.

4. *Operation DEFECTOR:*

a. *Objective:* To induce elements or individuals of the Cuban military to defect with equipment.

b. *Concept:* This activity when properly planned and implemented has the effect of decreasing military capability. In a totalitarian system the immediate reaction is increased security accompanied by decreased activity. It also creates havoc in security and intelligence agencies. Could be accomplished by intelligence means and promise of rewards.

5. *Operation BREAK-UP*:

a. *Objective*: To clandestinely introduce corrosive materials to cause aircraft, vehicle or boat accidents.

b. *Concept*: This activity, if possible should be aimed primarily toward the Soviet-provided aircraft. If properly accomplished it would degrade confidence in the equipment, increase supply and maintenance problems and seriously affect combat capability.

6. *Operation COVER-UP*:

a. *Objective*: The objective is to convince the Communist government of Cuba that Naval Forces ostensibly assigned to the MERCURY project is merely a cover.

b. *Concept*: It should not be revealed as to what the cover is—this should be left to conjecture. This could tie in with Operation DIRTY TRICK.

7. *Operation DIRTY TRICK*:

a. *Objective*: The objective is to provide irrevocable proof that, should the MERCURY manned orbit flight fail, the fault lies with the Communists et al Cuba.

b. *Concept*: This to be accomplished by manufacturing various pieces of evidence which would prove electronic interference on the part of the Cubans.

8. *Operation FULL-UP*:

a. *Objective*: The objective is to destroy confidence in fuel supplied by the Soviet Bloc by indicating it is contaminated.

b. *Concept*: This to be accomplished by introducing a known biological agent into jet fuel storage facilities. This agent flourishes in jet fuel and grows until it consumes all the space inside the tank.

9. *Operation PHANTOM*:

a. *Objective*: The objective is to convince the Castro Government that clandestine penetration and resupply of agents is being regularly conducted.

b. *Concept*: This to be accomplished by [creating] the impression that landings have been made on beaches and air drops have been made in other areas.

10. *Operation BINGO*:

a. *Objective*: The objective is to create an incident which has the appearance of an attack on U.S. facilities (GMO) in Cuba, thus providing the excuse for use of U.S. military might to overthrow the current government of Cuba.

b. *Concept*: This to be accomplished by the use of SNAKES outside the confines of the Guantanamo Base. SNAKES simulate an actual fire-fight and upon hearing such a sound it is entirely feasible that the immediate reaction on G'Mo would be that the base is being attacked. This would, with proper preparation, be followed by a counterattack and with adequate planning the base at G'Mo could disgorge military force in sufficient number to sustain itself until other forces, which had been previously alerted, could attack in other areas. It is envisaged that a schedule of operations similar to the following would overwhelm the Cuban military and cause its defeat:

(1) Simulated attack on Guantanamo.

(2) Word flashed to the President.

(3) President orders counterattack to include:

    (a) Immediate launch of alerted aircraft whose targets are Cuban airfields.

    (b) Immediate launch of counterattack down strategic lines in communication in Cuba.

    (c) Fleet force standing by on alert would make way toward pre-selected targets/landing areas.

    (d) Immediate embarkation of airborne troops previously alerted to preselected targets.

    (e) Launch of additional combat aircraft to clear drop areas and further interdict lines of communication.

    (f) Ships and aircraft would land/airdrop troops and secure airfields, road/rail terminals, etc.

    (g) Resupply and replacement activities.

Properly executed, the above could overthrow the Cuban Government in a matter of hours, providing the plan is implemented within the next six months.

11. *Operation GOOD TIMES:*

a. *Objective:* To disillusion the Cuban population with Castro image by distribution of fake photographic material.

b. *Concept:* Prepare a desired photograph, such as an obese Castro with two beauties in any situation desired, ostensibly within a room in the Castro residence, lavishly furnished, and a table briming [sic] over with the most delectable Cuban food with an underlying caption (appropriately Cuban) such as "My ration is different." Make as many prints as desired on sterile paper and then distribute over the countryside by air drops or agents. This should put even a Commie Dictator in the proper perspective with the underprivileged masses.

12. *Operation HEAT IS ON:*

a. *Objective:* To create the impression with Castro Government that certain dyed-in-the-wool Red pilots are planning to defect, thus causing a detrimental tightening of security.

b. *Concept:* It is known that many Cuban refugee pilots are personally acquainted with many of the present CRAF pilots. Accordingly, by utilizing all sources available, determine by name those pilots considered to be dedicated Castro Reds. Then by use of agents, communications, etc. inject into the Castro intelligence system the fact that these pre-designated Reds are planning to defect for monetary and/or ideological reasons. Security crackdown should help destroy Castro image and also impose unacceptable restrictions on routine training activities. . . .

OPERATION: Invisible Bomb

    OBJECTIVE:

1. To create the impression that isolated bombings are taking place in Cuba thus maximizing harrassment [sic] and confusion of the Castro government.

CONCEPT OF OPERATIONS:

2. The Air Force can utilize the operational characteristics of F-101 or other Century series aircraft to create the impression that anti-Castro opposition is continuing. The aircraft operational characteristic to be exploited is the "sonic-boom."

3. The "sonic-boom" can be employed in several different ways such as an individual boom at selected spots or a continuous boom and performed at either high or low altitudes. It will cause not only apprehension but varying degrees of malicious damage as well, i.e. break all the windows on a street in Havana.

4. The "sonic-boom" effect can be maximized by planning missions for execution during the early morning hours when the populace is sleeping. The Cuban people are generally unfamiliar with this phenomenon, therefore it is felt that the impact for a time would be most beneficial.

5. The directional aspects of the "sonic-boom" also make it feasible for use in simulating U.S. Naval gun-fire in the immediate vicinity of the Cuban land mass.

6. This operation is considered relatively safe and leaves no tangible evidence. It can be planned and executed with a minimum of effort and expense.

21. Review of Mongoose by Chief of Operations Lansdale

Lansdale provides a timetable for the overthrow of Castro. He also raises the difficult issue of whether the United States should provide overt military assistance to any Mongoose-induced, anti-Castro uprising.

Washington, February 20, 1962.

THE CUBA PROJECT[1]

The Goal. In keeping with the spirit of the Presidential memorandum of 30 November 1961,[2] the United States will help the people of Cuba overthrow the Communist regime from within Cuba and institute a new government with which the United States can live in peace.

The Situation. We still know too little about the real situation inside Cuba, although we are taking energetic steps to learn more. However, some salient facts are known. It is known that the Communist regime is an active Sino-Soviet

---

[1]Copies of this memorandum were sent to John and Robert Kennedy, and other senior officials.
[2]See Document 7.

spearhead in our Hemisphere and that Communist controls inside Cuba are severe. Also, there is evidence that the repressive measures of the Communists, together with disappointments in Castro's economic dependency on the Communist formula, have resulted in an anti-regime atmosphere among the Cuban people which makes a resistance program a distinct and present possibility.

Time is running against us. The Cuban people feel helpless and are losing hope fast. They need symbols of inside resistance and of outside interest soon. They need something they can join with the hope of starting to work surely towards overthrowing the regime. Since late November, we have been working hard to re-orient the operational concepts within the U.S. government and to develop the hard intelligence and operational assets required for success in our task. . . .

Premise of Action. Americans once ran a successful revolution. It was run from within, and succeeded because there was timely and strong political, economic, and military help by nations outside who supported our cause. Using this same concept of revolution from within, we must now help the Cuban people to stamp out tyranny and gain their liberty.

On 18 January, the Chief of Operations assigned thirty-two tasks to Departments and Agencies of the U.S. government, in order to provide a realistic assessment and preparation of U.S. capabilities.[3] The Attorney General and the Special Group were apprised of this action. The answers received on 15 February provided the basis for planning a realistic course of action. The answers also revealed that the course of action must contain continuing coordination and firm overall guidance.

The course of action set forth herein is realistic within present operational estimates and intelligence. *Actually, it represents the maximum target timing which the operational people jointly considered feasible.* It aims for a revolt which can take place in Cuba by October 1962. It is a series of target actions and dates, not a rigid time-table. The target dates are timed as follows:

Phase I, *Action*, March 1962. Start moving in.

Phase II, *Build-up*, April–July 1962. Activating the necessary operations inside Cuba for revolution and concurrently applying the vital political, economic, and military-type support from outside Cuba.

Phase III, *Readiness*, 1 August 1962, check for final policy decision.

Phase IV, *Resistance*, August–September 1962, move into guerrilla operations.

Phase V, *Revolt*, first two weeks of October 1962. Open revolt and overthrow of the Communist regime.

Phase VI, *Final*, during month of October 1962. Establishment of new government.

Plan of Action. Attached is an operational plan for the overthrow of the Communist regime in Cuba, by Cubans from within Cuba, with outside help from the U.S. and elsewhere. Since this is an operation to prompt and support a revolt by the people in a Communist police state, flexibility is a must for success. De-

[3]See Document 15.

cisions on operational flexibility rest with the Chief of Operations, with consultation in the Special Group when policy matters are involved. Target actions and dates are detailed in the attached operational plans, which cover:

A. Basic Action Plan Inside Cuba
B. Political Support Plan
C. Economic Support Plan
D. Psychological Support Plan
E. Military Support Plan
F. Sabotage Support Plan
G. Intelligence Support Plan

Early Policy Decisions. The operational plan for clandestine U.S. support of a Cuban movement inside Cuba to overthrow the Communist regime is within policy limits already set by the President. A vital decision, still to be made, is on the use of open U.S. force to aid the Cuban people in winning their liberty. If conditions and assets permitting a revolt are achieved in Cuba, and if U.S. help is required to sustain this condition, will the U.S. respond promptly with military force to aid the Cuban revolt? The contingencies under which such military deployment would be needed, and recommended U.S. responses, are detailed in a memorandum being prepared by the Secretaries of State and of Defense. An early decision is required, prior to deep involvement of the Cubans in this program.

22. Memorandum from Director of the Bureau of Intelligence and Research Roger Hilsman to Deputy Under Secretary of State for Political Affairs Alexis Johnson

A State Department official echoes the concerns about Mongoose expressed earlier by John McCone.

Washington, February 20, 1962.

SUBJECT

The Cuba Project

Although I am not familiar with the context in which the paper dated 18 January 1962[1] has been discussed and developed, I think it may be useful for you to have a few observations on it from a bystander's viewpoint.

[1]See Document 15.

1. I believe that the Objective as stated is sound and desirable.

2. With regard to the Concept of Operations, I have serious misgivings. The concept appears to depend in large measure on building up an internal political action organization *in Cuba* which would enjoy the support of the majority of the Cuban people. Presumably, it would be primarily CIA's job to build such an organization. I have seen no hard intelligence which would lead me to suppose that there exists, or that the Agency [CIA] has assets for bringing into existence in the near future, an internal political action organization which would assure the support of the majority of the Cuban people against the Castro regime. On the contrary, the evidence we have points toward the present regime's tightening its controls. This leads me to conclude, as others have, that unless a popular uprising in Cuba is promptly supported by overt U.S. military action, it would probably lead to another Hungary. Briefly, I do not believe we can unseat the present regime in Havana by anything short of outright military intervention.

3. There exist, of course, contingency plans for taking Cuba over in a matter of days. What does not exist, to my knowledge, is any agreement (a) to carry out such an intervention, (b) on a means of provoking it, or (c) an analysis of the possible consequences of intervention. I think we should bite the bullet and address ourselves to these points. Unless we are at least willing seriously to consider such a course of action, I am afraid we may be heading for a fiasco that could be worse for us than the ill-fated [Bay of Pigs] operation of last year. In a word, on the basis of the information available to me on the Lansdale approach, which is fragmentary to say the least, I tend to agree with the position taken by John McCone in the Special Group as reflected in the minutes of the meeting of January 25.[2]

23. Review of Operation Mongoose by Chief of Operations Lansdale

A summary of Mongoose's development shows that Lansdale's superiors had instructed him to center the operation, initially at least, on intelligence collection.

Washington, March 2, 1962.

THE CUBA PROJECT[1]

The Goal: The United States will help the people of Cuba overthrow the Communist regime from within Cuba and institute a new government with which the United States can live in peace.

[2]See Document 18.
[1]Robert Kennedy and other senior officials received a copy of this memorandum.

Developments:

30 November 1961: The above goal was set for the United States, with Brig. General Lansdale as Chief of Operations and with operational lieutenants appointed as direct representatives of the Secretary of State, the Secretary of Defense, and the Director, Central Intelligence. The Special Group (NSC 5412) was to be kept informed and be available for advice and recommendation.

December–January. Decisive effort was made to re-orient the operational concepts within the U.S. government and to develop the hard intelligence and operational assets required for success. A joint effort was mounted to obtain intelligence in depth from refugees at Opa-Locka, Florida, and to provide more thorough access to operational assets. At the same time, reports from significant population groups, including religious and labor groups, indicated that the spirit of the Cuban people was dying under the Communist police-state controls and that some evidence on which to base hope for a better future was needed promptly to prevent this death of spirit. A review of operational assets dictated that the U.S. was powerless to hamper the sugar harvest, without U.S. attribution.

18 January 1962. The Chief of Operations assigned thirty-two tasks to Departments and Agencies, for a realistic assessment and preparation of U.S. capabilities.[2]

15 February 1962. Detailed staff papers were received from Departments and Agencies, responding to assigned tasks. A basic action plan was then made, for the step-by-step development of an internal revolution, by the Chief of Operations with joint consideration and approval by the operational representatives (CIA, State, Defense, and USIA).

20 February 1962. Completed basic plan for paced operations inside Cuba, and support plans for political, economic, psychological, military, sabotage, and intelligence actions.[3] The outlined concept would develop assets inside Cuba for a popular revolution in October (judged to be the earliest possible date by those responsible for operations), with U.S. and Latin American help from the outside. Each step would be taken as operationally feasible, collecting intelligence, building revolutionary assets, and taking advantage of targets of opportunity.

21 February 1962. Plan was discussed by Special Group (NSC 5412) and decision was made to meet again on it the following Monday, with Secretary McNamara.

26 February 1962. Special Group (NSC 5412) met with Secretary McNamara. Chief of Operations was asked to submit a plan for an initial intelligence collection program only.

1 March 1962. Special Group (NSC 5412) agreed that the immediate objective of the U.S. during March, April, and May will be the acquisition of intelligence, and that other U.S. actions must be inconspicuous and consistent with an overt policy of isolating Castro and of neutralizing his influence in the Western Hemisphere. At the end of May, the situation will be reviewed and a decision made as to the next phase. The Chief of Operations is to report to the Pres-

---

[2]See Document 15.
[3]See Document 21.

ident through the Special Group (NSC 5412 augmented by the Attorney General and the Chairman, JCS); the Special Group will be responsible for providing policy guidance for approving important operations, and for monitoring progress.

Intelligence Plan

As requested by the Special Group (NSC 5412), a plan for basic intelligence collection, upon which to base the decision to undertake actions to cause the overthrow of Castro, is submitted herewith.[4] In view of the new requirement for a comprehensive and definitive intelligence finding concerning the Cuban population vis-à-vis the regime, CIA requested that the initial period be extended through July 1962. This practical realism is reflected in the plan. Also, responsible CIA operational officers noted that at least 6 months should be added to the timing of phases set forth in the original basic action plan,[5] if a decision to seek an internal revolution is deferred until the end of the collection and reporting period.

24. Memorandum from Chairman of the JCS Lemnitzer to Secretary of Defense McNamara

The Joint Chiefs provide a variety of pretexts that might be used to justify an attack on Cuba.

13 March 1962

Subject: Justification for US Military Intervention in Cuba

1. The Joint Chiefs of Staff have considered the attached Memorandum for the Chief of Operations [Lansdale], Cuba Project, which responds to a request of that office for brief but precise description of pretexts which would provide justification for US military intervention in Cuba.

2. The Joint Chiefs of Staff recommend that the proposed memorandum be forwarded as a preliminary submission suitable for planning purposes. It is assumed that there will be similar submissions from other agencies and that these inputs will be used as a basis for developing a time-phased plan. Individual projects can then be considered on a case-by-case basis.

3. Further, it is assumed that a single agency will be given the primary responsibility for developing military and para-military aspects of the basic plan. It

[4]Not found attached.
[5]See Document 21.

is recommended that this responsibility for both overt and covert military operations be assigned the Joint Chiefs of Staff.

1 Enclosure
    Memo for Chief of Operations, Cuba Project

REPORT BY THE DEPARTMENT OF DEFENSE AND JOINT CHIEFS
OF STAFF REPRESENTATIVE[1] ON THE CARIBBEAN SURVEY GROUP
to the
JOINT CHIEFS OF STAFF
on
CUBA PROJECT

JUSTIFICATION FOR US MILITARY INTERVENTION IN CUBA

THE PROBLEM

1. As requested[2] by Chief of Operations, Cuba Project, the Joint Chiefs of Staff are to indicate brief but precise description of pretexts which they consider would provide justification for US military intervention in Cuba. . . .

DISCUSSION

5. The suggested courses of action are based on the premise that US military intervention will result from a period of heightened US-Cuban tensions which place the United States in the position of suffering justifiable grievances. World opinion, and the United Nations forum should be favorably affected by developing the international image of the Cuban government as rash and irresponsible, and as an alarming and unpredictable threat to the peace of the Western Hemisphere.

6. While the foregoing premise can be utilized at the present time it will continue to hold good only as long as there can be reasonable certainty that US military intervention in Cuba would not directly involve the Soviet Union. There is as yet no bilateral mutual support agreement binding the USSR to the defense of Cuba, Cuba has not yet become a member of the Warsaw Pact, nor have the Soviets established Soviet bases in Cuba in the pattern of US bases in Western Europe. Therefore, since time appears to be an important factor in resolution of the Cuba problem, all projects are suggested within the time frame of the next few months.

CONCLUSION

7. The suggested courses of action satisfactorily respond to the statement of the problem. However, these suggestions should be forwarded as a preliminary submission suitable for planning purposes, and together with similar inputs from other agencies, provide a basis for development of a single, integrated, time-

---

[1]William Craig.
[2]Memorandum from Lansdale to Craig, subject "Operation MONGOOSE," dated March 5, 1962.

phased plan to focus all efforts on the objective of justification for US military intervention in Cuba. . . .

PRETEXTS TO JUSTIFY US MILITARY INTERVENTION IN CUBA . . .

1. Since it would seem desirable to use legitimate provocations as the basis for US military intervention in Cuba a cover and deception plan, to include requisite preliminary actions . . . could be executed as an initial effort to provoke Cuban reactions. Harassment plus deceptive actions to convince the Cubans of imminent invasion would be emphasized. Our military posture throughout execution of the plan will allow a rapid change from exercise to intervention if Cuban response justifies.

2. A series of well coordinated incidents will be planned to take place in and around Guantanamo to give genuine appearance of being done by hostile Cuban forces.

    a. Incidents to establish a credible attack (not in chronological order):

        (1) Start rumors (many). Use clandestine radio.

        (2) Land friendly Cubans in uniform "over-the-fence" to stage attack on base.

        (3) Capture Cuban (friendly) saboteurs inside the base.

        (4) Start riots near the base main gate (friendly Cubans).

        (5) Blow up ammunition inside the base; start fires.

        (6) Burn aircraft on air base (sabotage).

        (7) Lob mortar shells from outside of base into base. Some damage to installations.

        (8) Capture assault teams approaching from the sea or vicinity of Guantanamo City.

        (9) Capture militia group which storms the base.

        (10) Sabotage ship in harbor; large fires—napthalene.

        (11) Sink ship near harbor entrance. Conduct funerals for mock-victims (may be lieu of (10)).

    b. United States would respond by executing offensive operations to secure water and power supplies, destroying artillery and mortar emplacements which threaten the base.

    c. Commence large scale United States military operations.

3. A "Remember the Maine" incident could be arranged in several forms:

    a. We could blow up a US ship in Guantanamo Bay and blame Cuba.

    b. We could blow up a drone (unmanned) vessel anywhere in the Cuban waters. We could arrange to cause such incident in the vicinity of Havana or Santiago as a spectacular result of Cuban attack from the air or sea, or both. The presence of Cuban planes or ships merely investigating the intent of the vessel could be fairly compelling evidence that the ship was taken under attack. The nearness to Havana or Santiago would add credibility especially to those people that might have heard the blast or have seen the fire. The US could follow up with an air/sea rescue operation covered by US fighters to "evacuate" remaining members of the non-existent crew. Casualty lists in US newspapers would cause a helpful wave of national indignation.

4. We could develop a Communist Cuban terror campaign in the Miami area, in other Florida cities and even in Washington. The terror campaign could be pointed at Cuban refugees seeking haven in the United States. We could sink a boatload of Cubans enroute to Florida (real or simulated). We could foster attempts on lives of Cuban refugees in the United States even to the extent of wounding in instances to be widely publicized. Exploding a few plastic bombs in carefully chosen spots, the arrest of Cuban agents and the release of prepared documents substantiating Cuban involvement also would be helpful in projecting the idea of an irresponsible government.

5. A "Cuban-based, Castro-supported" filibuster could be simulated against a neighboring Caribbean nation. . . . We know that Castro is backing subversive efforts clandestinely against Haiti, Dominican Republic, Guatemala, and Nicaragua at present and possible others. These efforts can be magnified and additional ones contrived for exposure. For example, advantage can be taken of the sensitivity of the Dominican Air Force to intrusions within their national air space. "Cuban" B–26 or C–46 type aircraft could make cane-burning raids at night. Soviet Bloc incendiaries could be found. This could be coupled with "Cuban" messages to the Communist underground in the Dominican Republic and "Cuban" shipments of arms which would be found, or intercepted, on the beach.

6. Use of MIG type aircraft by US pilots could provide additional provocation. Harassment of civil air, attacks on surface shipping and destruction of US military drone aircraft by MIG type planes would be useful as complementary actions. An F-86 properly painted would convince air passengers that they saw a Cuban MIG, especially if the pilot of the transport were to announce such fact. The primary drawback to this suggestion appears to be the security risk inherent in obtaining or modifying an aircraft. However, reasonable copies of the MIG could be produced from US resources in about three months.

7. Hijacking attempts against civil air and surface craft should appear to continue as harassing measures condoned by the government of Cuba. Concurrently, genuine defections of Cuban civil and military air and surface craft should be encouraged.

8. It is possible to create an incident which will demonstrate convincingly that a Cuban aircraft has attacked and shot down a chartered civil airliner enroute from the United States to Jamaica, Guatemala, Panama or Venezuela. The destination would be chosen only to cause the flight plan route to cross Cuba. The passengers could be a group of college students off on a holiday or any grouping of persons with a common interest to support chartering a non-scheduled flight.

    a. An aircraft at Eglin AFB would be painted and numbered as an exact duplicate for a civil registered aircraft belonging to a CIA proprietary organization in the Miami area. At a designated time the duplicate would be substituted for the actual civil aircraft and would be loaded with the selected passengers, all boarded under carefully prepared aliases. The actual registered aircraft would be converted to a drone.

    b. Take off times of the drone aircraft and the actual aircraft will be scheduled to allow a rendezvous south of Florida. From the rendezvous point the passenger-carrying aircraft will descend to minimum altitude and go directly into an auxiliary field at Eglin AFB where arrangements will have been made to evacuate the passengers and return the aircraft to its original status. The drone aircraft meanwhile will continue to fly the filed flight plan. When over Cuba the drone will being [sic] transmitting on the international distress frequency a "MAY DAY" message stating he is under attack by Cuban MIG aircraft. The transmission will be interrupted by destruction of the aircraft which will be triggered by radio signal. This will allow . . . radio stations in the Western Hemisphere to tell the US what has happened to the aircraft instead of the US trying to "sell" the incident.

9. It is possible to create an incident which will make it appear that Communist Cuban MIGs have destroyed a USAF aircraft over international waters in an unprovoked attack.

a. Approximately 4 or 5 F-101 aircraft will be dispatched in trail from Homestead AFB, Florida, to the vicinity of Cuba. Their mission will be to reverse course and simulate fakir aircraft for an air defense exercise in southern Florida. These aircraft would conduct variations of these flights at frequent intervals. Crews would be briefed to remain at least 12 miles off the Cuban coast; however, they would be required to carry live ammunition in the event that hostile actions were taken by the Cuban MIGs.

b. On one such flight, a pre-briefed pilot would fly tail-end Charley at considerable interval between aircraft. While near the Cuban Island this pilot would broadcast that he had been jumped by MIGs and was going down. No other calls would be made. The pilot would then fly directly west at extremely low altitude and land at a secure base, an Eglin auxiliary. The aircraft would be met by the proper people, quickly stored and given a new tail number. The pilot who had performed the mission under an alias, would resume his proper identity and return to his normal place of business. The pilot and aircraft would then have disappeared.

c. At precisely the same time that the aircraft was presumably shot down a submarine or small surface craft would disburse F-101 parts, parachute, etc., at approximately 15 to 20 miles off the Cuban coast and depart. The pilots returning to Homestead would have a true story as far as they knew. Search ships and aircraft could be dispatched and parts of aircraft found.

FACTS BEARING ON THE PROBLEM

1. The Joint Chiefs of Staff have previously stated that US unilateral military intervention in Cuba can be undertaken in the event that the Cuban regime commits hostile acts against US forces or property which would serve as an incident upon which to base overt intervention.

2. The need for positive action in the event that current covert efforts to foster an internal Cuban rebellion are unsuccessful was indicated by the Joint Chiefs of Staff on 7 March 1962, as follows:

"—determination that a credible internal revolt is impossible of attainment during the next 9–10 months will require a decision by the United States to develop a Cuba "provocation" as justification for positive US military action."

3. It is understood that the Department of State also is preparing suggested courses of action to develop justification for US military intervention in Cuba.

25. Guidelines for Operation Mongoose

After months of planning and discussion, the first phase of Mongoose receives final definition.

Washington, March 14, 1962.

1. Operation Mongoose will be developed on the following assumptions:

a. In undertaking to cause the overthrow of the target government, the U.S. will make maximum use of indigenous resources, internal and external,[1] but recognizes that final success will require decisive U.S. military intervention.

b. Such indigenous resources as are developed will be used to prepare for and justify this intervention, and therefore to facilitate and support it.

2. The immediate priority objective of U.S. efforts during the coming months will be the acquisition of hard intelligence on the target area. Concurrently, all other political, economic and covert actions will be undertaken short of those reasonably calculated to inspire a revolt within the target area, or other development which would require U.S. armed intervention. These actions, insofar as possible, will be consistent with overt policies of isolating the local leader and of neutralizing his influence in the Western Hemisphere, and will be taken in such a way as to permit disengagement with minimum losses in assets and U.S. prestige. The JCS will continue the planning and essential preliminary actions to assure a decisive U.S. military capability for intervention. At the end of this first period, or earlier if conditions permit, the situation will be reviewed and a decision taken as to the next phase of the program.

3. In order to get the covert phase of this program in motion, it will be necessary at the outset to use U.S. personnel, bases and equipment for the support of operations inside the target area. However, the CIA will concurrently expedite the development of non-attributable resources in order to reduce or eliminate this dependence should it become necessary after the initial phase.

4. During this period, General Lansdale will continue as chief of operations, calling directly on the participating departments and agencies for support and implementation of agreed tasks. The heads of these departments and agencies

[1]"Internal" is a reference to Cubans in Cuba, while "external" refers to Cuban exiles.

are responsible for performance through normal command channels to higher authority. General Lansdale is responsible for coordinating combined planning and execution, reporting to higher authority[2] through the Special Group (5412), augmented by the Attorney General and the Chairman, JCS. The Special Group (5412 augmented) is responsible for providing policy guidance to the project, for approving important operations and for monitoring progress.[3]

26. Memorandum Prepared by Under Secretary of State Johnson

JFK endorses the March 14 guidelines but shows caution when considering the idea of an American attack on Cuba.

March 16, 1962.

Discussed with the President today—McCone, Gen. Taylor, Gilpatric, Attorney General, Mac Bundy, & Gen. Lemnitzer present.

The President expressed general approval [of the March 14 guidelines for Operation Mongoose] on the understanding there will be further examination of use of Americans for airdrops etc. during first phase when risk estimates are completed.

The President also expressed skepticism that in so far as can now be foreseen circumstances will arise that would justify and make desirable the use of American forces for overt military action. It was clearly understood no decision was expressed or implied approving the use of such forces although contingency planning would proceed.

27. National Intelligence Estimate

Rather like the intelligence estimate produced in November 1961 (see Document 3), this reports casts doubt on the notion that the Cuban people were likely to revolt.

[2]Namely, the president.
[3]General Maxwell D. Taylor, the president's military representative, drafted this paper on March 5. It was revised slightly according to recommendations by McCone and McGeorge Bundy.

Washington, March 21, 1962.

THE SITUATION AND PROSPECTS IN CUBA[1]

Summary and Conclusions . . .

7. The initial popular enthusiasm for the revolution has steadily waned. Many men who fought against Batista have been alienated by the even more dictatorial character of the Castro regime and its increasingly Communist complexion. The vaunted agrarian reform has done little to improve the lot of the peasants. Moreover, people are becoming fed up with the privations, exactions, and regimentation that characterize life in Castro's Cuba.

8. Nevertheless, Fidel Castro and the Revolution retain the positive support of at least a quarter of the population. The hard core of this support consists principally of those who now have a vested interest in the regime: the new managerial class and the Communists. These are reinforced by the substantial numbers of Cubans, especially those in the mass organizations, who are still under the spell of Castro's charismatic leadership or are convinced the Revolution has been to their advantage.

9. There is active resistance in Cuba, but it is limited, uncoordinated, unsupported, and desperate. The regime, with all the power of repression at its disposal, has shown that it can contain the present level of resistance activity.

10. The majority of the Cuban people neither support the regime nor resist it, in any active sense. They are grumbling and resentful, but apparently hopeless and passive, resigned to acceptance of the present regime as the effective government in being with which they must learn to live for lack of a feasible alternative.

11. The next year or two will be a critical period for the Castro regime. The 1962 sugar crop will be the smallest in years; the difficulty of acquiring convertible foreign exchange will be greater than ever. Want of convertible exchange will limit Cuba's ability to purchase foodstuffs and other needed supplies in the Free World. No substantial increase in the supplies provided by the [Soviet] Bloc is likely during 1962. In these circumstances it is unlikely that the total output of the Cuban economy in 1962 can rise above the 1961 level. Under consequent privations, the Cuban people are likely to become more restive. Much will depend on whether the regime succeeds in directing their resentment toward the US, or whether it comes to focus on the regime.

12. The regime's apparatus for surveillance and repression should be able to cope with any popular tendency toward active resistance. Any impulse toward widespread revolt is inhibited by the fear which this apparatus inspires, and also by the lack of dynamic leadership and of any expectation of liberation within the foreseeable future. In these circumstances, increasing antagonism toward the regime is likely to produce only a manageable increase in isolated acts of sabotage or of open defiance on the part of a few desperate men. A sequence of disaffection-repression-resistance could conceivably be set in motion, but would

[1]The CIA and the intelligence organizations of various other government departments and branches of the military produced this estimate.

be unlikely to cause major difficulties for the regime in the absence of considerable external support. . . .

28. Memorandum from Chairman of the JCS Lemnitzer to Secretary of Defense McNamara

Moving beyond the idea of support for a Mongoose-induced anti-Castro uprising, the Joint Chiefs recommend immediate American military action against Cuba.

10 April 1962.

1. The Joint Chiefs of Staff believe that the Cuban problem must be solved in the near future. Further, they see no prospect of early success in overthrowing the present communist regime either as a result of internal uprisings or external political, economic or psychological pressures. Accordingly they believe that military intervention by the United States will be required to overthrow the present communist regime.

2. The United States cannot tolerate permanent existence of a communist government in the Western Hemisphere. The present regime in Cuba provides communism with a base of operations for espionage, sabotage and subversion against Latin America. The stability of some governments in Latin America is already threatened by the overt and covert actions of the Cuban government. Continued existence of this communist government increases the probability that one or more other nations in Latin America will become communist or communist dominated. This will greatly increase the problems currently facing the United States and the Organization of American States. While considered unlikely, it is possible for the Sino-Soviet Bloc to establish military bases in Cuba similar to US installations around the bloc periphery. Establishment of such bases would increase US defense costs as forces were developed or shifted to meet the threat.

3. Time favors the Cuban regime and the communist bloc. They are provided with the opportunity to continue with their subversive efforts in Latin America. Increasing internal security measures by police state methods decrease the possibility of internal uprisings within Cuba. The steady improvement in military defenses strengthens the resistance which must be overcome in the event of US military intervention and could lengthen the time required to secure control of the government and the island. The continuing indoctrination of the Cuban youth creates a growing nucleus for a communist underground after the elimination of the present government. This creates a problem for the future which is steadily increasing in magnitude.

4. The Joint Chiefs of Staff believe that the United States can undertake military intervention in Cuba without risk of general war. They also believe that the intervention can be accomplished rapidly enough to minimize communist opportunities for solicitation of UN action. Forces available would assure rapid essential military control of Cuba. Continued police action would be required.

5. In view of the increasing military and subversive threat to the United States and the nations of the Western Hemisphere posed by the communist regime in Cuba, the Joint Chiefs of Staff recommend that a national policy of early military intervention in Cuba be adopted by the United States. They also recommend that such intervention be undertaken as soon as possible and preferably before the release of National Guard and Reserve forces presently on active duty.

For the Joint Chiefs of Staff[1]

29. Memorandum for the Special Group (Augmented)

Mongoose officials are instructed to respond to a concern expressed earlier by Robert Kennedy about how to react should the Russians build a military base in Cuba—an issue that would become salient later in the year.

Washington, May 31, 1962.

SUBJECT

US Policy in the Event USSR Establishes a Base(s) in Cuba[1]

1. At the 22 March meeting, Mr. Robert Kennedy asked the Special Group (Augmented)—what would be an appropriate course of action for the United States to take in the event that the Soviets establish a military base in Cuba.

2. The Department of Defense is most desirous that a considered response to this question be prepared by each agency concerned, for the establishment of a Soviet military base(s) of any kind in Cuba would increase our national vulnerability and defense costs as forces would have to be developed or shifted to meet this threat from the South.[2] At the same time, it is logical to assume that a Soviet military base in Cuba would result in further economic, managerial and technical assistance for Cuba which would virtually assure, for the foreseeable future, the continuation of the Cuban-Communist base of operations for espionage, sabotage and subversion throughout the entire Western Hemisphere.

---

[1]The Joint Chiefs produced this memorandum in response to a request from Maxwell Taylor at an April 5 Special Group meeting for their views on military intervention.

[1]Lansdale probably drafted this memorandum.

[2]On May 31 the CIA distributed a report of a possible Russian submarine base being established in Cuba.

3. Since the Special Group (Augmented) has assumed that overt US military force will have to be used to end Communist control of Cuba, Mr. Kennedy's question is particularly pertinent. For should the Soviets choose to exercise their option of establishing a military base under a Soviet flag in Cuba, it is possible that this would act to prevent any future US decision to intervene with US military force, just as the Soviets have refrained from applying military force against countries on which US bases are established.

4. Furthermore, establishment of a military base(s) in Cuba would cost the Soviets very little in terms of world public opinion. For example, they could explain that they were simply taking a page from our book, and would remove their base(s) from Cuba if we would remove ours from Berlin, Turkey or Formosa.

5. Consequently, I believe national security considerations require that all participating agencies prepare a written response to Mr. Robert Kennedy's question. I recommend that these responses be prepared in time for presentation at our next meeting.

30. Memorandum from Chief of Operations Lansdale

Further contingency planning for military action against Cuba is requested.

Washington, June 14, 1962.

MEMORANDUM FOR

Edwin Martin, State
General Craig, Defense
William Harvey, CIA
Donald Wilson, USIA

SUBJECT

Spontaneous Revolts in Cuba, Contingency Planning

This confirms the oral assignment of tasks for further contingency planning.

The Defense operational representative is responsible for the preparation of a contingency plan for U.S. actions in a situation of open, widespread revolt in Cuba. This contingency is seen as a non-U.S.-initiated situation, similar to that rumored as being activated for mid-June 1962.[1] U.S. actions are seen as including the use of U.S. military force.

---

[1]The historian James G. Hershberg speculates that this talk of an anti-Castro uprising was disingenuous, that "what Lansdale really had in mind was the possibility that one of several assassination plots against Castro set in motion by the Kennedy administration might succeed." So this would be American military planning for that eventuality. See Hershberg, "Before the 'Missiles of October': Did Kennedy Plan a Military Strike Against Cuba?" *Diplomatic History* 14 (Spring 1990): 178–179.

The State operational representative is responsible for the preparation of a contingency plan for U.S. actions in a situation of open revolt in one or a few localities in Cuba. This contingency is seen as a non-U.S.-initiated situation where the people in one Cuban locality (or several neighboring localities) openly defy the Communist regime, are being suppressed with force, and U.S. help is requested (by the Cuban revolters or Latin American opinion).

All U.S. Departments and Agencies participating in Operation Mongoose will assist in the preparation of these plans, as required. . . .

31. Memorandum from Deputy Secretary of Defense Roswell L. Gilpatric to the Special Group (Augmented)

The Pentagon asserts that the United States should respond with force if a Russian military base is built in Cuba.

June 28, 1962.

Subject: Soviet Base in Cuba

1. In response to a memorandum for the Special Group (Augmented) from the Director of Operations,[1] Operation Mongoose, subject: "Status of Requested Studies, Operation Mongoose," dated 8 June 1962, the Department of Defense has considered the problem of an appropriate course of action for the United States to take in [the] event that the Soviets should take steps to establish a military base in Cuba.

2. In the event of such a contingency, the choice of US counteraction is between long term acceptance of a communist state in the Caribbean with an increasing military threat to the United States from the South or US military intervention. Our present view is that the latter course of action would be the only solution compatible with the security interests of the United States.

[1]Lansdale.

32. Memorandum Prepared by CIA Director McCone of Discussion at Dinner on the Evening of July 18, 1962, with Attorney General Kennedy

Bobby Kennedy reflects on Mongoose as the operation's first phase draws to a close.

Washington, July 18, 1962.

. . . 3. The Cuban situation was reviewed in considerable detail, AG [Attorney General] expressing the opinion that the last six months' effort had been worthwhile inasmuch as we had gained a very substantial amount of intelligence which was lacking, but that the effort was disappointing inasmuch as the program had not advanced to the point we had hoped. He urged intensified effort but seemed inclined to let the situation "worsen" before recommending drastic action. We discussed several leaders such as [*less than 1 line of source text not declassified*] however, there was no specific recommendation as to whom we should support or who represented the most dynamic leadership of the Cuban group.[1] . . .

33. Memorandum from Chief of Operations Lansdale to the Special Group (Augmented)

Lansdale reviews the first phase of Mongoose and calls for a more ambitious second phase.

Washington, July 25, 1962.

SUBJECT

Review of Operation Mongoose

This is the Operations report at the end of Phase I. It has been compiled to assist you in reviewing Operation Mongoose thus far and in determining the best course of U.S. action for the future.

This Operations report contains the contribution of each major participant,

---

[1]Presumably a reference to the Cuban exile group.

on objectives, on the planning and operational activity to win these objectives, and on future possibilities to be governed by the policy framework. . . .

Objectives

As desired by higher authority[1] on 30 November 1961, the U.S. undertook a special effort "in order to help Cuba overthrow the Communist regime."[2] After a review of operational planning and programming concepts, the Special Group (Augmented) provided guidelines on 14 March 1962 for Phase I, Operation Mongoose (roughly until the end of July 1962).[3] The main objectives were seen as:

a. The acquisition of hard intelligence on the target area.

b. Undertaking all other political, economic, and covert actions, short of inspiring a revolt in Cuba or developing the need for U.S. armed intervention.

c. Be consistent with U.S. overt policy, and remain in position to disengage with minimum loss in assets and U.S. prestige.

d. Continue JCS planning and essential preliminary actions for a decisive U.S. capability for intervention.

Accomplishment

Elements of the U.S. government were organized to reach the goals set for Phase I. My assessment of where we are on each objective is noted under appropriate sub-headings below. In general, this has been a remarkably quiet operation, well within the "noise" and "visibility" limits imposed.

Higher authority has been kept informed of progress through the Special Group (Augmented), by frequent reports. The Special Group has provided policy guidance, as required, in Phase I.

The Chief of Operations has coordinated the efforts of participating departments and agencies, through meetings of the Operational Representatives and by constant review of progress. The Operational Representative of each major U.S. participant in Operation Mongoose are William Harvey (CIA), Robert Hurwitch (State), Brig. Gen. Benjamin Harris (Defense), and Don Wilson (USIA).

My assessment of the organization, planning, and actions to reach the goals in Phase I:

Intelligence. CIA had the main assignment to acquire the "hard-intelligence" desired. The headquarters and field staff of CIA are now well organized for a major effort for this aspect of Operation Mongoose, being strengthened by a number of CIA officers experienced in "denied area" operations elsewhere in the world. Planning and actions rate superior, in a professional sense of intelligence collection.

CIA established the Caribbean Admission Center at Opa-Locka, Florida. . . . It undertook a priority plan to collect information on the target from third country areas in Latin America and Europe. Inside Cuba, the recruitment and placement of third country nationals and initiation of Cuban collection nets, particularly in urban centers, has made Operation Mongoose numerically the

---

[1] A reference to JFK.
[2] See Document 7.
[3] See Document 25.

largest U.S. intelligence agent effort inside a Communist state. However, the effort in more remote provincial areas of Cuba, where guerrilla resistance was expected to be spotted, recruited, and organized, was short of the hoped-for goal; this was due to the regime's security precautions and, to some degree, to policy limitations on the risks to be assumed. . . .

Political. State appointed a representative to devote full-time to Operation Mongoose and to develop the required political actions. . . . Two Operation Mongoose efforts in political action were attempted in Phase I: to counter Castro-Communist propaganda exploitation of May Day[4] and to arouse strong Hemisphere reaction to Cuban military suppression of the hunger demonstration at Cardenas,[5] in June. Ambassadors in Latin America were asked to undertake a special effort, as possible, with the help of their Country Teams; political action results in both instances were mostly negative, due to lack of capability and the local attitude in Latin American countries.

State is responsible for refugee political policy matters, assisted by CIA in daily liaison. This is an area of major interest to Operation Mongoose, since the Cuban refugees have an open objective of overthrowing the Communist regime in Havana and recapturing their homeland. They are given open U.S. assistance to remain in this country, yet are participating in covert actions in a limited way. Only a fractional opening has been made to release the frustrated energy of these refugees in freeing their homeland and in creating a favorable political climate in Latin America for the liberation of Cuba. Policy limitations of "audibility" and "visibility" apply directly in considering the handling and use of this dynamic refugee potential.

As a working document for U.S. operational guidance, State developed a definition of a political program for a free Cuba, with the understanding that any real political program must be developed by the Cubans themselves.

Psychological. Psychological activities for Operation Mongoose make use of existing assignments of responsibilities within the U.S. government: State, having the policy role, chairs an inter-agency Cuba Psychological Operations Group which meets weekly; USIA disseminates any U.S. government information (VOA and Press Service) and generates "gray" or non-official information (5 million cartoon books and thousands of Spanish books on Cuba disseminated in Latin America); CIA passes information appropriate for "gray" and covert psychological channels (radio, mailings to Cuba, and dissemination inside Cuba).

Conditions and events in Cuba have provided many effective themes, which have been promptly and sharply exploited by available means in the Western Hemisphere. However, the U.S. still lacks the capability of effectively getting information to the majority of the Cuban people. Our short-wave broadcasts are highly regarded by the Cuban people, but short-wave receiver sets are limited inside Cuba. Our medium-wave broadcasts compete against stronger Cuban signals; it was felt that greater U.S. competition in medium-wave broadcasts could lead to Cuban interference of U.S. commercial broadcasts over a fairly wide area

---

[4]A holiday in honor of workers.
[5]Cardenas is in northern Cuba.

of the U.S. Clandestine broadcasts from a submarine (appearing as broadcasts by Cuban guerrillas inside Cuba) have been initiated; they are in their infancy, and have a long way to develop before their messages are believed and get passed among Cubans by word-of-mouth. Dissemination of leaflets and propaganda inside Cuba by balloon or aircraft has not received policy approval.

Economic. State has the main responsibility for developing economic actions. State has chaired an inter-agency working group, which generated the U.S. trade embargo,[6] denial of bunkering facilities, increased port security, and control procedures on transshipment, technical data, and customs inspection. Diplomatic means were used to frustrate Cuban trade negotiations in Israel, Jordan, Iran, Greece, and possibly Japan. Under Resolution VIII adopted at Punta del Este,[7] the OAS has established a special committee to study "the feasibility and desirability of extending the suspension of trade with Cuba to other items (than arms)," State has prepared a program to be submitted to this OAS committee in the future.

The evidence is that Cuba's economy is suffering. Trade with the Communist Bloc and others has kept it limping along, despite scarcity of U.S. goods, the bad drought limiting agrarian crops, increased worker non-cooperation and the regime's bungling of economic control measures. Critical spare parts still arrive in Cuba, including shipments from British and Canadian firms. Chartered shipping from Free World sources still plays a major role in Cuba's trade, and the U.S. has little hope of cutting this life-line to Castro.

Guerrilla. CIA had the main responsibility for assessing resistance potential inside Cuba and to start quietly organizing such resistance as feasible. The CIA plan has been to set about doing this through introducing small teams into the Cuban countryside, "over the beach" from boats. Each team is tasked first to stay alive, while getting established in an area. Once able to live in an area, it then starts a cautious survey of potential recruits for a resistance group. Names of such recruits are sent to CIA for checking. As recruits join, they are trained on the ground by the team, and then continue the survey. This is slow and dangerous work.

CIA reports that 11 teams will have been infiltrated by the end of July and that 19 maritime operations have aborted. Of the teams in, the most successful is the one in Pinar del Rio in western Cuba; its success was helped greatly by a maritime re-supply of arms and equipment; the fact that it is a "going concern" and receives help from outside has attracted recruits. Its potential has been estimated at about 250, which is a sizable guerrilla force. With equally large guerrilla forces in other Cuban provinces, guerrilla warfare could be activated with a good chance of success, if assisted properly. However, the teams in other provinces have not been so successful; our best hope is that we will have viable teams in all the potential resistance areas by early October. Bad weather, high seas, and increased security patrols will make the infiltration of teams and their re-supply from small boats a hard task.

[6] Imposed on Cuba in February 1962.
[7] A meeting of OAS foreign ministers in January 1962.

Sabotage has not taken place, on a U.S.-sponsored basis. Planning for such action by CIA has been thorough, including detailed study of the structures and vulnerabilities of key targets. Sophisticated actions, such as the contamination of POL has been frustrated by lack of cooperation of nations where POL would be vulnerable to action. Commando type raids would take maritime means which now have priority use in support of CIA teams being infiltrated inside to survey and create a guerrilla potential. CIA has reported that there is now some capability inside Cuba for sabotage action, that target selection has been under further careful review, and that a proposal is forthcoming to be submitted for policy approval.

Intervention Planning. The JCS were given the responsibility for planning and undertaking essential preliminary actions for a decisive U.S. capability for intervention in Cuba. This "Guidelines" objective has been met, fully. Also, U.S. military readiness for intervention in Cuba has been under continuing review within Defense, being improved wherever feasible. In addition, rumors during June of a possible uprising inside Cuba led to further planning for a contingency where a non-U.S. inspired revolt might start inside Cuba; interagency staffing of U.S. planning for such a Cuban contingency is being completed, under Defense leadership.

Assets. Whatever we decide to do in the future depends, to a large degree, on the assets available to us. Our own U.S. assets in organization, personnel, and equipment are sufficient to liberate Cuba, given the decision to do so. Assets among the Cubans, to liberate themselves, are capable of a greater effectiveness once a firm decision is made by the U.S. to provide maximum support of Cubans to liberate Cuba, and the Cubans start being helped towards that goal by the U.S. There are enough able-bodied and properly motivated Cubans inside Cuba and in exile to do the job. There is wide-spread disaffection in Cuba, with strong indications that economic distress and demoralization of population is causing real concern and strain for the regime's control officials. Firm U.S. intention to help free Cuba is the key factor in assessing the Cubans themselves as an operational asset for Operation Mongoose.

At the close of Phase I, my concern is strong that time is running out for the U.S. to make a free choice on Cuba, based largely on what is happening to the will of the Cuban people. Rightly or wrongly, the Cubans have looked and are looking to the U.S. for guidance on what to aspire to and do next. They wonder if we are not merely watching Cuba closely, as a matter of our own security, undertaking some economic proscription, and isolating the Castro/Communist gang from contaminating the Hemisphere. Along with recognition of our humanitarian sympathies, this seems to be the fear among Cuban refugees, although they are still hopeful.

If Cubans become convinced that the U.S. is not going to do more than watch and talk, I believe they will make other plans for the future. The bulk of Cuban refugees in the U.S. are most likely to start getting serious about settling down for life in the U.S., dulling their desire to return home with personal risk involved. The bulk of disaffected people inside Cuba will lose hope and incentive for futile protests against the regime and start accepting their status as captives of the Communists. Some Cuban activists will not accept the loss of their homeland so easily and may seek release from frustration by liberation operations outside U.S. territory and control. . . .

Our probes of the guerrilla potential inside Cuba have been hampered by similar morale factors. Cubans sent to risk their lives on missions inside Cuba feel very much alone, except for their communications link back to the U.S. They are unable to recruit freedom fighters aggressively by the time-proven method of starting an active resistance and thus attracting recruits; U.S. guidelines to keep this short of a revolt have made the intention behind the operation suspect to local Cubans. The evidence of some intent is seen in the recent maritime re-supply of the team in Pinar del Rio. We brought in extra weapons, for which there were immediate recruits; if we were to exploit the evident guerrilla potential in this province, it appears likely that we would have to furnish supplies by air and probably open the U.S. to strong charges of furnishing such support to Cuban resistance elements.

Therefore, we have been unable to surface the Cuban resistance potential to a point where we can measure it realistically. The only way this can be done, accurately, is when resistance actually has a rallying point of freedom fighters who appear to the Cuban people to have some chance of winning, and that means at least an implication that the U.S. is in support. Word-of-mouth information that such a freedom movement is afoot could cause the majority of the Cuban people to choose sides. It would be the first real opportunity for them to do so since Castro and the Communists came to power. There was little opportunity for the Cuban people to join an active resistance in April 1961; there is less opportunity today. If the Cuban people are to feel they have a real opportunity, they must have something which they can join with some belief in its success.

Projection (Phase II).

As a help towards the making of a U.S. decision on a future course of action, the Operational Representatives developed working statements of four possibilities; at my request they have commented on the positive and negative factors worth considering for each possible course, and it is suggested that these thoughtful statements are worth reading in full. The working statements of the choices open to the U.S. are as follows:

a. Cancel operational plans; treat Cuba as a Bloc nation; protect Hemisphere from it, or

b. Exert all possible diplomatic, economic, psychological, and other pressures to overthrow the Castro-Communist regime without overt employment of U.S. military, or

c. Commit U.S. to help Cubans overthrow the Castro-Communist regime, with a step-by-step phasing to ensure success, including the use of U.S. military force if required at the end, or

d. Use a provocation and overthrow the Castro-Communist regime by U.S. military force.

Recommendation

It is recommended that this review of Phase I be considered by the Special Group as providing the operational basis for guidelines and objectives for Phase II. It is a matter of urgency that these be arrived at by the Special Group, to permit developing specific plans and schedules for Phase II.

34. Memorandum from Chief of Operations Lansdale to the Special Group (Augmented)

The contingency planning for the use of force against Cuba, requested in June, is produced.

Washington, July 31, 1962.

SUBJECT

Contingency Plan

Transmitted herewith is a copy of "United States Contingency Plan No. 2, Cuba (S)," which is submitted for your consideration. The plan has been approved by the Secretary of Defense and by the Joint Chiefs of Staff.

This plan was developed as a result of reports in mid-June 1962 that the Cuban people were about to revolt against the Castro-Communist regime, without U.S. sponsorship, and the desire expressed by the Special Group that the U.S. be ready for such a contingency. The DOD/JCS representative was tasked by me to develop a plan with the assistance of Operation Mongoose representatives from participating departments and agencies. The DOD/JCS representative did so, and the attached plan is the result.

Attachment

UNITED STATES CONTINGENCY PLAN NO. 2, CUBA (S)

REFERENCE

Memorandum for Representatives of State, Defense, CIA and USIA, from Chief of Operations [Lansdale], Operation Mongoose, subject: "Spontaneous Revolts in Cuba, Contingency Planning," dated 14 June 1962

TASK AGENCIES

Department of State
Department of Defense
Central Intelligence Agency
US Information Agency

1. *Situation.*

a. The purpose of this plan is to define the courses of action to be pursued by affected agencies of the US Government in the event that a decision is made that the United States undertake military intervention in Cuba.

b. The assumed situation in Cuba is open, wide-spread revolt. This contingency may be a non-US initiated situation, similar to that rumored as being activated for mid-June 1962. US actions to exploit the situation include the use of US military force.

c. It is assumed that this plan would be implemented under the following conditions, and would be considered for implementation under situations less severe. An internal revolt has created a chaotic situation in Cuba where:

(1) The revolution is open and threatens the Communist regime;

(2) Areas are taken and held by the revolutionaries, and;

(3) Leadership of the revolt, unable to overthrow the government or sustain the revolution indefinitely requests assistance from the United States and/or the Organization of American States (OAS).

d. The United States may, or may not, be able to determine that a rebellion is imminent before actual outbreak. However, it is unlikely that the assumed situation will occur all at once and without notice. More probably it will evolve from a localized revolt which will provide some advance notice and the opportunity to initiate necessary diplomatic, propaganda, covert and military preparations.

e. The strength, morale, disposition and equipage of unfriendly forces will be assumed to be as described in current estimates of the United States Intelligence Board (USIB).

2. *Mission.*

The United States will support and sustain the rebellion in Cuba through all its resources including the use of US military force to assure replacement of the Communist regime with a new Cuban government acceptable to the United States.

3. *Execution.*

a. *Concept of Operations.*

(1) When the likelihood or emergence of a Cuban revolt becomes apparent to the US intelligence community it will be immediately brought to the attention of the 5412 Special Group (Augmented) through the Officer of the Chief of Operations, Operation Mongoose. Evaluation of the situation by the Special Group will determine whether or not the President's decision should be sought to implement this plan.

(2) The initial stages of a spontaneous revolt will be supported by the United States through propaganda, covert operations and other actions as necessary, but maintaining the appearance of non-US involvement should the revolt fail. In the event that the revolt spreads as a popular movement against the Communist regime, the United States should be capable of rapid military action to forestall

a concerted and drastic reprisal program in the interest of humanity and the mission of this plan.

(3) US Military Reaction.

(a) With no prior warning and with eighteen (18) days of preparation a coordinated airborne-amphibious assault could be executed which, it is anticipated, would gain control of key military installations and the principal centers of population of Cuba within ten (10) days and result in minimum US and Cuban casualties.

(b) A requirement to reduce significantly the pre-assault period would necessitate incremental commitment of US forces as they could be assembled and employed. Under this circumstance the time required to gain essential US military control of Cuba could be appreciably extended. However, reduction of US military reaction time may be of overriding importance. In such case, air and naval forces could attack in support of the rebel Cubans with little delay from the time a decision is made. An air assault could be initiated within eight (8) hours, an airborne assault could be initiated within five (5) days and a Navy/Marine amphibious force could be committed three (3) days later with a build up to the full-scale effort to follow.

(4) Execution of this plan will be in two (2) phases:

(a) Phase I. After Presidential decision, this phase will be undertaken by the Department of Defense supported by other agencies of the government. It will be initiated by overt US military assault on Cuba under the direction of the Joint Chiefs of Staff and will be terminated at such time as essential military control is gained over the island. The operation is to be conducted as rapidly as possible, quickly to confront Cuban forces with sufficient strength to be clearly beyond enemy capability to resist and to reduce risk to US units initially deployed, with a view toward early capitulation of Cuban military units and avoidance of needless loss of life.

(b) Phase II. Following the establishment of essential US military control of the island, this phase will be primarily concerned with the restoration of law and order and the establishment of a new Cuban government friendly to the US. US military efforts will be directed primarily to matters of civil affairs and military government in accordance with policy established by the Department of State. Military operations essential for the elimination of small pockets of resistance and restoration of law and order throughout the island will continue. Major US combat forces will be withdrawn as early as security may permit. Operational responsibility of the Department of Defense will cease at the time the Department of State assumes responsibility for civil administration of Cuba.

b. *Department of Defense Operations.*

(1) When directed by higher authority,[1] or as the situation demands, the Department of Defense will initiate preparatory actions for US military intervention in Cuba. These actions may include pre-positioning forces and equipment by execution of current cover and deception plans.

[1] The president.

(2) Upon final decision of the President, the Joint Chiefs of Staff will direct execution of military intervention plans for Cuba.

(3) In concept, initial military operations commence with a blockade, concentrated air strikes and coordinated Naval gunfire to effect destruction of enemy air power and to neutralize and destroy as much as possible of the enemy tank, armor, artillery, and anti-air capability. . . .

PART 3

Before the Storm: Autumn 1962

THE FOLLOWING DOCUMENTS reveal the split between public pronouncement and private action that characterized the Kennedy administration's Cuban policies in the late summer and fall of 1962. As it had during the 1960 presidential campaign between JFK and Republican nominee Richard Nixon, Cuba became a fiercely partisan issue. The Russian military buildup in Cuba, which initially involved conventional equipment (the nuclear weapons did not start arriving until September), was reported in the American press and soon seized upon by politicians. Republicans assailed the administration over the buildup, forcing JFK to respond publicly. Extracts from speeches by Senator Kenneth Keating of New York, the leading GOP critic on this issue, are included here, as are the public statements issued by President Kennedy in partial response to his domestic adversaries.

In those statements Kennedy sought to diminish anxieties over developments in Cuba, noting that no nuclear missiles had been deployed. Behind closed doors, however, the administration's reaction to the Russian military initiative was far less moderate. As the documents make clear, the administration kept close tabs on Cuba; intelligence reports assessed the buildup there, the motives behind it, and the implications for the United States. Considerable time was devoted to establishing the guidelines and producing a plan of action for a more ambitious second phase of Operation Mongoose. In early October 1962 John and Robert Kennedy intensified Mongoose still further. Contingency plans for military action against Cuba were advanced, and the circumstances that would necessitate the implementation of those plans were considered.

These documents also show Moscow's deception over the buildup in Cuba. Khrushchev and other Soviet officials lied by insisting in conversations with Kennedy's aides that only defensive weapons were being sent to the Caribbean island. When John and Robert Kennedy learned in mid-October that there were nuclear missiles in Cuba, they were furious, in large measure because of this mendacity on the part of the Russians.

1. Memorandum of a Special Group (Augmented) Meeting on Mongoose Prepared by CIA Director McCone

In the summer of 1962 the Kennedy administration charted a course for the second phase of Operation Mongoose. *The Special Group (Augmented) (SGA) requested a "possible stepped up Course B," which Edward Lansdale produced on August 8, as well as "an Alternative Course B," completed by Lansdale on August 14. Here the SGA reviews Lansdale's ideas for Mongoose's second phase.*

Washington, August 16, 1962.

1. General Lansdale presented his paper of 15 August[1] expressing the caveats that the program (a) did not place us in a position to take advantage of internal uprisings and (b) the program made no reference to the use of third country assets. The paper was approved subject to the submission by General Lansdale of detailed actions.

2. The meeting was generally unsatisfactory from my standpoint. In the first place, the reservations of General Lansdale seem to indicate a difference between Lansdale and CIA growing out of the position that I took on his Plan B Augmented. Secondly, the policy implications were not acted upon: strong opposition to utilization of Guantanamo was expressed by Lemnitzer, and McCone stated that he too was concerned about the use of Guantanamo and he felt that the operation should be planned so that Guantanamo would not be used. Bundy expressed strong reservations concerning use of Navy submarines and some reservations concerning overflights [of Cuba]. Alexis Johnson questioned the level of sabotage operations, Taylor favoring approval by the [Special] Group [Augmented] of each important sabotage action and Johnson favoring modest rather than violent acts of sabotage. McCone stated that proposal involved substantial sabotage actions and that the Lansdale Task Force[2] should be permitted

---

[1] This refers to the memorandum produced by Lansdale on August 14 for the Special Group (Augmented).

[2] A reference to Task Force W, the CIA unit that carried out Operation Mongoose.

to proceed without further reference to the Special Group. DCI stated he did not feel we could sit in judgment on each sabotage operation and expect Lansdale with his supporting staff of 500 or 1,000 people to work effectively. Bundy brought up the question of the "noise level." McCone stated that operations anticipated would raise the noise level very substantially and there would be a very considerable attribution. In general the meeting was unsatisfactory, lacked both purpose and direction and left me with a feeling that very considerable reservation exists as to just where we are going with Operation Mongoose.

Action: A detailed plan of operation specifying the acts of sabotage, planned infiltrations, . . . propaganda effort, etc., should be presented by Lansdale at the earliest moment. Any differences between Lansdale and CIA should be straightened out by Harvey with the assistance of Helms or others. McCone should discuss this subject privately with the Attorney General.

3. The attached memorandum to the President and the guidelines on Phase II, dated August 16th,[3] was approved with only modest modification.

2. Memorandum from CIA Operations Officer for Operation Mongoose William K. Harvey and Acting Chairman of the Board of National Estimates Abbot Smith to Chief of Operations Lansdale

With the Soviet military buildup in Cuba, authorized by Khrushchev and approved by Castro in the spring of 1962, under way by this time, a U.S. intelligence estimate takes stock of the situation.

Washington, August 17, 1962.

SUBJECT

Operation Mongoose—The Soviet Stake in Cuba

For your information, set out below is the substance of a memorandum dated 15 August 1962 prepared by the Board of National Estimates for the information and assistance of the DCI.

The Soviet Stake in Cuba

1. The USSR's primary stake in Cuba is political. The Soviets regard Castro's revolution, and his subsequent alignment with the Communists, as one of the

---

[3]The memorandum and guidelines were sent to JFK the next day. See Document 3.

most telling blows to the prestige of the US which has occurred in the entire postwar period. In their eyes, it is a compelling demonstration of a major thesis which they are urging upon the underdeveloped countries everywhere: that the "colonial" peoples can throw off the "imperialist yoke" and, with the indispensable help of the USSR, successfully maintain their independence against their former masters.

2. In specific application to Latin America, the Soviets value the Cuban example as showing:

a. That a small but dedicated revolutionary group, with the sympathy and support of the oppressed masses, can prevail against the military power of a ruthless dictatorship supported by the Yankee imperialists.

b. That the [Soviet] Bloc will provide such a revolutionary regime with the economic aid required to offset anticipated US economic warfare and to develop the country.

c. That Soviet support, and especially Soviet missile power, will deter the US from military intervention to overthrow the revolutionaries.

d. That Latin American radicals can safely cooperate with local Communists, who will facilitate the securing of Soviet support without insisting upon seizing the leadership of the revolution for themselves.

3. Cuba is also of value to the USSR as an operational base from which the revolution in Latin America can be furthered by propaganda, the indoctrination and training of militants, gun-running, and other clandestine operations. For the Soviets, however, this use is incidental and auxiliary to the political impact of the Cuban revolutionary example.

4. With the passage of time, the Soviet stake in Cuba has come to be defensive as well as offensive. The USSR's prestige has become involved with Castro's fortunes, and Moscow's political commitment to the survival and success of the Cuban revolution is deepening. In the past year the Soviets have reluctantly acquiesced in several moves—Castro's proclamation that he is a Communist, his attack upon Moscow-oriented Communists seeking to undermine his leadership—which have considerably reduced their freedom of maneuver. They have done this in large part because they are not prepared to accept the setback to their policies which would result from a breach with Castro.

5. Cuba could be used by the USSR as a military base from which to threaten the US. With the growth of Soviet strategic capabilities, however, installations on Cuba would add little to the weight of attack which the Soviets could direct against the US. The USSR's chief motive for the establishment of, for example, a medium-range missile base on Cuba would therefore be to deter an anticipated US military intervention against Castro.

6. The USSR almost certainly recognizes, however, that such an undertaking would be as likely to provoke as to deter American intervention. Further, the Soviets would either have to share control of such a base with the Cubans, in which case the risks of war would pass beyond their exclusive control, or affront Cuban sovereignty by denying Havana any role at all. Most important of all, by such an act the Soviets would firmly commit themselves to the military protection of Cuba, a step which they have thus far refrained from taking and which,

we believe, they will continue to avoid. In this connection, it is notable that Soviet military aid to Cuba, while heavy, has thus far been confined to the development of essentially defensive capabilities.

7. In sum, we believe that the Soviets' stake in Castro, composed of both the great hopes they place in his revolution and the heavy loss of prestige which they would suffer upon its downfall, is high. They would probably be willing to accept further assertions of Cuban independence, and to increase the scale of their aid if this were necessary to insure the viability of the Castro regime. If its existence were threatened, the Soviets would deploy all the political weapons at their command in its defense. But we think it highly unlikely that they would undertake actions on Cuba's behalf which, in their view, involved any considerable risk of war with the US. Instead, we believe that they would try to make the regime's downfall as costly as possible, in political terms, to the US, and at the same time seek to repair their prestige rapidly with some visible triumph elsewhere in the world.

3. Memorandum from the President's Military Representative Maxwell Taylor to President Kennedy

Maxwell Taylor provides JFK with the Special Group (Augmented)'s guidelines for Phase II of Mongoose. Kennedy would endorse them three days later.

Washington, August 17, 1962.

The Special Group (Augmented) has reviewed the results achieved in Phase I (March to August, 1962) of the Mongoose program. The priority objective in this period was the acquisition of hard intelligence bearing on the internal situation, accompanied by political, economic and covert actions short of those calculated to inspire a revolt in the target area.

The responsible agencies have worked vigorously to accomplish this objective, generating the largest intelligence effort directed at any Soviet Bloc country and attacking the target country broadly across the political, economic and psychological fronts. However, in spite of some progress in intelligence collection, the Special Group (Augmented) does not feel that the information obtained has been adequate to assess accurately the internal conditions. Nevertheless, from what we know we perceive no likelihood of an overthrow of the government by internal means and without the direct use of U.S. military force.

As we look ahead in the Mongoose program, we have considered several alternative courses of action. We have ruled out those which would commit us to deliberate military intervention although we recognize that an unanticipated revolt might at any time force a decision for or against the support of such a revolt by U.S. forces. For the coming period, we favor a somewhat more aggressive program than the one carried on in Phase I, wherein we continue to press for intelligence, attempt to hurt the local regime as much as possible on the economic front and work further to discredit the regime locally and abroad.

We have approved an outline plan drawn up under the direction of General Lansdale, which is designed to carry out this concept. General Lansdale will work with the Special Group (Augmented) as he has during Phase I, submitting to us for approval schedules of specific actions based on the outline plan. While we believe that this new course of action will create added difficulties for the regime and will increase the visibility of its failures, there is no reason to hope that it will cause the overthrow of the regime from within. Also, the "noise level" of Mongoose operations will probably rise in the course of the new phase and there will always be the chance that the participation of some U.S. citizens may become known. However, the Special Group (Augmented) considers that these are tolerable risks which they will seek to control by close attention to the implementation of the program.

Attached hereto are revised guidelines for Phase II which, with your concurrence, we propose to promulgate for the guidance of General Lansdale and his associates.

Attachment

GUIDELINES[1] FOR OPERATION MONGOOSE, PHASE II

(August 1, 1962 until_____)
Terminal date to be set later

1. While retaining as its eventual objective the overthrow of the target government, the objective of the Mongoose program during Phase II will be the further containment, undermining and discrediting of the target regime while isolating it from other Hemisphere nations.

2. In view of the growing weakness of the economy of the country, special efforts will be directed at accentuating the difficulties in this sector, and at increasing the demands on Bloc resources. Sabotage will be employed for this purpose on a selective basis.

3. Continued priority will be given to the intelligence collection program, with renewed emphasis on the establishment of viable agent assets inside the target country.

4. Efforts will be increased to inspire frictions and schisms both within the target regime and between its leaders and the Bloc.

5. Consideration will be given to assisting Cuban exile groups and other Latin American governments to perform actions and operations in support of the Mongoose program.

6. It is recognized that this program may cause the "noise level" to rise; however, the importance of maintaining non-attributability remains unchanged.

---

[1]These guidelines are dated August 16.

7. While a revolt is not sought at this time, we must be prepared to exploit it should one unexpectedly occur. The JCS will maintain plans for U.S. military intervention.

8. General Lansdale will continue as Chief of Operations during Phase II, following the procedures which have been worked out during Phase I.

4. Memorandum of Discussion in Secretary of State Rusk's Office

Concern over the Russian military buildup in Cuba prompts McNamara and Robert Kennedy to call for more forceful action.

Washington, August 21, 1962.

IN ATTENDANCE

Secretary Rusk, Secretary McNamara, Alexis Johnson, the Attorney General, DCI [McCone], General Taylor, General Lemnitzer and McGeorge Bundy.

McCone stated that the purpose of the meeting was to again review the situation in Cuba in light of the most recent intelligence findings.

DCI recalled that in the August 10th [SGA] Meeting he had reported such information as was then available on the accelerated Soviet supply of personnel and matériel to Cuba. However, information available to the Agency since August 10th indicated that the extent of the Soviet supply operations was much greater than had been reported on August 10th. . . .

There was general agreement that the situation was critical and that the most dynamic action was indicated.

There was discussion of various courses of action open to us in case the Soviets place MRBM missiles on Cuban territory. There was also discussion of blockades of Soviet and Bloc shipping into Cuba or alternatively a total blockade of Cuba.

Throughout these discussions, it was abundantly clear that in the minds of State, and Mr. Bundy, speaking for the White House, there is a very definite inter-relationship between Cuba and other trouble spots, such as Berlin. It was felt that a blockade of Cuba would automatically bring about a blockade of Berlin; that drastic action on a missile site or other military installation of the Soviets in Cuba would bring about similar action by the Soviets with respect to our bases and numerous missile sites, particularly Turkey and southern Italy. Also, there is a reluctance, as previously, to the commitment of military forces because of the task involved and also because of retaliatory actions of the Soviets elsewhere throughout the world.

McNamara expressed strong feelings that we should take every possible aggressive action in the fields of intelligence, sabotage and guerrilla warfare, utilizing Cubans and do such other things as might be indicated to divide the Castro regime. McCone pointed out that all of these things could be done. Efforts to date with agent teams had been disappointing. Sabotage activities were planned on a priority basis and in all probability, we would witness more failures than successes. To date we had experienced a very tight internal security situation and probably this would become more so in the future.

The Attorney General queried the meeting as to what other aggressive steps could be taken, questioning the feasibility of provoking an action against Guantanamo which would permit us to retaliate, or involving a third country in some way.

It was Mr. Bundy's opinion that all overt actions would involve serious consequences throughout the world and therefore our operations must be covert at this time, although we should expect a high degree of attribution.

The meeting was inconclusive with respect to any particular course of action. It was felt that the President should be informed on the evolving situation and the DCI agreed to brief him at the Meeting on Wednesday, August 22nd at 6 o'clock.[1]

We further agreed that the entire matter should be reviewed with the President by Rusk, McNamara, Bundy and McCone. Mr. Bundy undertook to arrange for this meeting following the Special Meeting scheduled for ten o'clock on Thursday, August 23rd.[2] . . .

5. Memorandum Prepared by CIA Director McCone of Meeting Between President Kennedy and Senior U.S. Officials

JFK and his advisers explore their options.

Washington, August 23, 1962.

ATTENDED BY

Secretaries Rusk, McNamara, Gilpatric, General Taylor, Messrs. [McGeorge] Bundy, McCone

---

[1]This meeting took place, with McCone informing JFK of the concerns expressed at this August 21 meeting.

[2]McCone prepared this memorandum.

1. McCone advised that President had been briefed on the Cuban situation.[1] . . .

Rusk advocated informing Canadians and all NATO allies of growing seriousness of situation; also advocated removal of restrictions on use of Guantanamo by the Lansdale group.

Action: This point not cleared and should be pursued as strongly opposed by [the Joint] Chiefs.

2. The President requested a continuing analysis of the number and type of Soviet and Oriental personnel imported into Cuba; quantity and type of equipment and its probable use; all construction—particularly anxious to know whether construction involving SAM sites might differ from the ground sites. McCone stated we probably could not differentiate between surface-to-air and 350 mile ground-to-ground offensive missiles. McNamara observed portable ground missiles could not be located under any circumstances.

Action: DDCI should have Board of National Estimates working continuously on this analysis.

3. President requested analysis of the danger to the United States and the effect on Latin America of missile installations.

Action: DDCI should arrange for preparation of such estimates.

4. President raised the question of whether we should make a statement in advance of our position, should the Soviets install missiles and the alternative actions open to us in such event. In the course of the discussion, apparent many in the room related action in Cuba to Soviet actions in Turkey, Greece, Berlin, Far East and elsewhere. McCone questioned value of [America's] Jupiter missiles in Turkey and Italy. McNamara agreed they were useless but difficult politically to remove them.

Action: He agreed to study this possibility.

5. President raised question of what we could do against Soviet missile sites in Cuba. Could we take them out by air or would a ground offensive be necessary or alternatively could they be destroyed by a substantial guerrilla effort.

6. President raised question of what we should do in Cuba if Soviets precipitated a Berlin crisis. This is the alternative to the proposition of what Soviets would do in Berlin if we moved in Cuba.

7. During the conversation I raised substance of my plan of action as outlined in the attached paper.[2] There was no disagreement that we must solve the Cuban problem. However, we should not start the political action and propaganda effort now until we had decided on the policy of following through to the complete solution of the Cuban problem.

8. After the meeting in a private conversation with Robert Kennedy, I stated that I felt Cuba was our most serious problem. . . . I also added, in my opinion, Cuba was the key to all of Latin America; if Cuba succeeds, we can expect most of Latin America to fall.

---

[1]Presumably a reference to the JFK-McCone meeting of August 22.
[2]Not included here.

6. National Security Action Memorandum No. 181

JFK issues a series of policy directives in response to the Russian military buildup in Cuba.

Washington, August 23, 1962.

TO

Secretary of State [Rusk]
Secretary of Defense [McNamara]
Attorney General [Robert Kennedy]
Acting Director, CIA [Marshall S. Carter][1]
General Taylor

The President has directed that the following actions and studies be undertaken in the light of evidence of new [Soviet] bloc activity in Cuba.

1. What action can be taken to get Jupiter missiles out of Turkey? (*Action:* Department of Defense)

2. What information should be made available in the U.S. and abroad with respect to these new bloc activities in Cuba? (*Action:* Department of State, in consultation with USIA and CIA)

3. There should be an organized effort to bring home to governments of our NATO allies in particular the meaning of this new evidence of Castro's subservience to the Soviets, and the urgency of action on their part to limit their economic cooperation with Cuba. (*Action:* Department of State)

4. The line of activity projected for Operation Mongoose Plan B plus should be developed with all possible speed. (*Action:* General Taylor)

5. An analysis should be prepared of the probable military, political and psychological impact of the establishment in Cuba of either surface-to-air missiles or surface-to-surface missiles which could reach the U.S. (*Action:* White House, in consultation with Department of State, Department of Defense, and CIA)

6. A study should be made of the advantages and disadvantages of making a statement that the U.S. would not tolerate the establishment of military forces (missile or air, or both?) which might launch a nuclear attack from Cuba against the U.S. (*Action:* Department of State, in consultation with Department of Defense with respect to the study in item 7 below)

7. A study should be made of the various military alternatives which might be adopted in executing a decision to eliminate any installations in Cuba capable of launching nuclear attack on the U.S. What would be the pros and cons, for example, of pinpoint attack, general counter-force attack, and outright invasion? (*Action:* Department of Defense)

8. A study should be made of the advantages and disadvantages of action to

---

[1]From August 23 to September 23 McCone was on his honeymoon. During his absence from Washington, CIA Deputy Director Carter served as acting director.

liberate Cuba by blockade or invasion or other action beyond Mongoose B plus, in the context of an aggravated Berlin crisis. (*Action:* Department of State, in consultation with Department of Defense)

To facilitate coordination of these efforts, I should like to receive an immediate report from action Departments indicating which officer of the Department will be directly responsible for items in which action is assigned to that Department. Insofar as practicable, except for item 1, item 3, and item 5, these assignments should be made from among senior officers already informed of Mongoose. . . .

The President emphasizes again the sensitive character of these instructions.[2]

7. Memorandum from Chief of Operations Lansdale to the Special Group (Augmented)

Lansdale, as requested by the SGA, produces a detailed plan of action for Mongoose according to the guidelines established two weeks earlier for the operation's second phase (see Document 3).

Washington, August 31, 1962.

SUBJECT

Phase II, Operation Mongoose

Pursuant to your instructions,[1] transmitted herewith is a proposed projection of actions to be undertaken as Phase II, Operation Mongoose. This projection incorporates the suggestions of the operations team designated by the major departments and agencies charged with Mongoose planning and implementation.

The format employed is responsive to the 16th August 1962 guidelines for Phase II, Operation Mongoose,[2] and to your comments at recent meetings. The projection is divided into each objective contained in the 16 August guidelines, and then lists proposed actions to attain that objective. The guideline objectives have been given short titles as follows:

A. Discredit and isolate the regime
B. Harass the economy
C. Intensify intelligence collection
D. Split regime leadership and relations with Bloc
E. Assist Cuban exile groups and Latin American governments to take actions

[2]McGeorge Bundy prepared this memorandum.
[1]See Document 1.
[2]See Document 3.

F. Be prepared to exploit a revolt

In preparing this projection of actions for Phase II, Operation Mongoose, an effort was made to restrict proposals to the "B plus" frame of reference provided and to assume that a broader frame of programming under the NSAM[3] would supplement Mongoose by separate planning.

PHASE II
(1 August 1962 until _____)

Objective A: Discredit and Isolate the Regime

Political

1. Encourage Latin American nations, bilaterally and through the OAS Special Consultative Committee (SCCS), to establish controls over the travel of their nationals to Cuba. (State, with CIA support) . . .

2. Encourage Latin American nations, bilaterally and through the SCCS, to limit or prohibit entry of Cuban propaganda. (State, with CIA and USIA support) . . .

3. Provide intelligence of arms smuggling from Cuba to other Hemisphere nations. (CIA, State, Defense) . . .

4. As opportune, initiate action or support another nation's initiative in the OAS with respect to countering the Communist regime in Cuba. (State, with CIA support) . . .

5. Continue the program of excluding Cuba from Hemisphere organizations. (State, with CIA support) . . .

6. Stimulate manifestations critical of the Castro/Communist regime by Latin American political, labor, religious, and student and other significant impact groups. (State, with CIA and USIA support) . . .

7. Encourage and exploit the defection of Cuban diplomats, officials, and delegates abroad. (CIA) . . .

8. Keep friendly nations fully informed of the nature of the Castro/Communist regime and of U.S. policy with respect to it. (State, with CIA and USIA support) . . .

Psychological

9. Beamed to Cuba, initiate a planned series of statements by U.S. and other free world official and nonofficial spokesmen which support developing and maintaining the will to resist within Cuba. (USIA, with State and CIA support) . . .

10. Continue Voice of America shortwave broadcasts to Cuba (USIA). To maintain regular, overt communication with the Cuban people. . . .

11. Continue U.S. broadcasting to the Western Hemisphere (USIA). To keep the people of the Hemisphere awake to the Cuban situation. . . .

12. Produce propaganda cartoon books (USIA). To build and reinforce a negative image of Castro/Communism among youth, labor, and other groups in Latin America. . . .

13. Produce photo-novels carrying the propaganda story. (USIA) . . .

[3]See National Security Action Memorandum No. 181, Document 6.

14. Supply TV outlets in Latin America with materials (USIA). . . . In addition to supplying documentaries and news clips, a series of one-minute puppet shorts will be tried. . . .

15. Produce short films for commercial outlets and impact groups in Latin America. (USIA) . . .

16. Produce propaganda exhibits ("before" and "after") for public and organizational display (USIA). Same purpose as 12 above. Three such exhibits are now being developed. The first one contrasts Castro's promises with his actions. An electric motor turns the slats on a venetian blind exhibit, changing the picture.

17. Publish books in Spanish and Portuguese, with distribution through commercial sales and presentation (USIA and CIA). Same purpose as 12 above, plus impact on intellectuals and other opinion leaders. . . .

18. Special propaganda exploitation of U.S. information about the agricultural, labor, and public health situation in Cuba. (State, with CIA and USIA support) . . .

19. Expand the delivery of propaganda material into Cuba via the open mails, legal travellers, and controlled couriers (CIA). To disaffect the Cuban people and to help maintain the will to resist. . . .

20. Develop specific proposal for use of balloons to deliver propaganda (CIA). To provide a means of distributing propaganda inside Cuba. . . .

21. Direct propaganda at Soviet and other Bloc personnel in Cuba (CIA). To make them disaffected with their role in Cuba.

22. "Voice of Free Cuba" broadcasts from submarine (CIA, with Defense support). To have a "voice" for resistance inside Cuba. . . .

23. Continue "Radio Americas" broadcasts from Swan Island as appropriate (CIA). To provide an irritant to the Castro/Communist regime. . . .

24. Make available to the International Narcotics Commission documented evidence of Cuban exportation/importation of narcotics (State). To create increased awareness in Latin America of Cuban subversive activities. . . .

25. [4 lines of source text not declassified] . . .

Objective B: Harass the Economy

26. Encourage the Cuban people, as appropriate, to engage in minor acts of sabotage (CIA). . . . "Minor acts of sabotage" include such actions as excessive use of electricity or short-circuiting of telephone equipment, immobilizing vehicles (stealing parts, puncturing tires, contaminating gas tanks), material spoilage, and crop burning. . . .

27. Conduct selected major sabotage operations against key Cuban industries and public utilities, with priority attention being given to transportation, communication, power plants, and utilities (CIA). . . . Depending upon circumstances, the sabotage will be conducted either by especially trained, carefully selected commando/sabotage teams infiltrated especially for the operation and exfiltrated at the completion of the operation, or by internal assets if such can be developed with the necessary access to the target. The following are currently selected targets:

Matahambre Mine–Santa Lucia
Texaco Refinery–Santiago
Shell/Esso Refinery–Habana
Regla Steam Electric Plant–Habana
Matanzas Steam Electric Plant–Mantanzas
[*1 line of source text not declassified*]
Moa Bay Nickel Plant
Paper Mill–Cardenas
Micro Wave Towers . . .

28. Sabotage Cuban assets outside Cuba as targets of opportunity, provided this does not unduly affect food and medical supplies, or the Cuban people, as such (CIA). . . . Targets are seen mostly as shipments of products into or from Cuba. Sabotage would be to cause undue delay of shipment, using additives to spoil a commodity, fire or water damage, etc. A recent example was reported, post-action, on a shipment to the USSR.

29. Inspire labor groups outside Cuba to obstruct free world trade with Cuba (CIA and State). . . .

30. Discourage free world trade with Cuba (State, supported by CIA). . . .

31. Encourage the OAS Special Committee to recommend further trade measures against Cuba by Latin American countries (State). To provide a basis for renewed pressures upon NATO to recommend trade controls to NATO members. . . .

32. Reduce production of export agricultural commodities in Cuba, by covert means (CIA). . . . The main export commodities are sugar, tobacco, tropicals, and coffee. Activities would include . . . hampering of harvests by work slow-downs, destruction of bags, cartons, and other shipping containers, sabotage of sugar mill machinery, etc.

33. [*2 lines of source text not declassified*] . . .

Objective C: Intensify Intelligence Collection

34. Spot, recruit, and train legally established Cubans in Cuba or in Cuban Government Posts abroad. (CIA, supported by State and Defense) . . .

35. Spot, recruit, and train third country nationals resident in Cuba. (CIA, supported by State and Defense) . . .

36. Spot, recruit and train legal travellers who have potential access to significant information. (CIA, supported by State and Defense) . . .

37. Continue Caribbean Admissions Center, Opa-locka, Florida (CIA, with Defense, USIA, and other support). . . . The continuation of the refugee flow and the selective debriefing of refugees provide the most significant source of intelligence. . . .

38. [*2 lines of source text not declassified*] . . .

39. Maintain PAA service between the U.S. and Cuba (State, with CIA support) . . . to continue the exodus of skilled manpower from Cuba. PAA requires financial assistance to continue this activity.

40. [*3-1/2 lines of source text not declassified*] . . .

41. Continue monitoring overt Cuban broadcasts. (CIA) . . .

42. [4 *lines of source text not declassified*] . . .

43. [3 *lines of source text not declassified*] . . .

44. Establish program of periodic reports from U.S. Embassies in Hemisphere analyzing the effects of existence of the target area regime on host country. (State) . . .

Objective D: Split Regime Leadership and Relations With Bloc

45. Collect personality information on key Cuban individuals, their personalities, their attitudes, their associations, and their influences (CIA and others). To identify channels to key individuals and to identify frictions between the individuals. . . .

46. Develop channels of communications to selected key individual and "power centers" of the regime (CIA). To permit exploitation of the key individuals.

47. Conduct psychological and political action (CIA and State). . . . Activity will include:

a.   By public and private comment, to stimulate distrust and disaffection in the leadership and ranks of the supporters of the Castro regime, principally among the militia, the government bureaucracy, by organized labor, youth and students, farmers. . . .

Objective E: Assist Cuban Exile Groups and Latin American Governments to Undertake Actions

48. Stimulate, support and guide covertly the propaganda and political activities of all Cuban exile groups and individuals offering useful impact inside Cuba and upon world opinion. (CIA, with State and USIA support) . . .

49. Provide covert support to the Cuban Revolutionary Council (CRC). (CIA) . . .

50. Encourage and support other governments in the hemisphere to undertake programs for Cuba along lines of our own effort. (State, CIA) . . .

Objective F: Be Prepared To Exploit a Revolt

51. Continue to develop and refine contingency plans (Defense). To assure maximum readiness from the standpoint of military planning for military intervention if directed. These plans are well advanced.

52. Continue planning with Defense and the various sub-commanders for the participation of others in military contingency plans for Cuba (State, CIA and USIA). To provide support to the military in the event of execution of military contingency plans.

53. Establish and maintain in being the necessary communication and crypto links between CIA and Defense, including various sub-commands (CIA). To provide the communications capability to support the military contingency plans. These links have been or are in the process of being established.

54. Develop post-Castro concepts, leaders, and political groups (State, with support of others). To provide a focal point for anti-Castro resistance elements and to facilitate the transition of a post-Castro government in the event of a successful overthrow of Castro/Communism. . . .

55. Cache arms, ammunition, and other supplies in areas of Cuba accessible to known resistance elements and in potential resistance areas (CIA). . . . This will require extensive maritime infiltration/exfiltration operations. It is considered likely that Cuban maritime patrolling will be such that in the near future if the job is to be done, submarines must be used in lieu of surface craft.

56. Recruit, train, and supply small resistance cells in the major cities and in other selected areas of Cuba (CIA). To provide controlled intelligence sources and to be available in the event of an uprising. . . .

8. Comments by Senator Kenneth B. Keating in the U.S. Senate

Senator Keating of New York became the focal point of the Republican attack directed at JFK's response to the Russian military buildup in Cuba. Keating claimed to have access to special sources of information. Here he addresses his fellow senators.

August 31, 1962.

Mr. KEATING: Mr. President, I have prepared some remarks for delivery today on the subject of Cuba and the activities of Russian military personnel, which are probably in an effort to interfere with our operations at Cape Canaveral.

This morning additional facts came to my attention which indicate the danger of the stepped-up flow of Soviet so-called technicians to Cuba and the threat which their activities pose to the security of the United States, largely as a result of their effort to interfere with our operations at Cape Canaveral.

I am reliably informed—when I say "reliably informed," I mean that has been checked out from five different sources, and I am certain I can state it as a fact—that between the dates of August 4 and August 15, 10 or 12 Soviet vessels anchored at the Marante dock area at Mariel. The dock area previously had been surrounded by the construction of a high cinder-block wall. The Soviet ships unloaded 1,200 troops. Troops is what I mean, and not technicians. They were wearing Soviet fatigue uniforms. . . .

So far no action has been taken by our Government. The President has said that he has no evidence of Soviet troops in Cuba. If he has no evidence, I am giving him evidence this afternoon, Mr. President.

The American people have not been informed of the dangerous situation which exists 90 miles off our mainland.

Mr. President, the American people are asking with new urgency, What is going on in Cuba? So far the answers received are unsatisfactory. . . .

In my judgment, Mr. President, all the Soviet equipment, which undeniably includes radar and other electronic devices, is not only to prop up Castro economically; it is not only to build missile bases, which could easily be sabotaged; but it is also designed deliberately to put the Communists in a position where they can interfere with the American space effort at Cape Canaveral. The thousands of technicians are arriving, not only to teach the Cubans how to build their economy, not only to fight dissidents, not only to discourage common action by all the nations of this hemisphere, but above all to build and to man espionage and interference stations and to keep a constant eye on, and very possibly also a finger in the important U.S. launchings scheduled to take place at Cape Canaveral through the coming years.

Mr. President, so far the American people have not had a frank answer from their Government as to what the real dangers of a Communist buildup in Cuba are. Our present policy is just to look the other way in the hope that somehow Castro will just disappear. The present influx of Soviet men and technicians shows what a vain, blind, and misleading hope this has been. Castro is not a bad dream or a nightmare that will go away when morning comes. He is a dangerous reality. He will not go away merely because we rub Aladdin's lamp and wish for his disappearance. And he is not very likely to fall, no matter how much he abuses and antagonizes the people of Cuba, for the Soviet forces that stand behind him are now too much for mere refugees and rebels.

Therefore, at this point, Mr. President, Castro has virtually handed the Communists a gigantic monkeywrench that can be turned right through the middle of our entire space effort, that can endanger the lives of our astronauts, and that can critically slowdown vital defense developments. It is time for the people of this country and of this hemisphere to have the truth, the whole truth, about what Castro and his Soviet cohorts are up to. Only with full knowledge of the seriousness of the situation can we develop a strong national policy with the support of the people of the United States.

Our present look-the-other-way policy in Cuba depends to a large extent on popular ignorance of the facts and wishful underestimation of the dangers that are involved. Will we have to wait until more and more of our launchings at Canaveral go wrong before we suspect the worst? Will we have to wait until the Russians have established a space monopoly before we weigh the dangers of their activities in Cuba? Will we have to wait until Castro dies of old age before we recognize that the Soviet stronghold which is being established at this minute on the island of Cuba is undoubtedly a loaded gun that can be aimed directly at our military and space efforts?

Mr. President, the time for the truth is now and I hope the American people will be provided with the truth while there is still time to deal with it, before it is too late.

In my judgment, the first step which should be taken—immediately—would be to present the matter to the Organization of American States. We should lay the facts before them and urge upon them the necessity for prompt and vigorous action in a concerted way to meet this threat to their future security as well as to the security of the United States. Time is short. The situation is growing worse. I urge upon my Government that prompt action be taken.

9. News Conference at the White House with Press Secretary Pierre Salinger

A presidential statement warns the Russians not to push the envelope too far in Cuba, and seeks to refute Republican charges that the administration was underestimating the seriousness of the Soviet buildup there. It implicitly commits JFK to vigorous action should nuclear missiles be deployed on the Caribbean island.

September 4, 1962.

MR. SALINGER: I am going to read a statement, which is a statement of the President.

"All Americans, as well as all of our friends in this hemisphere, have been concerned over the recent moves of the Soviet Union to bolster the military power of the Castro regime in Cuba. Information has reached this Government in the last four days from a variety of sources which establishes without doubt that the Soviets have provided the Cuban Government with a number of anti-aircraft defense missiles. Along with these missiles, the Soviets are apparently providing the extensive radar and other electronic equipment which is required for their operation. We can also confirm the presence of several Soviet-made motor torpedo boats carrying ship-to-ship guided missiles having a range of 15 miles. The number of Soviet military technicians now known to be in Cuba or enroute—approximately 3,500—is consistent with assistance in setting up and learning to use this equipment. As I stated last week, we shall continue to make information available as fast as it is obtained and properly verified.

"There is no evidence of any organized combat force in Cuba from any Soviet-bloc country; of military bases provided to Russia; of a violation of the 1934 treaty relating to Guantanamo; of the presence of offensive ground-to-ground missiles; or of other significant offensive capability either in Cuban hands or under Soviet direction and guidance. Were it to be otherwise, the gravest issues would arise.

"The Cuban question must be considered as a part of the worldwide challenge posed by Communist threats to the peace. It must be dealt with as a part of that larger issue as well as in the context of the special relationships which have long characterized the inter-American system.

"It continues to be the policy of the United States that the Castro regime will not be allowed to export its aggressive purposes by force or the threat of force. It will be prevented by whatever means may be necessary from taking action against any part of the Western Hemisphere. The United States, in conjunction with other hemisphere countries, will make sure that while increased Cuban armaments will be a heavy burden to the unhappy people of Cuba themselves, they will be nothing more."

10. Memorandum for the Files Prepared by Special Counsel to the President Theodore C. Sorensen

Unwittingly—he had not been briefed about the decision to put missiles in Cuba–Soviet Ambassador to the United States Anatoly F. Dobrynin deceives a close Kennedy aide about Russian intentions.

Washington, September 6, 1962.

SUBJECT

Conversation with Ambassador Dobrynin–#2[1]

In response to his repeated telephone requests, I saw Soviet Ambassador Dobrynin at the Embassy today from 12:30 to 1:00 P.M. He told me that he had sent a report of our "informal conversation" on August 23 to Moscow and that (somewhat to his own surprise, I gathered) he had received a personal message from Chairman Khrushchev directing him to make known directly to me the following:

1. First, "nothing will be undertaken before the American Congressional elections[2] that could complicate the international situation or aggravate the tension in the relations between our two countries. We shall follow this course, provided there are no actions taken on the other side which would change the situation. This includes a German peace settlement and West Berlin." (The quotation is approximately, although not precisely, correct, inasmuch as the Ambassador urged me to take notes as he read from his own message.)

2. Chairman Khrushchev is definitely not coming to the opening of the United Nations General Assembly. "If the necessity arises for him to speak" this would be possible "only in the second half of November" and therefore not before the election. The Chairman does not wish to become involved in our internal political affairs.

I told the Ambassador that I appreciate his conveying the message to us; but that he should understand the President's feeling that the recent Soviet actions in Cuba had already caused considerable political turmoil—that this was a far more difficult problem for the administration politically because of the frustration felt by many Americans over the Cuban situation—and that the Chairman's message therefore seemed both hollow and tardy. (Dobrynin demurred at this point that he had tried to reach me with the message a week ago, before the Cuban issue became so hot.) The President, I said, had understood that the Chairman would not want to offer any grounds for attack to our political opponents—he regarded the Cuban action, therefore, as something of a deliberate

---

[1]Sorensen had also met with Dobrynin on August 23 at the latter's request. Their conversation then had not touched on Cuba.

[2]The elections were to take place on November 6.

and personal affront—and, given the current situation in Berlin and elsewhere, the President could hardly be expected to take a very accommodating attitude in the months ahead . . .

With respect to Cuba, Dobrynin said that he would report this conversation in full to the Chairman and that he was aware himself of the political and press excitement regarding this matter. He repeated several times, however, that they had done nothing new or extraordinary in Cuba—that the events causing all the excitement had been taking place somewhat gradually and quietly over a long period of time—and that he stood by his assurances that all of these steps were defensive in nature and did not represent any threat to the security of the United States. He neither contradicted nor confirmed my reference to large numbers of Soviet military personnel, electronic equipment and missile preparations.

11. Transcript of Conversation Between Secretary of the Interior Stewart Udall and Chairman Khrushchev at Petsunda in the Soviet Union

During a visit to Khrushchev's villa, a Kennedy cabinet member receives misleading assurances from the Soviet premier himself on the defensive nature of the military buildup in Cuba—and a complaint about the belligerence of U.S. congressmen.

September 6, 1962.

"U: The President is the commander of the military in our country, just as you are in the Soviet Union.

"K: It is true that irresponsible actions occasionally take place. It's up to me to make the decision on going to war, but fools in airplanes do exist, I realize. Now as to Cuba—here is an area that could really lead to some unexpected consequences. I have been reading what some irresponsible Senators have been saying on this. A lot of people are making a big fuss because we are giving aid to Cuba. But you are giving aid to Japan. Just recently I was reading that you have placed atomic warheads on Japanese territory, and surely this is not something the Japanese need. So when Castro comes to us for aid, we give him what he needs for defense. He hasn't much modern military equipment, so he asked us to supply some. But only for defense. However, if you attack Cuba, that would create an entirely different situation. And it is unthinkable, of course, that a tiny nation like Cuba would ever attack the United States.

"U: The responsible people prevail in our country unless intolerable provocations occur.

"K: You have surrounded us with military bases. If you attack Cuba, then we will attack one of the countries next to us where you have placed your bases.

"U: The President has made his position on Cuba clear. A few people in Congress may call for an invasion, but the President makes the policy.

"K: These Congressmen do not see with their eyes, but with their asses. All they can see is what's behind them. Yesterday's events are not today's realities. I remember Gorky recounting in his memoirs how he had a conversation with Tolstoy.[1] Tolstoy asked him how he got along with women, and then ventured his own opinion. 'Men are poorly designed. When they're young, they can satisfy their sexual desires. But as they grow old, the ability to reap this satisfaction disappears. The desires, however, do not.' So it is with your Congressmen. They do not have power, but they still have the same old desires.

"U: Nevertheless, most Congressmen are responsible. I used to be a Congressman myself. But there are only a few who are irresponsible.

"K: I'm speaking of the latter. America is no longer the strongest nation in the world. The President knows and understands this. Relations between countries must be built on political and economic realities. If your Congressmen want to attack Cuba, they are like Tolstoy's aging man. I have stated that we could support Cuba even from our own territory. So this shows that some of your Congressmen are stronger in their asses than their heads.

"U: The irresponsible people have a right to speak out but they do not control policy. For example, one of the noisiest Senators is Goldwater[2] from my own state of Arizona. He's a Republican, while I'm a Democrat. He doesn't understand modern times. But the President does, and he makes our policies on foreign relations."[3]

12. Presidential News Conference

JFK again makes clear in public his determination to act should offensive missiles be installed in Cuba.

September 13, 1962.

JFK: I have a preliminary statement.

There has been a great deal of talk on the situation in Cuba in recent days both in the Communist camp and in our own, and I would like to take this opportunity to set the matter in perspective.

[1] Eminent Russian writers Maxim Gorky and Leo Tolstoy were close friends.
[2] Barry M. Goldwater, the GOP nominee for president in 1964.
[3] Udall produced this transcript, which he summarized for American officials in a telegram from Moscow on September 7. The Udall-Khrushchev conversation also touched on issues other than Cuba.

In the first place, it is Mr. Castro and his supporters who are in trouble. In the last year his regime has been increasingly isolated from this hemisphere. His name no longer inspires the same fear or following in other Latin American countries. He has been condemned by the OAS. . . . By his own monumental economic mismanagement, supplemented by our refusal to trade with him, his economy has crumbled, and his pledges for economic progress have been discarded, along with his pledges for political freedom. His industries are stagnating, his harvests are declining, his own followers are beginning to see that their revolution has been betrayed.

So it is not surprising that in a frantic effort to bolster his regime he should try to arouse the Cuban people by charges of an imminent American invasion, and commit himself still further to a Soviet takeover in the hope of preventing his own collapse.

Ever since communism moved into Cuba in 1958, Soviet technical and military personnel have moved steadily onto the island in increasing numbers at the invitation of the Cuban Government.

Now that movement has been increased. It is under our most careful surveillance. But I will repeat the conclusion that I reported last week: that these new shipments do not constitute a serious threat to any other part of this hemisphere.

If the United States ever should find it necessary to take military action against communism in Cuba, all of Castro's Communist-supplied weapons and technicians would not change the result or significantly extend the time required to achieve that result.

However, unilateral military intervention on the part of the United States cannot currently be either required or justified, and it is regrettable that loose talk about such action in this country[1] might serve to give a thin color of legitimacy to the Communist pretense that such a threat exists. But let me make this clear once again: If at any time the Communist buildup in Cuba were to endanger or interfere with our security in any way, including our base at Guantanamo, our passage to the Panama Canal, our missile and space activities at Cape Canaveral, or the lives of American citizens in this country, or if Cuba should ever attempt to export its aggressive purposes by force or the threat of force against any nation in this hemisphere, or become an offensive military base of significant capacity for the Soviet Union, then this country will do whatever must be done to protect its own security and that of its allies.

We shall be alert, too, and fully capable of dealing swiftly with any such development. As President and Commander in Chief I have full authority now to take such action, and I have asked the Congress to authorize me to call up reserve forces should this or any other crisis make it necessary.[2]

In the meantime, we intend to do everything within our power to prevent such a threat from coming into existence.

Our friends in Latin America must realize the consequences such develop-

[1]An obvious reference to those Republicans then pressing JFK to take forceful action against Cuba.
[2]A request JFK made on September 7.

ments hold out for their own peace and freedom, and we shall be making further proposals to them. Our friends in NATO must realize the implications of their ships engaging in the Cuban trade.

We shall continue to work with Cuban refugee leaders who are dedicated as we are to that nation's future return to freedom. We shall continue to keep the American people and the Congress fully informed. We shall increase our surveillance of the whole Caribbean area. We shall neither initiate nor permit aggression in this hemisphere.

With this in mind, while I recognize that rash talk is cheap, particularly on the part of those who do not have the responsibility, I would hope that the future record will show that the only people talking about a war or an invasion at this time are the Communist spokesmen in Moscow and Havana, and that the American people defending as we do so much of the free world, will in this nuclear age, as they have in the past, keep both their nerve and their head.

Q. Mr. President, coupling this statement with the one of last week,[3] at what point do you determine that the buildup in Cuba has lost its defensive character and become offensive? Would it take an overt act?

THE PRESIDENT. I think if you read last week's statement and the statement today, I made it quite clear, particularly in last week's statement, when we talked about the presence of offensive military missile capacity or development of military bases and other indications which I gave last week, all those would, of course, indicate a change in the nature of the threat.

Q. Well, Mr. President, in this same line, have you set for yourself any rule or set of conditions at which you will determine the existence of an offensive rather than a defensive force in Cuba, and, in that same connection, in your reading of the Monroe Doctrine,[4] how do you define "intervention"? Will it require force to contravene the Monroe Doctrine or does the presence of a foreign power in any force, but not using that force in this hemisphere, amount to contravention of the Doctrine?

THE PRESIDENT. Well, I have indicated that if Cuba should possess a capacity to carry out offensive actions against the United States, that the United States would act. I've also indicated that the United States would not permit Cuba to export its power by force in the hemisphere. The United States will make appropriate military judgments after consultation with the Joint Chiefs of Staff and others, after carefully analyzing whatever new information comes in, as to whether that point has been reached where an offensive threat does exist. And at that time the country and the Congress will be so notified. . . .

---

[3]A probable reference to Kennedy's statement on September 4. See Document 9.

[4]Enunciated by President James Monroe in December 1823 in his annual message to Congress, warning European powers against intervention in the Western Hemisphere; and regarded as a cornerstone of American foreign policy ever since.

13. Memorandum of Mongoose Meeting

Lansdale's plan of action for Phase II of Mongoose (see Document 7) is, with minor modifications, approved.

Washington, September 14, 1962.

. . . The 12 September addendum[1] to the Phase Two Mongoose Operation was discussed and the entire Phase Two was approved in principle as a platform from which to proceed. Activities which may be especially sensitive are to be brought before the Group,[2] and this body wishes to be kept generally advised on progress.

General Lansdale indicated that papers on a "blockade" [of Cuba] are being generated outside Mongoose channels. (Elder talked to George Carroll on Saturday who identified such papers as part of the DOD contingency planning exercise and indicated that there is very little interest or steam in them.)

CIA Headquarters and all WH stations are to be especially alert for any shipments of arms or other subversive material from Cuba to other Latin American countries. (Chief, Task Force W[3] says this alert has been laid on and is in force.)

There was some discussion of a State–JCS meeting with McGeorge Bundy on contingency plans for Cuba.

Bruce Cheever attended for the Agency.[4] He reports that no decisions were made, no new ideas were brought up, and nothing useful emerged from the meeting. . . .

The Attorney General expressed concern that activities by certain Cuban exiles are reaching the point where the Government may be forced to take action against them rather than to simply state that "we are investigating." The Agency is requested to see what it can do to help reduce the noise level of these activities.[5]

14. Special National Intelligence Estimate Submitted by the CIA

An intelligence estimate claims that the Russian military buildup in Cuba was motivated by a desire to deter an American attack on the island, and that the deployment of offensive missiles in Cuba is not likely.

[1]This provided for a few minor changes to the plan of action for Mongoose's second phase described by Lansdale in his August 31 memorandum (see Document 7).
[2]A reference to the Special Group (Augmented).
[3]A reference to William Harvey.
[4]Namely, the CIA.
[5]Walter Elder, executive assistant to the CIA director, drafted this memorandum.

Washington, September 19, 1962.

THE MILITARY BUILDUP IN CUBA

The Problem

To assess the strategic and political significance of the recent military buildup in Cuba and of the possible future development of additional military capabilities there.

Conclusions

A. We believe that the USSR values its position in Cuba primarily for the political advantages to be derived from it, and consequently that the main purpose of the present military buildup in Cuba is to strengthen the Communist regime there against what the Cubans and the Soviets conceive to be a danger that the US may attempt by one means or another to overthrow it. The Soviets evidently hope to deter any such attempt by enhancing Castro's defensive capabilities and by threatening Soviet military retaliation. At the same time, they evidently recognize that the development of an offensive military base in Cuba might provoke US military intervention and thus defeat their present purpose.

B. In terms of military significance, the current Soviet deliveries are substantially improving air defense and coastal defense capabilities in Cuba. Their political significance is that, in conjunction with the Soviet statement of 11 September[1] they are likely to be regarded as ensuring the continuation of the Castro regime in power, with consequent discouragement to the opposition at home and in exile. The threat inherent in these developments is that, to the extent that the Castro regime thereby gains a sense of security at home, it will be emboldened to become more aggressive in fomenting revolutionary activity in Latin America.

C. As the buildup continues, the USSR may be tempted to establish in Cuba other weapons represented to be defensive in purpose, but of a more "offensive" character: e.g., light bombers, submarines, and additional types of short-range surface-to-surface missiles (SSMs). A decision to provide such weapons will continue to depend heavily on the Soviet estimate as to whether they could be introduced without provoking a US military reaction.

D. The USSR could derive considerable military advantage from the establishment of Soviet medium and intermediate range ballistic missiles in Cuba, or from the establishment of a Soviet submarine base there. As between these two, the establishment of a submarine base would be the more likely. Either development, however, would be incompatible with Soviet practice to date and with Soviet policy as we presently estimate it. It would indicate a far greater willingness to increase the level of risk in US-Soviet relations than the USSR has displayed thus far, and consequently would have important policy implications with respect to other areas and other problems in East-West relations.

E. The Latin American reaction will be [to] the evidence of an increased So-

---

[1] TASS, the Soviet news agency, had released a statement on September 11 saying the military buildup in Cuba was defensive, and that any American aggression in the Caribbean would lead to war.

viet commitment to Cuba, rather than to the technical implications of the military buildup. Many Latin Americans will fear and resent a Soviet military intrusion into the Hemisphere, but will regard the problem as one to be met by the US and not their responsibility. We estimate the chances are better now than they were at Punta del Este[2] to obtain the necessary two-thirds OAS majority for sanctions and other steps of direct military action aimed at Cuba. If it became clear that the USSR was establishing an "offensive" base in Cuba, most Latin American governments would expect the US to eliminate it, by whatever means were necessary, but many of them would still seek to avoid direct involvement.[3]

15. Memorandum from President Kennedy to Secretary of Defense McNamara

JFK shows interest in the contingency planning for military action against Cuba. (McNamara would respond to this memorandum on October 4, assuring JFK that contingency plans for Cuba were up to date.)

Washington, September 21, 1962.

At the meeting with you and the Joint Chiefs of Staff on Friday, 14 September,[1] there seemed to be lack of unanimity between General LeMay and Admiral Anderson as to losses our aircraft would incur in attacking an SA2 missile site.

Would it be useful to build a model of such a site for exercises to be observed by an objective and disinterested party? Judgement as to losses to be incurred should include those that would result from the addition of anti-aircraft guns to protect the site. If you believe such a program would be useful, would you provide me with an estimate as to its cost.

Would you assure that contingency plans with relation to Cuba are kept up-to-date, taking into account the additions to their armaments resulting from the continuous influx of Soviet equipment and technicians.

---

[2] A conference of OAS foreign ministers met there in January 1962.
[3] CIA Director McCone submitted this estimate.
[1] JFK had met with McGeorge Bundy and the Joint Chiefs on September 14.

16. Message from Chairman Khrushchev to President Kennedy

An indignant Khrushchev complains to JFK about American rhetoric and actions, warning that an attack on Cuba will trigger world war.

Moscow, September 28, 1962.

Recently I had a talk with your Secretary of the Interior Mr. S. Udall.[1] He made a good impression on me. Our conversation was friendly. And I never expected that at the time I talked with him you would take a decision to request from the Congress an authority to call up 150.000 reservists.[2] Motivating that step of yours you referred to the red-hot state of international atmosphere and to a necessity for you in that connection to react promptly to the dangers that may arise in any part of "the free world." Everybody understands that when the President of the U.S. demands an increase in armed forces and explains that demand by an aggravation of the situation, it means that he considers that the situation is aggravated by the other side, that is by us, the Soviet Union. But we haven't done anything that could give a pretext for that. We did not carry out any mobilization, and did not make any threats.

I must tell you straightforwardly, Mr. President, that your statement with threats against Cuba[3] is just an inconceivable step. Under present circumstances, when there exist thermonuclear weapons, your request to the Congress for an authority to call up 150.000 reservists is not only a step making the atmosphere red-hot, it is already a dangerous sign that you want to pour oil in the flame, to extinguish that red-hot glow by mobilizing new military contingents. And that, naturally, forces the other side to respond in kind. What could it lead to, all the more that you consider that the U.S. has right to attack Cuba whenever it wishes? But nowadays is not the Middle Ages, though even at the time it was considered brigandage, and measures were taken against such actions. And in our time such actions are absolutely unthinkable. That is what made us to come out with the TASS statement[4] and later at the session of the UN General Assembly to qualify your act, to remind of the norms of international law and to say about West Berlin.

If there were not statement[s] by you on Cuba, we, naturally, . . . would not say anything on West Berlin. Your statement forced us to do so.

We regret that this dangerous line is being continued in the United States now. What is going on, for example, in the U.S. Congress. How can one, for example, fail to notice the decision of the House of Representatives to stop giving U.S. aid to any country that trades with Cuba or whose ships are used for trading

---

[1]See Document 11.
[2]JFK made this request on September 7.
[3]A probable reference to JFK's statement on September 13. See Document 12.
[4]See Document 14, footnote 1.

with Cuba.[5] Isn't that an act of an unpermissible arbitrariness against freedom of international trade, an act of crude interference into domestic affairs of other countries?

Very serious consequences may [arise from] the resolution adopted by the U.S. Senate on the Cuban question.[6] The contents of that resolution gives [sic] ground to draw a conclusion that the U.S. is evidently ready to assume responsibility for unleashing thermonuclear war. We consider that if what is written in that resolution were actually carried out it would mean the beginning of war because no country can agree with such interpretation of rights, with such arbitrariness. Then there would be no UN, everything would collapse and roll into abyss as it happened once when the League of Nations collapsed. Who wrecked it then? Japan and Hitler, who quit the League of Nations to untie their hands and start war. And they did start it. Could it be that the US wants to embark on such road?

We would greatly regret if it were so. We still do not lose hope that we will be able to normalize our relations. But this can be achieved only when the United States and its allies will strictly adhere to the generally recognized norms of international law and will not interfere into the domestic affairs of other states, will not threaten other countries. This is the main thing. And this is the coexistence of which we spoke more than once.[7] You spoke of it too.[8] But what kind of coexistence is this if the United States would attack countries whose government or socio-political system are not to its liking? In our time the world has split into two camps—capitalist and socialist: you have neighbors whom, as you say, you do not like while we have neighbors whom we do not like, but they are your friends and allies. How can one, especially under these circumstances, consider it to be one's right to attack another country merely because its government and internal order are not to your liking? If we conduct such a policy, where this will lead to—to world war.

---

[5]The House of Representatives passed this appropriations bill on September 20.

[6]The Cuba Resolution, passed by the Senate on September 20, sanctioned the use of force to combat Cuban aggression in the Western Hemisphere, and expressed a determination to prevent the development of a Russian military base in Cuba that threatened the United States.

[7]During his time as leader, Khrushchev had called for peaceful coexistence between East and West—a nonmilitary, economic competition.

[8]A probable reference to Kennedy's comments at the Vienna summit in June 1961 about the need to maintain a balance of power in the cold war in the early 1960s that would keep the United States and Russia from war.

17. Memorandum from Secretary of Defense McNamara to Chairman of the JCS Taylor[1]

In September and early October, plans to blockade, invade, and carry out air strikes against Cuba are advanced. Here McNamara considers the circumstances that would make such action necessary.

Washington, October 2, 1962.

During my meeting with the Joint Chiefs of Staff on October 1, 1962, the question arose as to the contingencies under which military action against Cuba may be necessary and toward which our military planning should be oriented. The following categories would appear to cover the likely possibilities:

(a) Soviet action against Western rights in Berlin calling for a Western response including among other actions a blockade of Communist or other shipping en route to Cuba.

(b) Evidence that the Castro regime has permitted the positioning of bloc offensive weapon systems on Cuban soil or in Cuban harbors.

(c) An attack against the Guantanamo base, or against U.S. planes or vessels outside Cuban territorial air space or waters.

(d) A substantial popular uprising in Cuba, the leaders of which request assistance in recovering Cuban independence from the Castro Soviet puppet regime.

(e) Cuban armed assistance to subversion in other parts of the Western Hemisphere.

(f) A decision by the President that affairs in Cuba have reached a point inconsistent with continuing U.S. national security.

May I have the views of the Chiefs as to the appropriateness of the above list of contingencies and answers to the following three sets of questions:

(a) The operational plans considered appropriate for each contingency.

(b) The preparatory actions which should now and progressively in the future be undertaken to improve U.S. readiness to execute these plans.

(c) The consequences of the actions on the availability of forces and on our logistics posture to deal with threats in other areas, i.e. Berlin, Southeast Asia, etc.

We can assume that the political objective in any of these contingencies may be either:

(a) the removal of the threat to U.S. security of Soviet weapon systems in Cuba, or

(b) the removal of the Castro regime and the securing in the island of a new regime responsive to Cuban national desires.

Inasmuch as the second objective is the more difficult objective and may be

---

[1]Maxwell Taylor had just been appointed chairman of the Joint Chiefs.

required if the first is to be permanently achieved, attention should be focused upon a capability to assure the second objective.

I have asked ISA to initiate discussion with State as to the political actions which should precede or accompany the various military actions being planned.

18. Memorandum of Mongoose Meeting

Robert Kennedy conveys to Mongoose officials JFK's dissatisfaction with the operation's lack of progress. Also discussed is the need for reconnaissance flights over Cuba to monitor the Russian military buildup.

Washington, October 4, 1962.

Chaired by Attorney General [Robert Kennedy]

Attended by: Gilpatric, [Alexis] Johnson, General Taylor, General Carter, McCone, Scoville, General Lansdale and Colonel Steakley (part of the time).

The Attorney General reported on discussions with the President on Cuba; dissatisfied with lack of action in the sabotage field, went on to stress that nothing was moving forward, commented that one effort attempted had failed, expressed general concern over developing situation.

General Lansdale reviewed operations, pointing out that no sabotage had been attempted and gave general impression that things were all right.

McCone then stated that phase one was principally intelligence gathering, organizing and training, that no sabotage was authorized, that one operation against a powerhouse had been contemplated but was discouraged by [the Special] group [(Augmented)], that he had called a meeting to review matters this morning and that he had observed a lack of forward motion due principally to "hesitancy" in government circles to engage in any activities which would involve attribution to the United States.

AG took sharp exception stating the Special Group had not withheld approval on any specified actions to his knowledge, but to the contrary had urged and insisted upon action by the Lansdale operating organization.

There followed a sharp exchange which finally was clarifying inasmuch as it resulted in a reaffirmation of a determination to move forward. In effect it seemed to be the consensus that phase two as approved on September 6,[1] was now outmoded, that more dynamic action was indicated, that hesitancy about overflights [over Cuba] must be reconsidered . . . , that actions which could be attributed to indigenous Cubans would not be important or very effective, and that a very considerable amount of attribution and "noise" must be expected.

[1]For the formulation and approval of Operation Mongoose's Phase II, see Documents 7 and 13. The September 6 date refers to a meeting of senior officials at which Lansdale was asked to make some minor changes to Phase II's plan of action.

As a result, General Lansdale was instructed to give consideration to new and more dynamic approaches, the specific items of sabotage should be brought forward immediately and new ones conceived, that a plan for mining harbors should be developed and presented, and the possibility of capturing Castro forces for interrogation should be studied.

With respect to overflights, the NRO and Colonel Steakley were instructed to prepare and present to the Special Group on next Tuesday[2] at a special meeting alternate recommendations for overflights. These to include the use of U–2s[3] on complete sweeps (as contrasted with peripheral or limited missions). . . .

Consideration was given to stating publicly that we propose to overfly Cuba in the interest of our own security and the security of the Western Hemisphere, and then to proceed even though doing so involved risk.

It was the consensus that we could not accept restrictions which would foreclose gaining all reasonable knowledge of military installations in Cuba.

During the meeting McCone reviewed the earlier meeting with General Lansdale, and pointed out to the group that this meeting clarified General Lansdale's authority over the entire Mongoose operation and that the CIA organization was responsive to his policy and operational guidance, and this was thoroughly understood.

Consideration was given to the existing guidelines and it was the consensus that the August 1st guidelines for phase two[4] were inadequate and new guidelines must be considered.[5]

19. Comments by Senator Keating in the U.S. Senate

The Russian buildup in Cuba, which began in July, initially involved conventional military equipment. But in September the deployment of nuclear missiles commenced. Here Senator Keating claims that such weapons are in Cuba, six days before JFK learned this was indeed the case.

October 10, 1962.

Mr. KEATING: Mr. President, yesterday I spoke on the subject of Cuba. At that time I did not have fully confirmed the matter to which I shall address myself now. I now have it fully confirmed. As a result, I call upon the appropriate Government officials to confirm or to deny reports of intermediate range missile bases in Cuba.

Construction has begun on at least a half dozen launching sites for interme-

---

[2]October 9.
[3]High-altitude American reconnaissance planes.
[4]Presumably a reference to the guidelines endorsed by JFK on August 20. See Document 3.
[5]John McCone prepared this memorandum.

diate range tactical missiles. Intelligence authorities must have advised the President and top Government officials of this fact, and they must now have been told that ground-to-ground missiles can be operational from the island of Cuba within 6 months.

My own sources on the Cuban situation, which have been 100 percent reliable, have substantiated this report completely.

When are the American people going to be given all of the facts about the military buildup in Cuba?

Yesterday I pointed out, for either the 19th or 20th time, that we are not getting the whole story on Cuba. I referred to the recent testimony by Under Secretary of State George Ball before the House Select Committee on Export Control.[1] Presumably the report was supposed to be in line with the President's commitment of September 4[2] that, "We shall continue to make information available as fast as it is obtained and properly verified."

I stated that Mr. Ball had confirmed facts which some of us had previously reported: that he had identified three, possibly four, short-range missile sites in Cuba. I commented, however, that the significant sentence in his testimony, which was buried away, perhaps in the hope that no one would notice it, was this: "Quite likely several more such sites will be installed."

The fact of the matter is, according to my reliable sources, that six launching sites are under construction—pads which will have the power to hurl rockets into the American heartland and as far as the Panama Canal Zone.

Why would Under Secretary Ball give the committee the impression that new missile sites were a possibility rather than a fact? Even as possibilities, he indicated they would be short range rather than intermediate range missile sites. Why has such a veil been thrown around Cuba, keeping this new information from the American people? Are they still trying to perpetuate the myth that the buildup is defensive? Is it possible anyone in Government is childish enough to believe this?

According to Mr. Walter Lippmann's[3] column of yesterday, the United States has "an elaborate system of surveillance by sea, by air, and by land and there is every reason to think that its accuracy is very high. Little of military interest can happen without our knowing it. We do not have to guess. We know."

If this is true, our Government is well aware of the fact that within a matter of months, Cuba may have the capability of launching intermediate range missiles, but the American people are being kept in the dark. The Soviets know the fact. The Cubans know this fact. But in the view of the administration our people are not entitled to know it.

Mr. President, let us have all the facts, and have them now.

---

[1]On October 3 Ball started open congressional testimony on the Russian military buildup in Cuba.

[2]For JFK's September 4 statement, see Document 9.

[3]Lippmann was one of the most distinguished journalists of the twentieth century.

20. Memorandum by CIA Director McCone of Meeting with President Kennedy[1]

In a conversation with John McCone, JFK shows an interest in concealing the extent of the Cuban problem from the American public. His striking comment at the end seems to suggest he would have seriously considered the use of force against Cuba even if the presence of nuclear weapons on the island had not been detected by the CIA.

Washington, October 11, 1962.

I showed the President photographs of the crates which presumably would carry, or were carrying, IL 28s, Soviet medium bombers, and were deck loaded on a ship which had arrived in Havana in the early days of October. The President requested that such information be withheld at least until after [the November congressional] elections as if the information got into the press, a new and more violent Cuban issue would be injected into the campaign and this would seriously affect his independence of action.

McCone stated that these particular photographs could not be restricted as they had been disseminated to the Intelligence Community and several joint and specified commands, such as CINCLANT, SAC, NORAD, and others and would be reported in the CIA Bulletin on Thursday morning. The President then requested that the report be worded to indicate a probability rather than an actuality because in the final analysis we only saw crates, not the bombers themselves. DCI agreed. The President further requested that all future information be suppressed. DCI stated that this was extremely dangerous.

It was then agreed that future information would be disseminated to members of USIB, with appropriate instructions that only those responsible for giving the President advice be given the information. Furthermore, that within CIA circles a minimum number of experts be informed. McCone stated there was no problem in CIA, that it was secure. It was therefore agreed that the USIB members would be instructed to restrict the information to their personal offices and fully and currently inform the Chiefs of Staff, the Chairman, the Service Secretaries and the Secretary of Defense. Similar restrictive action would be taken in State. Therefore all those involved in "giving advice to the President" would be fully informed. However operational divisions and the joint and specified commands would not be informed at this time, except at the direction of the above people who are receiving the information.

At this point the President mentioned that "we'll have to do something drastic about Cuba" and I am anxiously looking forward to the JCS operational plan which is to be presented to me next week. . . .

[1]McGeorge Bundy also attended this meeting.

21. Memorandum from Director for Operations of the Joint Staff F. T. Unger to Assistant Secretary of Defense for International Security Affairs Paul H. Nitze

In response to a memorandum from McNamara (see Document 17), an administration official outlines contingency plans to blockade or attack Cuba.

Washington, October 12, 1962.

SUBJECT

Political Actions/Military Actions Concerning Cuba

REFERENCE

SecDef[1] Memo of 2 October 1962

1. In furtherance of our discussion of last evening concerning the project included in the reference, we are having a meeting at 1300 hours today of operational and logistical planners from CINCLANT and CINSTRIKE for the purpose of developing our responses to the contingencies and other matters requested by the SecDef.

2. Pending completion of the requirement given us by the SecDef, a general picture of each of our military contingency plans for Cuba is tabulated below as a basis for your initial discussions with State. On the other hand, it may be better to delay discussions with State until we have completed our part of the requirement and have submitted it to the SecDef and the JCS on Monday, 15 October.

a. Blockade Plan—employs 24 to 36 destroyers, a carrier task force, etc., which can marshal significant strength to blockade Cuba, both air and maritime.

b. Air Strike Plan—currently being revised, but employs between 450 and 500 aircraft. In the event of any execution of this plan steps would be taken to alert all forces allocated to the other assault plans.

c. Fast Reaction Assault Plan—employs both air-borne and amphibious assault with about 32,000 troops in initial phase, with balance of assault forces arriving in increments as they become available. Ultimately builds up to about 80,000 troops in Cuba around D+18 days.

d. Full-Scale Deliberate Assault Plan—employs simultaneous air-borne and amphibious assault with around 49,000 troops engaged on D-Day, building to about 60,000 by D+5 days, and again to 80,000 by D+16 days.

3. For your consideration, following are some of the political actions which

[1]A reference to Secretary of Defense McNamara.

might be undertaken in connection with the implementation of one or more of the foregoing plans: final arrangements for the tactical use of Mayaguana Island in the Bahamas; perhaps a request for token participation by Latin American military forces; in the case of blockade, notification of "neutral" shipping and publication of U.S. intent; in all cases, possibly, the preliminary political arrangements attendant to a state of war; and, of course, coordination with international organizations, such as the OAS and the UN during the execution of military action.

PART 4

The Missile Crisis

A U–2 FLIGHT over Cuba on October 14, 1962, revealed that the Soviet Union was deploying nuclear missiles on the Caribbean island. National Security Adviser McGeorge Bundy conveyed this somber news to President Kennedy on the morning of Tuesday, October 16. The Cuban missile crisis, the most dangerous episode of the entire cold war epoch, was under way.

The documents in this chapter show how the October 1962 crisis was managed and defused. A number of them are records of the meetings of the Executive Committee of the National Security Council (ExComm), a group of senior advisers which JFK established to handle the crisis.[1] Also included is the exchange of letters between Kennedy and Khrushchev, initiated by the president's October 22 public address in which he told the American people about the missiles in Cuba and his plans to blockade the island. The documents also shed light on Robert Kennedy's role—as an increasingly committed supporter of the blockade option and an opponent of the air-strike-on-Cuba alternative—during the first week of the crisis; and as an intermediary between President Kennedy and Anatoly Dobrynin, Soviet ambassador in Washington, during the second week. Other important matters are touched on, including UN Ambassador Adlai Stevenson's dissent on how to meet the Russian challenge in Cuba (he wanted a greater emphasis on diplomacy), the congressional response to the crisis, and the so-called Cordier ploy regarding the removal of American missiles from Turkey.

In the first two ExComm meetings, on October 16, JFK gave every indication that he intended to launch a military strike on Cuba. The main story of the

[1]For the full record of these ExComm sessions, see the excellent book edited by Ernest R. May and Philip D. Zelikow, *The Kennedy Tapes: Inside the White House During the Cuban Missile Crisis* (Cambridge, Mass., 1997).

missile crisis, from an American perspective, is how the president moved from this initially belligerent stance to a far more prudent one, selecting the blockade instead of an air strike, deciding against retaliation when an American U–2 plane was shot down over Cuba on October 27, agreeing to withdraw the Jupiter missiles from Turkey in order to end the crisis. These documents tell this story.

1. Memorandum for the Record Prepared by CIA Deputy Director for Plans Richard M. Helms

With the missile crisis under way, Robert Kennedy calls for an acceleration of Operation Mongoose.

Washington, October 16, 1962.

SUBJECT

Mongoose Meeting with the Attorney General

1. At 2:30 this afternoon, the Attorney General convened in his office a meeting on Operation Mongoose consisting of General Lansdale and Colonel Patchell, General Johnson of the Joint Staff, Robert Hurwitch of State (vice Ed Martin who was unable to attend), Hewson Ryan of USIA, and the undersigned.[1]

2. The Attorney General opened the meeting by expressing the "general dissatisfaction of the President" with Operation Mongoose. He pointed out that the Operation had been under way for a year, that the results were discouraging, that there had been no acts of sabotage, and that even the one which had been attempted had failed twice. He indicated that there had been noticeable improvement during the year in the collection of intelligence but that other actions had failed to influence significantly the course of events in Cuba. He spoke of the weekly meetings of top officials on this problem and again noted the small accomplishments despite the fact that Secretaries Rusk and McNamara, General Taylor, McGeorge Bundy, and he personally had all been charged by the President with finding a solution. He traced the history of General Lansdale's personal appointment by the President a year ago. The Attorney General then stated that in view of this lack of progress, he was going to give Operation Mongoose more personal attention. In order to do this, he will hold a meeting every morning at 0930 with the Mongoose operational representatives from the various agencies (Lansdale, Harvey, Hurwitch, Ryan, and General Johnson).

3. The Attorney General spoke favorably of the sabotage paper which had

[1]A reference to Helms.

171

been presented by General Carter this morning to the meeting of the Special Group (Augmented).[2] He obviously did not like the earlier memorandum,[3] since he felt it showed no "push" in getting on with the acts of sabotage.

4. When asked for my comments, I stated that we were prepared to get on with the new action program and that we would execute it aggressively. I pointed out, however, that the objective of Operation Mongoose would have to be determined at some point since the Cubans with whom we have to work were seeking a reason for risking their lives in these operations. I related my conversation with the young Cuban from the DRE who pointed out that they were willing to commit their people only on operations which they regarded as sensible. I defined "sensible" in Cuban terminology these days as meaning an action which would contribute to the liberation of their country, another way of saying that the United States, perhaps in conjunction with other Latin countries, would bail them out militarily. My point was specifically echoed by Hewson Ryan. The Attorney General's rejoinder was a plea for new ideas of things that could be done against Cuba. In passing, he made reference to the change in atmosphere in the United States Government during the last twenty-four hours,[4] and asked some questions about the percentage of Cubans whom we thought would fight for the regime if the country were invaded.

5. The meeting concluded with the reaffirmation by the Attorney General of his desire to hold a meeting each day, beginning tomorrow. He said that these meetings might later be changed to every other day when and if he finds a daily get-together is not necessary. . . .

2. Memorandum by CIA Director McCone, "Brief Discussion with the President—9:30 a.m.— 17 October 1962"

The inclination to use force shown by JFK in the initial ExComm meetings on October 16 is still evident the following morning.

Confirmed the situation and explored possible actions. . . .

President seemed inclined to act promptly if at all, without warning, targeting on MRBM's and possibly airfields. Stated Congressional Resolution[1] gave him all authority he needed and this was confirmed by [McGeorge] Bundy, and therefore seemed inclined to act.

President asked McCone to see Eisenhower promptly.

[2]Not included.
[3]Not included.
[4]Meaning, of course, that the CIA had now identified missiles in Cuba.
[1]See Chapter 3, Document 16, footnote 6.

3. Memorandum of ExComm Meeting

In the absence of JFK, who had decided to keep his prior commitments to campaign on behalf of Democrats running for Congress, ExComm officials discuss diplomacy, the use of force, and blockading Cuba as the administration's main options.

Washington, October 17, 1962.

Memorandum of Meeting, Wednesday, October 17th, at 8:30 a.m., and again at 4:00 p.m. . . .

The purpose of the discussion was to develop a plan of action in connection with Cuba. . . .

Ambassador Bohlen warned against any action against Cuba, particularly an air strike without warning, stating such would be divisive with all allies and subject us to criticism throughout the world. He advocated writing both Khrushchev and Castro; if their response was negative or unsatisfactory then we should plan action; advise our principal allies, seek a two-thirds vote from the OAS and then act. The Attorney General [Robert Kennedy] and Bohlen exchanged views as to just what type of an answer we could expect from Khrushchev and what he might do if we threatened an attack. During this discussion Secretary Rusk seemed to favor asking Congress for a declaration of a state of war against Cuba and then proceed with OAS, NATO,[1] etc., but always preserve flexibility as to the type of action. Bohlen consistently warned that world opinion would be against us if we carried out a military strike. Secretary Ball emphasized the importance of time, stating that if action was over quickly, the repercussions would not be too serious.

The Attorney General raised the question of the attitude of Turkey, Italy, Western European countries, all of which have been "under the gun" for years, and would take the position that now that the U.S. has a few missiles in their backyard, they become hysterical. This point was discussed back and forth by various people throughout both days of discussion.

Secretary McNamara made the point that missiles in Cuba had no great military consequence. . . . General Taylor supported this view in the early parts of the discussion, but in the later meetings expressed increasing concern over the importance of the missile threat from Cuba. Gilpatric supported McNamara's position. McCone doubted it, stating that McNamara's facts were not new. . . .

Bohlen and Thompson questioned the real purpose of the Soviet's actions in Cuba and seemed to feel that their acts may be in preparation for a confrontation with President Kennedy at which time they would seek to settle the entire subject [of] overseas bases as well as the Berlin question. McCone indicated this might be one of several objectives and undoubtedly would be the subject of discussion at the time of confrontation; however, McCone doubted that this was

---

[1] Rusk means to initiate consultations with the OAS and NATO.

the prime purpose of such an elaborate and expensive installation as the Soviets were going forward with in Cuba. Bohlen seemed to favor precipitating talks, and was supported by Thompson.

SecDef [McNamara] and Taylor both objected to political talks because it would give time for threatening missiles to become operational and also give the Soviets an opportunity to camouflage the missiles. McCone presented most recent photographs and indicated CIA opinion that the first missiles will be operational within one or two weeks.

Bohlen again raised the question of opening up discussions. McNamara agreed that this would be desirable but emphasized the importance of developing sequence of events which would lead to military action.

There followed an extensive discussion of the advantages and disadvantages of a military blockade, total or partial.

It was at this point that McNamara and Taylor presented their schedule of alternative military strikes, which was the subject of continual discussion in the ensuing meetings.

Dean Acheson then expressed his views as follows:

We should proceed at once with the necessary military actions and should do no talking. The Soviets will react some place. We must expect this; take the consequences and manage the situations as they evolve. We should have no consultations with Khrushchev, Castro, or our allies, but should fully alert our allies in the most persuasive manner by high level people. This would include all NATO partners, and the OAS. The President should forget about the [upcoming congressional] elections and should cancel all future campaign speeches.

As an alternate to military action, a plan was discussed involving a declaration of war and the creation of an all-out blockade. Thompson spoke strongly in favor of a blockade. General Taylor at this point indicated that he favored a blockade although in subsequent meetings he seemed inclined towards a military strike. McCone gave an intelligence estimate on the effects of a blockade, indicating its seriousness would depend upon how "hard" a blockade it turned out to be, and finally stated that the main objective of taking Cuba away from Castro had been lost and we have been overly consumed with the missile problem. McCone stated that we must all bear in mind that we have two objectives, one, disposing of the missile sites, and the other, getting rid of Castro's communism in the Western Hemisphere.

The meeting adjourned for dinner and in the evening Secretary Rusk came forward with the following plan.

The United States cannot accept operational MRBMs in Cuba. There is not much profit in preliminary exchanges with Khrushchev and Castro because the President has said that the establishment of Soviet bases and offensive weapons in the Western Hemisphere would raise serious problems and therefore on September 5th [4th] and 13th[2] the President has in effect warned both Khrushchev and Castro.

Rusk continued that more talks with Khrushchev would result in extended

[2]See Chapter 3, Documents 9 and 12.

parlays and therefore he recommended against such an approach. Rusk then proposed that we hold until the middle of next week and then follow the OD course No. 1 (52 sorties against MRBMs). Prior, we inform key allies probably on Tuesday [October 23] (Macmillan, de Gaulle, Adenauer, possibly the Turks and a few Latin American Presidents). On Wednesday, we strike with missiles and simultaneously send a message to Khrushchev, NATO, OAS, etc. We should be alert for an attack on Turkey and be prepared for the consequences in Berlin, Quemoy, Matsu, Korea, etc. Rusk made the estimate that world opinion would go along, 42 allies would go along and some neutrals would be favorable. Latin Americans must be told that we are acting in the interests of the Western Hemisphere. Rusk advocated that the first step—we take out the missiles and thus remove the immediate problem of the establishment of an offensive capability, but that we be prepared for subsequent steps. He emphasized the United States cannot accept missiles in our security interests and in view of statements made by the President and others and our various policy declarations. Bohlen continued to persist for [a] diplomatic approach but Rusk and several others were not at this point persuaded. McNamara raised innumerable questions concerning military operations.

Both Ambassador Thompson and Secretary Martin in discussing the Rusk proposal favored a blockade, coupled with a declaration of war.

General Taylor at this point spoke in favor of a military strike taking out the MRBMs and the planes as well, and was supported by McCone.

At the conclusion of the meetings, which served the purpose of airing the views of all parties responsible for giving advice to the President, the alternatives open to us were summarized by the Attorney General.[3] . . .

4. Letter from UN Ambassador Adlai E. Stevenson to President Kennedy

Fearing a nuclear catastrophe, Adlai Stevenson implores JFK to be cautious in responding to the missiles in Cuba.

Washington, October 17, 1962.

DEAR MR. PRESIDENT: I have reviewed the planning thus far and have the following comments for you:

As I have said I think your *personal* emissaries should deliver your messages to C and K.[1] There is no disagreement as to C. As to K an emissary could better

---

[3]McCone prepared this memorandum.
[1]Meaning Castro and Khrushchev.

supplement the gravity of the situation you have communicated to Gromyko.[2] And *talking* with K would afford a chance of uncovering his motives and objectives far better than correspondence thru the "usual channels."

As to your announcement, assuming it becomes imperative to say something soon, I think it would be a mistake at this time to disclose that an attack was imminent and that merely reciting the facts, emphasizing the gravity of the situation and that further steps were in process would be enough for the *first* announcement.

Because an attack would very likely result in Soviet reprisals somewhere — Turkey, Berlin, etc. — it is most important that we have as much of the world with us as possible. To start or risk starting a nuclear war is bound to be divisive at best and the judgments of history seldom coincide with the tempers of the moment.

If war comes, in the long run our case must rest on stopping while there was still time the Soviet drive to world domination, our obligations under the Inter-American system, etc. We must be prepared for the widespread reaction that if we have a missile base in Turkey and other places around the Soviet Union surely they have a right to one in Cuba. If we attack Cuba, an ally of the USSR, isn't an attack on NATO bases equally justified. One could go on and on. While the explanation of our action may be clear to us it won't be clear to many others. Moreover, if war is the consequence, the Latin American republics may well divide and some say that the U.S. is not acting with their approval and consent. Likewise unless the issue is very clear there may be sharp differences with our Western Allies who have lived so long under the same threat of Soviet attack from bases in the satellite countries[3] by the same IRBMs.

But all these considerations and obstacles to clear and universal understanding that we are neither rash, impetuous or indifferent to the fate of others are, I realize, only too familiar to you.

I know your dilemma is to strike before the Cuban sites are operational or to risk waiting until a proper groundwork of justification can be prepared. The national security must come first. *But the means adopted have such incalculable consequences that I feel you should have made it clear that the existence of nuclear missile bases anywhere is negotiable[4] before we start anything.*

Our position, then, is that we can't negotiate with a gun at our head, a gun that imperils the innocent, helpless Cuban people as much as it does the U.S., and that if they won't remove the missiles and restore the status quo ante we will have to do it ourselves — and then we will be ready to discuss bases in the context of a disarmament treaty or anything else with them. In short it is they, not the U.S., that have upset the balance and created this situation of such peril to the whole world.

I confess I have many misgivings about the proposed course of action, but to discuss them further would add little to what you already have in mind. So I will only repeat that it should be clear as a pikestaff that the U.S. was, is and will be

---

[2]A meeting between JFK and Soviet Foreign Minister Gromyko scheduled for the following day.
[3]Stevenson was mistaken on this. All Soviet missile bases, before the Cuban deployment, were in the USSR; none were located in the Soviet satellite states in Eastern Europe.
[4]The word "negotiable" is double underlined in the original document.

ready to negotiate the elimination of bases and anything else; that it is they who have upset the precarious balance in the world in arrogant disregard of your warnings—by threats against Berlin and now from Cuba—and that we have no choice except to restore that balance, i.e., blackmail and intimidation *never*, negotiation and sanity *always*.

5. Memorandum of ExComm Meeting at 11:00 a.m. on October 18, 1962

The hawkishness shown by JFK at the start of the missile crisis starts to evaporate.

Washington, October 19, 1962.

. . . Secretary Rusk then stated that developments in the last 24 hours had substantially changed his thinking. He first questioned whether it is necessary to move against Cuba, and then concluded that it was because Cuba can become a formidable military threat. He also referred to the President's recent public statements[1] and indicated a feeling that if no action was taken, we would free the Soviets to act any place they wished and at their own will. Also, Rusk stated the failure on our part to act would make our situation unmanageable elsewhere in the world. He furthermore indicated that this would be an indication of weakness which would have serious effect on our Allies. Secretary pointed out to the President that action would involve risks. We could expect counter action and the cost may be heavy. The President must expect action in Berlin, Korea and possibly against the United States itself. Rusk felt a quick strike would minimize the risk of counter action. He raised the question of solidarity of the Alliance and seemed to dismiss this question, feeling that the Alliance would hold together. Rusk stated that if we enter upon positive action, we can not say for sure what the final Soviet response will be and therefore what the final outcome will be. However he felt that the American people will accept danger and suffering if they are convinced doing so is necessary and that they have a clear conscience. The Secretary reviewed the circumstances surrounding the outbreak of World War I, World War II, and the Korean war. These factors militated in favor of consulting with Khrushchev and depending on the Rio pact.[2] This, he indicated, might have the possibility of prevention of action and settlement by political means. The other course open was the declaration of war. Rusk expressed himself in favor of leaning upon the Rio pact, but does not dismiss the alternative of

[1]On September 4 and 13. See Chapter 3, Documents 9 and 12.
[2]A 1947 security pact between the United States and Latin American countries.

a unilateral declaration of war as the ultimate action we must take. The alternate is a quick strike.

Ambassador Bohlen was not present but his views were expressed in a message which was read in which he strongly advocated diplomatic effort and stated that military action prior to this would be wrong.[3] He urged against action first and then decisive value of discussion. He also stated that limited quick military action was an illusion and that any military action would rapidly escalate into an invasion. McNamara at this point presented the alternatives referred to the previous day, stating that alternatives one and two were not conclusive and that we would have to resort to alternative 3 and in fact this would lead us ultimately into an invasion.[4]

General Taylor generally reviewed the situation stating that the Chiefs looked upon Cuba as a forward base of serious proportions, that it cannot be taken out totally by air; that the military operation would be sizeable, nevertheless necessary.

Ambassador Thompson urged that any action be preceded by a declaration of war, he strongly advocated that we institute a blockade and not resort to military action unless and until it is determined that Castro and Khrushchev refuse to reverse their activities and actually remove the missiles which are now in place.

Secretary Dillon questioned what would be accomplished by talking to Khrushchev. He pointed out that we would probably become engaged in discussions from which we could not extract ourselves and therefore our freedom of action would be frustrated. Dillon was very positive that whatever action we take should be done without consultation with Khrushchev. Rusk seemed to disagree indicating there was a possibility that Khrushchev might be persuaded to reduce his efforts but he admitted also that he might step them up as a result of discussions.

President Kennedy was non-committal, however he seemed to continually raise questions of reactions of our allies, NATO, South America, public opinion and others. Raised the question whether we should not move the [American Jupiter] missiles out of Turkey. All readily agreed they were not much use but a political question was involved. Bundy thought this a good idea either under conditions of a strike or during a preliminary talk.

McNamara discussed in some detail the effects of a strike indicating that we could expect several hundred Soviet citizens to be killed; he pointed out that all of the SAM sites were manned exclusively by Soviets and a great many Soviet technicians were working on the MRBMs and at the air fields. He agreed that we could move out of Turkey and Italy; pointed out the political complications. At this point McNamara seemed to be reconsidering his prior position of advocating military action and laid special emphasis on the fact that the price of Soviet

---

[3]Bohlen was heading for Paris, as JFK had recently appointed him ambassador to France.

[4]An apparent reference to an October 17 memorandum by CIA Director McCone, which described the three main options as (1) doing nothing, (2) blockading Cuba, and (3) carrying out an air strike on Cuba.

retaliation, whether in Berlin or elsewhere, would be very high and we would not be able to control it.

Secretary Ball throughout the conversation maintained the position that strike without warning was not acceptable and that we should not proceed without discussion with Khrushchev. President Kennedy then said that he thought at some point Khrushchev would say that if we made a move against Cuba, he would take Berlin. McNamara surmised perhaps that was the price we must pay and perhaps we'd lose Berlin anyway. There followed an exchange of view on the possibility of the Soviets taking Berlin and our prospect of retaining it.

President Kennedy rather summed up the dilemma stating that action of a type contemplated would be opposed by the alliance—on the other hand, lack of action will create disunity, lack of confidence and disintegration of our several alliances and friendly relations with countries who have confidence in us.

As a result of discussions of the "price" of a strike, there followed a long discussion of the possibilities of a blockade, the advantages of it, and manner in which it would be carried out, etc. There seemed to be differences of opinion as to whether the blockade should be total, or should only involve military equipment which would mean blockading Soviet ships. Also there were continued references to blockading ships carrying offensive weapons and there seemed to be a differentiation in the minds of some in the policy of blockading offensive weapons as contrasted to blockading all weapons.

There followed discussions as to policies the President should follow with respect to calling Congress into session, asking for a declaration of war, advising the country and authorizing action. Thompson continued to insist that we must communicate with Khrushchev. There was a discussion concerning the President's meeting with Gromyko[5] and the position he should take should the Cuban question come up. The President was advised to draw Gromyko out and it was indicated he probably would receive a flat denial that there were any offensive weapons in Cuba.

Meeting adjourned with the President requesting that we organize into two groups. One to study the advantages of what might be called a slow course of action which would involve a blockade to be followed by such further actions as appeared necessary as the situation evolved. Second would be referred to as a fast dynamic action which would involve the strike of substantial proportions with or without notice.[6]

---

[5]See Document 6.
[6]McCone prepared this memorandum.

6. Memorandum of Conversation Between President Kennedy and Foreign Minister Andrei Gromyko

In a White House meeting arranged before the missile crisis, JFK decides against informing the Soviet foreign minister that the CIA has detected missile sites in Cuba.

Washington, October 18, 1962, 5 p.m.

. . . After a discussion on Germany and Berlin, Mr. Gromyko stated he wished to set forth the Soviet position on Cuba and to voice the views of the Soviet Government with regard to US actions relating to Cuba. Continuing to read from his prepared text, he asserted that the Soviet Government stood for peaceful coexistence and was against interference by one state in the internal affairs of another state, and this also applied to relations between big and small states. This, he said, was the basic core, the credo of Soviet foreign policy, and it was not just a statement.

The President was surely fully familiar with the attitude of the Soviet Government, and of Mr. Khrushchev personally, toward recent developments and toward actions by the United States Government in relation to Cuba. For quite some time there had been an unabated anti-Cuban campaign in the United States, a campaign which was apparently backed by the United States Government. Now the United States Government wished to institute a blockade against trade with Cuba, and there had also been some talk of organized piracy under the aegis of the United States. All this could only lead to great misfortunes for mankind. The United States Government seemed to believe that the Cubans must settle their internal affairs not at their own discretion, but at the discretion of the United States. Yet Cuba belonged to Cubans and not to the United States. If this was so, why then were statements being made in the United States advocating invasion of Cuba? What did the United States want to do with Cuba?

Mr. Gromyko said he knew that the President appreciated frankness. Mr. Khrushchev's conversation with the President at Vienna[1] had been frank and therefore, with the President's permission, he himself wished to be frank, too. The situation today could not be compared to that obtaining in the middle of the 19th century. Modern times were not the same as those when colonies had been divided among colonial powers. Modern times could not be compared to those when it took weeks or months for the voice of the attacked to be heard. Statements had been made that the US was a powerful and great nation; this was true, but what kind of a nation was the USSR? Mr. Khrushchev had been favorably impressed with the President's statement at Vienna regarding the equality of forces of our two nations. Since this was so, i.e., since the USSR was also a great and strong nation, it could not stand by as a mere observer when aggression was

[1]In June 1961.

planned and when a threat of war was looming. The US Government was surely aware of the Soviet Government's attitude toward the recent call-up of 150,000 Reservists in the United States.[2] The Soviet Government believed that if both sides were for relaxation of international tensions and for solving the outstanding international problems, such demonstrations could be designed only for the purpose of increasing tensions and should therefore be avoided. If worse should come to worse and if war should occur, then surely 150,000 soldiers would be of no significance. As the President was surely aware, today was not 1812, when Napoleon had relied on the number of soldiers, sabres and rifles. Neither could today's situation be compared to 1941, when Hitler had relied on the number of tanks and guns. Today, life itself and military technology had created an entirely different situation, where it was better not to rely on arms. As to Soviet assistance to Cuba, Mr. Gromyko stated that he was instructed to make it clear, as the Soviet Government had already done, that such assistance, pursued solely for the purpose of contributing to the defense capabilities of Cuba and to the development of Cuba, toward the development of its agriculture and land amelioration, and training by Soviet specialists of Cuba nationals in handling defensive armaments were by no means offensive. If it were otherwise, the Soviet Government would have never become involved in rendering such assistance. This applied to any other country as well. Laos was a good and convincing illustration of this point.[3] If the Soviet Government had pursued a different policy, the situation in that country today would be quite different. It was quite evident that the Soviet Union and its friends had broader opportunities of influencing the situation in that country than had the United States. However, the USSR had sought an understanding on that question, since it could not go back on the basic principle of its foreign policy, which was designed to alleviate tensions, to eliminate outstanding problems and to resolve them on a peaceful basis.

Such was the position of the Soviet Government with regard to Cuba. The Soviet Government and Mr. Khrushchev personally appealed to the President and the United States Government not to allow such steps as would be incompatible with peace, with relaxation of tensions, and with United Nations Charter under which both the US and the USSR had solemnly affixed their signatures. The Soviet Government addressed its appeal to the United States on this question because both our countries were major powers and should direct their efforts only to ensuring peace.

The President said he was glad that Mr. Gromyko had referred to Laos because he believed that the Soviet policy on that problem was as Mr. Gromyko had described it. So far the Soviet Union had apparently met its obligations just as the United States had met them. However, a most serious mistake had been made last summer with respect to Cuba. The US had not pressed the Cuban problem and had attempted to push it aside although of course a number of people in this country opposed the regime now prevailing in Cuba and there were

---

[2]On September 7 Kennedy had asked permission from Congress to call up 150,000 reservists as a precautionary step in handling the situation in Berlin.

[3]The superpowers had agreed to seek a neutralist government in Laos, a country with a strong Communist presence.

many refugees coming to this country. However, there was no intention to invade Cuba. But then last July the USSR, without any communication from Mr. Khrushchev to the President, had embarked upon the policy of supplying arms to Cuba. The President said he did not know the reasons for that shift in Soviet policy, because there was no threat of invasion and he would have been glad to give appropriate assurances to that effect had Mr. Khrushchev communicated with him. Soviet arms supply had had a profound impact in the United States; Ambassador Dobrynin was surely aware of how the American people and the Congress felt on this matter. The administration had tried to calm this reaction and he, the President, had made a statement that in view of the nature of Soviet assistance to Cuba at this time coolness was required.[4] Yet, the President said, he wished to stress that Soviet actions were extremely serious and he could find no satisfactory explanation for them. The Soviet Union was surely aware of US feelings with regard to Cuba, which was only 90 miles away from the United States. The President continued that the US planned no blockade of Cuba; it was only a question of ships taking arms to Cuba not being able to stop in the United States with their return cargo. Thus a very unfortunate situation had developed. The President said he did not know where it was taking us but it was the most dangerous situation since the end of the war. The US had taken the Soviet statement concerning the nature of armaments supplied to Cuba at its face value. He, the President, had attacked last Sunday in Indianapolis a Senator who was advocating invasion, and he had stated that the Cuban problem must be kept in perspective.[5] The President reiterated that this was a dangerous situation, and said he did not know where the USSR planned to have it end.

Mr. Gromyko said that there had already been an invasion, and it was well known how it ended.[6] It was well known now, both from facts and statements, including the President's own, under what circumstances and by whom that invasion had been organized. Everyone knew that if the United States had merely lifted its little finger, Cuban émigrées [sic] and smaller Caribbean countries which had helped them would not have dared undertake any invasion.

The President interjected that he had discussed with Mr. Khrushchev the April 1, 1961, invasion and had said that it was a mistake.[7] He also pointed out he would have given assurances that there would be no further invasion, either by refugees or by US forces. But last July the Soviet Union took certain actions and the situation changed.

Mr. Gromyko continued that Cubans and the Cuban Government had before them the vital question of whether they should remain unprepared to resist attack or to take steps to defend their country. He said he wished to reiterate that the Soviet Union had responded to appeals for assistance only because that assistance pursued the sole objective of giving bread to Cuba and preventing

[4]Either JFK's September 4 or 13 statement.
[5]A reference to Senator Homer E. Capehart of Indiana.
[6]An obvious reference to the Bay of Pigs invasion.
[7]JFK or Alexander Akalovsky, the president's interpreter who drafted this memorandum on October 21, meant April 15 or perhaps April 17. The discussion with Khrushchev of which JFK talks took place at the Vienna summit meeting.

hunger in that country; also, as far as armaments were concerned, Soviet specialists were training Cubans in handling certain types of armaments which were only defensive—and he wished to stress the word defensive—in character, and thus such training could not constitute a threat to the United States. He reiterated that if it were otherwise the Soviet Union would never have agreed to render such assistance.

The President said that in order to be clear on this Cuban problem he wanted to state the following: The US had no intention of invading Cuba. Introduction last July of intensive armaments had complicated the situation and created grave danger. His own actions had been to prevent, unless US security was endangered, anything from being done that might provoke the danger of war. The President then read a portion of his September 4 statement on Cuba[8] and stated that this had been US position and policy on this question. He noted that the Attorney General had discussed the Cuban situation with Ambassador Dobrynin so that the latter must be aware of what it was. The President again recalled his Indianapolis speech of last Sunday and said that we were basing our present attitude on facts as they had been described by Mr. Gromyko; our presumption was that the armaments supplied by USSR were defensive.

Mr. Gromyko stated the Soviet Union proceeded from the assumption that on the basis of Soviet Government's statements and his own today the US Government and the President had a clear idea of the Soviet policy on this matter and of the Soviet evaluation of US action in relation to Cuba. He said he had nothing to add to what he had already said.

7. Record of ExComm Meeting Drafted by the State Department's Deputy Legal Adviser Leonard C. Meeker

With JFK again on the campaign trail, Robert Kennedy urges other officials to support the idea of a naval blockade of Cuba rather than a military attack on the island. By this point his impassioned arguments are beginning to prevail.

Washington, October 19, 1962, 11 a.m.

. . . There followed a discussion covering the meeting held the night before with the President. One participant looked back on the meeting as having arrived at a tentative conclusion to institute a blockade, and thought the President

[8]See Chapter 3, Document 9.

had been satisfied at the consensus by then arrived at among his advisers. General Taylor quickly indicated that he had not concurred and that the Joint Chiefs had reserved their position.

Mr. [McGeorge] Bundy then said that he had reflected a good deal upon the situation in the course of a sleepless night, and he doubted whether the strategy group was serving the President as well as it might, if it merely recommended a blockade. He had spoken with the President this morning, and he felt there was further work to be done. A blockade would not remove the missiles. Its effects were uncertain and in any event would be slow to be felt. Something more would be needed to get the missiles out of Cuba. This would be made more difficult by the prior publicity of a blockade and the consequent pressures from the United Nations for a negotiated settlement. An air strike would be quick and would take out the bases in a clean surgical operation. He favored decisive action with its advantages of surprises and confronting the world with a fait accompli.

Secretary Rusk asked Mr. Acheson for his views. Mr. Acheson said that Khrushchev had presented the United States with a direct challenge, we were involved in a test of wills, and the sooner we got to a showdown the better. He favored cleaning the missile bases out decisively with an air strike. There was something else to remember. This wasn't just another instance of Soviet missiles aimed at the United States. Here they were in the hands of a madman[1] whose actions would be perfectly irresponsible; the usual restraints operating on the Soviets would not apply. We had better act, and act quickly. . . .

Secretary Dillon said he agreed there should be a quick air strike. Mr. McCone was of the same opinion.

General Taylor said that a decision now to impose a blockade was a decision to abandon the possibility of an air strike. A strike would be feasible for only a few more days; after that the missiles would be operational. Thus it was now or never for an air strike. He favored a strike. If it were to take place Sunday morning,[2] a decision would have to be made at once so that the necessary preparations could be ordered. For a Monday morning strike, a decision would have to be reached tomorrow. Forty-eight hours' notice was required.

Secretary McNamara said that he would give orders for the necessary military dispositions, so that if the decision were for a strike the Air Force would be ready. He did not, however, advocate an air strike, and favored the alternative of blockade.

Under Secretary Ball said that he was a waverer between the two courses of action.

The Attorney General said with a grin that he too had had a talk with the President, indeed very recently this morning. There seemed to be three main possibilities as the Attorney General analyzed the situation: one was to do nothing, and that would be unthinkable; another was an air strike; the third was a blockade. He thought it would be very, very difficult indeed for the President if

[1]A reference to Castro.
[2]October 21.

the decision were to be for an air strike, with all the memory of Pearl Harbor and with all the implications this would have for us in whatever world there would be afterward. For 175 years we had not been that kind of country. A sneak attack was not in our traditions. Thousands of Cubans would be killed without warning, and a lot of Russians too. He favored *action*, to make known unmistakably the seriousness of United States determination to get the missiles out of Cuba, but he thought the action should allow the Soviets some room for maneuver to pull back from their over-extended position in Cuba.

Mr. Bundy, addressing himself to the Attorney General, said this was very well but a blockade would not eliminate the bases; an air strike would.

I asked at this point: who would be expected to be the government of Cuba after an air strike? Would it be anyone other than Castro? If not, would anything be solved, and would we not be in a worse situation than before? After a pause, Mr. Martin replied that, of course, a good deal might be different after a strike, and Castro might be toppled in the aftermath. Others expressed the view that we might have to proceed with invasion following a strike. Still another suggestion was that US armed forces seize the base areas alone in order to eliminate the missiles. Secretary McNamara thought this a very unattractive kind of undertaking from the military point of view.

Toward one o'clock Secretary Rusk said he thought this group could not make the decision as to what was to be done; that was for the President in consultation with his constitutional advisers. The Secretary thought the group's duty was to present to the President, for his consideration, fully staffed-out alternatives. Accordingly, two working groups should be formed, one to work up the blockade alternative and the other to work up air strike. Mr. [Alexis] Johnson was designated to head the former, and Mr. Bundy the latter. Mr. Johnson was to have with him Ambassador Thompson, Deputy Secretary Gilpatric, Mr. Martin, Mr. Nitze, and Mr. Meeker. Mr. Bundy was to have Secretary Dillon, Mr. Acheson, and General Taylor. . . .

Mr. Sorensen commented that he thought he had absorbed enough to start on the draft of a speech for the President. There was some inconclusive discussion on the timing of such a speech, on the danger of leaks before then, and on the proper time for meeting with the President once more, in view of his current Western campaign trip.[3]

Before the whole group dispersed, Ambassador Thompson said the Soviets attached importance to questions of legality and we should be able to present a strong legal case. The Attorney General, as he was about to leave the room, said he thought there was ample legal basis for a blockade. I said: yes, that is so provided the Organ of Consultation under the Rio Treaty adopted an appropriate resolution. The Attorney General said: "That's all political; it's not legal." . . .

The two groups met separately until four o'clock. They then reconvened and were joined once more by the cabinet officers who had been away in the earlier afternoon.

[3]On October 19 JFK had left for Ohio and Illinois, as scheduled, to campaign for Democrats running for Congress.

The Johnson group scenario, which was more nearly complete and was ready earlier, was discussed first. Numerous criticisms were advanced. Some were answered; others led to changes. There was again a discussion of timing, now in relation to a Presidential radio address. Mr. Martin thought Sunday might be too early, as it would be virtually impossible to get to all the Latin American heads of state on Sunday. Ambassador Thompson made the point that 24 hours must be allowed to elapse between announcement of the blockade and enforcement, so as to give the Soviet Government time to get instructions to their ship captains.

Approximately two hours were spent on the Johnson scenario. About 6 o'-clock the Bundy approach was taken up, its author saying, "It's been much more fun for us up to this point, since we've had a chance to poke holes in the blockade plan; now the roles will be reversed." Not much more than half an hour was spent on the Bundy scenario.

More than once during the afternoon Secretary McNamara voiced the opinion that the US would have to pay a price to get the Soviet missiles out of Cuba. He thought we would at least have to give up our missile bases in Italy and Turkey and would probably have to pay more besides. At different times the possibility of nuclear conflict breaking out was referred to. The point was made that, once the Cuban missile installations were complete and operational, a new strategic situation would exist, with the United States more directly and immediately under the gun than ever before. A striking Soviet military push into the Western Hemisphere would have succeeded and become effective. The clock could not be turned back, and things would never be the same again. During this discussion, the Attorney General said that in looking forward into the future it would be better for our children and grandchildren if we decided to face the Soviet threat, stand up to it, and eliminate it, now. The circumstances for doing so at some future time were bound to be more unfavorable, the risks would be greater, the chances of success less good.

Secretary Rusk, toward the end of the afternoon, stated his approach to the problem as follows: the US needed to move in a way such that a planned action would be followed by a pause in which the great powers could step back from the brink and have time to consider and work out a solution rather than be drawn inexorably from one action to another and escalate into general nuclear war. The implication of his statement was that he favored blockade rather than strike.

In the course of the afternoon discussion, the military representatives, especially Secretary McNamara, came to expressing [sic] the view that an air strike could be made some time after the blockade was instituted in the event the blockade did not produce results as to the missile bases in Cuba. The Attorney General took particular note of this shift, and toward the end of the day made clear that he firmly favored blockade as the first step; other steps subsequently were not precluded and could be considered; he thought it was now pretty clear what the decision should be.

At about six-thirty Governor Stevenson came into the room. After a few minutes, Secretary Rusk asked him if he had some views on the question of what to do. He replied: "Yes, most emphatic views." When queried as to them, he said that in view of the course the discussion was taking he didn't think it was necessary to express them then. When asked: "But you are in favor of blockade, aren't you?", he answered affirmatively. He went on to say he thought we must look beyond the particular immediate action of blockade; we need to develop a plan for solution of the problem—elements for negotiation designed to settle the current crisis in a stable and satisfactory way and enable us to move forward on wider problems; he was working on some ideas for a settlement. One possibility would be the demilitarization of Cuba under effective international supervision, perhaps accompanied by neutralization of the island under international guaranties [sic] and with UN observers to monitor compliance.

Once again there was discussion of when another meeting with the President should be held. It was generally agreed that the President should continue on his trip until Sunday morning. He would be reachable by telephone prior to that time.

8. Minutes of ExComm Meeting

Returning from Chicago, JFK holds a crucial meeting with his ExComm advisers. They decide to proceed with a blockade but also to advance preparations for an air strike in case the quarantine has no impact on the Soviets. This meeting is famous for the vain attempt by Adlai Stevenson to persuade JFK to try not only the blockade but also diplomatic concessions to Khrushchev.

Washington, October 20, 1962, 2:30–5:10 p.m.

. . . The first twenty minutes were spent in the presentation and discussion of photographic intelligence establishing the presence in Cuba of Soviet intermediate-range and medium-range missiles, mobile missile launchers and missile sites. . . .

In summary, the Council was informed that sixteen SS–4 missiles, with a range of 1020 nautical miles were now operational in Cuba and could be fired approximately eighteen hours after a decision to fire was taken. The bearing of these launchers was 315 degrees, i.e. toward the central area of the United States.

The President summarized the discussion of the intelligence material as follows. There is something to destroy in Cuba now and, if it is destroyed, a strategic missile capability would be difficult to restore. . . .

Secretary McNamara explained to the President that there were differences among his advisers which had resulted in the drafting of alternative courses of action. He added that the military planners are at work on measures to carry out all recommended courses of action in order that, following a Presidential decision, fast action could be taken.

Secretary McNamara described his view as the "blockade route." This route is aimed at preventing any addition to the strategic missiles already deployed to Cuba and eventually to eliminate these missiles. He said to do this we should institute a blockade of Cuba and be prepared to take armed action in specified instances.

(The President was handed a copy of Ted Sorensen's "blockade route" draft of a Presidential message, which he read.)

Secretary McNamara concluded by explaining that following the blockade, the United States would negotiate for the removal of the strategic missiles from Cuba. He said we would have to be prepared to accept the withdrawal of United States strategic missiles from Turkey and Italy and possibly agreement to limit our use of Guantanamo to a specified limited time. He added that we could obtain the removal of the missiles from Cuba only if we were prepared to offer something in return during negotiations. He opposed as too risky the suggestion that we should issue an ultimatum to the effect that we would order an air attack on Cuba if the missiles were not removed. He said he was prepared to tell Khrushchev we consider the missiles in Cuba as Soviet missiles and that if they were used against us, we would retaliate by launching missiles against the USSR.

Secretary McNamara pointed out that SNIE 11–19–62,[1] dated October 20, 1962, estimates that the Russians will not use force to push their ships through our blockade. He cited Ambassador Bohlen's view that the USSR would not take military action, but would limit its reaction to political measures in the United Nations.

Secretary McNamara listed the disadvantages of the blockade route as follows:

1. It would take a long time to achieve the objective of eliminating strategic missiles from Cuba.

2. It would result in serious political trouble in the United States.

3. The world position of the United States might appear to be weakening.

The advantages which Secretary McNamara cited are:

1. It would cause us the least trouble with our allies.

2. It avoids any surprise air attack on Cuba, which is contrary to our tradition.

3. It is the only military course of action compatible with our position as a leader of the free world.

4. It avoids a sudden military move which might provoke a response from the USSR which could result in escalating actions leading to general war.

The President pointed out that during a blockade, more missiles would become operational, and upon the completion of sites and launching pads, the threat would increase. He asked General Taylor how many missiles we could destroy by air action on Monday [October 22].

General Taylor reported that the Joint Chiefs of Staff favor an air strike on

---

[1] A special national intelligence estimate that updated an October 19 intelligence estimate regarding Cuba.

Tuesday when United States forces could be in a state of readiness. He said he did not share Secretary McNamara's fear that if we used nuclear weapons in Cuba, nuclear weapons would be used against us.

Secretary Rusk asked General Taylor whether we dared to attack operational strategic missile sites in Cuba.

General Taylor responded that the risk of these missiles being used against us was less than if we permitted the missiles to remain there.

The President pointed out that on the basis of the intelligence estimate there would be some fifty strategic missiles operational in mid-December, if we went the blockade route and took no action to destroy the sites being developed.

General Taylor said that the principal argument he wished to make was that now was the time to act because this would be the last chance we would have to destroy these missiles. If we did not act now, the missiles would be camouflaged in such a way as to make it impossible for us to find them. Therefore, if they were not destroyed, we would have to live with them with all the consequent problems for the defense of the United States.

The President agreed that the missile threat became worse each day, adding that we might wish, looking back, that we had done earlier what we are now preparing to do.

Secretary Rusk said that a blockade would seriously affect the Cuban missile capability in that the Soviets would be unable to deploy to Cuba any missiles in addition to those now there. . . .

The President asked whether the institution of a blockade would appear to the free world as a strong response to the Soviet action. He is particularly concerned about whether the Latin American countries would think that the blockade was an appropriate response to the Soviet challenge.

The Attorney General returned to the point made by General Taylor, i.e. that now is the last chance we will have to destroy Castro and the Soviet missiles deployed in Cuba.

Mr. Sorensen said he did not agree with the Attorney General or with General Taylor that this was our last chance. He said a missile buildup would end if, as everyone seemed to agree, the Russians would not use force to penetrate the United States blockade.

Mr. [McGeorge] Bundy handed to the President the "air strike alternative," which the President read. It was also referred to as the Bundy plan.

The Attorney General told the President that this plan was supported by Mr. Bundy, General Taylor, the Joint Chiefs of Staff, and with minor variations, by Secretary Dillon and Director McCone.

General Taylor emphasized the opportunity available now to take out not only all the missiles, but all the Soviet medium bombers (IL–28) which were neatly lined up in the open on airbases in Cuba. . . .

Mr. McNamara cautioned that an air strike would not destroy all the missiles and launchers in Cuba, and, at best, we could knock out two-thirds of these missiles. Those missiles not destroyed could be fired from mobile launchers not destroyed. . . .

The President stated flatly that the Soviet planes in Cuba did not concern

him particularly. He said we must be prepared to live with the Soviet threat as represented by Soviet bombers. However, the existence of strategic missiles in Cuba had an entirely different impact throughout Latin America. In his view the existence of fifty planes in Cuba did not affect the balance of power, but the missiles already in Cuba were an entirely different matter.

The Attorney General said that in his opinion a combination of the blockade route and the air strike route was very attractive to him. He felt we should first institute the blockade. In the event that the Soviets continued to build up the missile capability in Cuba, then we should inform the Russians that we would destroy the missiles, the launchers, and the missile sites. He said he favored a short wait during which time the Russians could react to the blockade. If the Russians did not halt the development of the missile capability, then we would proceed to make an air strike. The advantage of proceeding in this way, he added, was that we would get away from the Pearl Harbor surprise attack aspect of the air strike route.

Mr. Bundy pointed out that there was a risk that we would act in such a way as to get Khrushchev to commit himself fully to the support of Castro.

Secretary Rusk doubted that a delay of twenty-four hours in initiating an air strike was of any value. He said he now favored proceeding on the blockade track.

Secretary Dillon mentioned seventy-two hours as the time between instituting the blockade and initiating an air strike in the event we receive no response to our initial action.

Director McCone stated his opposition to an air strike, but admitted that in his view a blockade was not enough. He argued that we should institute the blockade and tell the Russians that if the missiles were not dismantled within seventy-two hours, the United States would destroy the missiles by air attack. He called attention to the risk involved in a long drawn-out period during which the Cubans could, at will, launch the missiles against the United States. Secretary Dillon said that the existence of strategic missiles in Cuba was, in his opinion, not negotiable. He believed that any effort to negotiate the removal of the missiles would involve a price so high that the United States could not accept it. If the missiles are not removed or eliminated, he continued, the United States will lose all of its friends in Latin America, who will become convinced that our fear is such that we cannot act. He admitted that the limited use of force involved in a blockade would make the military task much harder and would involve the great danger of the launching of these missiles by the Cubans.

Deputy Secretary Gilpatric saw the choice as involving the use of limited force or of unlimited force. He was prepared to face the prospect of an air strike against Cuba later, but he opposed the initial use of all-out military force such as a surprise air attack. He defined a blockade as being the application of the limited use of force and doubted that such limited use could be combined with an air strike.

General Taylor argued that a blockade would not solve our problem or end the Cuban missile threat. He said that eventually we would have to use military force and, if we waited, the use of military force would be much more costly.

Secretary McNamara noted that the air strike planned by the Joint Chiefs involved 800 sorties. Such a strike would result in several thousand Russians being killed, chaos in Cuba, and efforts to overthrow the Castro government. In his view the probability was high that an air strike would lead inevitably to an invasion. He doubted that the Soviets would take an air strike on Cuba without resorting to a very major response. In such an event, the United States would lose control of the situation which could escalate to general war.

The President agreed that a United States air strike would lead to a major Soviet response, such as blockading Berlin. He agreed that at an appropriate time we would have to acknowledge that we were willing to take strategic missiles out of Turkey and Italy if this issue was raised by the Russians. He felt that implementation of a blockade would also result in Soviet reprisals, possibly the blockade of Berlin. If we instituted a blockade on Sunday,[2] then by Monday or Tuesday we would know whether the missile development had ceased or whether it was continuing. Thus, we would be in a better position to know what move to make next.

Secretary Dillon called attention to the fact that even if the Russians agreed to dismantle the missiles now in Cuba, continuing inspection would be required to ensure that the missiles were not again made ready.

The President said that if it was decided to go the Bundy route, he would favor an air strike which would destroy only missiles. He repeated this view that we would have to live with the threat arising out of the stationing in Cuba of Soviet bombers.

Secretary Rusk referred to an air strike as chapter two. He did not think we should initiate such a strike because of the risk of escalating actions leading to general war. He doubted that we should act without consultation of our allies. He said a sudden air strike had no support in the law or morality, and, therefore, must be ruled out. Reading from notes, he urged that we start the blockade and only go on to an air attack when we knew the reaction of the Russians and of our allies. . . .

The President asked what we would say to those whose reaction to our instituting a blockade now would be to ask why we had not blockaded last July.

Both Mr. Sorensen and Mr. Ball made the point that we did not institute a blockade in July because we did not then know of the existence of the strategic missiles in Cuba.

Secretary Rusk suggested that our objective was an immediate freeze of the strategic missile capability in Cuba to be inspected by United Nations observation teams stationed at the missile sites. He referred to our bases in Turkey, Spain and Greece as being involved in any negotiation covering foreign bases. He said a United Nations group might be sent to Cuba to reassure those who might fear that the United States was planning an invasion.

Ambassador Stevenson stated his flat opposition to a surprise air strike, which he felt would ultimately lead to a United States invasion of Cuba. He supported the institution of the blockade and predicted that such action would reduce the

[2]The following day.

chance of Soviet retaliation of a nature which would inevitably escalate. In his view our aim is to end the existing missile threat in Cuba without casualties and without escalation. He urged that we offer the Russians a settlement involving the withdrawal of our missiles from Turkey and our evacuation of Guantanamo base.

The President sharply rejected the thought of surrendering our base at Guantanamo in the present situation. He felt that such action would convey to the world that we had been frightened into abandoning our position. He was not opposed to discussing withdrawal of our missiles from Turkey and Greece,[3] but he was firm in saying we should only make such a proposal in the future.

The Attorney General thought we should convey our firm intentions to the Russians clearly and suggested that we might tell the Russians that we were turning over nuclear weapons and missiles to the West Germans.

Ambassador Thompson stated his view that our first action should be the institution of a blockade. Following this, he thought we should launch an air strike to destroy the missiles and sites, after giving sufficient warning so that Russian nationals could leave the area to be attacked.

The President said he was ready to go ahead with the blockade and to take actions necessary to put us in a position to undertake an air strike on the missiles and missile sites by Monday or Tuesday.

General Taylor summarized the military actions already under way, including the quiet reinforcement of Guantanamo by infiltrating marines and the positioning of ships to take out United States dependents from Guantanamo on extremely short notice.

The Attorney General said we could implement a blockade very quickly and prepare for an air strike to be launched later if we so decided.

The President said he was prepared to authorize the military to take those preparatory actions which they would have to take in anticipation of the military invasion of Cuba. He suggested that we inform the Turks and the Italians that they should not fire the strategic missiles they have even if attacked. The warheads for missiles in Turkey and Italy could be dismantled. He agreed that we should move to institute a blockade as quickly as we possibly can.

In response to a question about further photographic surveillance of Cuba, Secretary McNamara recommended, and the President agreed, that no low level photographic reconnaissance should be undertaken now because we have decided to institute a blockade.

Secretary Rusk recommended that a blockade not be instituted before Monday in order to provide time required to consult our allies.

Mr. Bundy said the pressure from the press was becoming intense and suggested that one way of dealing with it was to announce shortly that we had obtained photographic evidence of the existence of strategic missiles in Cuba. This announcement would hold the press until the President made his television speech.

The President acknowledged that the domestic political heat following his television appearance would be terrific. He said he had opposed an invasion of

[3]JFK or the unknown drafter of these minutes might have meant Italy instead of Greece.

Cuba but that now we were confronted with the possibility that by December there would be fifty strategic missiles deployed there. In explanation as to why we have not acted sooner to deal with the threat from Cuba, he pointed out that only now do we have the kind of evidence which we can make available to our allies in order to convince them of the necessity of acting. Only now do we have a way of avoiding a split with our allies.

It is possible that we may have to make an early strike with or without warning next week. He stressed again the difference between the conventional military buildup in Cuba and the psychological impact throughout the world of the Russian deployment of strategic missiles to Cuba. General Taylor repeated his recommendation that any air strike in Cuba included attacks on the MIGs and medium bombers.

The President repeated his view that our world position would be much better if we attack only the missiles. He directed that air strike plans include only missiles and missile sites, preparations to be ready three days from now.

Under Secretary Ball expressed his view that a blockade should include all shipments of POL to Cuba. Secretary Rusk thought that POL should not now be included because such a decision would break down the distinction which we want to make between elimination of strategic missiles and the downfall of the Castro government. Secretary Rusk repeated his view that our objective is to destroy the offensive capability of the missiles in Cuba, not, at this time, seeking to overthrow Castro!

The President acknowledged that the issue was whether POL should be included from the beginning or added at a later time. He preferred to delay possibly as long as a week.

Secretary Rusk called attention to the problem involved in referring to our action as a blockade.[4] He preferred the use of the word "quarantine."

Parenthetically, the President asked Secretary Rusk to reconsider present policy of refusing to give nuclear weapons assistance to France. He expressed the view that in light of present circumstances a refusal to help the French was not worthwhile. He thought that in the days ahead we might be able to gain the needed support of France if we stopped refusing to help them with their nuclear weapons project. . . .

The President made clear that in the United Nations we should emphasize the subterranean nature of the missile buildup in Cuba. Only if we were asked would we respond that we were prepared to talk about the withdrawal of missiles from Italy and Turkey. In such an eventuality, the President pointed out that we would have to make clear to the Italians and the Turks that withdrawing strategic missiles was not a retreat and that we would be prepared to replace these missiles by providing a more effective deterrent, such as the assignment of Polaris submarines. The President asked Mr. Nitze to study the problems arising out of the withdrawal of missiles from Italy and Turkey, with particular reference to complications which would arise in NATO. The President made clear that our emphasis should be on the missile threat from Cuba.

Ambassador Stevenson reiterated his belief that we must be more forthcom-

[4]The problem was that, technically, blockade was an act of war.

ing about giving up our missile bases in Turkey and Italy. He stated again his belief that the present situation required that we offer to give up such bases in order to induce the Russians to remove the strategic missiles from Cuba.

Mr. Nitze flatly opposed making any such offer, but said he would not object to discussing this question in the event that negotiations developed from our institution of a blockade.

The President concluded the meeting by stating that we should be ready to meet criticism of our deployment of missiles abroad but we should not initiate negotiations with a base withdrawal proposal.

9. Notes on Meeting with President Kennedy

General Walter Sweeney, commander-in-chief of the Tactical Air Command, tells JFK that no air strike will destroy all the missiles in Cuba. Hence the Soviets could respond with a nuclear attack on the United States from Cuba whether the president chooses a blockade of Cuba or an air strike on the Soviet missile sites. This information strengthens JFK's resolve to implement a blockade.

Washington, October 21, 1962.

1. The meeting was held in the Oval Room at the White House and lasted from 11:30 a.m. to approximately 12:30 p.m. In attendance were the Attorney General [Robert Kennedy], General Taylor, General Sweeney and the Secretary of Defense [McNamara]. [McCone joined later.] . . .

5. General Sweeney outlined the following plan of air attack, the object of which would be the destruction of the known Cuban missile capability.

a. The 5 surface-to-air missile installations in the vicinity of the known missile sites would each be attacked by approximately 8 aircraft; the 3 MIG airfields defending the missile sites would be covered by 12 U.S. aircraft per field. In total, the defense suppression operations, including the necessary replacement aircraft, would require approximately 100 sorties.

b. Each of the launchers at the 8 or 9 known sites (a total of approximately 32 to 36 launchers) would be attacked by 6 aircraft. For the purpose, a total of approximately 250 sorties would be flown.

c. The U.S. aircraft covering the 3 MIG airfields would attack the MIG's if they became airborne. General Sweeney strongly recommended attacks on each of the airfields to destroy the MIG aircraft.

6. General Sweeney stated that he was certain the air strike would be "successful"; however, even under optimum conditions, it was not likely that all of

the known missiles would be destroyed. (The known missiles are probably no more than 60% of the total missiles on the Island.) General Taylor stated, "The best we can offer you is to destroy 90% of the known missiles." General Taylor, General Sweeney and the Secretary of Defense all strongly emphasized that in their opinion the initial air strike must be followed by strikes on subsequent days and that these in turn would lead inevitably to an invasion. . . .

8. General Sweeney strongly recommended that any air strike include attacks on the MIG aircraft and, in addition, the IL–28s. To accomplish the destruction of these aircraft, the total number of sorties of such an air strike should be increased to 500. The President agreed that if an air strike is ordered, it should probably include in its objective the destruction of the MIG aircraft and the IL–28s.

9. The President directed that we be prepared to carry out the air strike Monday[1] morning or any time thereafter during the remainder of the week. The President recognized that the Secretary of Defense was opposed to the air strike Monday morning, and that General Sweeney favored it. He asked the Attorney General and Mr. McCone for their opinions:

a. The Attorney General stated he was opposed to such a strike because:

(1) "It would be a Pearl Harbor type of attack."

(2) It would lead to unpredictable military responses by the Soviet Union which could be so serious as to lead to general nuclear war.

He stated we should start with the initiation of the blockade and thereafter "play for the breaks."

b. Mr. McCone agreed with the Attorney General, but emphasized he believed we should be prepared for an air strike and thereafter an invasion.[2]

10. Minutes of ExComm Meeting

As they discuss the draft for a presidential address to the nation, JFK and his advisers touch on a cluster of issues: the concessions that may ultimately need to be made to the Russians, the feasibility of a summit meeting, preparations for any military action that may be authorized, and related matters.

Washington, October 21, 1962, 2:30–4:50 p.m.

. . . *Substantial Issues in a Draft Presidential Speech*
The Council members read the third draft of the President's speech.[1] . . .

[1]October 22.
[2]McNamara made these notes.
[1]Written by Theodore Sorensen.

The Attorney General wanted to be certain that the text as drafted did not preclude us from giving nuclear weapons to Western Germany, West Berlin, and France in the event we decided to do so. . . . .

The question of whether our actions should be described as a blockade or a quarantine was debated. Although the legal meaning of the two words is identical, Secretary Rusk said he preferred "quarantine" for political reasons in that it avoids comparison with the [1948] Berlin blockade [by the Russians]. The President agreed to use "quarantine" and pointed out that if we so desired we could later institute a total blockade. . . . .

Secretary Rusk commented that our objective was to "put out the fire" in Cuba and get United Nations teams to inspect all missile activity in Cuba. The President felt that a better tactic was for us initially to frighten the United Nations representatives with the prospect of all kinds of actions and then, when a resolution calling for the withdrawal of missiles from Cuba, Turkey and Italy was proposed, we could consider supporting such a resolution.

Ambassador Stevenson said we should take the initiative by calling a U.N. Security Council meeting to demand an immediate missile standstill in Cuba.

The President agreed that the [idea of an] invitation to a summit meeting should be deleted [from the draft of his speech].

Ambassador Stevenson repeated that he favored an early conference with the Russians on terms acceptable to us, to be held in an atmosphere free of threat. The President responded that he did not want to appear to be seeking a summit meeting as a result of Khrushchev's actions. Ambassador Thompson agreed. The President added that we should not look toward holding a meeting until it is clear to us what Khrushchev really thinks he will obtain worldwide as a result of his actions in Cuba.

Secretary Rusk said our first objective was to get a fully inspected missile standstill in Cuba before we sit down to talk with the Russians. Mr. McCone was concerned that if we let it be known that we are prepared to talk to the Russians now, it would appear to outsiders that our only response to Khrushchev's challenge was to negotiate.

The Attorney General said that in his view we should anticipate a Soviet reaction involving a movement in Berlin. Secretary Dillon felt that the Soviet reaction in Berlin would be governed by the actions we would take in response to the Russian missile deployment in Cuba. . . . .

In response to a Presidential question, General Taylor said an invasion of Cuba could be carried out seven days after the decision to invade had been taken. Secretary McNamara said the President had asked a question which was difficult to answer precisely. Present plans called for invasion to follow seven days after an initial air strike. The timing could be reduced, depending upon whether certain decisions were taken now. Some actions which were irreversible would have to be taken now in order to reduce the time when forces could be landed. He promised the President a breakdown of the decisions which he would have to take immediately in order to reduce the seven-day period.

The President said that in three or four days we might have to decide to act in order that we would not have to wait so long prior to the landing of our forces.

As he understood the situation, a decision taken today would mean that an air strike could not be undertaken before seven days, and then seven days later the first forces could be ashore. . . .

The President told General Taylor that he wanted to do those things which would reduce the length of time between a decision to invade and the landing of the first troops.

The President said that as soon as he had finished his speech, the Russians would: (a) hasten the construction and the development of their missile capability in Cuba, (b) announce that if we attack Cuba, Soviet rockets will fly, and (c) possibly make a move to squeeze us out of Berlin.

Secretary Dillon said that in his view a blockade would either inevitably lead to an invasion of Cuba or would result in negotiations, which he believes the Soviets would want very much. To agree to negotiations now would be a disaster for us. We would break up our alliances and convey to the world that we were impotent in the face of a Soviet challenge. Unless the Russians stop their missile buildup at once, we will have to invade Cuba in the next week, no matter what they say, if we are to save our world position. We cannot convey firm intentions to the Russians otherwise and we must not look to the world as if we were backing down.

Secretary McNamara expressed his doubt that an air strike would be necessary within the next week.

Admiral Anderson described, in response to the President's question, the way the blockade would be instituted. . . .

Diplomatic Measures . . .

The President asked Assistant Secretary of Defense Nitze to study the problem of withdrawing United States missiles from Turkey and Italy. Mr. Nitze said such a withdrawal was complicated because we must avoid giving the Europeans the impression that we are prepared to take nuclear weapons of all kinds out of Europe.

Secretary McNamara stated his firm view that the United States could not lift its blockade as long as the Soviet weapons remained in Cuba.

The President asked why we could not start with a demand for the removal or the withdrawal of the missiles [from Cuba] and if at a later time we wanted to negotiate for a less favorable settlement, we could then decide to do so. The Attorney General said we should take the offensive in our presentation to the United Nations. Our attitude should not be defensive, especially in view of the fact that Soviet leaders had lied to us about the deployment of strategic missiles to Cuba.

The President interjected a directive that we reverse our policy on nuclear assistance to France in the light of the present situation.

Ambassador Stevenson repeated his view that the United States would be forced into a summit meeting and preferred to propose such a meeting.

The President disagreed, saying that we could not accept a neutral Cuba and the withdrawal from Guantanamo without indicating to Khrushchev that we were in a state of panic. An offer to accept Castro and give up Guantanamo must not be made because it would appear to be completely defensive. He said we should be clear that we would accept nothing less than the ending of the missile capability now in Cuba, no reinforcement of that capability, and no further construction of missile sites.

Secretary McNamara stated his view that in order to achieve such a result we would have to invade Cuba.

The President said what he was talking about was the dismantlement of missiles now in Cuba.

Ambassador Stevenson thought that we should institute a blockade, and when the Russians rejected our demand for a missile standstill in Cuba, we should defer any air strike until after we had talked to Khrushchev. . . .

[JFK] requested that reference to a meeting with Khrushchev be deleted from the draft letter [then being prepared for dispatch to the Soviet leader].

11. Minutes of ExComm Meeting

JFK explains his reasons for selecting the blockade option instead of an air strike.

Washington, October 22, 1962, 3 p.m.

. . . The President discussed the reasons why he had decided against an air strike now. First, there was no certainty that an air strike would destroy all missiles now in Cuba. We would be able to get a large percentage of these missiles, but could not get them all.

In addition we would not know if any of these missiles were operationally ready with their nuclear warheads and we were not certain that our intelligence had discovered all the missiles in Cuba. Therefore, in attacking the ones we had located, we could not be certain that others unknown to us would not be launched against the United States. The President said an air strike would involve an action comparable to the Japanese attack on Pearl Harbor. Finally, an air strike would increase the danger of a worldwide nuclear war.

The President said he had given up the thought of making an air strike only yesterday morning. In summary, he said an air strike had all the disadvantages of Pearl Harbor. It would not insure the destruction of every strategic missile in Cuba, and would up end eventually in our having to invade. . . .

12. Memorandum of Meeting Between President Kennedy and the Congressional Leadership on October 22

Shortly before his address to the nation, the president attempts to win the support of congressional leaders for his blockade strategy. It proved to be a hard sell.

Washington, October 24, 1962.

SUBJECT

Leadership meeting on October 22nd at 5:00 p.m.

ATTENDED BY

The [Congressional] Leadership, except for Senator Hayden,
The President, Rusk, McNamara, McCone and Ambassador Thompson

. . . The President reviewed the chronology of the situation, starting on Tuesday, October 16th, when the first information was received from the photographic flight of October 14th. He stated that he immediately ordered extensive overflights; that McCone briefed President Eisenhower;[1] that we must recognize that these missiles might be operational and therefore military action on our part might cause the firing of many of them with serious consequences to the United States; furthermore the actions taken, and further actions which might be required, might cause the Soviets to react in various areas, most particularly Berlin, which they could easily grab and if they do, our European Allies would lay the blame in our lap. The President concluded whatever we do involves a risk; however we must make careful calculations and take a chance. To do nothing would be a great mistake. The blockade of Cuba on the importation of offensive weapons was to be undertaken, all ships would be stopped and those containing offensive weapons would not be permitted to proceed. We have no idea how the [Soviet] Bloc will react but the indications are, from unconfirmed sources, they will attempt to run the blockade. Initially the blockade would not extend to petroleum. This might be a further step. We are taking all military preparations for either an air strike or an invasion. It was the President's considered judgment that if we have to resort to active military actions, then this would involve an invasion. Rusk then stated that our proposed action gave the other side a chance to pause. They may pull back or they may rapidly intensify the entire situation existing between the Soviet Union and the United States.

Senator [Richard] Russell then demanded stronger steps, stated he did not think we needed time to pause. The President had warned them in September

---

[1]McCone had done so on October 17 and 21.

and no further warning was necessary. We must not take a gamble and must not temporize; Khrushchev has once again rattled his missiles; he can become firmer and firmer, and we must react. If we delay, if we give notification, if we telegraph our punches, the result will be more a difficult military action and more American lives will be sacrificed. The thrust of Senator Russell's remarks were [sic] to demand military action. He did not specifically say by surprise attack; however he did not advocate warning.

McNamara then described the blockade, indicating that this might lead to some form of military action; that there would be many alternative courses open to us. The President then reviewed in some detail time required to assemble an invasion force which would involve 90,000 men in the actual landings and a total of about 250,000 men. He stated this could not be done in 24 or 36 hours but would take a number of days and that many preliminary steps had been taken.

[Representative Charles] Halleck recalled a recent briefing by Secretary McNamara in which he stated it would take three months to prepare adequately to invade Cuba. McNamara then reaffirmed the 250,000-man figure, with 90,000 of them actually involved in the landing force. He stated that he could be ready in 7 days and that the landing would be preceded by substantial air strike. Russell again questioned the delay. . . .

[Representative Carl] Vinson then asked if the Joint Chiefs of Staff actually approved the plans for the invasion. McNamara answered, "Yes." The plans had been developed over a 10-month period and had been submitted to the President by the JCS on a number of occasions.

Note: This question did *not* refer to whether the JCS did or did not approve the proposed actions of blockade against Cuba.

The President then reviewed matters again, read an intelligence note from a United Nations source which indicated Soviet intention to grab Berlin. Russell promptly replied that Berlin will always be a hostage. He then criticized the decision, stated we should go now and not wait.

Halleck questioned whether we were absolutely sure these weapons were offensive. The President answered affirmatively. . . .

Questions were then raised concerning the attitude of our Allies. The President advised steps taken to inform our major Allies. He then read the message received from the [British] Prime Minister which in effect agreed to support us in the United Nations and then raised many warnings including the dangers to Berlin, Turkey, Pakistan, Iran, etc., etc.

Senator [Leverett] Saltonstall brought up the question of the legality of the blockade. A great many Senators expressed concern over the proposed action with the OAS, indicating that they felt the OAS would delay rather than act.[2] Saltonstall then asked whether a blockade would be legal if the OAS did not support it. The President answered that it probably would not; however we would proceed anyway.

---

[2]Kennedy administration officials intended to seek OAS backing for its handling of the crisis. They obtained it on October 23.

[Senator William] Fulbright then stated that in his opinion the blockade was the worst of the alternatives open to us and it was a definite affront to Russia and that the moment that we had to damage or sink a Soviet ship because of their failure to recognize or respect the blockade we would be at war with Russia and the war would be caused because of our own initiative. The President disagreed with this thinking. Fulbright then repeated his position and stated in his opinion it would be far better to launch an attack and to take out the bases from Cuba. McNamara stated that this would involve the spilling of Russian blood since there were so many thousand Russians manning these bases. Fulbright responded that this made no difference because they were there in Cuba to help on Cuban bases. These were not Soviet bases. There was no mutual defense pact between the USSR and Cuba. Cuba was not a member of the Warsaw Pact.[3] Therefore he felt the Soviets would not react if some Russians got killed in Cuba. The Russians in the final analysis placed little value on human life. The time has come for an invasion under the President's statement of February 13th.[4] Fulbright repeated that an act [attack] on Russian ships is an act of war against Russia and on the other hand, an attack or an invasion of Cuba was an act against Cuba, not Russia. Fulbright also expressed reservations concerning the possible OAS action.

The President took issue with Fulbright, stating that he felt that an attack on these bases, which we knew were manned by Soviet personnel, would involve large numbers of Soviet casualties and this would be more provocative than a confrontation with a Soviet ship.

Vinson urged that if we strike, we strike with maximum force and wind the matter up quickly as this would involve the minimum of American losses and insure the maximum support by the Cuban people at large who, he reasoned, would very quickly go over to the side of the winner.

The meeting was concluded at 6:35 to permit the President to prepare for his 7:00 o'clock talk to the nation. . . .[5]

13. Letter from President Kennedy to Chairman Khrushchev

JFK sends the first of what would become a series of letters between the superpower leaders during the missile crisis.

---

[3]The Warsaw Pact was a military alliance between the Soviet Union and its Eastern European satellite states, formed in 1955.
[4]A reference presumably to JFK's September 13 statement. See Chapter 3, Document 12.
[5]John McCone prepared this memorandum.

Washington, October 22, 1962.

DEAR MR. CHAIRMAN: A copy of the statement I am making tonight concerning developments in Cuba and the reaction of my Government thereto has been handed to your Ambassador in Washington.[1] In view of the gravity of the developments to which I refer, I want you to know immediately and accurately the position of my Government in this matter.

In our discussions and exchanges on Berlin and other international questions, the one thing that has most concerned me has been the possibility that your Government would not correctly understand the will and determination of the United States in any given situation, since I have not assumed that you or any other sane man would, in this nuclear age, deliberately plunge the world into war which it is crystal clear no country could win and which could only result in catastrophic consequences to the whole world, including the aggressor.

At our meeting in Vienna and subsequently, I expressed our readiness and desire to find, through peaceful negotiation, a solution to any and all problems that divide us. At the same time, I made clear that in view of the objectives of the ideology to which you adhere, the United States could not tolerate any action on your part which in a major way disturbed the existing over-all balance of power in the world. I stated that an attempt to force abandonment of our responsibilities and commitments in Berlin would constitute such an action and that the United States would resist with all the power at its command.

It was in order to avoid any incorrect assessment on the part of your Government with respect to Cuba that I publicly stated that if certain developments in Cuba took place, the United States would do whatever must be done to protect its own security and that of its allies.

Moreover, the Congress adopted a resolution expressing its support of this declared policy.[2] Despite this, the rapid development of long-range missile bases and other offensive weapons systems in Cuba has proceeded. I must tell you that the United States is determined that this threat to the security of this hemisphere be removed. At the same time, I wish to point out that the action we are taking is the minimum necessary to remove the threat to the security of the nations of this hemisphere. The fact of this minimum response should not be taken as a basis, however, for any misjudgment on your part.

I hope that your Government will refrain from any action which would widen or deepen this already grave crisis and that we can agree to resume the path of peaceful negotiation.

[1]At 6 p.m., October 22, Rusk handed Ambassador Dobrynin a copy of JFK's speech to the nation.

[2]See Chapter 3, Document 16, footnote 6.

14. Radio and Television Report by President Kennedy to the American People on the Soviet Arms Buildup in Cuba

JFK informs the nation of the existence of nuclear weapons in Cuba, and of his plan to blockade the island. The missile crisis was now a public affair.

October 22, 1962.

[Delivered from the President's Office at 7 p.m.]

Good evening, my fellow citizens:

This Government, as promised, has maintained the closest surveillance of the Soviet military buildup on the island of Cuba. Within the past week, unmistakable evidence has established the fact that a series of offensive missile sites is now in preparation on that imprisoned island. The purpose of these bases can be none other than to provide a nuclear strike capability against the Western Hemisphere.

Upon receiving the first preliminary hard information of this nature last Tuesday morning[1] at 9 a.m., I directed that our surveillance be stepped up. And having now confirmed and completed our evaluation of the evidence and our decision on a course of action, this Government feels obliged to report this new crisis to you in fullest detail.

The characteristics of these new missile sites indicate two distinct types of installations. Several of them include medium range ballistic missiles, capable of carrying a nuclear warhead for a distance of more than 1,000 nautical miles. Each of these missiles, in short, is capable of striking Washington, D.C., the Panama Canal, Cape Canaveral, Mexico City, or any other city in the southeastern part of the United States, in Central America, or in the Caribbean area.

Additional sites not yet completed appear to be designed for intermediate range ballistic missiles—capable of traveling more than twice as far—and thus capable of striking most of the major cities in the Western Hemisphere, ranging as far north as Hudson Bay, Canada, and as far south as Lima, Peru. In addition, jet bombers, capable of carrying nuclear weapons, are now being uncrated and assembled in Cuba, while the necessary air bases are being prepared.

This urgent transformation of Cuba into an important strategic base—by the presence of these large, long-range, and clearly offensive weapons of sudden mass destruction—constitutes an explicit threat to the peace and security of all the Americas, in flagrant and deliberate defiance of the Rio Pact of 1947,[2] the traditions of this Nation and hemisphere, the joint resolution of the 87th Congress,[3] the Charter of the United Nations, and my own public warnings to the So-

[1]October 16.
[2]See Document 5, footnote 2.
[3]See Chapter 3, Document 16, footnote 6.

viets on September 4 and 13.[4] This action also contradicts the repeated assurances of Soviet spokesmen, both publicly and privately delivered, that the arms buildup in Cuba would retain its original defensive character, and that the Soviet Union had no need or desire to station strategic missiles on the territory of any other nation.

The size of this undertaking makes clear that it has been planned for some months. Yet only last month, after I had made clear the distinction between any introduction of ground-to-ground missiles and the existence of defensive antiaircraft missiles,[5] the Soviet Government publicly stated on September 11 that, and I quote, "the armaments and military equipment sent to Cuba are designed exclusively for defensive purposes," that, and I quote the Soviet Government, "there is no need for the Soviet Government to shift its weapons . . . for a retaliatory blow to any other country, for instance Cuba," and that, and I quote their government, "the Soviet Union has so powerful rockets to carry these nuclear warheads that there is no need to search for sites for them beyond the boundaries of the Soviet Union." That statement was false.

Only last Thursday,[6] as evidence of this rapid offensive buildup was already in my hand, Soviet Foreign Minister Gromyko told me in my office that he was instructed to make it clear once again, as he said his government had already done, that Soviet assistance to Cuba, and I quote, "pursued solely the purpose of contributing to the defense capabilities of Cuba," that, and I quote him, "training by Soviet specialists of Cuban nationals in handling defensive armaments was by no means offensive, and if it were otherwise," Mr. Gromyko went on, "the Soviet Government would never become involved in rendering such assistance." That statement also was false.

Neither the United States of America nor the world community of nations can tolerate deliberate deception and offensive threats on the part of any nation, large or small. We no longer live in a world where only the actual firing of weapons represents a sufficient challenge to a nation's security to constitute maximum peril. Nuclear weapons are so destructive and ballistic missiles are so swift, that any substantially increased possibility of their use or any sudden change in their deployment may well be regarded as a definite threat to peace.

For many years, both the Soviet Union and the United States, recognizing this fact, have deployed strategic nuclear weapons with great care, never upsetting the precarious status quo which insured that these weapons would not be used in the absence of some vital challenge. Our own strategic missiles have never been transferred to the territory of any other nation under a cloak of secrecy and deception; and our history—unlike that of the Soviets since the end of World War II—demonstrates that we have no desire to dominate or conquer any other nation or impose our system upon its people. Nevertheless, American citizens have become adjusted to living daily on the bull's-eye of Soviet missiles located inside the U.S.S.R. or in submarines.

In that sense, missiles in Cuba add to an already clear and present danger—

[4]See Chapter 3, Documents 9 and 12.
[5]JFK refers here to his September 4 and 13 public statements.
[6]October 18; see Document 6.

although it should be noted the nations of Latin America have never previously been subjected to a potential nuclear threat.

But this secret, swift, and extraordinary buildup of Communist missiles—in an area well known to have a special and historical relationship to the United States and the nations of the Western Hemisphere, in violation of Soviet assurances, and in defiance of American and hemispheric policy—this sudden, clandestine decision to station strategic weapons for the first time outside of Soviet soil—is a deliberately provocative and unjustified change in the status quo which cannot be accepted by this country, if our courage and our commitments are ever to be trusted again by either friend or foe.

The 1930's taught us a clear lesson: aggressive conduct, if allowed to go unchecked and unchallenged, ultimately leads to war. This nation is opposed to war. We are also true to our word. Our unswerving objective, therefore, must be to prevent the use of these missiles against this or any other country, and to secure their withdrawal or elimination from the Western Hemisphere.

Our policy has been one of patience and restraint, as befits a peaceful and powerful nation, which leads a worldwide alliance. We have been determined not to be diverted from our central concerns by mere irritants and fanatics. But now further action is required—and it is under way; and these actions may only be the beginning. We will not prematurely or unnecessarily risk the costs of worldwide nuclear war in which even the fruits of victory would be ashes in our mouth—but neither will we shrink from that risk at any time it must be faced.

Acting, therefore, in the defense of our own security and of the entire Western Hemisphere, and under the authority entrusted to me by the Constitution as endorsed by the resolution of the Congress, I have directed that the following *initial* steps be taken immediately:

First: To halt this offensive buildup, a strict quarantine on all offensive military equipment under shipment to Cuba is being initiated. All ships of any kind bound for Cuba from whatever nation or port will, if found to contain cargoes of offensive weapons, be turned back. This quarantine will be extended, if needed, to other types of cargo and carriers. We are not at this time, however, denying the necessities of life as the Soviets attempted to do in their Berlin blockade of 1948.

Second: I have directed the continued and increased close surveillance of Cuba and its military buildup. The foreign ministers of the OAS, in their communique of October 6, rejected secrecy on such matters in this hemisphere. Should these offensive military preparations continue, thus increasing the threat to the hemisphere, further action will be justified. I have directed the Armed Forces to prepare for any eventualities; and I trust that in the interest of both the Cuban people and the Soviet technicians at the sites, the hazards to all concerned of continuing this threat will be recognized.

Third: It shall be the policy of this Nation to regard any nuclear missile launched from Cuba against any nation in the Western Hemisphere as an attack by the Soviet Union on the United States, requiring a full retaliatory response upon the Soviet Union.

Fourth: As a necessary military precaution, I have reinforced our base at Guantanamo, evacuated today the dependents of our personnel there, and ordered additional military units to be on a standby alert basis.

Fifth: We are calling tonight for an immediate meeting of the Organ of Consultation under the Organization of American States, to consider this threat to hemispheric security and to invoke articles 6 and 8 of the Rio Treaty in support of all necessary action. The United Nations Charter allows for regional security arrangements—and the nations of this hemisphere decided long ago against the military presence of outside powers. Our other allies around the world have also been alerted.

Sixth: Under the Charter of the United Nations, we are asking tonight that an emergency meeting of the Security Council be convoked without delay to take action against this latest Soviet threat to world peace. Our resolution will call for the prompt dismantling and withdrawal of all offensive weapons in Cuba, under the supervision of U.N. observers, before the quarantine can be lifted.

Seventh and finally: I call upon Chairman Khrushchev to halt and eliminate this clandestine, reckless, and provocative threat to world peace and to stable relations between our two nations. I call upon him further to abandon this course of world domination, and to join in an historic effort to end the perilous arms race and to transform the history of man. He has an opportunity now to move the world back from the abyss of destruction—by returning to his government's own words that it had no need to station missiles outside its own territory, and withdrawing these weapons from Cuba—by refraining from any action which will widen or deepen the present crisis—and then by participating in a search for peaceful and permanent solutions.

This Nation is prepared to present its case against the Soviet threat to peace, and our own proposals for a peaceful world, at any time and in any forum—in the OAS, in the United Nations, or in any other meeting that could be useful—without limiting our freedom of action. We have in the past made strenuous efforts to limit the spread of nuclear weapons. We have proposed the elimination of all arms and military bases in a fair and effective disarmament treaty. We are prepared to discuss new proposals for the removal of tensions on both sides—including the possibilities of a genuinely independent Cuba, free to determine its own destiny. We have no wish to war with the Soviet Union—for we are a peaceful people who desire to live in peace with all other peoples.

But it is difficult to settle or even discuss these problems in an atmosphere of intimidation. That is why this latest Soviet threat—or any other threat which is made either independently or in response to our actions this week—must and will be met with determination. Any hostile move anywhere in the world against the safety and freedom of peoples to whom we are committed—including in particular the brave people of West Berlin—will be met by whatever action is needed.

Finally, I want to say a few words to the captive people of Cuba, to whom this speech is being directly carried by special radio facilities. I speak to you as a friend, as one who knows of your deep attachment to your fatherland, as one who shares your aspirations for liberty and justice for all. And I have watched and the American people have watched with deep sorrow how your nationalist revolution was betrayed—and how your fatherland fell under foreign domination. Now your leaders are no longer Cuban leaders inspired by Cuban ideals. They are puppets and agents of an international conspiracy which has turned Cuba against your friends and neighbors in the Americas—and turned it into the first Latin American country to become a target for nuclear war—the first Latin American country to have these weapons on its soil.

These new weapons are not in your interest. They contribute nothing to your peace and well-being. They can only undermine it. But this country has no wish to cause you to suffer or to impose any system upon you. We know that your lives and land are being used as pawns by those who deny your freedom.

Many times in the past, the Cuban people have risen to throw out tyrants who destroyed their liberty. And I have no doubt that most Cubans today look forward to the time when they will be truly free—free from foreign domination, free to choose their own leaders, free to select their own system, free to own their own land, free to speak and write and worship without fear or degradation. And then shall Cuba be welcomed back to the society of free nations and to the associations of this hemisphere.

My fellow citizens: let no one doubt that this is a difficult and dangerous effort on which we have set out. No one can foresee precisely what course it will take or what costs or casualties will be incurred. Many months of sacrifice and self-discipline lie ahead—months in which both our patience and our will will be tested—months in which many threats and denunciations will keep us aware of our dangers. But the greatest danger of all would be to do nothing.

The path we have chosen for the present is full of hazards, as all paths are—but it is the one most consistent with our character and courage as a nation and our commitments around the world. The cost of freedom is always high—but Americans have always paid it. And one path we shall never choose, and that is the path of surrender or submission.

Our goal is not the victory of might, but the vindication of right—not peace at the expense of freedom, but both peace *and* freedom, here in this hemisphere, and, we hope, around the world. God willing, that goal will be achieved.

Thank you and good night.

15. Alternative Draft of President Kennedy's Speech on October 22

Speechwriter Theodore Sorensen produced another draft of JFK's address to the nation, one that would have been used had the president opted for an air strike on the missile sites in Cuba. This document gives an ominous sense of how the missile crisis might have turned out had cooler heads not prevailed.

My fellow Americans:

With a heavy heart, and in necessary fulfillment of my oath of office, I have ordered—and the United States Air Force has now carried out—military operations, with conventional weapons only, to remove a major nuclear weapons build-up from the soil of Cuba. This action has been taken under Article 51 of the Charter of the United Nations[1] and in fulfillment of the requirements of the national safety. Further military action has been authorized to ensure that this threat is fully removed and not restored. . . .

The tragedy here—self-evidently—is in the loss of innocent lives on all sides. For the United States Government I hereby accept responsibility for this action and pledge that all appropriate efforts will be made, on request, to assist the families of these innocent victims. Neither Cubans nor Russians, as individuals, can be held accountable for the extraordinary and irresponsible conspiracy which has required this action. This was Communist militarism in action—neither more nor less. . . .

We are, of course, reporting our actions at once to the Organization of American States and the United Nations. We shall ask the first for support and the second for understanding. We believe that the world will be relieved that a new threat of nuclear terror has been kept out of the Americas. . . .

16. Message from Chairman Khrushchev to President Kennedy

The Soviet leader responds to JFK's decision to blockade Cuba by charging his American counterpart with recklessness. At this point Khrushchev shows no sign of backing down.

Moscow, October 23, 1962.

Mr. President:

I have just received your letter, and have also acquainted myself with the text of your speech of October 22 regarding Cuba.[1]

I must say frankly that the measures indicated in your statement constitute a serious threat to peace and to the security of nations. The United States has openly taken the path of grossly violating the United Nations Charter, the path of violating international norms of freedom of navigation on the high seas, the path of aggressive actions both against Cuba and against the Soviet Union.

The statement by the Government of the United States of America can only be regarded as undisguised interference in the internal affairs of the Republic of

[1]Article 51 permits a nation or nations to use force if needed for self-defense.
[1]See Documents 13 and 14.

Cuba, The [sic] Soviet Union and other states. The United Nations Charter and international norms give no right to any state to institute in international waters the inspection of vessels bound for the shores of the Republic of Cuba.

And naturally, neither can we recognize the right of the United States to establish control over armaments which are necessary for the Republic of Cuba to strengthen its defense capability.

We reaffirm that the armaments which are in Cuba, regardless of the classification to which they may belong, are intended solely for defensive purposes in order to secure the Republic of Cuba against the attack of an aggressor.

I hope that the United States Government will display wisdom and renounce the actions pursued by you, which may lead to catastrophic consequances [sic] for world peace. . . .[2]

17. Memorandum of ExComm Meeting at 6:00 p.m. on October 23, 1962

JFK and his advisers focus on the implementation of the blockade, which was to come into effect the next day, and on civil defense issues.

Washington, October 23, 1962.

Committee reviewed the blockade proclamation and approved it. It was signed by the President at 6:00 p.m.

The President instructed McNamara to review all details of instructions to the Fleet Commanders regarding procedures to be followed in the blockade. There was an extended discussion of actions to be taken under various assumed Soviet resistance activities such as (a) failing to stop, (b) refusing right to board, (c) ships turning around, heading in another direction, etc. . . .

In the prolonged discussion of report on Civil Defense problems, the President seemed particularly concerned over the situation if we should launch attacks which might result in four or five missiles being delivered on the United States. DOD spokesmen stated that the area covered by the 1100-mile missiles involved 92 million people. They felt that fall-out space was available though not equipped for about 40 million. The President asked what emergency steps could be taken. Replied that many arrangements could be made without too much publicity, such as repositioning food, actually obtaining space, putting up shelter signs, etc. I got the conclusion that not very much could or would be done; that whatever was done would involve a great deal of publicity and public alarm. . . .[1]

---

[2]This document is a State Department translation of Khrushchev's message.
[1]McCone prepared this memorandum.

18. Message from President Kennedy to Chairman Khrushchev

JFK tells the Soviet premier that the missile crisis is Moscow's fault, and urges him to be cautious.

Washington, October 23, 1962.

Dear Mr. Chairman:

I have received your letter of October twenty-third.[1] I think you will recognize that the steps which started the current chain of events was the action of your Government in secretly furnishing offensive weapons to Cuba. We will be discussing this matter in the Security Council. In the meantime, I am concerned that we both show prudence and do nothing to allow events to make the situation more difficult to control than it already is.

I hope that you will issue immediately the necessary instructions to your ships to observe the terms of the quarantine, the basis of which was established by the vote of the Organization of American States this afternoon, and which will go into effect at 1400 hours Greenwich time October twenty-four.

19. Memorandum from Attorney General Kennedy to President Kennedy

Contrary to what he says in this report, Robert Kennedy goes to see the Russian ambassador on October 23 on JFK's instructions. Dobrynin would inform his superiors in Moscow that the attorney general arrived in "an obviously excited condition and his speech was rich in repetitions and digressions."[1] Here Bobby Kennedy reports to his brother on the meeting.

Washington, October 24, 1962.

I met with Ambassador Dobrynin [at 9:30] last evening on the third floor of the Russian Embassy and as you suggested made the following points:

I told him first that I was there on my own and not on the instructions of the President. I said that I wanted to give him some background on the decision of the United States Government and wanted him to know that the duplicity of the

---

[1]Document 16.
[1]For Dobrynin's full report on this meeting, see Cold War International History Project *Bulletin* 5 (Spring 1995), 71–73.

Russians had been a major contributing factor. When I had met with him some six weeks before,[2] I said, he had told me that the Russians had not placed any long-range missiles in Cuba and had no intention to do so in the future. He interrupted at that point and confirmed this statement and said he specifically told me they would not put missiles in Cuba which would be able to reach the continental United States.

I said based on that statement which I had related to the President plus independent intelligence information at that time, the President had gone to the American people and assured them that the weapons being furnished by the Communists to Cuba were defensive and that it was not necessary for the United States to blockade or take any military action.[3] I pointed out that this assurance of Dobrynin to me had been confirmed by the TASS statement[4] and then finally, in substance, by Gromyko when he visited the President on Thursday.[5] I said that based on these assurances the President had taken a different and far less belligerent position than people like Senators Keating and Capehart,[6] and he had assured the American people that there was nothing to be concerned about.

I pointed out, in addition, that the President felt he had a very helpful personal relationship with Mr. Khrushchev. Obviously, they did not agree on many issues, but he did feel that there was a mutual trust and confidence between them on which he could rely. . . .

I said that with the background of this relationship, plus the specific assurances that had been given to us, and then the statement of Dobrynin from Khrushchev to Ted Sorensen[7] and to me that no incident would occur before the American elections were completed, we felt the action by Khrushchev and the Russians at this time was hypocritical, misleading and false. I said this should be clearly understood by them as it was by us.

Dobrynin's only answer was that he had told me no missiles were in Cuba but that Khrushchev had also given similar assurances through TASS and as far as he (Dobrynin) knew, there were still no missiles in Cuba.

Dobrynin in the course of the conversation made several other points. The one he stressed was why the President did not tell Gromkyo the facts on Thursday. He said this was something they could not understand and that if we had the information at the time why didn't we tell Gromyko.

I answered this by making two points:

Number one, there wasn't anything the President could tell Gromyko that Gromyko didn't know already and after all, why didn't Gromyko tell the President this instead of, in fact, denying it. I said in addition the President was so shocked at Gromyko's presentation and his failure to recite these facts that he felt that any effort to have an intelligent and honest conversation would not be profitable.

[2] They had met on September 4.
[3] A reference no doubt to JFK's September 4 and 13 public statements. See Chapter 3, Documents 9 and 12.
[4] See Chapter 3, Document 14, footnote 1.
[5] October 18; see Document 6 in this chapter.
[6] Republican Homer E. Capehart, senator from Indiana, had called for an invasion of Cuba.
[7] Dobrynin and Sorensen had met on September 6. See Chapter 3, Document 10.

Dobrynin went on to say that from his conversations with Gromyko he doesn't believe Gromyko thought there were any missiles in Cuba. He said he was going to contact his government to find out about this matter.

I expressed surprise that after all that had appeared in the papers, and the President's speech, that he had not had a communication on that question already.

Dobrynin seemed extremely concerned. When I left I asked him if ships were going to go through to Cuba. He replied that was their instructions last month and he assumed they had the same instructions at the present time. He also made the point that although we might have pictures, all we really knew about were the sites and not missiles and that there was a lot of difference between sites and the actual missile itself. I said I did not have to argue the point—there were missiles in Cuba—we knew that they were there and that I hoped he would inform himself also.

I left around 10:15 p.m. and went to the White House and gave a verbal report to the President.

20. Record of Action of ExComm Meeting

Here is one of the most dramatic moments of the missile crisis. As the quarantine takes effect, two Russian ships and one submarine approach the blockade line. Then the news arrives during this ExComm meeting that the Soviet vessels are respecting the blockade by not crossing that line. For the time being at least, war is averted.

Washington, October 24, 1962, 10 a.m.

. . . The Secretary of Defense [McNamara] reported the plans for naval interception, noted the presence of a [Russian] submarine near the more interesting [Soviet] ships, and warned that radio silence might be imposed. There was discussion of the problem of dealing with such submarines, and it was understood that in the event of intervention by a submarine in the process of interception the submarine might have to be destroyed.

In the middle of the meeting there were reports that certain Soviet ships had appeared to have stopped or turned back, and the President directed that there be no interception of any target for at least another hour while clarifying information was sought. . . .

The President directed that State and USIA should give immediate attention to increasing understanding in Europe of the fact that any Berlin crisis would be fundamentally the result of Soviet ambition and pressure, and that inaction by the United States in the face of the challenge in Cuba would have been more and not less dangerous for Berlin. . . .[1]

21. Telegram from Secretary of State Rusk to U.S. Ambassador to Turkey Raymond Hare and to U.S. Ambassador to NATO Thomas Finletter

Early in the second week of the crisis, this message shows the willingness of administration officials to consider a diplomatic settlement involving withdrawal of American Jupiter missiles from Turkey.

Washington, October 24, 1962, 11:24 a.m.

For Ambassadors Hare and Finletter from Secretary [Rusk]. Soviet reaction Cuban quarantine likely involve efforts compare missiles in Cuba with Jupiters in Turkey. While such comparison refutable, possible that negotiated solution for removal Cuban offensive threat may involve dismantling and removal Jupiters. Recognize this would create serious politico-military problems for US-Turkish relations and with regard to Turkey's place in NATO Alliance. Therefore need prepare carefully for such contingency order not harm our relations with this important ally.

Urgently request Ambassador Hare's assessment political consequences such removal under various assumptions, including outright removal, removal accompanied by stationing of Polaris submarine in area, or removal with some other significant military offset, such as seaborn multilateral nuclear force within NATO.

Ambassador Finletter also requested comment standpoint NATO aspect problem. Do not discuss with any foreigners.[1]

[1]McGeorge Bundy prepared this memorandum.
[1]George Ball drafted this telegram, and Rusk approved it. A few hours later the State Department dispatched a similar telegram to American officials in Rome.

22. Message from Chairman Khrushchev to President Kennedy

In his correspondence with JFK, Khrushchev continues to express his indignation. His comment that Russian ships would not respect the American blockade around Cuba did not square, however, with the fact that Soviet vessels had not crossed the quarantine line that day.

Moscow, October 24, 1962.

DEAR MR. PRESIDENT: I have received your letter of October 23,[1] have studied it, and am answering you.

Just imagine, Mr. President, that we had presented you with the conditions of an ultimatum which you have presented us by your action. How would you have reacted to this? I think that you would have been indignant at such a step on our part. And this would have been understandable to us.

In presenting us with these conditions, you, Mr. President, have flung a challenge at us. Who asked you to do this? By what right did you do this? Our ties with the Republic of Cuba, like our relations with other states, regardless of what kind of states they may be, concern only the two countries between which these relations exist. And if we now speak of the quarantine to which your letter refers, a quarantine may be established, according to accepted international practice, only by agreement of states between themselves, and not by some third party. Quarantines exist, for example, on agricultural goods and products. But in this case the question is in no way one of quarantine, but rather of far more serious things, and you yourself understand this.

You, Mr. President, are not declaring a quarantine, but rather are setting forth an ultimatum and threatening that if we do not give in to your demands you will use force. Consider what you are saying! And you want to persuade me to agree to this! What would it mean to agree to these demands? It would mean guiding oneself in one's relations with other countries not by reason, but by submitting to arbitrariness. You are no longer appealing to reason, but wish to intimidate us.

No, Mr. President, I cannot agree to this, and I think that in your own heart you recognize that I am correct. I am convinced that in my place you would act the same way.

Reference to the decision of the Organization of American States[2] cannot in any way substantiate the demands now advanced by the United States. This Organization has absolutely no authority or basis for adopting decisions such as the one you speak of in your letter. Therefore, we do not recognize these decisions. International law exists and universally recognized norms of conduct exist. We

---

[1]See Document 18.
[2]See Document 12, footnote 2.

firmly adhere to the principles of international law and observe strictly the norms which regulate navigation on the high seas, in international waters. We observe these norms and enjoy the rights recognized by all states.

You wish to compel us to renounce the rights that every sovereign state enjoys, you are trying to legislate in questions of international law, and you are violating the universally accepted norms of that law. And you are doing all this not only out of hatred for the Cuban people and its government, but also because of considerations of the [congressional] election campaign in the United States. What morality, what law can justify such an approach by the American Government to international affairs? No such morality or law can be found, because the actions of the United States with regard to Cuba constitute outright banditry or, if you like, the folly of degenerate imperialism. Unfortunately, such folly can bring grave suffering to the peoples of all countries, and to no lesser degree to the American people themselves, since the United States has completely lost its former isolation with the advent of modern types of armament.

Therefore, Mr. President, if you coolly weigh the situation which has developed, not giving way to passions, you will understand that the Soviet Union cannot fail to reject the arbitrary demands of the United States. When you confront us with such conditions, try to put yourself in our place and consider how the United States would react to these conditions. I do not doubt that if someone attempted to dictate similar conditions to you—the United States—you would reject such an attempt. And we also say—no.

The Soviet Government considers that the violation of the freedom to use international waters and international air space is an act of aggression which pushes mankind toward the abyss of a world nuclear-missile war. Therefore, the Soviet Government cannot instruct the captains of Soviet vessels bound for Cuba to observe the orders of American naval forces blockading that Island. Our instructions to Soviet mariners are to observe strictly the universally accepted norms of navigation in international waters and not to retreat one step from them. And if the American side violates these rules, it must realize what responsibility will rest upon it in that case. Naturally we will not simply be bystanders with regard to piratical acts by American ships on the high seas. We will then be forced on our part to take the measures we consider necessary and adequate in order to protect our rights. We have everything necessary to do so.

23. Message from President Kennedy to Chairman Khrushchev

In response to Khrushchev's October 24 message, Kennedy insists that Russian deceit is the root cause of the missile crisis.

Washington, October 25, 1962.

Dear Mr. Chairman:

I have received your letter of October 24, and I regret very much that you still do not appear to understand what it is that has moved us in this matter.

The sequence of events is clear. In August there were reports of important shipments of military equipment and technicians from the Soviet Union to Cuba. In early September I indicated very plainly that the United States would regard any shipment of offensive weapons as presenting the gravest issues.[1] After that time, this Government received the most explicit assurance from your Government and its representatives, both publicly and privately, that no offensive weapons were being sent to Cuba. If you will review the statement issued by TASS in September,[2] you will see how clearly this assurance was given.

In reliance on these solemn assurances I urged restraint upon those in this country who were urging action in this matter at that time. And then I learned beyond doubt what you have not denied—namely, that all these public assurances were false and that your military people had set out recently to establish a set of missile bases in Cuba. I ask you to recognize clearly, Mr. Chairman, that it was not I who issued the first challenge in this case, and that in the light of this record these activities in Cuba required the responses I have announced.

I repeat my regret that these events should cause a deterioration in our relations. I hope that your Government will take the necessary action to permit a restoration of the earlier situation.

24. Summary of ExComm Meeting

By October 25 JFK was giving more thought to what further action might be needed in order to bring about a removal of the missiles from Cuba. In that morning's ExComm meeting he asked his advisers to consider three options: extending the blockade (so that POL as well as Russian weaponry was intercepted), a diplomatic settlement, and an air strike on Cuba. Later in the day he decided to permit an East German passenger ship, the Volker Freundschaft, *to pass through the quarantine line. Robert Kennedy, meanwhile, was exhibiting less moderation. In a late afternoon ExComm session he stated that an air strike on the missile sites in Cuba might be preferable to a confrontation at sea with Soviet ships. On October 26 JFK and his ExComm advisers continue to consider steps that might be taken in addition to enforcing the blockade.*

[1]See Chapter 3, Documents 9 and 12.
[2]See Chapter 3, Document 14, footnote 1.

Washington, October 26, 1962, 10 a.m.

. . . Secretary McNamara reported on the status of the quarantine. The Defense Department was authorized to release information on the boarding of the Lebanese ship, the *Marucla*, the first dry cargo ship which had been loaded in a Soviet port. In the event that comparisons were made between stopping the Lebanese ship and permitting an East German ship to go through the quarantine line, the point will be made that the East German ship carried only passengers.[1]

Secretary McNamara read a list of Bloc ships and their locations and noted that there would be no intercepts at sea today. The tanker *Graznyy* is apparently moving but will not cross the line today. He suggested that shortly we should embargo fuel used by bombers and substances from which airplane fuel is made, i.e. petroleum products.

The President suggested that if we decide to embargo bomber fuel, we should also mention the fact that we were embargoing fuel which was contributing to the operational capability of the strategic missiles.

Secretary Rusk asked that POL not be embargoed for at least twenty-four hours in order to avoid upsetting the U Thant talks now under way in New York.[2]

Under Secretary Ball asked for agreement on the embargo of petroleum as the next step in the effort to increase pressures—the timing of the embargo to be decided later in relation to the New York talks.

Secretary Dillon stated his reservations concerning this course of action. He said it ended up in stopping Soviet ships. Thus, a confrontation with the Russians would not be over the missiles, but over Soviet ships. He believed we should go for the missiles rather than force a confrontation with the USSR at sea.

A decision on adding petroleum to the embargo list was delayed until the political path was decided upon.

Secretary McNamara pointed out that construction on the strategic missile sites in Cuba was continuing. He asked that public announcement be made of our continuation of air surveillance. He recommended that daylight reconnaissance measures be flown today and a night mission tonight, including the dropping of flares.

Secretary Rusk asked that the night mission not be flown because of the unfortunate effect which it might have on the U Thant negotiations in New York.

Secretary McNamara thought that one way of avoiding reaction to night reconnaissance was to inform the Cubans and the Russians in advance that we were initiating such flights.

---

[1]The East German passenger ship was the *Volker Freundschaft*, which JFK permitted to pass through the blockade line on October 25. Early in the morning of October 26, the *Marucla*, of Lebanese registration, became the first Russian ship to be stopped and boarded by the American navy since the imposition of the quarantine.

[2]UN Secretary General U Thant was by this time playing an important role in the crisis. On October 24 he had sent letters to Kennedy and Khrushchev calling for a suspension of both the quarantine and the delivery of missiles to Cuba. But JFK had not responded enthusiastically. The following day U Thant sent a revised proposal, this time suggesting that Khrushchev keep Russian ships away from the quarantine line and that Kennedy do all he could for a few days to avoid a clash on the seas with Soviet vessels. Both Kennedy and Khrushchev found this October 25 plan acceptable.

Ambassador Stevenson opposed any public announcement of our surveillance activities.

The President directed that we dramatize the fact that the missile buildup in Cuba is continuing. He authorized daylight reconnaissance measures but decided to delay night flights. . . .

Secretary Rusk summarized political actions now under way. He said the object of the talks with U Thant today was to set up some form of negotiations with the Russians in New York. The objective would be to obtain a commitment from the Russians that there would be no further construction at the missile sites in Cuba, no further Soviet military shipments, the defusing of existing weapons in Cuba, UN inspection of all nuclear-capable missiles, and an observer corps on the ground in Cuba of 350 technically able inspectors. The U.S. quarantine would continue until a UN quarantine is in place. UN teams would be put into specified Cuban ports. U.S. Navy ships would stay close to all Cuban ports to ensure that there were no landings unknown to the UN inspectors and no cargoes anywhere which UN inspectors did not see.

Mr. McCloy stated that our quarantine was vital and should be kept in place until the Russians had accepted all of our conditions.

Secretary Rusk pointed out that we must make clear to U Thant that the quarantine is related to the Soviet missiles rather than to Soviet military shipments to Cuba.

With respect to the proposed atomic-free zone in Latin America,[3] Secretary Rusk said that Puerto Rico and the Canal Zone would be exempted, but that possibly we might have to accept a ban on the storage of nuclear weapons in the Canal Zone. Conceivably, the proposal would hinder the transit by air of nuclear weapons in Latin America.

Secretary McNamara said the Joint Chiefs were very cool toward the proposal of a Latin American atomic-free zone, but, personally, he favored the idea if it was conditioned on the elimination of Soviet missiles in Cuba.

General Taylor said the Chiefs had no formal position on the proposal, but they were very sceptical as to its efficacy. He felt that discussion of this proposal would divert attention from the Soviet missile program. He was also concerned about its effect on the defense of Panama and on our submarine defense system. . . .

Mr. Sorensen pointed out that if the OAS would support the atomic-free zone proposal, Cuba would be in violation and action could be taken to remove nuclear weapons from Cuba.

Secretary Rusk felt that it was better for us not to participate in such action as would be necessary if it were done by an organization, i.e. the OAS, to which we belong.

The President noted that the plan proposed by Brazil not only calls for an atomic-free zone in Latin America, but also encompasses a guarantee of the territorial integrity on all Latin American States. He asked whether we could com-

---

[3]In a September 20 address to the UN General Assembly, the Brazilian representative had called for a ban on nuclear weapons in Latin America.

mit ourselves not to invade Cuba. Secretary Rusk commented that we are committed not to invade Cuba, having signed the UN Charter and the Rio Treaty.

Secretary Rusk read a draft cable which he wished to send to the Brazilian Ambassador in Cuba outlining an approach to Castro, with a view to persuading him to break with the Russians. In commenting on the draft cable, Mr. Nitze called attention to the importance of getting Soviet missiles out urgently.

Mr. McCone expressed his dislike of a situation involving continued control of Cuba by Castro. Even if the Soviet missiles are removed, Castro, if he is left in control, will be in an excellent position to undertake the Communization of Latin America.

Secretary Rusk said the present position is that Cuba ties to the USSR are not negotiable. Mr. Bundy pointed out, and the President agreed, that our objective was to get the Soviet missiles out of Cuba.

The President said work on the missile sites has to cease and we have to verify what is going on at the sites every day during the talks in New York. As to the message to Castro, he agreed in general, but wanted to have another look at it. He doubted that it would do any good, but it might be undertaken if done now with the greatest urgency.

Ambassador Stevenson discussed the immediate negotiations now under way with U Thant and the longer talks which would follow if agreement can be reached with the Russians in New York. He said the immediate talks were aimed at getting a 24–48-hour standstill on the missile buildup in Cuba. He acknowledged that in these talks it would be impossible to obtain an agreement to make the weapons inoperable. He wanted to know whether he should seek a standstill on all Soviet arms or only offensive weapons. He would seek to get a commitment that there be no further construction, but it would not be possible to set up a system to ensure that the weapons were made inoperable and kept inoperable. In addition, he needed to know whether in return we would be prepared to suspend the quarantine.

Ambassador Stevenson said the aim of the longer term talks would be the withdrawal from this hemisphere of the strategic missiles and the dismantlement of existing sites. He predicted that the Russians would ask us for a new guarantee of the territorial integrity of Cuba and the dismantlement of U.S. strategic missiles in Turkey.

Mr. McCone disagreed with Ambassador Stevenson's linking of Soviet missiles in Cuba to U.S. missiles in Turkey. He said the Soviet weapons in Cuba were pointed at our heart and put us under great handicap in continuing to carry out our commitments to the free world. He urged that we do not drop the quarantine until the Soviet missiles are out of Cuba. He believed that we must keep up the momentum so far achieved by the quarantine.

The President said we will get the Soviet strategic missiles out of Cuba only by invading Cuba or by trading. He doubted that the quarantine alone would produce a withdrawal of the weapons. He said our objective should be to prevent further military shipments, further construction at missile sites, and to get some means of inspection. . . .

The President said he understood Ambassador Stevenson to be asking for time during which he would try to negotiate the withdrawal of the missiles.

Secretary Rusk doubted that we could get any pre-conditions to negotiation.

Secretary Dillon agreed that the Soviets could not back down merely in return for dropping the quarantine.

Mr. Nitze called attention to the importance of obtaining a guarantee that the nuclear missiles would be disassembled from their launchers.

Mr. Bundy said negotiations for a standstill or a standdown were not enough for our security because we must press, in addition, for guaranteed inspection of Cuba.

Secretary Dillon said we could not negotiate for two weeks under the missile threat which now exists in Cuba.

The President noted that there appeared to be little support for Ambassador Stevenson's plan. If the quarantine would not result in the Soviets withdrawing the missiles, what will we do if negotiations break down?

Mr. Bundy said when the interim 24–48-hour talks fail, then our choice would be to expand the blockade or remove the missiles by air attack. . . .[4]

25. Message from Chairman Khrushchev to President Kennedy

For the Kennedy team, the entire equation was changed by the arrival on the evening of October 26 of a candid and remarkably emotional letter from the Soviet premier. Although somewhat vague, it appeared to advance a settlement to the crisis: an American pledge not to invade Cuba in return for removal of the Russian missiles. (The Kennedy administration's belief that Khrushchev's letter included this offer was reinforced when the same deal was discussed at a secret meeting between Washington-based KGB officer Aleksandr Feklisov and ABC reporter John Scali, a development reported immediately by Scali to the State Department. American officials assumed that Feklisov was following orders from Khrushchev, but this was not in fact the case. The KGB official had been working on his own initiative. Hence the similarity between the Feklisov and Khrushchev proposals was pure coincidence.)

[4]Bromley Smith, executive secretary of the National Security Council, wrote this summary of the meeting.

Moscow, October 26, 1962.

Dear Mr. President:

I have received your letter of October 25.[1] From your letter I got the feeling that you have some understanding of the situation which has developed and a sense of responsibility. I appreciate this.

By now we have already publicly exchanged our assessments of the events around Cuba and each of us has set forth his explanation and his interpretation of these events. Therefore, I would think that, evidently, continuing to exchange opinions at such a distance, even in the form of secret letters, would probably not add anything to what one side has already said to the other.

I think you will understand me correctly if you are really concerned for the welfare of the world. Everyone needs peace: both capitalists, if they have not lost their reason, and all the more, communists—people who know how to value not only their own lives but, above all else, the life of nations. We communists are against any wars between states at all, and have been defending the cause of peace ever since we came into the world. We have always regarded war as a calamity, not as a game or a means for achieving particular purposes, much less as a goal in itself. Our goals are clear, and the means of achieving them is work. War is our enemy and a calamity for all nations.

This is how we Soviet people, and together with us, other peoples as well, interpret questions of war and peace. I can say this with assurance at least for the peoples of the Socialist countries, as well as for all progressive people who want peace, happiness, and friendship among nations.

I can see, Mr. President, that you also are not without a sense of anxiety for the fate of the world, not without an understanding and correct assessment of the nature of modern warfare and what war entails. What good would a war do you? You threaten us with war. But you well know that the very least you would get in response would be what you had given us; you would suffer the same consequences. And that must be clear to us—people invested with authority, trust and responsibility. We must not succumb to light-headedness and petty passions, regardless of whether elections are forthcoming in one country or another.[2] These are all transitory things, but should war indeed break out, it would not be in our power to contain or stop it, for such is the logic of war. I have taken part in two wars, and I know that war ends only when it has rolled through cities and villages, sowing death and destruction everywhere.

I assure you on behalf of the Soviet Government and the Soviet people that your arguments regarding offensive weapons in Cuba are utterly unfounded. From what you have written me it is obvious that our interpretations on this point are different, or rather that we have different definitions for one type of military means or another. And indeed, the same types of armaments may in actuality have different interpretations.

You are a military man, and I hope you will understand me. Let us take a

---

[1]See Document 23.

[2]Khrushchev clearly suggests that Kennedy's tough stance on Cuba derives from concerns about the upcoming congressional elections.

simple cannon for instance. What kind of a weapon is it—offensive or defensive? A cannon is a defensive weapon if it is set up to defend boundaries or a fortified area. But when artillery is concentrated and supplemented by an appropriate number of troops, then the same cannon will have become an offensive weapon, since they prepare and clear the way for infantry to advance. The same is true for nuclear missile weapons, for any type of these weapons.

You are mistaken if you think that any of our armaments in Cuba are offensive. However, let us not argue at this point. Evidently, I shall not be able to convince you. But I tell you: You, Mr. President, are a military man and you must understand: How can you possibly launch an offensive even if you have an enormous number of missiles of various ranges and power on your territory, using these weapons alone? These missiles are a means of annihilation and destruction. But it is impossible to launch an offensive by means of these missiles, even nuclear missiles of 100 megaton yield, because it is only people—troops—who can advance. Without people any weapons, whatever their power, cannot be offensive.

How can you, therefore, give this completely wrong interpretation, which you are now giving, that some weapons in Cuba are offensive, as you say? All weapons there—and I assure you of this—are of a defensive nature; they are in Cuba solely for purposes of defense, and we have sent them to Cuba at the request of the Cuban Government. And you say that they are offensive weapons.

But, Mr. President, do you really seriously think that Cuba could launch an offensive upon the United States and that even we, together with Cuba, could advance against you from Cuban territory? Do you really think so? How can that be? We do not understand. Surely, there has not been any such new development in military strategy that would lead one to believe that it is possible to advance that way. And I mean advance, not destroy; for those who destroy are barbarians, people who have lost their sanity.

I hold that you have no grounds to think so. You may regard us with distrust, but you can at any rate rest assured that we are of sound mind and understand perfectly well that if we launch an offensive against you, you will respond in kind. But you too will get in response whatever you throw at us. And I think you understand that too. It is our discussion in Vienna that gives me the right to speak this way.[3]

This indicates that we are sane people, that we understand and assess the situation correctly. How could we, then, allow [ourselves] the wrong actions which you ascribe to us? Only lunatics or suicides, who themselves want to perish and before they die destroy the world, could do this. But we want to live and by no means do we want to destroy your country. We want something quite different: to compete with your country in a peaceful endeavor. We argue with you; we have differences on ideological questions. But our concept of the world is that questions of ideology, as well as economic problems, should be settled by other than military means; they must be solved in peaceful contest, or as this is interpreted in capitalist society—by competition. Our premise has been and remains

[3]A reference to their summit meeting in June 1961.

that peaceful coexistence, of two different sociopolitical systems—a reality of our world—is essential, and that it is essential to ensure lasting peace. These are the principles to which we adhere.

You have now declared piratical measures, the kind that were practiced in the Middle Ages when ships passing through international waters were attacked, and you have called this a "quarantine" around Cuba. Our vessels will probably soon enter the zone patrolled by your Navy. I assure you that the vessels which are now headed for Cuba are carrying the most innocuous peaceful cargoes. Do you really think that all we spend our time on is transporting so-called offensive weapons, atomic and hydrogen bombs? Even though your military people may possibly imagine that these are some special kind of weapons, I assure you that they are the most ordinary kind of peaceful goods.

Therefore, Mr. President, let us show good sense. I assure you that the ships bound for Cuba are carrying no armaments at all. The armaments needed for the defense of Cuba are already there. I do not mean to say that there have been no shipments of armaments at all. No, there were such shipments. But now Cuba has already obtained the necessary weapons for defense.

I do not know whether you can understand me and believe me. But I wish you would believe yourself and agree that one should not give way to one's passions; that one should be master of them. And what direction are events taking now? If you begin stopping vessels it would be piracy, as you yourself know. If we should start doing this to your ships you would be just as indignant as we and the whole world are now indignant. Such actions cannot be interpreted otherwise, because lawlessness cannot be legalized. Were this allowed to happen then there would be no peace; nor would there be peaceful coexistence. Then we would be forced to take the necessary measures of a defensive nature which would protect our interests in accordance with international law. Why do this? What would it all lead to?

Let us normalize relations. We have received an appeal from U Thant, Acting Secretary General of the U.N., containing his proposals.[4] I have already answered him. His proposals are to the effect that our side not ship any armaments to Cuba for a certain period of time while negotiations are being conducted—and we are prepared to enter into such negotiations—and the other side not undertake any piratical actions against vessels navigating on the high seas. I consider these proposals reasonable. This would be a way out of the situation which has evolved that would give nations a chance to breathe easily.

You asked what happened, what prompted weapons to be supplied to Cuba? You spoke of this to our Minister of Foreign Affairs.[5] I will tell you frankly, Mr. President, what prompted it.

We were very grieved by the fact—I spoke of this in Vienna—that a landing was effected and an attack made on Cuba, as a result of which many Cubans were killed.[6] You yourself told me then that this had been a mistake. I regarded

---

[4]For U Thant's role, see Document 24, footnote 2.

[5]A reference to the JFK-Gromyko meeting on October 18. For a record of this discussion, see Document 6.

[6]Khrushchev is talking about the Bay of Pigs invasion.

that explanation with respect. You repeated it to me several times, hinting that not everyone occupying a high position would acknowledge his mistakes as you did. I appreciate such frankness. For my part I told you that we too possess no less courage; we have also acknowledged the mistakes which have been made in the history of our state, and have not only acknowledged them but have sharply condemned them.

While you really are concerned for peace and for the welfare of your people—and this is your duty as President—I, as Chairman of the Council of Ministers, am concerned for my people. Furthermore, the preservation of universal peace should be our joint concern, since if war broke out under modern conditions, it would not be just a war between the Soviet Union and the United States, which actually have no contentions between them, but a world-wide war, cruel and destructive.

Why have we undertaken to render such military and economic aid to Cuba? The answer is: we have done so only out of humanitarian considerations. At one time our people accomplished its own revolution, when Russia was still a backward country. Then we were attacked. We were the target of attack by many countries. The United States took part in that affair. This has been documented by the participants in aggression against our country. An entire book has been written on this by General Graves, who commanded the American Expeditionary Force at that time. Graves entitled it *American Adventure in Siberia*.[7]

We know how difficult it is to accomplish a revolution and how difficult it is to rebuild a country on new principles. We sincerely sympathize with Cuba and the Cuban people. But we do not interfere in questions of internal organization; we are not interfering in their affairs. The Soviet Union wants to help the Cubans build their life, as they themselves desire, so that others would leave them alone.

You said once that the United States is not preparing an invasion. But you have also declared that you sympathize with the Cuban counterrevolutionary emigrants, support them, and will help them in carrying out their plans against the present government of Cuba. Nor is it any secret to anyone that the constant threat of armed attack and aggression has hung and continues to hang over Cuba. It is only this that has prompted us to respond to the request of the Cuban Government to extend it our aid in strengthening the defense capability of that country.

If the President and Government of the United States would give their assurances that the United States would itself not take part in an attack upon Cuba and would restrain others from such action; if you recall your Navy—this would immediately change everything. I do not speak for Fidel Castro, but I think that he and the Government of Cuba would, probably, announce a demobilization and would call upon the people to commence peaceful work. Then the question of armaments would also be obviated, because when there is no threat, armaments are only a burden for any people. This would also change the approach to

[7]The Soviet premier writes here of American intervention in the Russian Civil War that broke out shortly after the Bolshevik Revolution.

the question of destroying not only the armaments which you call offensive, but of every other kind of armament.

I have spoken on behalf of the Soviet Government at the United Nations and introduced a proposal to disband all armies and to destroy all weapons. How then can I stake my claims on these weapons now?

Armaments bring only disasters. Accumulating them damages the economy, and putting them to use would destroy people on both sides. Therefore, only a madman can believe that armaments are the principal means in the life of society. No, they are a forced waste of human energy, spent, moreover, on the destruction of man himself. If people do not display wisdom, they will eventually reach the point where they will clash, like blind moles, and then mutual annihilation will commence.

Let us therefore display statesmanlike wisdom. I propose: we, for our part, will declare that our ships bound for Cuba are not carrying any armaments. You will declare that the United States will not invade Cuba with its tropps [sic] and will not support any other forces which might intend to invade Cuba. Then the necessity for the presence of our military specialists in Cuba will be obviated.

Mr. President, I appeal to you to weigh carefully what the aggressive, piratical actions which you have announced the United States intends to carry out in international waters would lead to. You yourself know that a sensible person simply cannot agree to this, cannot recognize your right to such action.

If you have done this as the first step towards unleashing war—well then— evidently nothing remains for us to do but to accept this challenge of yours. If you have not lost command of yourself and realize clearly what this could lead to, then, Mr. President, you and I should not now pull on the ends of the rope in which you have tied a knot of war, because the harder you and I pull, the tighter the knot will become. And a time may come when this knot is tied so tight that the person who tied it is no longer capable of untying it, and then the knot will have to be cut. What that would mean I need not explain to you, because you yourself understand perfectly what dread forces our two countries possess.

Therefore, if there is no intention of tightening this knot, thereby dooming the world to the catastrophe of thermonuclear war, let us not only relax the forces straining on the ends of the rope, let us take measures for untying this knot. We are agreeable to this.

We welcome all forces which take the position of peace. Therefore, I both expressed gratitude to Mr. Bertrand Russell,[8] who shows alarm and concern for the fate of the world, and readily responded to the appeal of the Acting Secretary General of the U.N., U Thant.

These, Mr. President, are my thoughts, which, if you should agree with them, could put an end to the tense situation which is disturbing all peoples.

These thoughts are governed by a sincere desire to alleviate the situation and remove the threat of war.

---

[8]British philosopher Bertrand Russell had written both Khrushchev and Kennedy during the crisis, calling for a compromise solution.

26. Message from Chairman Khrushchev to President Kennedy

Before JFK and his advisers responded to Khrushchev's October 26 offer, they received another letter from the Soviet premier, changing the proposed terms of settlement. Khrushchev now made the additional request that American Jupiter missiles be removed from Turkey. His earlier message had been sent secretly, but Khrushchev decided to broadcast this one over Moscow radio.

Moscow, October 27, 1962.

DEAR MR. PRESIDENT, I have studied with great satisfaction your reply to Mr. Thant[1] concerning measures that should be taken to avoid contact between our vessels and thereby avoid irreparable and fatal consequences. This reasonable step on your part strengthens my belief that you are showing concern for the preservation of peace, which I note with satisfaction.

I have already said that our people, our Government, and I personally, as Chairman of the Council of Ministers, are concerned solely with having our country develop and occupy a worthy place among all peoples of the world in economic competition, in the development of culture and the arts, and in raising the living standard of the people. This is the most noble and necessary field for competition, and both the victor and the vanquished will derive only benefit from it, because it means peace and an increase in the means by which man lives and finds enjoyment.

In your statement[2] you expressed the opinion that the main aim was not simply to come to an agreement and take measures to prevent contact between our vessels and consequently a deepening of the crisis which could, as a result of such contacts, spark a military conflict, after which all negotiations would be superfluous because other forces and other laws would then come into play—the laws of war. I agree with you that this is only the first step. The main thing that must be done is to normalize and stabilize the state of peace among states and among peoples.

I understand your concern for the security of the United States, Mr. President, because this is the primary duty of a President. But we too are disturbed about these same questions; I bear these same obligations as Chairman of the Council of Ministers of the U.S.S.R. You have been alarmed by the fact that we have aided Cuba with weapons, in order to strengthen its defense capability— precisely defense capability—because whatever weapons it may possess, Cuba cannot be equated with you since the difference in magnitude is so great, particularly in view of modern means of destruction. Our aim has been and is to

[1]See Document 24, footnote 2. Kennedy had sent his reply to U Thant on October 25.
[2]JFK's address to the nation on October 22. See Document 14.

help Cuba, and no one can dispute the humanity of our motives, which are oriented toward enabling Cuba to live peacefully and develop in the way its people desire.

You wish to ensure the security of your country, and this is understandable. But Cuba, too, wants the same thing; all countries want to maintain their security. But how are we, the Soviet Union, our Government, to assess your actions which are expressed in the fact that you have surrounded the Soviet Union with military bases; surrounded our allies with military bases; placed military bases literally around our country; and stationed your missile armaments there? This is no secret. Responsible American personages openly declare that it is so. Your missiles are located in Britain, are located in Italy, and are aimed against us. Your missiles are located in Turkey.

You are disturbed over Cuba. You say that this disturbs you because it is 90 miles by sea from the coast of the United States of America. But Turkey adjoins us; our sentries patrol back and forth and see each other. Do you consider, then, that you have the right to demand security for your own country and the removal of the weapons you call offensive, but do not accord the same right to us? You have placed destructive missile weapons, which you call offensive, in Turkey, literally next to us. How then can recognition of our equal military capacities be reconciled with such unequal relations between our great states? This is irreconcilable.

It is good, Mr. President, that you have agreed to have our representatives meet and begin talks, apparently through the mediation of U Thant, Acting Secretary General of the United Nations.[3] Consequently, he to some degree has assumed the role of a mediator and we consider that he will be able to cope with this responsible mission, provided, of course, that each party drawn into this controversy displays good will.

I think it would be possible to end the controversy quickly and normalize the situation, and then the people could breathe more easily, considering that statesmen charged with responsibility are of sober mind and have an awareness of their responsibility combined with the ability to solve complex questions and not bring things to a military catastrophe.

I therefore make this proposal: We are willing to remove from Cuba the means which you regard as offensive. We are willing to carry this out and to make this pledge in the United Nations. Your representatives will make a declaration to the effect that the United States, for its part, considering the uneasiness and anxiety of the Soviet State, will remove its analogous means from Turkey. Let us reach agreement as to the period of time needed by you and by us to bring this about. And, after that, persons entrusted by the United Nations Security Council could inspect on the spot the fulfillment of the pledges made. Of course, the permission of the Governments of Cuba and of Turkey is necessary for the entry into those countries of these representatives and for the inspection of the fulfillment of the pledge made by each side. Of course it would be best if these representatives enjoyed the confidence of the Security Council, as well as yours and

[3]By this time discussion of the Cuban situation was under way at the UN.

mine—both the United States and the Soviet Union—and also that of Turkey and Cuba. I do not think it would be difficult to select people who would enjoy the trust and respect of all parties concerned.

We, in making this pledge, in order to give satisfaction and hope [to] the peoples of Cuba and Turkey and to strengthen their confidence in their security, will make a statement within the framework of the Security Council to the effect that the Soviet Government gives a solemn promise to respect the inviolability of the borders and sovereignty of Turkey, not to interfere in its internal affairs, not to invade Turkey, not to make available our territory as a bridgehead for such an invasion, and that it would also restrain those who contemplate committing aggression against Turkey, either from the territory of the Soviet Union or from the territory of Turkey's other neighboring states.

The United States Government will make a similar statement within the framework of the Security Council regarding Cuba. It will declare that the United States will respect the inviolability of Cuba's borders and its sovereignty, will pledge not to interfere in its internal affairs, not to invade Cuba itself or make its territory available as a bridgehead for such an invasion, and will also restrain those who might contemplate committing aggression against Cuba, either from the territory of the United States or from the territory of Cuba's other neighboring states.

Of course, for this we would have to come to an agreement with you and specify a certain time limit. Let us agree to some period of time, but without unnecessary delay—say within two or three weeks, not longer than a month.

The means situated in Cuba, of which you speak and which disturb you, as you have stated, are in the hands of Soviet officers. Therefore, any accidental use of them to the detriment of the United States is excluded. These means are situated in Cuba at the request of the Cuban Government and are only for defense purposes. Therefore, if there is no invasion of Cuba, or attack on the Soviet Union or any of our other allies, then of course these means are not and will not be a threat to anyone. For they are not for purposes of attack.

If you are agreeable to my proposal, Mr. President, then we would send our representatives to New York, to the United Nations, and would give them comprehensive instructions in order that an agreement may be reached more quickly. If you also select your people and give them the corresponding instructions, then this question can be quickly resolved.

Why would I like to do this? Because the whole world is now apprehensive and expects sensible actions of us. The greatest joy for all peoples would be the announcement of our agreement and of the eradication of the controversy that has arisen. I attach great importance to this agreement in so far as it could serve as a good beginning and could in particular make it easier to reach agreement on banning nuclear weapons tests. The question of the tests could be solved in parallel fashion, without connecting one with the other, because these are different issues. However, it is important that agreement be reached on both these issues so as to present humanity with a fine gift, and also to gladden it with the news that agreement has been reached on the cessation of nuclear tests and that consequently the atmosphere will no longer be poisoned. Our position and yours on this issue are very close together.[4]

All of this could possibly serve as a good impetus toward the finding of mutually acceptable agreements on other controversial issues on which you and I have been exchanging views. These views have so far not been resolved, but they are awaiting urgent solution, which would clear up the international atmosphere. We are prepared for this.

These are my proposals, Mr. President.

27. Summary Record of ExComm Meeting

Now the issue for ExComm officials was how to respond to Khrushchev's October 26 and 27 messages. In this discussion, the question of what to do about the Jupiter missiles in Turkey looms large.

Washington, October 27, 1962, 10 a.m.

... The discussion then turned to the question of U.S. missiles in Turkey. Mr. Nitze said it would be an anathema to the Turks to pull the missiles out. He feared the next Soviet step would be a demand for the denuclearization of the entire NATO area. He urged us to focus attention on Cuba rather than on U.S. bases in other countries.

Under Secretary Ball reported that the Turks would be very difficult about withdrawal of their strategic missiles, but the Italians would be easier to persuade if we chose to withdraw Jupiters from Italy.

At this point in the meeting the partial text of a Soviet public statement was read by the President as it was received in the room.[1] The President commented that the statement was a very tough position and varied considerably from the tone of Khrushchev's personal letter to the President received last night.[2] The President felt that the Soviet position would get wide support and said we should consider making public the Khrushchev private letter.

Secretary Rusk returned to the question of U.S. missiles in Turkey and pointed out that this subject must be kept separate from Soviet missiles in Cuba. The Turkish missile problem should be dealt with in the context of NATO vs. Warsaw Pact.

---

[4]Khrushchev and Kennedy had been corresponding before the missile crisis on the possibility of a nuclear test-ban treaty. See Michael R. Beschloss, *The Crisis Years: Kennedy and Khrushchev, 1960–1963* (New York, 1991), 424–425.

[1]Khrushchev's October 27 message (see Document 26).

[2]Khrushchev's October 26 message (see Document 25).

Mr. Bundy said we could not accept the Soviet proposal on Turkish missiles because the Soviet missiles were not out of Cuba.

The President recalled that he had asked that consideration be given to the withdrawal of U.S. missiles from Turkey some days previously.

Under Secretary Ball replied that the [State] Department had decided it could not raise this question with the Turks at this time for fear of a disastrous Turkish reaction. He said the question had been raised with Finletter in Paris and study was being given to whether any method could be worked out to reassure the Turks if we were going to offer to withdraw the Jupiter missiles.

Mr. Bundy said we cannot get into the position of appearing to sell out an ally, i.e. Turkey, to serve our own interests, i.e. getting the Soviet missiles out of Cuba.

The President commented that the Russians had made the Turkish missile withdrawal proposal in the most difficult possible way. Now that their proposal is public, we have no chance to talk privately to the Turks about the missiles, which, for a long time, we have considered to be obsolete.

Secretary Dillon said that it was possible that the Russians had made their public statement as part of a stalling tactic to provide them with sufficient time for a full-fledged confrontation with us.

The President read a draft statement telephoned from New York by Ambassador Stevenson commenting on the Soviet statement. Ambassador Stevenson argued for releasing his statement in an effort to keep the "peace offensive" from going to the Soviets.

The President left the meeting at this point with Mr. Sorensen. There ensued a discussion of how to handle the discrepancy between the Khrushchev private letter and the Russian offer made public in the Soviet statement. A suggestion was made that the Russian proposals contained in the private Khrushchev letter be made public.

The President returned to the meeting. He said we must ensure that the construction work on the missile sites in Cuba be stopped at once. He suggested that we talk to the Turks about the missiles, pointing out to them the great peril facing them during the next week. He acknowledged that the Turks were now in no position to make a statement to the effect that they would ask that the Jupiters be withdrawn.

Secretary Rusk suggested that we tell the Turks they must say that the Jupiter problem is a NATO problem and is not associated with the Cuban missile problem.

Secretary McNamara called attention to the fact that the missiles belonged to Turkey and that only the nuclear warheads are under our total control.

The President returned to a discussion of where we now find ourselves, i.e. we now have Soviet public proposals and Khrushchev's private proposals. What we must seek is an immediate cessation of the work on offensive missiles in Cuba. Once this work stopped we could talk to the Russians.

Mr. Bundy reiterated the view that the threat to us is Cuba. One explanation for the varying Soviet proposals is that the hard line Russians wanted to make public their preferred demands in order to make impossible progress toward the

Khrushchev private offer which may have been drafted by those who are less hard-nosed.

The President noted that it appeared to him that the Russians were making various proposals so fast, one after the other, that they were creating a kind of shield behind which work on the missile sites in Cuba continued. He said we had a perfectly defensible position, i.e. work on the missile sites must stop. Secretary McNamara added the thought that these offensive weapons must be made inoperable.

Mr. Bundy suggested that we tell Khrushchev privately that the position in their public statement was impossible for us, but that the position Khrushchev took in his private letter was different and we were studying these proposals. In the meantime, however, time is running out.

The President interrupted to take a telephone call from Ambassador Stevenson in New York. He resumed the discussion by saying that Khrushchev obviously is attempting to limit our freedom of action in Cuba by introducing the question of the missile bases outside this hemisphere. . . .

Mr. Alexis Johnson reported that he had just been informed that the Turkish Government had issued a press statement saying that the Russian proposal with respect to Jupiters in Turkey was not conceivable.

(As the remainder of the Soviet public statement was received in the Cabinet Room, it appeared that the Russian base proposal involved not merely Turkey but all of NATO.) . . .

[Robert Kennedy] desired that we make doubly clear that Turkish NATO missiles were one problem and that Cuba was an entirely separate problem.

Mr. Gilpatric stated that it was crucial for us to stand on the position that we will not negotiate with the Russians while the Soviet missile threat is growing in Cuba.

The President recalled that over a year ago we wanted to get the Jupiter missiles out of Turkey because they had become obsolete and of little military value. If the missiles in Cuba added 50% to Soviet nuclear capability, then to trade these missiles for those in Turkey would be of great military value. But we are now in the position of risking war in Cuba and in Berlin over missiles in Turkey which are of little military value. From the political point of view, it would be hard to get support on an airstrike against Cuba because many would think that we would make a good trade if we offered to take the missiles out of Turkey in the event the Russians would agree to remove the missiles from Cuba. We are in a bad position if we appear to be attacking Cuba for the purpose of keeping useless missiles in Turkey. We cannot propose to withdraw the missiles from Turkey, but the Turks could offer to do so. The Turks must be informed of the great danger in which they will live during the next week and we have to face up to the possibility of some kind of a trade over missiles.

The President left the meeting to meet the State Governors who had been waiting for one-half hour to see him.

The discussion continued in the President's absence. It was not possible to say with certainty whether the Soviet public offer included all NATO basses [sic] or referred specifically to Turkey.

The Attorney General expressed his concern as to what our position would be if we talked to the Russians for sixty days and then the Cubans refused to permit UN inspectors to continue to ensure that missiles in Cuba were inoperable. The reply was that we could then decide to attack the bases by air. . . .

The group agreed to meet at the State Department without the President at 2:30 PM and meet with the President again at 4:00 PM.

(Note: At the meeting at the State Department, the Attorney General repeated his view that we should keep the focus on the missile bases. He preferred to let the Soviet tankers through the quarantine line in order to avoid a confrontation with the Soviets over one of their ships. He said if we attack a Soviet tanker, the balloon would go up. He urged that we buy time now in order to launch an air attack Monday or Tuesday.[3])

Secretary McNamara expressed his view that before we attack Cuba we must notify the Cubans.[4]

28. Summary Record of ExComm Meeting

The Kennedy team continues its discussion in the late afternoon of October 27.

Washington, October 27, 1962, 4 p.m.

. . . There followed a discussion of a draft letter from the President to Khrushchev.[1] The President added to the draft an offer to discuss with the Russians the proposals they had made public.[2] He predicted that Khrushchev would say we had rejected his proposal. The formulation included a comment that Khrushchev must realize that matters relating to NATO must be discussed at a later time. The letter was approved in a revised form.

A message to U Thant was discussed and approved. The purpose of the message was to obtain the halting of work on the bases in Cuba as a condition to discussion of various other problems.

Secretary Rusk reported that one of our U–2 planes had overflown the Soviet Union by accident due to navigational error. Soviet fighters were scrambled from a base near Wrangel Island. The Secretary thought that the Russians would make a loud fuss about this incident.

The President decided not to make the incident public, but [to] be prepared to do so as soon as the Soviets publicized it.

---

[3] October 29 or 30.
[4] Bromley Smith drafted this memorandum.
[1] For the final version of this letter to Khrushchev, see Document 29.
[2] A reference to Khrushchev's October 27 message to JFK (Document 26).

The President asked whether we wanted to continue to say that we would talk only about the missiles in Cuba. He believed that for the next few hours we should emphasize our position that if the Russians will halt missile activity in Cuba we would be prepared to discuss NATO problems with the Russians. He felt that we would not be in a position to offer any trade for several days. He did feel that if we could succeed in freezing the situation in Cuba and rendering the strategic missiles inoperable, then we would be in a position to negotiate with the Russians.

Mr. Bundy pointed out that there would be a serious reaction in NATO countries if we appeared to be trading withdrawal of missiles in Turkey for withdrawal of missiles from Cuba. The President responded that if we refuse to discuss such a trade and then take military action in Cuba, we would also be in a difficult position.

The President left the room to talk to General Norstad on the KY–9 secure telephone to Paris.

In the President's absence the message to U Thant was further discussed. The Attorney General felt we should say to U Thant: "While these and other proposals are being discussed, would you urgently ascertain whether the Soviet Union is prepared to cease work on the bases and render the missiles inoperable?" U Thant would be asked to convey the President's message to the Russians in New York most urgently.

Secretary Rusk questioned whether the Russians are trying at the last minute to obtain more of a quid pro quo from us or whether they are introducing new elements in the picture merely to weaken our public position worldwide.

Secretary McNamara pointed out, in connection with the current military situation, that a limited airstrike on Cuba was now impossible because our reconnaissance planes were being fired on.[3] He felt that we must now look to the major airstrike to be followed by an invasion of Cuba. To do so he said we would need to call up the reserves now. . . .

Ambassador Thompson commented that it was impossible to draw any conclusions from the fact that one of our reconnaissance planes over Cuba had been shot at.

The President returned to the meeting, accompanied by General Lemnitzer.

The President approved the final revision of the statement to U Thant, which was to be phoned to U Thant and released here publicly.

The President asked whether we should call together the representatives of NATO to report to them what we had done and were planning to do. If we reject Soviet efforts to tie in NATO problems to the Cuban situation, then we could persuade NATO to take the same position. An additional reason for a NATO meeting then is that if the Russians do attack the NATO countries we do not want them to say that they had not been consulted about the actions we were taking in Cuba.

Secretary McNamara said that current military planning provided for 500

---

[3]On the morning of October 27 a U–2 plane was shot down over Cuba and the American pilot killed. Khrushchev had not authorized this provocative act; a Soviet commander had made the decision on his own initiative.

sorties to take out the SAM sites, the MIGs in Cuba, and the missiles and missile sites.

The President expressed his concern that the alternatives we are facing have not been presented to NATO. NATO does not realize what may be coming and the Europeans do not realize that we may face a choice of invading Cuba or taking the missiles out of Turkey.

Secretary McNamara urged that a NATO meeting be held tomorrow only if we have decided to launch our strike tomorrow. He repeated his hope that we can act in such a way as to reduce the pressure on the Russians to hit Turkey.

Secretary Rusk recommended that mobilization measures be authorized immediately.

The President suggested that we talk immediately to the Turks, explaining to them what we were planning to do with our missiles and then explain the entire situation to the North Atlantic Council.

Secretary Rusk then read a Stevenson draft of a letter to Khrushchev.[4]

The President said that the key to any letter to Khrushchev was the demand that work cease on the missile sites in Cuba. He predicted that if we make no mention of Turkey in our letter, Khrushchev will write back to us saying that if we include Turkey, then he would be prepared to settle the Cuban situation. The President said this would mean that we would lose twenty-four hours while they would continue to work on the bases and achieve an operational status for more of their missiles. He suggested that we would be willing to guarantee not to invade Cuba if the Soviet missiles were taken out.

Secretary Rusk returned to the Stevenson draft, which the President approved as revised. . . . The President also agreed not to call a meeting of the North Atlantic Council.

The Attorney General commented that in his opinion the Stevenson draft letter was defensive. It sounded as if we had been thrown off balance by the Russians. The State Department draft[5] merely said that we accepted Khrushchev's offer.

General Taylor summarized the conclusions of the Joint Chiefs. Unless the missiles are defused immediately, the Chiefs recommended implementation on Monday[6] of OP Plan 312, i.e. a major air strike, and, seven days later, OP Plan 316, which is the invasion plan.

Secretary McNamara asked what we should do about air surveillance tomorrow. He stated his recommendation, i.e. if our reconnaissance planes are fired on, we will attack the attackers. General Taylor noted that in order to be ready to invade on Monday, we must continue intensive air surveillance.

The President directed that our air reconnaissance missions be flown tomorrow without fighter escort. If our planes are fired on, we must be prepared for a general response or an attack on the SAM site which fired on our planes. We will decide tomorrow how we return fire after we know if they continue their at-

---

[4]The letter sent by JFK to Khrushchev on October 27 was based in part on this draft produced by Adlai Stevenson.

[5]Kennedy's October 27 message to Khrushchev was based not only on a Stevenson draft but also on a draft produced by State Department officials George Ball and Alexis Johnson.

[6]October 29.

tacks on our planes and after we hear from U Thant the Russian reply to our offer.[7]

The President considered a draft message to the Turks about their missile[s]. His objective was to persuade the Turks to suggest to us that we withdraw our missiles. He noted that negotiations with the Turks were very difficult if there was any life left in the proposal which we had asked U Thant to make to the Russians.

General Taylor read a late report of the shooting down of the U–2 reconnaissance plane in Cuba which said that the wreckage of the U–2 was on the ground and that the pilot had been killed. He felt that we should make an air attack tomorrow on the SAM site responsible for shooting down the U–2 plane.

Secretary McNamara said that we must now be ready to attack Cuba by launching 500 sorties on the first day. Invasion had become almost inevitable. If we leave U.S. missiles in Turkey, the Soviets might attack Turkey. If the Soviets do attack the Turks, we must respond in the NATO area. The minimum NATO response to Soviet attack on Turkey would be to use U.S. forces in Turkey to attack, by sea, and by air, the Soviet Black Sea fleet. However, we should make every effort to reduce the chance of a Soviet attack on Turkey.

In an informal discussion following the formal end of the meeting, the Vice President asked why we were not prepared to trade the withdrawal of U.S. missiles from Turkey for the withdrawal of the Soviet missiles from Cuba, if we were prepared to give up the use of U.S. missiles in Turkey. Under Secretary Ball responded that last week we thought it might be acceptable to trade the withdrawal of the missiles in Turkey if such action would save Berlin. He felt that we could accept the Soviet offer and replace the missiles in Turkey by assigning Polaris submarines to the area.[8]

29. Message from President Kennedy to Chairman Khrushchev

Following the advice of ExComm officials, JFK decides to accept Khrushchev's October 26 offer rather than his October 27 proposals. No explicit mention is made of the Jupiter missiles in this correspondence with the Soviet premier.

Washington, October 27, 1962, 8:05 p.m.

Dear Mr. Chairman:
I have read your letter of October 26[1] with great care and welcomed the state-

---

[7] Presumably a reference to the message to U Thant mentioned earlier in this meeting.
[8] Bromley Smith drafted this memorandum.
[1] Document 25.

ment of your desire to seek a prompt solution to the problem. The first thing that needs to be done, however, is for work to cease on offensive missile bases in Cuba and for all weapons systems in Cuba capable of offensive use to be rendered inoperable, under effective United Nations arrangements.

Assuming this is done promptly, I have given my representatives in New York instructions that will permit them to work out this week and—in cooperation with the Acting Secretary General[2] and your representative—an arrangement for a permanent solution to the Cuban problem along the lines suggested in your letter of October 26. As I read your letter, the key elements of your proposals— which seem generally acceptable as I understand them—are as follows:

1. You would agree to remove these weapons systems from Cuba under appropriate United Nations observation and supervision; and undertake, with suitable safeguards, to halt the further introduction of such weapons systems into Cuba.

2. We, on our part, would agree—upon the establishment of adequate arrangements through the United Nations to ensure the carrying out and continuation of these commitments—(a) to remove promptly the quarantine measures now in effect and (b) to give assurances against an invasion of Cuba and I am confident that other nations of the Western Hemisphere would be prepared to do likewise.

If you will give your representative similar instructions, there is no reason why we should not be able to complete these arrangements and announce them to the world within a couple of days. The effect of such a settlement on easing world tensions would enable us to work toward a more general arrangement regarding "other armaments," as proposed in your second letter which you made public.[3] I would like to say again that the United States is very much interested in reducing tensions and halting the arms race; and if your letter signifies that you are prepared to discuss a détente affecting NATO and the Warsaw Pact, we are quite prepared to consider with our allies any useful proposals.

But the first ingredient, let me emphasize, is the cessation of work on missile sites in Cuba and measures to render such weapons inoperable, under effective international guarantees. The continuation of this threat, or a prolonging of this discussion concerning Cuba by linking these problems to the broader questions of European and world security, would surely lead to an intensification of the Cuban crisis and a grave risk to the peace of the world. For this reason I hope we can quickly agree along the lines outlined in this letter and in your letter of October 26.

[2]U Thant.
[3]Khrushchev's October 27 message to JFK. See Document 26.

30. Memorandum from Attorney General Kennedy to Secretary of State Rusk

Although not mentioning the Jupiters in his message to Khrushchev, JFK decides on Rusk's advice to dispatch Robert Kennedy to Ambassador Dobrynin so that the Russians may be informed off the record that the Jupiters will be removed from Turkey in due course. What Robert Kennedy's report to Rusk on this meeting does not make clear is the explicitness of the promise made by the attorney general about withdrawing the Jupiters. (Robert Kennedy's original draft of this memorandum did make this clear— see footnote 3.)

Washington, October 30, 1962.

At the request of Secretary Rusk, I telephoned Ambassador Dobrynin at approximately 7:15 p.m. on Saturday, October 27th. I asked him if he would come to the Justice Department at a quarter of eight.

We met in my office. I told him first that we understood that the work was continuing on the Soviet missile bases in Cuba. Further, I explained to him that in the last two hours we had found that our planes flying over Cuba had been fired upon and that one of our U–2's had been shot down and the pilot killed. I said these men were flying unarmed planes.

I told him that this was an extremely serious turn in events. We would have to make certain decisions within the next 12 or possibly 24 hours. There was a very little time left. If the Cubans were shooting at our planes, then we were going to shoot back. This could not help but bring on further incidents and that he had better understand the full implications of this matter.

He raised the point that the argument the Cubans were making was that we were violating Cuban air space. I replied that if we had not been violating Cuban air space then we would still be believing what he and Khrushchev had said— that there were no long-range missiles in Cuba. In any case I said that this matter was far more serious than the air space over Cuba and involved peoples all over the world.

I said that he had better understand the situation and he had better communicate that understanding to Mr. Khrushchev. Mr. Khrushchev and he had misled us. The Soviet Union had secretly established missile bases in Cuba while at the same time proclaiming, privately and publicly, that this would never be done. I said those missile bases had to go and they had to go right away. We had to have a commitment by at least tomorrow that those bases would be removed. This was not an ultimatum, I said, but just a statement of fact. He should understand that if they did not remove those bases then we would remove them. His country might take retaliatory action but he should understand that before this was over, while there might be dead Americans there would also be dead Russians.

He asked me then what offer we were making. I said a letter had just been transmitted to the Soviet Embassy which stated in substance that the missile bases should be dismantled and all offensive weapons should be removed from Cuba.[1] In return, if Cuba and Castro and the Communists ended their subversive activities in other Central and Latin American countries, we would agree to keep peace in the Caribbean and not permit an invasion from American soil.

He then asked me about Khrushchev's other proposal dealing with the removal of the missiles from Turkey.[2] I replied that there could be no quid pro quo—no deal of this kind could be made. This was a matter that had to be considered by NATO and that it was up to NATO to make the decision. I said it was completely impossible for NATO to take such a step under the present threatening position of the Soviet Union.[3]

Per your instructions I repeated that there could be no deal of any kind and that any steps toward easing tensions in other parts of the world largely depended on the Soviet Union and Mr. Khrushchev taking action in Cuba and taking it immediately.

I repeated to him that this matter could not wait and that he had better contact Mr. Khrushchev and have a commitment from him by the next day to withdraw the missile bases under United Nations supervision for otherwise, I said, there would be drastic consequences.

31. Cable from Soviet Ambassador to the United States Anatoly F. Dobrynin to the Soviet Foreign Ministry

Ambassador Dobrynin's report on this meeting provides more detail on Robert Kennedy's assurances regarding the Jupiters.

October 27, 1962.

. . . "In this regard," R. Kennedy said, "the president considers that a suitable basis for regulating the entire Cuban conflict might be the letter N. S. Khrushchev sent on October 26 and the letter in response from the President,[1] which was sent off today to N. S. Khrushchev through the US Embassy in Moscow. The most important thing for us," R. Kennedy stressed, "is to get as soon as possible the agreement of the Soviet government to halt further work on the construction of the missile bases in Cuba and take measures under international control that would make it impossible to use these weapons. In exchange

[1]See Document 29.
[2]Khrushchev's October 27 message to JFK. See Document 26.
[3]In the original document there follows at this point, typed and crossed out, the following sentence: "If some time elapsed—and per your instructions, I mentioned four or five months—I said I was sure that these matters could be resolved satisfactory [sic]."
[1]See Documents 25 and 29.

the government of the USA is ready, in addition to repealing all measures on the 'quarantine,' to give the assurances that there will not be any invasion of Cuba and that other countries of the Western Hemisphere are ready to give the same assurances—the US government is certain of this."

"And what about Turkey?" I asked R. Kennedy.

"If that is the only obstacle to achieving the regulation I mentioned earlier, then the president doesn't see any unsurmountable difficulties in resolving this issue," replied R. Kennedy. "The greatest difficulty for the president is the public discussion of the issue of Turkey. Formally the deployment of missile bases in Turkey was done by a special decision of the NATO Council. To announce now a unilateral decision by the president of the USA to withdraw missile bases from Turkey—this would damage the entire structure of NATO and the US position as the leader of NATO, where, as the Soviet government knows very well, there are many arguments. In short, if such a decision were announced now it would seriously tear apart NATO."

"However, President Kennedy is ready to come to agree on that question with N. S. Khrushchev, too. I think that in order to withdraw these bases from Turkey," R. Kennedy said, "we need 4–5 months.[2] This is the minimal amount of time necessary for the US government to do this, taking into account the procedures that exist within the NATO framework. On the whole Turkey issue," R. Kennedy added, "if Premier N. S. Khrushchev agrees with what I've said, we can continue to exchange opinions between him and the president, using him, R. Kennedy and the Soviet ambassador." "However, the president can't say anything public in this regard about Turkey," R. Kennedy said again. R. Kennedy then warned that his comments about Turkey are extremely confidential; besides him and his brother, only 2–3 people know about it in Washington.

"That's all that he asked me to pass on to N. S. Khrushchev," R. Kennedy said in conclusion. "The president also asked N. S. Khrushchev to give him an answer (through the Soviet ambassador and R. Kennedy) if possible within the next day (Sunday) on these thoughts in order to have a business-like, clear answer in principle. [He asked him] not to get into a wordy discussion, which might drag things out. The current serious situation, unfortunately, is such that there is very little time to resolve this whole issue. Unfortunately, events are developing too quickly. The request for a reply tomorrow," stressed R. Kennedy, "is just that—a request, and not an ultimatum. The president hopes that the head of the Soviet government will understand him correctly." . . .

Then I told R. Kennedy that the President's thoughts would be brought to the attention of the head of the Soviet government. I also said that I would contact him as soon as there was a reply. In this regard, R. Kennedy gave me a number of a direct telephone line to the White House. . . .

I should say that during our meeting R. Kennedy was very upset; in any case, I've never seen him like this before. True, about twice he tried to return to the topic of "deception," (that he talked about so persistently during our previous meeting[3]), but he did so in passing and without any edge to it. He didn't even try

[2]See Document 30, footnote 3.
[3]On October 23 (see Document 19).

to get into fights on various subjects, as he usually does, and only persistently returned to one topic: time is of the essence and we shouldn't miss the chance.

After meeting with me he immediately went to see the president, with whom, as R. Kennedy said, he spends almost all his time now.

32. Telegram from United Kingdom Representative to the UN Sir Patrick H. Dean to the British Foreign Office

In 1987 Dean Rusk disclosed that on the evening of October 27, JFK instructed him to ask Andrew Cordier of Columbia University to be ready to provide UN Secretary General U Thant with a statement that would call publicly for the removal of missiles from Turkey and Cuba. This was an important revelation, as it suggested that Kennedy was prepared as a last resort to accept that the deal on the Jupiters be public knowledge if the Russians insisted on this. Hence this contributed to a stronger impression of JFK's determination to end the crisis by diplomacy, not force. The following document from a British archive, however, indicates that the Cordier ploy had been devised earlier, and would have entailed sending UN observation teams to the missile sites in Cuba and Turkey, not the actual removal of the nuclear weapons. Rusk's revelation may nonetheless have been accurate, in which case the October 27 plan was a case of JFK reworking this earlier version of the Cordier ploy.

October 25, 1962.

I have heard from a most reliable source that Cordier (lately United Nations Under-Secretary) has been in touch with top level persons in the United States Government about U Thant's statement on Cuba.[1] Cordier says that if a United Nations Commission could be introduced to keep a watch on Russian bases in Cuba under satisfactory guarantees, the United States might be prepared to consider allowing a similar United Nations Commission to look at some bases elsewhere, e.g. the United States bases in Turkey. If a satisfactory arrangement about Cuba could be reached they would be prepared for the United Nations Commission to go to other places but not to all the other American missile and other bases around the world.

2. Adlai Stevenson dropped a hint to this effect to me last night. If these ideas

---

[1] Possibly a reference to either U Thant's October 24 or 25 proposals to Kennedy and Khrushchev. See Document 24, footnote 2.

are being seriously considered, the biggest problem may be how to decide how many United States bases should be brought under the surveillance of the United Nations Commission.

33. Message from Chairman Khrushchev to President Kennedy

By October 28 a number of developments made Khrushchev fear that the crisis was spiraling out of control, that nuclear war was imminent. An American U–2 reconnaissance plane had been shot down over Cuba the previous day, action that Khrushchev had not authorized. His intelligence services were reporting that an American attack on Cuba was near, a view endorsed by Castro in a message to Khrushchev (in which the Cuban leader also recommended a nuclear strike on the United States if Kennedy decided to invade Cuba). Dobrynin's report on his conversation with Robert Kennedy the previous evening (Document 31) confirmed for Khrushchev the need to end the crisis immediately in order to prevent an American assault on Cuba and thus a superpower war. Accordingly, here the Soviet leader informs Kennedy, in a message broadcast by Radio Moscow, that he finds the proposals in the president's October 27 message acceptable.

Moscow, October 28, 1962.

DEAR MR. PRESIDENT: I have received your message of October 27.[1] I express my satisfaction and thank you for the sense of proportion you have displayed and for realization of the responsibility which now devolves on you for the preservation of the peace of the world.

I regard with great understanding your concern and the concern of the United States people in connection with the fact that the weapons you describe as offensive are formidable weapons indeed. Both you and we understand what kind of weapons these are.

In order to eliminate as rapidly as possible the conflict which endangers the cause of peace, to give an assurance to all people who crave peace, and to reassure the American people, who, I am certain, also want peace, as do the people of the Soviet Union, the Soviet Government, in addition to earlier instructions on the discontinuation of further work on weapons construction sites, has given a new order to dismantle the arms which you described as offensive, and to crate and return them to the Soviet Union.

Mr. President, I should like to repeat what I had already written to you in my

[1] See Document 29.

earlier messages—that the Soviet Government has given economic assistance to the Republic of Cuba, as well as arms, because Cuba and the Cuban people were constantly under the continuous threat of an invasion of Cuba. . . .

I regard with respect and trust the statement you made in your message of October 27, 1962, that there would be no attack, no invasion of Cuba, and not only on the part of the United States, but also on the part of other nations of the Western Hemisphere, as you said in your same message. Then the motives which induced us to render assistance of such a kind to Cuba disappear.

It is for this reason that we instructed our officers—these means as I had already informed you earlier are in the hands of the Soviet officers—to take appropriate measures to discontinue construction of the aforementioned facilities, to dismantle them, and to return them to the Soviet Union. As I had informed you in the letter of October 27,[2] we are prepared to reach agreement to enable United Nations Representatives to verify the dismantling of these means.

Thus in view of the assurances you have given and our instructions on dismantling, there is every condition for eliminating the present conflict.

I note with satisfaction that you have responded to the desire I expressed with regard to elimination of the aforementioned dangerous situation, as well as with regard to providing conditions for a more thoughtful appraisal of the international situation, fraught as it is with great dangers in our age of thermonuclear weapons, rocketry, spaceships, global rockets, and other deadly weapons. All people are interested in insuring peace.

Therefore, vested with trust and great responsibility, we must not allow the situation to become aggravated and must stamp out the centers where a dangerous situation fraught with grave consequences to the cause of peace has arisen. If we, together with you, and with the assistance of other people of good will, succeed in eliminating this tense atmosphere, we should also make certain that no other dangerous conflicts which could lead to a world nuclear catastrophe would arise.

In conclusion, I should like to say something about a détente between NATO and the Warsaw Treaty countries that you have mentioned. We have spoken about this long since and are prepared to continue to exchange views on this question with you and to find a reasonable solution.

We should like to continue the exchange of views on the prohibition of atomic and thermonuclear weapons, general disarmament, and other problems relating to the relaxation of international tension.

Although I trust your statement, Mr. President, there are irresponsible people who would like to invade Cuba now and thus touch off a war. If we do take practical steps and proclaim the dismantling and evacuation of the means in question from Cuba, in so doing we, at the same time, want the Cuban people to be certain that we are with them and are not absolving ourselves of responsibility for rendering assistance to the Cuban people.

We are confident that the people of all countries, like you, Mr. President, will understand me correctly. We are not threatening. We want nothing but peace. Our country is now on the upsurge. . . .

[2]See Document 26.

I should like to remind you, Mr. President, that military reconnaissance planes have violated the borders of the Soviet Union. In connection with this there have been conflicts between us and notes exchanged. In 1960 we shot down your U–2 plane, whose reconnaissance flight over the USSR wrecked the summit meeting in Paris. At that time, you took a correct position and denounced that criminal act of the former U.S. Administration.[3]

But during your term of office as President another violation of our border has occurred, by an American U–2 plane in the Sakhalin area. We wrote you about that violation on 30 August. . . .

A still more dangerous case occurred on 28 October, when one of your reconnaissance planes intruded over Soviet borders in the Chukotka Peninsula area in the north and flew over our territory.[4] The question is, Mr. President: How should we regard this? What is this: A provocation? One of your planes violates our frontier during this anxious time we are both experiencing, when everything has been put into combat readiness. Is it not a fact that an intruding American plane could be easily taken for a nuclear bomber, which might push us to a fateful step? And all the more so since the U.S. Government and Pentagon long ago declared that you are maintaining a continuous nuclear bomber patrol.

Therefore, you can imagine the responsibility you are assuming, especially now, when we are living through such anxious times. . . .

I should like to consider, Mr. President, that violation of Cuban airspace by American planes could also lead to dangerous consequences. And if you do not want this to happen, it would be better if no cause is given for a dangerous situation to arise.

We must be careful now and refrain from any steps which would not be useful to the defense of the states involved in the conflict, which could only cause irritation and even serve as a provocation for a fateful step. Therefore, we must display sanity, reason, and refrain from such steps.

We value peace perhaps even more than other peoples because we went through a terrible war with Hitler. But our people will not falter in the face of any test. Our people trust their Government, and we assure our people and world public opinion that the Soviet Government will not allow itself to be provoked. But if the provocateurs unleash a war, they will not evade responsibility and the grave consequences a war would bring upon them. But we are confident that reason will triumph, that war will not be unleashed and peace and the security of the peoples will be insured. . . .

---

[3]Khrushchev refers here to Kennedy's statement, made during the 1960 presidential campaign, that the Eisenhower administration should express regret for the episode in which Gary Powers's U–2 plane was brought down over the Soviet Union, the pilot captured, and the Paris summit meeting aborted.

[4]An American U–2 plane had strayed off course and entered Soviet airspace on October 27 (American time) but had managed to leave without triggering a confrontation with Soviet military aircraft. Kennedy responded to this news by saying, "There is always some son of a bitch who doesn't get the word."

34. Summary Record of ExComm Meeting

Kennedy and his advisers receive the good news of Khrushchev's October 28 message.

Washington, October 28, 1962, 11:10 a.m.

The full TASS text of the Khrushchev reply[1] to the President offering to withdraw Soviet offensive weapons from Cuba under UN supervision had been read by all prior to the opening of the meeting. (It had been received over the FBIS ticker beginning about 9:00 AM.)

Secretary Rusk began by making general comments to the effect that everyone present had helped to bring about the highly advantageous resolution of the Cuban missile crisis. Mr. Bundy interrupted to say that everyone knew who were hawks and who were doves, but that today was the doves' day.

Secretary McNamara said we would not have to face a decision on halting a Bloc ship today because the Soviet tanker *Graznyy* was lying dead in the water outside the quarantine zone and no other Bloc ships, if they continued toward Cuba, would be reaching the barrier.

Secretary McNamara and Secretary Rusk recommended, and the President agreed, that no air reconnaissance missions be flown today.

The President asked what we would substitute for our air surveillance of Cuba.

Secretary McNamara said this surveillance might be by the UN or a joint inspection of U.S./UN inspectors in a neutral plane, flown by Brazilians or Canadians. He said our objective should be to have reconnaissance carried out by the UN tomorrow. Technically, this could be arranged, but we do not know whether the UN would undertake the task.

The President suggested that we tell the UN they must carry out reconnaissance or else we will. He authorized the release to UN officials of classified information on Cuba, including photographs and refugee reports. . . . The purpose of the release of this information on Soviet armaments in Cuba was to facilitate the inspection task which we expected the UN to promptly undertake.

Secretary Rusk, in commenting on Khrushchev's reply, called attention to the text which said the Russians would "come to an agreement." He said [Soviet official Vasily] Kuznetsov was coming to New York to conduct the negotiations. He suggested that we pick up and accept Khrushchev's description of what he was prepared to withdraw from Cuba, i.e. "offensive weapons."

The President called attention to the IL–28 bombers which he said we should ask the Russians to withdraw by making a private approach to Khrushchev. He said we should not get "hung up" on the IL–28 bombers, but we should seek to include them in the Soviet definition of "offensive weapons" or "weapons we call offensive."

[1] See Document 33.

General Taylor said our objective should be the status quo ante.

The President agreed, but added that he did not want to get into a position where we would appear to be going back on our part of the deal. The IL–28 bombers were less important than the strategic missiles. Admittedly, we would face the problem of Soviet armaments in Cuba if the Russians continued to build up their defensive capability there.

At this point the Attorney General arrived.[2]

The President agreed to a statement to be made public, as revised in the meeting.[3] He asked that a draft reply to Khrushchev's statement be prepared for him to consider.[4] He directed that comments by everyone on the Soviet statement be reserved. Our posture is to be one of welcoming the Soviet offer to take out the offensive weapons under UN inspection, but attention should be called to the many problems we would encounter in the implementation of Khrushchev's offer. We should point out that we were under no illusion that the problem of Soviet weapons in Cuba is solved. In addition, he said we should make clear that we can draw no general conclusions about how the Russians will act in the future in areas other than Cuba. He made specific mention of the problem of Communist subversion in Latin America and asked that we refer to this problem either in our letter to Khrushchev or in U Thant's letter to Khrushchev. He directed that Ambassador Stevenson be asked to talk to UN officials about this aspect of the Cuban problem.[5]

35. Message from President Kennedy to Chairman Khrushchev

JFK welcomes Khrushchev's October 28 message in correspondence with the Soviet leader.

Washington, October 28, 1962, 5:03 p.m.

[Text has been handed to Soviet Embassy and released by White House at 4:35 PM.]

Dear Mr. Chairman:

I am replying at once to your broadcast message of October twenty-eight[1] even though the official text has not yet reached me because of the great impor-

---

[2]Robert Kennedy had been meeting with Ambassador Dobrynin. See Document 37.

[3]This public statement, welcoming Khrushchev's decision to remove the missiles from Cuba, was issued later in the day.

[4]For the final text of this message to Khrushchev, see Document 35.

[5]Bromley Smith drafted this memorandum.

[1]See Document 33.

tance I attach to moving forward promptly to the settlement of the Cuban crisis. I think that you and I, with our heavy responsibilities for the maintenance of peace, were aware that developments were approaching a point where events could have become unmanageable. So I welcome this message and consider it an important contribution to peace.

The distinguished efforts of Acting Secretary General U Thant have greatly facilitated both our tasks. I consider my letter to you of October twenty-seventh[2] and your reply of today as firm undertakings on the part of both our governments which should be promptly carried out. I hope that the necessary measures can at once be taken through the United Nations as your message says, so that the United States in turn can remove the quarantine measures now in effect. I have already made arrangements to report all these matters to the Organization of American States, whose members share a deep interest in a genuine peace in the Caribbean area.

You referred in your letter to a violation of your frontier by an American aircraft in the area of the Chukotsk Peninsula. I have learned that this plane, without arms or photographic equipment, was engaged in an air sampling mission in connection with your nuclear tests. Its course was direct from Eielson Air Force Base in Alaska to the North Pole and return. In turning south, the pilot made a serious navigational error which carried him over Soviet territory. He immediately made an emergency call on open radio for navigational assistance and was guided back to his home base by the most direct route. I regret this incident and will see to it that every precaution is taken to prevent recurrence.

Mr. Chairman, both of our countries have great unfinished tasks and I know that your people as well as those of the United States can ask for nothing better than to pursue them free from the fear of war. Modern science and technology have given us the possibility of making labor fruitful beyond anything that could have been dreamed of a few decades ago.

I agree with you that we must devote urgent attention to the problem of disarmament, as it relates to the whole world and also to critical areas. Perhaps now, as we step back from danger, we can together make real progress in this vital field. I think we should give priority to questions relating to the proliferation of nuclear weapons, on earth and in outer space, and to the great effort for a nuclear test ban. But we should also work hard to see if wider measures of disarmament can be agreed and put into operation at an early date. The United States Government will be prepared to discuss these questions urgently, and in a constructive spirit, at Geneva or elsewhere.

[2]See Document 29.

36. Telegram from Soviet Foreign Minister Gromyko to Ambassador Dobrynin

Gromyko instructs Dobrynin to contact Robert Kennedy in order to assure him that Khrushchev is now prepared to remove the missiles from Cuba.

October 28, 1962.

Quickly get in touch with R. Kennedy and tell him that you passed on to N. S. Khrushchev the contents of your conversation with him.[1] N. S. Khrushchev sent the following urgent response.

The thoughts which R. Kennedy expressed at the instruction of the President finds understanding in Moscow. Today, an answer will be given by radio to the President's message of October 27, and that response will be the most favorable.[2] The main thing which disturbs the President, precisely the issue of the dismantling under international control of the rocket bases in Cuba—meets no objection and will be explained in detail in N. S. Khrushchev's message.

Telegraph upon implementation.

37. Telegram from Ambassador Dobrynin to the Soviet Foreign Ministry

Dobrynin reports to Moscow on Robert Kennedy's palpable relief at the end of the missile crisis.

October 28, 1962.

R. Kennedy, with whom I met, listened very attentively to N. S. Khrushchev's response. Expressing thanks for the report, he said that he would quickly return to the White House in order to inform the President about the "important response" of the head of the Soviet government. "This is a great relief," R. Kennedy added further, and it was evident that he expressed his words somehow involuntarily. "I," said R. Kennedy, "today will finally be able to see my kids, for I have been entirely absent from home."

According to everything it was evident that R. Kennedy with satisfaction, it is necessary to say, really with great relief met the report about N. S. Khrushchev's response.

[1]See Document 31.
[2]See Document 33.

In parting, R. Kennedy once again requested that strict secrecy be maintained about the agreement with Turkey. "Especially so that the correspondents don't find out. At our place for the time being even Salinger does not know about it" (It was not entirely clear why he considered it necessary to mention his name, but he did it).

I responded that in the Embassy no one besides me knows about the conversation with him yesterday. R. Kennedy said that in addition to the current correspondence and future exchange of opinions via diplomatic channels, on important questions he will maintain contact with me directly, avoiding any intermediaries.

Before departing, R. Kennedy once again gave thanks for N. S. Khrushchev's quick and effective response. . . .

PART 5

Loose Ends

AFTER OCTOBER 28, 1962, the world no longer teetered on the brink of war. But the period until early January 1963, and particularly the first month after the October crisis, remained tense. The settlement of the missile crisis, forged by JFK and Khrushchev on October 27 and 28, remained to be implemented. And that proved to be no easy task.

The superpowers had to answer a cluster of questions during this period. How could Soviet withdrawal of the nuclear missiles from Cuba be verified, given that Castro would not permit UN observers on Cuban soil? Would Khrushchev accept President Kennedy's demand that IL–28 bombers, as well as the missiles, be removed? Would Kennedy make an explicit, official promise not to invade Cuba, as Khrushchev insisted? Could the superpowers reach an agreement at the United Nations, codifying the commitments they had made at the end of the missile crisis?

The documents in this chapter relate chiefly to the roles played by John and Robert Kennedy. Much of the intense correspondence between JFK and Khrushchev is included, as are records of clandestine meetings between Robert Kennedy and Dobrynin, used by their leaders as intermediaries during these weeks. Instructions sent by JFK to United Nations negotiators in New York are also included, as are some records of ExComm meetings.

These documents demonstrate an emerging ambivalence on the part of the Kennedys toward the Cuban issue and the cold war in general. On the one hand, the pre-crisis notion that the United States must work for the overthrow of Castro had not been completely discarded, as indicated by the Kennedys' reluctance to offer the Russians an explicit promise not to invade Cuba. On the other hand, after the missile crisis there were signs that John and Robert Kennedy were deeply troubled by how close they had come to war in October 1962. Hence they were ready to embrace a more conciliatory approach to cold war issues.

1. Telegram from Ambassador Dobrynin to the Soviet Foreign Ministry

After the missile crisis, Robert Kennedy and the Soviet ambassador in Washington continued the clandestine dialogue they had developed. Here Bobby Kennedy insists that the part of the settlement relating to the removal of the Jupiter missiles from Turkey be kept secret.

October 30, 1962.

Today Robert Kennedy invited me to meet with him. He said that he would like to talk about N. S. Khrushchev's letter to the President yesterday.[1]

The President, Robert Kennedy said, confirms the understanding with N. S. Khrushchev on the elimination of the American missile bases in Turkey. Corresponding measures will be taken towards fulfilling this understanding within the period of time indicated earlier, in confidential observance of NATO guidelines, but of course without any mention that this is connected to the Cuban events.

We, however, said Robert Kennedy, are not prepared to formulate such an understanding in the form of letters, even the most confidential letters, between the President and the head of the Soviet government when it concerns such a highly delicate issue. Speaking in all candor, I myself, for example, do not want to risk getting involved in the transmission of this sort of letter, since who knows where and when such letters can surface or be somehow published—not now, but in the future—and any changes in the course of events are possible. The appearance of such a document could cause irreparable harm to my political career in the future. This is why we request that you take this letter back.[2]

It is possible, Robert Kennedy continued, that you do not believe us and through letters you want to put the understanding in writing. The issue of Soviet

---

[1]Dobrynin had provided Robert Kennedy on October 29 with a message from Khrushchev to JFK that sought to formalize the secret component of the settlement to the missile crisis, namely the removal of the Jupiters from Turkey.

[2]Bobby Kennedy did return Khrushchev's October 29 message to Dobrynin on this occasion, making clear that the Kennedy administration would not acknowledge the withdrawal of the Jupiters as a formal part of the settlement.

missile bases in Cuba has unfortunately introduced a real element of uncertainty and suspicion even into confidential channels of contact. We will however live up to our promise, even if it is given in this oral form. As you know, it was in precisely the same oral form that the President made his promise to N. S. Khrushchev regarding the removal of a certain number of American soldiers from Thailand.[3] That promise was kept. So too will this promise be kept.

As a guarantee, Robert Kennedy added, I can only give you my word. Moreover I can tell you that two other people besides the President know about the existing understanding: they are [Secretary of State Dean] Rusk and [adviser on Soviet affairs Llewellyn] Thompson. If you do not believe me, discuss it with them, and they will tell you the same thing. But it is better not to transfer this understanding into a formal, albeit confidential, exchange of letters (as can be noted, the greatest suspicion in the two Kennedy brothers was elicited by the part of Khrushchev's letter which speaks directly of a link between the Cuban events and the bases in Turkey). We hope that N. S. Khrushchev will understand us correctly. In regard to this Robert Kennedy insistently asked to take the letter back without delay.

I told Robert Kennedy that everything said above I would report to N. S. Khrushchev, emphasizing in doing so that even the President and he, Robert Kennedy, could be sure of the fact that the Soviet government is regarding the understanding that has been reached as strictly secret and not for publication. At the same time, in order to confirm Robert Kennedy's statement about the understanding, I asked him again about whether the President really confirms the understanding with N. S. Khrushchev on the elimination of American missile bases in Turkey. Robert Kennedy said once again that he confirmed it, and again that he hoped that their motivations would be properly understood in Moscow. Taking what they explained into account, I believed it conditionally possible — before receiving any instructions from Moscow — to take this letter [back], since a categorical refusal to do so would, in my opinion, only weaken Robert Kennedy's firm statements on the understanding that has been reached. Moreover, leaving the letter with him, after he had clearly expressed the President's desire not to exchange letters, could scarcely be in the interests of doing business [in the future].

In conclusion Robert Kennedy said that, in his opinion, the events connected with the Cuban issue have been developing quite favorably, and that he hoped that everything would eventually be settled. He added that, on the Turkish issue and other highly confidential issues he was prepared to maintain a direct contact with me as earlier, emphasizing in doing so that the point was the possible oral considerations of the President and the head of the Soviet government N. S. Khrushchev on the exchange of letters on such delicate issues as missile bases in Turkey, or issues which need to be handled more by the State Department than by him personally, taking into account the delicacy of his situation as the President's brother and as Attorney General of the United States. I

---

[3]Following a request from Khrushchev transmitted by KGB official Georgi Bolshakov to Robert Kennedy in June 1962, JFK agreed to remove the American troops that had been dispatched to Thailand in May 1962 in response to an assault by Communist forces in Laos.

do not want, Robert Kennedy added, to claim for myself the function of the State Department, but my "solitary diplomacy" may be needed several more times, and we will [be] meeting with each other periodically.

I answered to Robert Kennedy that I was prepared to maintain contact with him on highly important issues in the future, passing over the heads, as he himself suggested, of all intermediaries. Robert Kennedy confirmed this. From what Robert Kennedy said it was clear that the President is trying now to avoid exchanging any documents on issues of a highly delicate nature like Turkey which could leave a trace anywhere, but that he favors the continuation of a confidential exchange of opinions between the heads of the two governments.

We believe it expedient to visit Robert Kennedy once again and to issue a statement, in referring to our mission, that the Soviet government and N. S. Khrushchev personally are prepared to take into account the President's desire for maintaining the secrecy of the oral understanding on the removal of the American missile bases from Turkey. It is also expedient to tell of our willingness, if the President is also prepared for this, to continue the confidential exchange of opinions between the heads of the governments on many important unresolved issues, on whose resolution the lessing of international tension, and of the tension between our two countries in particular, is to a very great degree dependent.

2. Telegram from Soviet Official Georgy Zhukov to Moscow

Using a different pair of intermediaries, JFK tells Khrushchev that he must receive evidence that the missiles are being withdrawn from Cuba, but also optimistically predicts that the removal of these nuclear weapons will usher in a harmonious phase in Soviet-American relations.

November 1, 1962.

I am reporting about a meeting with [White House Press Secretary Pierre] Salinger on 31 October.

1. Salinger requested that I pass on to N. S. Khrushchev that Kennedy is thankful to him for the decision which he made to dismantle and remove the missiles, and expresses his confidence that the agreement which was reached, built on mutual trust, will open the way to the resolution of other ripe problems. "The President does not want to portray the matter as if we won a victory over the USSR," said Salinger. His version for the press is exactly reflected in [*New York Times* correspondent James] Reston's article of 29 October. Kennedy de-

clared to the members of the government that it makes no sense to try to use the situation that developed to Khrushchev's detriment. In this spirit, Rusk conducted talks with 50 of the most prominent and trusted observers in the USA and allied countries.

2. Kennedy, in Salinger's words, is now extremely preoccupied with somehow disarming his adversaries, who are asserting that he has once again "fallen into a trap. . . ." We must, he said, no matter what, publish evidence that the missiles have been dismantled and taken away. Let it be representatives of the UN or of the Red Cross, let it be observation photos taken from the air, it is all the same to us. In this regard we are not demanding access to the missiles themselves, they really are secret. We must publish evidence that they are no longer on the launching pads and that they have been taken away.

3. Kennedy, in Salinger's words, as in the past is under strong pressure from the "right-wingers," who are condemning him for the fact that he, for the first time in the history of the Western hemisphere has given a guarantee for the permanent preservation of a "Communist preserve" by the shores of the USA. In order to deflect these attacks, Kennedy must receive evidence to the effect that Castro has no "offensive" weapons.

4. Kennedy, as Salinger asserts, believes that achieving a resolution to the Cuban crisis "will open a completely new epoch in Soviet-American relations," when mutual trust will become the "basis of everything." One of the first issues to be resolved can and must be the issue of a [nuclear] test ban.

5. Regarding a meeting between Kennedy and Khrushchev, before the Cuban crisis a majority of members of the government spoke out against such a contact, although it had been publicly stated that Kennedy will meet with Khrushchev if he comes to the General Assembly. Kennedy himself had doubted that this meeting will bring any sort of positive results.

"Now—said Salinger—the situation has changed. The Cuban crisis showed that the issues on which the improvement of Soviet-American relations depends must be resolved urgently. Therefore, it will be necessary to review the position in relation to a meeting in light of the results of the settlement of the crisis. We were too close to war for it to be possible to forget about this and to allow ourselves to delay even longer in reaching a resolution to the problems which have become urgent. However, the President still does not have a prepared decision about the expediency of a meeting and about the issues which should be considered. We still have to think about that." . . .

7. Salinger stressed that even with all the "shortcomings" of Kennedy and Khrushchev's Vienna meeting,[1] it had given a positive result, at least insofar as on the basis of the agreement that had been achieved there the Laos problem had been settled,[2] which prompted confidence that it is possible to develop our relations on the basis of trust. For precisely this reason Kennedy had withdrawn the forces from Thailand.[3]

[1] In June 1961.
[2] See Chapter 4, Document 6, footnote 3.
[3] See Document 1, footnote 3.

"The Cuban crisis undermined this development of relations, but Khrushchev's wise decision may put the development of Soviet-American relations onto a basis of mutual trust," said Salinger. . . .

3. Telegram from Ambassador Dobrynin to the Soviet Foreign Ministry

In another tête-à-tête between Robert Kennedy and Dobrynin on the withdrawal of Russian missiles from Cuba, the crucial issue of verification is explored.

November 1, 1962.

[. . . Dobrynin] expressed the hope, in accordance with the letter sent by N. S. Khrushchev,[1] that the USA would renounce the quarantine without waiting for the introduction of a supplementary procedure for inspecting ships, and so on.

Robert Kennedy has said that this issue does not represent any difficulties. The important thing for us now (he implied that he was talking about public opinion, rather than the thoughts of the President himself), is to have some confirmation, from the UN for example, that the Soviet bases are being dismantled, and that the corresponding missile weaponry is being removed.

We and the USA government have essentially two possible courses of actions in this matter: first, to carry out reconnaissance flights over Cuba. But this entails the danger that the Cubans (he emphasized the Cubans, and not the Russians) may shoot down an American plane, and thus a possible new and highly undesirable chain reaction of events in the Cuban affair would be unleashed.

The second course of action is to get from the UN some information on the dismantling of the bases. The government of the USA could then be satisfied with this as a prerequisite for lifting the quarantine. Robert Kennedy emphasized that he was not yet prepared to talk about the details of this whole affair, since the President did not yet have any information on the results of U Thant's trip.[2] . . .

Robert Kennedy emphasized that the point was not that they do not trust our information on this account, but rather the question of how to present this whole affair to the public opinion of the USA in connection with the earlier statements

---

[1] A reference to a message sent by Khrushchev to JFK on October 30.

[2] U Thant had traveled to Havana for talks with Castro and other Cuban officials. On October 30 he presented various plans for verification of the removal of the missiles from Cuba. Castro rejected them all. U Thant returned to New York on October 31.

offered by the President.[3] It was felt that he had been somewhat worried by how Fidel Castro might hinder the carrying out of the agreement that had been reached.

4. Telegram from the State Department to the U.S. Mission at the United Nations

In his instructions to American officials at the UN, JFK himself stresses the importance of verification of the missile withdrawal. He was concerned about Soviet subterfuge and the concealment of missiles that might go undetected by photographic intelligence.

Washington, November 1, 1962.

Eyes only from Undersecretary Ball. President believes it essential that in conversation with Mikoyan (and Kuznetsov as appropriate) following points be made with utmost emphasis:

1. Kennedy-Khrushchev understanding based on assumption that Sovs would and could deliver on Khrushchev commitment to remove all offensive weapons systems in Cuba and through UN verification satisfy U.S. and other OAS countries. This in fact done and does not recur.

2. Although four days have now passed since understanding reached that U Thant has made best efforts,[1] all we have so far is verbal assurances by Sov reps in NY and Cuba to US and UN without element of verification which in view history of this affair US regards as essential.

3. US has acted expeditiously and in good faith, promptly accepting Soviet proposal that ICRC act as UN agent for inspection incoming vessels. (US believes we should promptly move to put this in effect with or without Cuban agreement. Further instructions on this will come later today.) US also promptly responded SYG [U Thant] request suspend quarantine and recon flights[2] during period his Havana visit. Also as Sovs aware USG has close watch to prevent anti-Castro Cubans from any action which would upset execution of agreement, e.g. arrest of group with boat in Florida yesterday.

4. On question verification USG has expressed willingness accept wide

[3]A reference perhaps to JFK's October 27 letter to Khrushchev or to a public statement the president released at the end of the crisis on October 28. Alternatively it may be a reference to Kennedy's September 4 and 13 public statements.

[1]A reference to U Thant's unproductive talks with Castro in Havana. See Document 3, footnote 2.

[2]A reference to U.S. reconnaissance flights over Cuba.

range of possible UN arrangements but there does not yet appear likelihood even any one of these can be implemented.

5. President's responsibility for US security demands that in absence UN verification, US undertake whatever steps it can to provide verification. Subordinate to this overriding consideration but nevertheless important is assurance to US and LA publics.

6. Thus, although much less satisfactory than UN verification on the ground and from the air with cooperation Sovs and Cuba, US must in elemental interests of safety continue aerial surveillance. This surveillance is being carried out in as unprovocative a manner and on as limited a scale as possible by unarmed aircraft. While US accepts that some conventional anti-aircraft guns may be under Cuban control, it cannot accept that sophisticated weapons and control systems, including SAM's, do not require participation of Sov technicians and thus are not or could not be made subject to Soviet control. If US reconnaissance aircraft fired on or destroyed, serious question appropriate means protect US aircraft will arise. We might thus face a cycle of action and reaction which would put us back where we were last week. Thus of utmost importance Sovs immediately take measures to assure reconnaissance aircraft not fired on.

7. Second sentence of President's letter to Chairman Khrushchev of October 27 is clear in covering "all weapons systems in Cuba capable of offensive use." This covers not only systems under Soviet control but also those allegedly under Cuban control. The President considers Khrushchev's reply of October 28 as clear acceptance that all of these arms are to be dismantled, crated and returned to Sov Union (or destroyed). You should seek to elicit a clear confirmation that the IL28's are included and are being dismantled for removal from Cuba.

8. In addition, you should point out that if Sov missiles and bombers are being removed, there seems no need for Soviets to leave in Cuba equipment and military technicians brought to Cuba primarily to protect the offensive weapons. (Note that SAM's use missile fuel which proscribed under quarantine regulations.) President's undertaking against invasion is adequate assurance that these weapons are not needed.

9. The President particularly desires that there should be no discussion of wider issue from our side until the offensive weapons in Cuba are clearly on their way home. You must therefore avoid any exploration of tempting fields like Berlin and disarmament, making it plain that while we look forward to such discussion later, we cannot get anywhere on anything else until we have successfully put in operation the Kennedy-Khrushchev agreement on this present matter.[3]

[3]Rusk's name was placed at the end of this message.

5. Message from President Kennedy to Chairman Khrushchev

Kennedy responds to a lengthy, wide-ranging message from Khrushchev of October 30.

Washington, November 3, 1962.

DEAR MR. CHAIRMAN: I wish to thank you for your letter of October 30.[1] I am commenting now only on a problem raised in your letter which relates to the Cuban affair.

With respect to the quarantine on shipments to Cuba, I am hopeful that arrangements can be worked out quickly by the United Nations which would permit its removal. We were happy to agree to your suggestion that the International Committee of the Red Cross undertake responsibility for inspection. You are, of course, aware that Premier Castro has announced his opposition to measures of verification on the territory of Cuba. If he maintains this position this would raise very serious problems. So far as incoming shipments are concerned, I understand that efforts are being made to have the International Red Cross carry out the necessary measures at sea and I hope that these will be successful. In the meantime, perhaps the existence of the quarantine can be of assistance to Mr. Mikoyan in his negotiations with Premier Castro.[2] I should also like to point out that in an effort to facilitate matters, I instructed our [UN] delegation in New York to inform your representative there, Mr. Kuznetsov, that for the next few days any Soviet ships in the quarantine area would be passed without inspection and only the hailing procedure which was carried out in the case of your vessel, the *Bucharest*, would be applied.[3]

I am hopeful we can dispose of this pressing matter quickly so that we can go on in a better atmosphere to the broader questions. We both must make our best efforts to this end.

---

[1]Not included in this chapter.

[2]Close Khrushchev aide Anastas Mikoyan arrived in Havana on November 2 for talks with Castro.

[3]The *Bucharest* was the Soviet tanker that on October 25 had been hailed and then permitted to cross the quarantine line.

6. Telegram from the State Department to the U.S. Mission at the United Nations

JFK seeks to stiffen the resolve of Adlai Stevenson and John McCloy, his senior officials involved in UN negotiations with the Russians aimed at tying up the loose ends of the missile crisis settlement. He tells them there must be verified removal of all offensive Soviet weapons from Cuba.

Washington, November 3, 1962.

Eyes only for Stevenson and McCloy. Following is text of an instruction from the President to all concerned with present negotiations in Cuba:

"It is time for a review of our basic position in these negotiations and for a clear restatement of our policy and purpose.

We have good evidence that the Russians are dismantling the missile bases.[1] We have no decisive evidence of what they will do with this equipment. The assembly of IL–28's continues. There is some evidence of an intent to establish a submarine-tending facility. The future of the SAM sites is unclear. We have no satisfactory assurances on verification. Our aerial surveillance still proceeds without guarantee of safety.

This crisis is likely to move in one of two major directions in the next few weeks. On the one hand, we may be able to make arrangements which will in fact ensure the verified removal of all Soviet offensive weapons systems from Cuba and establish reliable safeguards against their reintroduction. This is the object of our policy and it is precisely stated in my letter to Khrushchev of October 27:[2] 'You would agree to remove these weapons systems (previously defined as "all weapons systems in Cuba capable of offensive use") from Cuba under appropriate United Nations observation and supervision; and undertake, with suitable safeguards, to halt the further introduction of such weapons systems into Cuba.' Chairman Khrushchev's message of 28 October[3] contained an explicit undertaking to dismantle, crate and return to the Soviet Union 'the weapons which you describe as "offensive"' under UN verification. It is the position of the United States Government that this is a clear acceptance of my proposal of October 27.

This requirement means removal of all offensive missiles and supporting equipment, and of all bombers and their equipment. These items and associated equipment are generally described in my statement of September 13 and in my address of October 22; they are clearly defined in my Proclamation of October

---

[1]U.S. photo reconnaissance on November 1 had revealed that Soviet medium-range missile sites had been bulldozed and the missiles removed. In addition, construction of intermediate-range missile sites had been halted.

[2]See Chapter 4, Document 29.

[3]See Chapter 4, Document 33.

23.[4] All Americans should stick firmly to this position. We should add that a submarine base is equally unacceptable. . . .

In blunt summary, we want no offensive weapons and no Soviet military base in Cuba, and that is how we understand the agreements of October 27 and 28.

If in fact the Soviet Government executes this kind of removal with the associated and necessary inspection, supervision, and safeguards against reintroduction, then we in turn will hold with equal clarity to the undertaking given in my letter of October 27, as follows: '(a) to remove promptly the quarantine measures now in effect and (b) to give assurances against an invasion of Cuba.' We also have an obligation to work with other Western Hemisphere countries to get them to take a similar position. The exact terms and meaning of this undertaking require further work, but its broad implication is clear: in the absence of other provocation or justification, we will give an undertaking not to invade Cuba if we are properly assured that Cuba ceases to be a Soviet military base and ceases to harbor weapons. This commitment in no way derogates from our Hemispheric obligations to deal with aggressive or subversive activities by the present regime in Cuba.

There is another major course which events may take. It is one with which all who have negotiated with the Soviet Government in the past are familiar. It is a course in which bargains are fudged, secrecy prevents verification, agreements are reinterpreted, and by one means or another the Soviet Government seeks to sustain and advance the very policy which it has apparently undertaken to give up.

There is much evidence to support the conclusion that this is what is now beginning.

This second line of Soviet conduct is unacceptable to the United States. To prevent it we must make it very clear, at every stage, by both word and act, that the United States Government will not accept a mere gentlemen's agreement relating only to visible missiles on identified launch pads. We must have adequate arrangements for verification and inspection to be sure both that offensive weapons are removed and that no more are introduced. Without them, both surveillance and the quarantine must be continued and both may need to be extended. (This condition does not exclude temporary relaxation of either quarantine or surveillance in return for useful steps toward fully effective arrangements. Such a relaxation is foreseen in connection with our plans for ICRC inspection of certain inbound cargoes.) All the offensive weapons systems, including anything related to a submarine base, must be removed, or we shall have to consider further action of our own to remove them.

Finally, and most generally, the undertaking of the United States against invasion cannot take effect in any atmosphere of ambiguity or uncertainty such that the American Government or the American people would lack proper assurance against the existence in Cuba now, or at any future time, of any Soviet military base or offensive weapons. The Soviet Government must recognize that

[4]JFK's October 23 Proclamation formally established the blockade. For JFK's September 13 statement and October 22 address, see Chapter 3, Document 12, and Chapter 4, Document 14, respectively.

the events of the last three weeks have made it impossible for opinion in this Hemisphere to be satisfied with Soviet assurances alone. Verification is essential if the Governments of the Western Hemisphere are to be able to live with this situation without further action.

I repeat that this statement of policy should be taken as binding guidance by all who are engaged in the framing of instructions or the conduct of negotiations on this matter.[5] It is of fundamental importance that we speak as one voice and continue to keep it entirely clear to all Soviet representatives that the agreements of October 27 and 28 must be carried out in full—and that otherwise the United States Government will find it necessary to move again by its own means to insure itself against a repetition of the extraordinary act of deception which initiated this crisis. In this situation the Soviet Government has a clear choice between verified removal of all offensive weapons systems and renewed action by the United States. It has no middle choice, and we believe its own interests should lead it to accept the honest and full execution of the Kennedy–Khrushchev agreement, and to see to it that Castro provides the necessary cooperation.

Detailed guidance in support of this general policy has been provided in approved instructions to USUN earlier this week. . . . My only addition at present is that I now believe we should not be satisfied with aerial surveillance and post-removal ground inspection for departing offensive weapons. We must also have some way of verifying the reexport of the missiles, and the best practicable way seems to be to count them on departing ships. This can be done with no violation of Soviet security by reliable and nontechnical non-Americans, and we should insist on this or an equally effective verification."[6]

7. Memorandum from Attorney General Kennedy to President Kennedy

On November 2 Stevenson provided the Russians with a list of what the Kennedy administration regarded as those "offensive weapons" in Cuba that had to be removed. This list mentioned not only surface-to-surface missiles but also such equipment as IL–28 bombers and Komar torpedo boats. It showed that JFK and his advisers had decided to seek the removal of as much Russian military equipment from Cuba as possible. In the following two documents, Bobby Kennedy discusses this issue with Dobrynin, and Khrushchev takes umbrage at the American list in correspondence with JFK.

---

[5]This statement was probably aimed at Stevenson, thought by John and Robert Kennedy to be incorrigibly "soft" in dealings with the Soviets.

[6]Rusk's name was placed at the end of this telegram, but it was drafted by McGeorge Bundy and approved by U. Alexis Johnson.

Washington, November 5, 1962.

Dobrynin asked earlier this morning if I could see him and I made arrangements to have him come to the office at 12 o'clock Noon.

He delivered another letter from Mr. Khrushchev.[1] I read it and found that it concerned our list of offensive weapons that Stevenson had submitted.[2]

I explained to Dobrynin that from the first it had been made clear by the Soviet Union that they would get rid of any weapons which we considered offensive and certainly it was very clear that the bombers, the IL–28's, had to go.[3] Dobrynin replied that he was not familiar with that position and also did not know what was on the list that Khrushchev mentioned in his letter. I told him I would get a copy of it; that it was basically the same list of weapons that had been listed in the President's Quarantine Proclamation.[4] He replied he would obtain a copy from Kuznetsov.

During the middle of the conversation the President called and said that he had just received some preliminary information which indicated that several of our planes over Cuba had been fired upon. In ending my conversation with Dobrynin, therefore, I stressed the fact that any arrangements that were made were dependent upon there not being any incidents in the air above Cuba.

8. Message from Chairman Khrushchev to President Kennedy

Moscow, undated.[1]

DEAR MR. PRESIDENT, I have just received information from Mr. V. Kuznetsov, our representative at the negotiations in New York for liquidation of the tense situation around Cuba, that Mr. Stevenson handed him a list of weapons which your side calls offensive.[2] I have studied the list and, I must confess, the approach of the American side to this matter has seriously worried me. In such a move, I will say frankly, I see a wish to complicate the situation, because it is impossible indeed to place into the category of "offensive" weapons such types of weapons which have always been referred to as defensive weapons even by a man uneducated militarily—by a common soldier, not to say of an officer.

---

[1]See Document 8.
[2]On November 2 Stevenson dispatched to Mikoyan a letter listing those weapons considered offensive by the Kennedy administration.
[3]This represented a shift to some degree from the position on the IL–28s taken by JFK in the ExComm meeting on October 28. See Chapter 4, Document 34.
[4]Issued on October 23.
[1]Received by the Kennedy administration on November 5.
[2]See Document 7, footnote 2.

It is hard for us to understand what aim is being pursued by the introduction of that list, by setting forth such a demand—in any case it must be some other aim, but not a desire for a speediest clearing of the atmosphere. And it is being done at a moment when we have already agreed with you on the main questions and when we on our part have already fulfilled what we agreed upon—have dismantled rocket weapons, are loading them now on ships and these weapons will be soon shipped from Cuba. That is why I feel greatly concerned with the advancing of such [a] demand by the American side, concerned with its possible consequences, if necessary reasonableness is not displayed.

The demand which has been set forth is evidently pursuing, as I have already said, some other aims and that—I would wish, Mr. President, that you understand me correctly—can lead not to the betterment of our relations but, on the contrary, to their new aggravation. We should understand the position each side is in and take it into consideration but not overburden, not complicate our relations, especially at such an important moment when measures are being taken to eliminate the acute tension and bring these relations to a normal state.

That is why I would ask you, Mr. President, to meet our anxiety with understanding, to take measures on your side in order not to complicate the situation and to give your representatives a directive to eliminate the existing tension on the basis upon which both of us have agreed by having exchanged public messages. You spoke to the effect that missiles which you called offensive should be removed from Cuba. We agreed to that. You in your turn gave assurances that the so-called "quarantine" would be promptly removed and that no invasion of Cuba would be made, not only by the U.S. but by other countries of the Western hemisphere either.

Let us then bring the achieved understanding to a completion, so that we could consider that each side has fulfilled its pledges and the question has been settled. If, however, additional demands are made, then that means only one thing—the danger that the difficulties on the way to eliminating tension created around Cuba will not be removed. But that may raise then new consequences.

I think that you will understand me correctly. For you and I will evidently have to deal not only with elimination of the remnants of the present tension—there lies ahead for you and me a great, serious talk on other questions. Why then start now complicating the situation by minor things. May be there exist some considerations, but they are beyond our comprehension. As for us, we view the introduction of additional demands as a wish to bring our relations back again into a heated state in which they were but several days ago.

9. Telegram from the State Department to the U.S. Mission at the United Nations

JFK sends Stevenson and McCloy fresh instructions for negotiating with the Russians. These touch on such issues as verification and the American pledge not to invade Cuba.

Washington, November 5, 1962.

Eyes only Stevenson and McCloy from President. Your conversation with Kuznetsov[1] shows progress on one important point but raises a number of questions on which I wish to comment.

If we can see and count for ourselves departing missiles and associated equipment, that will be an important forward step and we see promise in the procedures Kuznetsov proposed[2] as long as it is clear that reliable observation, not Soviet photography alone, is essential.

One serious gap in Kuznetsov's proposal respecting missiles is the absence of any reference to nuclear warheads. Our interest in their absence is intense, and you should emphasize to all Soviets that since Khrushchev spoke to Knox of the presence of such warheads in Cuba,[3] we need assurances on warheads as much as on missiles themselves. Moreover, we need to know about possible warheads for IL–28's and even MIG–21's.

This warhead problem highlights the general importance of post-removal verification in Cuba itself. Forty-two missiles is a plausible number and not inconsistent with our own reports, but Soviet figures, while genuinely useful, are not a wholly reliable basis for action. In this connection you should not hesitate to press home with Kuznetsov the fact that past Soviet deception remains a major element in our reaction to this whole episode. It may be true, as Kuznetsov argues, that the Soviets had no obligation to tell us exactly what they were doing in a country like Cuba, but what actually happened in this case was that they repeatedly gave us assurances of what they were not doing. These assurances came from highest levels, and proved absolutely false.

Your insistence on the removal of IL–28's, the unacceptability of any submarine support facility, and obvious Soviet involvement in SAM complex are all correct and worth repeating insistently. You are also right to resist guarantees on subversion and to keep Guantanamo out of it.

With respect to U.S. guarantees, we are not yet ready to give you more detailed instructions, but these general points may be helpful:

(1) No long-term arrangements can be settled until after we have reached

---

[1]A conversation on November 4 between Kuznetsov and McCloy at the latter's Stamford, Connecticut, home.

[2]Kuznetsov had suggested, among other things, that American officials observe the Soviet ships departing from Cuba in order to count the missiles on board.

[3]Khrushchev and U.S. businessman William E. Knox had met on October 24.

clear understanding on verified removal of offensive weapons systems, including IL28's.

(2) OAS-approved right of surveillance will be kept intact. . . . In this connection you should report to Kuznetsov that today one of our low-level flights was harassed by MIG's apparently manned by Soviets.[4] No damage was done, and it is not clear that MIG's fired, but episode provides good basis for you to drive home our view of critical importance of unimpeded surveillance unless and until better arrangements can be made. You should remind Kuznetsov that surveillance must and will continue, and that further interference will be sure to bring prompt reaction including armed action if necessary.[5] . . .

10. Memorandum from President Kennedy to Secretary of Defense McNamara

Little more than a week after the missile crisis was defused, JFK moves to make sure that his contingency plans to attack Cuba are updated.

Washington, November 5, 1962.

As I have communicated to General Wheeler, through General Clifton, the plans for X[1] seem thin. Considering the size of the problem, the equipment that is involved on the other side, the nationalistic fervor which may be engendered, it seems to me we could end up bogged down.

I think we should keep constantly in mind the British in Boer War, the Russians in the last war with the Finnish and our own experience with the North Koreans. We are keeping, as I understand it, three divisions in reserve. I think we should plan to use them and call up any guard divisions we have available. This may require us to build additional divisions.

---

[4]An encounter occurred between MiG fighters and U.S. reconnaissance aircraft, though apparently no shots were fired.

[5]Rusk's name was placed at the end of this telegram, but it was drafted by McGeorge Bundy and cleared by George Ball.

[1]JFK was referring here to CINCLANT OPLAN 316, a U.S. contingency plan to exploit various developments in Cuba, including an anti-Castro uprising, by launching a military assault on the island.

11. Message from President Kennedy to Chairman Khrushchev

In correspondence with the Soviet premier, JFK focuses on what had by this time become a major bone of contention between the superpowers: the question of whether the Soviet IL–28 bombers, as well as the surface-to-surface nuclear missiles, would be removed from Cuba.

Washington, November 6, 1962.

DEAR MR. CHAIRMAN: I am surprised that in your letter, which I received yesterday,[1] you suggest that in giving your representative in New York a list of the weapons we consider offensive there was any desire on our part to complicate the situation. Our intention was just the opposite: to stick to a well-known list, and not to introduce any new factors. But there is really only one major item on the list, beyond the missiles and their equipment, and that is the light bombers with their equipment. This item is indeed of great importance to us.

The solution of the Cuban affair was established by my letter to you of October twenty-seventh and your reply of October twenty-eighth.[2] You will recall that in my letter of October twenty-seventh, I referred to "all weapons systems in Cuba capable of offensive use." You will also recall that in my broadcast address of October twenty-second,[3] in addition to medium-range ballistic missiles, I mentioned specifically "jet bombers capable of carrying nuclear weapons," as "an explicit threat to the peace and security of all the Americas." Finally, my proclamation of October twenty-third entitled "Interdiction of the Delivery of Offensive Weapons to Cuba"[4] specifically listed bomber aircraft. These facts were all known at the time of our exchange of letters on Cuba, and so it seems clear to me that our exchange of letters covers the IL–28s, since your undertaking was to remove the weapons we described as offensive.

Your letter says—and I agree—that we should not complicate the situation by minor things. But I assure you that this matter of IL–28s is not a minor matter for us at all. It is true, of course, that these bombers are not the most modern of weapons, but they are distinctly capable of offensive use against the United States and other Western Hemispheric countries, and I am sure your own military men would inform you that the continued existence of such bombers in Cuba would require substantial measures of military defense in response by the United States. Thus, in simple logic these are weapons capable of offensive use. But there is more in it than that, Mr. Chairman. These bombers could carry nuclear weapons for long distances, and they are clearly not needed, any more than

---

[1]See Document 8.
[2]See Chapter 4, Documents 29 and 33.
[3]See Chapter 4, Document 14.
[4]This proclamation formally established the quarantine.

missiles, for purely defensive purposes on the island of Cuba. Thus in the present context their continued presence would sustain the grave tension that has been created, and their removal, in my view, is necessary to a good start on ending the recent crisis.

I am not clear as to what items you object to on the list which Ambassador Stevenson handed to Mr. Kuznetsov. I can assure you I have no desire to cause you difficulties by any wide interpretation of the definitions of weapons which we consider offensive and I am instructing my representative in New York to confer promptly with Mr. Kuznetsov and to be as forthcoming as possible in order to meet any legitimate complaints you may have in order to reach a quick solution which would enable our agreement to be carried to completion. I entirely agree with your statement that we should wind up the immediate crisis promptly, and I assure you that on our side we are insisting only on what is immediately essential for progress in this matter. In order to make our position clear, I think I should go on to give you a full sense of the very strong feelings we have about this whole affair here in the United States.

These recent events have given a profound shock to relations between our two countries. . . . Not only did this action threaten the whole safety of this hemisphere, but it was, in a broader sense, a dangerous attempt to change the world-wide status quo. Secret action of this kind seems to me both hazardous and unjustified. But however one may judge that argument, what actually happened in this case was not simply that the action of your side was secret. Your Government repeatedly gave us assurances of what it was *not* doing; these assurances were announced as coming from the highest levels, and they proved inaccurate. . . .

We were specifically informed that no missiles would be placed in Cuba which would have a range capable of reaching the United States. In reliance upon these assurances I attempted, as you know, to restrain those who were giving warnings in this country about the trend of events in Cuba. Thus undeniable photographic evidence that offensive weapons were being installed was a deep and dangerous shock, first to this Government and then to our whole people.

In the aftermath of this shock, to which we replied with a measured but necessary response, I believe it is vital that we should re-establish some degree of confidence in communication between the two of us. If the leaders of the two great nuclear powers cannot judge with some accuracy the intentions of each other, we shall find ourselves in a period of gravely increasing danger—not only for our two countries but for the whole world.

I therefore hope that you will promptly recognize that when we speak of the need to remove missiles and bombers, with their immediate supporting equipment, we are not trying to complicate the situation but simply stating what was clearly included in our understanding of October twenty-seventh and twenty-eighth. I shall continue to abide fully by the undertakings in my letter of October twenty-seventh, and specifically, under the conditions stated in that letter I will hold to my undertaking "to give assurances against an invasion of Cuba." This undertaking has already come under attack here and is likely to become increasingly an object of criticism by a great many of my countrymen. And the very minimum that is necessary in regard to these assurances is, as we agreed, the verified removal of the missile and bomber systems, together with real safeguards against their reintroduction.

I should emphasize to you directly, Mr. Chairman, that in this respect there is another problem immediately ahead of us which could become very serious indeed, and that is the problem of continuing verification in Cuba. Your representatives have spoken as if this were entirely a problem for the Castro regime to settle, but the continuing verification of the absence of offensive weapons in Cuba is an essential safeguard for the United States and the other countries of this hemisphere, and is an explicit condition for the undertakings which we in our turn have agreed to. The need for this verification is, I regret to say, convincingly demonstrated by what happened in Cuba in the months of September and October.

For the present we are having to rely on our own methods of surveillance, and this surveillance will surely have to be continued unless, as we much prefer, a better and durable method can be found. We believe that it is a serious responsibility of your Government to insure that weapons which you have provided to Cuba are not employed to interfere with this surveillance which is so important to us all in obtaining reliable information on which improvements in the situation can be based. It was of great importance, for example, for me last week to be able to announce with confidence that dismantling of missiles has begun.

Finally, I would like to say a word about longer range matters. I think we must both recognize that it will be very difficult for any of us in this hemisphere to look forward to any real improvement in our relations with Cuba if it continues to be a military outpost of the Soviet Union. We have limited our action at present to the problem of offensive weapons, but I do think it may be important for you to consider whether a real normalization of the Cuba problem can be envisaged while there remains in Cuba large numbers of Soviet military technicians, and major weapons systems and communications complexes under Soviet control, all with the recurrent possibility that offensive weapons might be secretly and rapidly reintroduced. That is why I think there is much wisdom in the conclusion expressed in your letter of October 26th, that when our undertakings against invasion are effective the need for your military specialists in Cuba will disappear. That is the real path to progress in the Cuban problem. And in this connection in particular, I hope you will understand that we must attach the greatest importance to the personal assurances you have given that submarine bases will not be established in Cuba.

I believe that Cuba can never have normal relations with the other nations of this hemisphere unless it ceases to appear to be a foreign military base and adopts a peaceful course of non-interference in the affairs of its sister nations. These wider considerations may belong to a later phase of the problem, but I hope that you will give them careful thought.

In the immediate situation, however, I repeat that it is the withdrawal of the missiles and bombers, with their supporting equipment, under adequate verification, and with a proper system for continued safeguards in the future, that is essential. This is the first necessary step away from the crisis to open the door through which we can move to restore confidence and give attention to other problems which ought to be resolved in the interest of peace.

12. Telegram from Ambassador Dobrynin to the Soviet Foreign Ministry

Robert Kennedy offers a solution to the IL–28 bomber problem in another conversation with Dobrynin.

November 12, 1962.

Your instructions have been carried out. Robert Kennedy has familiarized himself attentively with the content of N. S. Khrushchev's confidential oral message to the President.[1] When he got to the place that spoke of Nixon's defeat in the elections,[2] he immediately grinned, saying: "Your chairman is a real master of colorful expression that expressed the true essence of the issue. Yes, we are quite satisfied with Nixon's defeat, and in general we are not complaining about the results of the election." It was felt that this portion of the message was received with definite satisfaction.

When Robert Kennedy had familiarized himself with the whole message, he said that for the President, for domestic policy considerations, it was very important to receive the Soviet Union's firm agreement to the removal of the IL–28 planes, especially now that there were essentially no inspections being conducted in Cuba itself. The correspondence between N. S. Khrushchev and President Kennedy of 27 and 28 October implied that an agreement between our countries had been reached. But we understand the difficulties in this area that have now arisen because of Premier Fidel Castro's position, and we are not insisting on this as an unalterable and fundamental condition. But the removal of the IL–28 planes—in an atmosphere of growing criticism within the USA—is a matter of great concern to the President. Let us reach an agreement, continued Robert Kennedy, on the following points: that the Soviet Union will remove its IL–28 planes by a definite date announced in advance, and that on that same day the USA will officially lift its quarantine. All this may be announced immediately.

I answered Robert Kennedy that his proposal is entirely unacceptable for the Soviet side. I then demonstrated the unacceptability of this proposal by using the

---

[1]See Document 13.

[2]Richard Nixon had been defeated in the November 1962 elections in his race for the governorship of California.

argument contained in N. S. Khrushchev's oral message that had been passed on to him. In conclusion I expressed my certainty that conveying his proposal to Moscow would prove fruitless.

Thinking a moment, Robert Kennedy said that he would like to confer with his brother the President, after which he would again contact me later the same day. I agreed.

After an hour and a half (all this happened in the evening), Robert Kennedy came to my residence. He said that now, after speaking with the President, he could formulate the American proposal in the following way:

N. S. Khrushchev and the President would reach an essential agreement that the IL–28 planes would be removed by a definite date. After such an agreement has been reached, the USA would, as early as the next day, lift any quarantine even before the removal of the planes had been completed. The Americans would of course prefer that the date agreed upon for the removal of the IL–28 planes be publicized. However, if the Soviets have any objections to the public disclosure of that date, then the President would not insist on it. For him a promise from N. S. Khrushchev would be entirely sufficient. As far as the date is concerned, it would be good if the planes were removed, let us say, within 30 days. We ask that N. S. Khrushchev be informed of this whole proposal.

Robert Kennedy was told that the President's proposal would of course be communicated to N. S. Khrushchev. As a personal opinion, however, I noted that it was unlikely that such an imminent date could be acceptable to us, all the more so since the fundamental USA obligations—guarantees of non-aggression against Cuba, and other obligations—remain, as before, unfulfilled; moreover, they themselves are pushing everything later and later. And this is happening in circumstances in which the Soviet government is sincerely fulfilling, and essentially has already fulfilled, its own obligations for the removal of the missiles. It is now the Americans' turn.

Robert Kennedy said that the time-frame he had referred to—30 days—is not in any way definitive. That time-frame had been "given to him," but he thought that there was room for negotiation here as long as the period was not too great, and as long as N. S. Khrushchev generally found the President's proposal acceptable. I want now to make note of one more condition, Robert Kennedy continued. After such an agreement has been reached, especially if it is not publicized, it would be important for us that, even if the end of the agreed-upon period for the removal of the IL–28 planes has not yet been reached, at least some planes will have been disassembled by this time, or if they have just been taken out of containers, that a portion of them be returned to their containers. We need all of this, Robert Kennedy remarked, so that we can satisfy our domestic public opinion by reporting that there has been some progress in the removal of the IL-28 planes. This is necessary, since even [West German Chancellor Konrad] Adenauer is starting now to criticize us publicly for trusting the word of the Soviet Union without inspections in Cuban territory—not to mention the Cuban emigres in certain . . . [states] who are making similar accusations. But the President, Robert Kennedy emphasized, has faith in N. S. Khrushchev's word, and is willing to lift the quarantine immediately if the agreement mentioned above can be reached, even though we really do not have any guarantees with regard to inspections in Cuban territory.

I answered Robert Kennedy that it would be much better if Adenauer kept his nose out of everyone else's business, and if the USA government told him so directly (here Robert Kennedy energetically nodded his head in a gesture of agreement). I then said that in the proposal that he had advanced, the issue is once again raised of a full elimination of all the tension that has existed, that is, beyond the immediate lifting of the blockade, the obligations of all the parties should be fixed in appropriate UN documents, and non-aggression against Cuba and a strict observation of its sovereignty should be guaranteed; there would also be UN posts established in the countries of the Caribbean region as guarantees against unexpected actions harming another state.

Robert Kennedy said that he believed that an agreement could be reached on all these points. It is important, from the point of view of American public opinion, to have some inspection conducted in Cuba, even in the form of several UN posts. Castro will scarcely go for this unless a similar procedure is imposed on the other countries of the Caribbean basin. But it is possible to resolve this too. . . . I can repeat the firm assurances of the President not to invade Cuba. He authorized me once again to say this now. He was grateful to N. S. Khrushchev for the latter's clarification that the IL–28 planes are manned by Soviet rather than Cuban pilots, but nevertheless the issue of the removal of these planes remains a very important one for the President, and he asks that we consider his proposal.

Further discussion came down to a reiteration of the positions of the parties. Robert Kennedy said in conclusion that he was flying now to New York on personal business, and that he would be willing to meet with me at any time.

When he left, he glimpsed a crowd of dancing couples in the embassy's parlor. Realizing that this was a friendly welcome party arranged by the embassy community for the Bolshoi Theater troupe that had just arrived in Washington, he said that he would like to meet with the troupe. Mingling with and greeting almost all the members of the troupe, he delivered a welcome speech in which he said that the President was preparing to attend their premier the following evening. At the end, he kissed Maya Plisetskaya when he found out that he and she had been born in the same year, month, and day, and said they would celebrate their birthdays in a week. None of this needs to be mentioned especially, but all in all the behavior of Robert Kennedy, who is ordinarily quite a reserved and glum man, reflects to some degree the calmer and more normal mood in the White House after the tense days that shook Washington, even though this fact is concealed in various ways by American propaganda.

13. Message from Chairman Khrushchev to President Kennedy[1]

From November 5 to 9 several vessels left Cuba with the nuclear missiles on board. Soviet personnel removed the tarpaulins covering the missiles, allowing U.S. officials to verify the withdrawal of the nuclear weapons. Here, in correspondence with JFK, Khrushchev makes the case that as the missiles were now out of Cuba, the American blockade of the island should cease. On the issue of the IL–28s the Soviet premier tried to fudge, saying that they will be removed in due course.

Moscow, November 12, 1962.

DEAR MR. PRESIDENT, I would like to express my satisfaction that the mutual obligations taken in accordance with the exchange of messages between us are being carried out both by your side and our side. One can say that certain favourable results are already seen at this time. We appreciate your understanding of the situation and your cooperation in carrying out the obligations taken by [y]our side. We, on our part, will as always honor our obligations. And I would like to inform you that our obligations with regard to dismantling and removal of both missiles and warheads have already been fulfilled.

We appreciate that we must come to an agreement with you regarding the mutually acceptable means for your side to ascertain that we really carry out our obligations. What has already been achieved in the course of negotiations between our representatives—Kuznetsov, McCloy and Stevenson—and the cooperation reached in the process of these negotiations is a good thing. The same should be said about the cooperation between captains of our ships, which were taking our missiles from Cuba, and corresponding U.S. ships. This is very good, this has created an impression that your side also wishes to cooperate, eliminating the remnants of the tension which only yesterday were very dangerous both for our two peoples and for the peoples of the whole world. Thus, if we proceed from our understanding which was expressed in your message of October 27[2] and in our reply of October 28,[3] then we, the Soviet side, have carried out our obligations and thereby have created possibility for complete elimination of tension in the Caribbean. Consequently, now it is your turn, it is for your side to carry out precisely your obligations. We have in mind that apart from the long term obligations that the United States itself will not attack Cuba and will restrain other countries of the Western Hemisphere from doing that, the most important thing which is required today is to give moral satisfaction to world public opinion and tranquility to peoples. And what is required from your side to that

---

[1]This message was first delivered orally by Ambassador Dobrynin to Robert Kennedy. See Document 12.

[2]See Chapter 4, Document 29.

[3]See Chapter 4, Document 33.

end is to lift the so-called quarantine and of course to stop violating the territorial waters and air space of Cuba. If this continues confidence in your obligations will thus be undermined which can only grieve world public and throw us back to the positions to which we must not return after the liquidation of such a dangerous situation. To say nothing of the fact that it would hamper us in the future.

At present, we must—and we are convinced in that—look forward and draw necessary conclusions from what has happened up till now and from the good which followed due to the efforts of both sides. Therefore, we believe that conditions are emerging now for reaching an agreement on the prohibition of nuclear weapons, cessation of all types of nuclear weapons tests and on all other questions which are ripe and require solution. You have already ended your tests and we shall probably also end our tests in November or at least before the end of this year. . . .

Now about the matter that, as you state, worries you today—about the IL–28 planes which you call an offensive weapon. We have already given you our clarification on this point and I think you can not but agree with us. However, if you do not agree—and this is your right—ask your intelligence after all and let it give you an answer based not on guesswork but on facts. . . .

If your intelligence is objective it must give a correct appraisal of these 12-year-old planes and report to you that they are incapable of offensive actions. We brought them to Cuba only because they can be used as a mobile means of coastal defense under the cover of anti-aircraft fire from their own territory. . . .

Nevertheless we regard your concern with understanding, though on our part we share the desire of the Government of Cuba to possess defensive weapons which would permit [it] to defend the territorial integrity of its country.

Therefore if you meet this with understanding and if we agreed with you on solving other questions in implementing the mutually assumed obligations then the question of IL–28 bombers would be solved without difficulties.

In what way should this cooperation, in our understanding, find its expression and what would facilitate the solution of this question?

We state to you that these bombers are piloted solely by our fliers. Consequently you should not have any fears that they can be used to do harm to the United States or other neighboring countries in Western Hemisphere. And since you and your allies in Western Hemisphere have taken an obligation not to invade Cuba then it would seem this weapon should not pose any threat for you. Moreover, we are aware of what military means are in your possession. If the enemy were threatening us with such weapon we would ignore that threat completely for it would cause us no anxiety whatsoever.

But because you express apprehension that this weapon can be some sort of a threat to the US or other countries of Western Hemisphere which do not possess adequate defensive means we state to you as a guarantee that those planes are piloted by our fliers and therefore there should be no misgivings that they could be used to the detriment of any state.

As you ascertained yourself we have removed the missiles, we also removed everything else related to missiles, all the equipment necessary for their use and recalled the personnel manning those missiles. Now that the missiles are removed the question of IL–28's is an incomprehensible argument because that weapon as I have already said is of no value as a combat weapon at present, to say nothing of the future. Let us come to an agreement on this question as well, let us do away with tension, let us fulfill the mutual pledges made in our messages. We will not insist on permanently keeping those planes on Cuba. We have our difficulties in this question. Therefore we give a gentleman's word that we will remove the IL–28 planes with all the personnel and equipment related to those planes, although not now but later. We would like to do that some time later when we determine that the conditions are ripe to remove them. We will advise you of that.

I think that an agreement on such basis will enable us to complete the elimination of all the tension that existed and will create conditions for life to resume its normal course, that is the blockade would be immediately removed; the pledges of the sides would be registered in the appropriate documents in the United Nations Organization; non-invasion of Cuba and strict observance of her sovereignty guaranteed; the UN posts established in the countries of the Caribbean so that neither one nor the other side would indeed undertake any unexpected actions to the detriment of another state.

This would be the best solution which can be anticipated especially having in mind the tension that we lived through and the abyss we came to. And I believe, Mr. President, that you yourself understand that we were very close to that abyss. But you and we soberly and wisely appraised the situation and maintained self-control. Let us now give a complete satisfaction to the public.

What happened should now prompt us to make new great efforts so that no repetition of such events should be allowed because if we succeeded in finding a way out of a dangerous situation this time, next time we might not safely untie the tightly made knot. And the knot that we are now untying has been tied rather tightly, almost to the limit.

We displayed an understanding with regard to the positions of each other and came out of a critical situation through mutual concessions to the satisfaction of all peoples of the world. Let us now give joy to all peoples of the world and show that this conflict really became a matter of yesterday, let us normalize the situation. And it would be good if on your part efforts were made to make the normalization a complete, real normalization and it is necessary to do this in the interests of all peoples and this is within our power.

14. Telegram from Ambassador Dobrynin to the Soviet Foreign Ministry

The next two documents relate to a message from Khrushchev to Kennedy, transmitted in person by Dobrynin to Robert Kennedy. The Soviet leader now seeks to tie Soviet cooperation on the IL–28 issue to American concessions in other areas, including termination of the blockade around Cuba.

November 14, 1962.

Having familiarized himself with our response,[1] Robert Kennedy said that he would pass it on to the President today. Then, saying that he would like to express a little of his own views provisionally, Robert Kennedy stated the following.

The President—he, Robert Kennedy, expects—will be disappointed by the answer when he receives it. The President's proposal was very simple: the USA would immediately and officially lift the blockade in exchange for assurances—public or not—that before some definite date the IL–28 planes would be removed. The President believes that this proposal of his serves the interests of both countries, and opens the way towards a resolution of the remaining aspects of the Cuban problem, creating a significantly less tense situation than the one that would arise if his proposal was approved[2] by the Soviets. The President intends to fulfill his obligations, which were stipulated by the correspondence between the heads of the two governments. But for this there must be a certain time in which all the details of the future agreement can be worked out. The President's proposal referred to above could be carried out immediately, without any delay. The insistence of the USA government in this matter of the IL–28 planes has been provoked by the growing pressure that has been brought to bear on the President by representatives of Congress, the press, and so on. It is important that this aspect be properly understood in Moscow, since the President himself has great difficulties in dealing with this issue (Robert Kennedy twice emphasized the "difficulties for the President").

I carried out the discussion with Robert Kennedy of these difficulties using the arguments advanced by N. S. Khrushchev's response. It was especially emphasized that we have removed from Cuba the missiles and warheads, in other words that we have fulfilled the obligations we assumed, while the USA is not fulfilling its own obligations; for this reason, in order to conduct assurance inspections [of Cuba] after the missiles and warheads have been removed, the quarantine should have already been lifted by now, the flights by American planes over the territory of Cuba should have already ceased, and the mutual obligations assumed by the parties should have been formalized in appropriate documents under the auspices of the UN.

Robert Kennedy stated that the USA government would not cease its flights over Cuba in circumstances in which he had no other guarantees that the government of Cuba would carry out its end of the agreement. Mr. Mikoyan's long stay in Cuba[3] shows—or at least this conviction has been created in us—that Premier Castro does not want to approve the agreement reached between the President and the head of the Soviet government on such guarantees. We understand

---

[1]Presumably a reference to Khrushchev's November 14 message to JFK. See Document 15.

[2]Dobrynin must have meant "rejected," not "approved," or else this is an error in translation from the Russian.

[3]See Document 5, footnote 2.

the circumstances that have been created, but this does not relieve the difficulties of our position, said Robert Kennedy. The issue of UN guarantees,[4] in the form of UN posts or something like them, would require a significant amount of time before concrete approval of the agreement could be reached. Let us take for example the issue of UN posts in the area of the Caribbean basin. Here Robert Kennedy asked, would the Soviet Union itself really agree to some foreign posts on its own territory? . . .

[Robert Kennedy added that the] President has put forth a proposal that he believes serves the interests of both parties, but that proposal is being rejected now by the Soviets, which can lead only to an extension, or perhaps even a complication, of the present situation which clearly does not satisfy us or, we believe, you. Both parties are equally uninterested in that. We hope nonetheless that Chairman N. S. Khrushchev will be able to approve the proposal put forth by the President, who himself had great confidence in it when he sent it to Khrushchev.

I told Robert Kennedy that the position of the Soviet government has been clearly laid out in today's response by N. S. Khrushchev. The Soviet Union has fulfilled its obligations. Now it is simply the USA government's turn to do the same, so that the situation of tension that has been created in the Caribbean Sea can be eased. For this it is necessary: to lift the quarantine without delay, to cease all flights by USA planes over Cuba, and to fix the mutual obligations deriving from the correspondence between the heads of both governments on 27 and 28 October. If corresponding instructions were given by the President to McCloy and Stevenson on the issue of UN posts in the Caribbean Sea area and the parts of the USA that border it—and the Soviet representatives already have such instructions—and if they could reach an agreement, then of course the issue of the time-frame for the removal of the IL–28 planes would not be any complex problem.

Since Robert Kennedy, who often refers to the President's opinion, has been stubbornly continuing to assert the necessity of first resolving the issue of the IL–28 planes' removal, connecting the lifting of the quarantine with that removal, he was directly asked, after mutually reiterating our arguments to each other, whether this meant that the President had already authorized him to give an answer, and that such an answer should be communicated to Moscow?

Robert Kennedy immediately answered that the views he had been expressing, although based on the opinions of the President, with whom he had just that evening discussed all these issues, are nonetheless exclusively his own, Robert Kennedy's, personal thoughts, and that there would be an answer to N. S. Khrushchev's address today from the President himself. Robert Kennedy promised to provide information on that answer immediately.

Towards the end, the conversation started to have a formalized and official

---

[4]In his October 27 message to Khrushchev, JFK had written of the need for UN observation of the withdrawal of the missiles from Cuba. By mid-November the idea of having UN posts throughout the Caribbean, including Cuban and American territory, had emerged—as a way of ensuring stability in the region.

air connected with the President's invitation, passed on to me via Robert Kennedy, to visit the White House on the following day along with the Bolshoi Theater troupe.

15. Message from Chairman Khrushchev to President Kennedy

Moscow, November 14, 1962.

I have read with great satisfaction the reply of the President of the United States[1] and I agree with the considerations expressed by the President. It is of particular pleasure to me that we seem to have the same desire to liquidate as soon as possible the state of tension and normalize the situation so that to untie our hands for normal work and for solving those questions that are awaiting their solution. And this depends in the main on agreement between us—the two greatest powers in the world with whom special responsibility for ensuring peace lies to a greater degree than with other countries.

The question of the withdrawal of the IL–28's within mentioned 30 days does not constitute any complicated question. Yet this period will probably not be sufficient. As I already said in my oral message[2] I can assure the President that those planes will be removed from Cuba with all the equipment and flying personnel. It can be done in 2–3 months. But for me, for our country, it would be a great relief if the state of tension that evolved in the Caribbean were liquidated as soon as possible. I have in mind what I have already said, namely: to lift immediately the quarantine, that is, blockade; to stop the flights of the US planes over Cuba; to write down the mutual commitments ensuing from the messages of the President and mine of October 27 and 28[3] to which end your representatives and ours have to prepare with the participation of the UN acting Secretary General U Thant an appropriate document. This is the main thing now.

You understand that when we say that it is necessary to announce now the withdrawal of the IL–28's at the time when your planes are flying over Cuba it creates for us no small difficulties. I have no doubt that you will understand—and the Cuban Government understands this—that such actions constitute violation of sovereignty of the Cuban state. Therefore it would be a reasonable step to create in this respect also conditions for the normalization of the situation and this in a great degree would make it easier to meet your wish of expediting the withdrawal of the IL–28 planes from Cuba.

If we attained all that now and if this were announced, then more favourable

[1]Apparently a reference to Document 11.
[2]See Document 13.
[3]See Chapter 4, Documents 29 and 33.

conditions would be created for our country to solve the question of time table for the withdrawal of IL–28 planes.

Now our main difficulties lie precisely in the fact that, as it is well known to everybody and it is being rightfully pointed out to us, we have removed from Cuba missiles and warheads, that is, we have fulfilled our commitments while the US is not carrying out its commitments—the quarantine continues, the US planes continue to fly over Cuba and there is no agreement that would register the pledges of the US. And all this finds ears that are listening and listening attentively. It is difficult for us to give explanations to [for] such [an] unjustifiable state of affairs. Therefore to carry out the final procedure after the missiles and warheads have been removed, already now the quarantine must be lifted, the flights of the American planes over Cuba must be stopped and mutual commitments of the sides must be written down in an appropriate document with the participation of the UN.

It is hard to say for me what specific agreement is possible on the question of UN observation posts. But we as well as the Government of Cuba have already expressed a desire to come to terms on this question. If the question of the observation posts is of interest to the US—and I think it must be of interest—then I consider it wise to come to an agreement on this. I think that the Government of Cuba will not object to the UN posts, of course on the condition of respect for the sovereignty of Cuba, on the condition of treating her as equal which must mean that on the territory of other countries of the Caribbean and in a corresponding region of the US there will be also set up similar UN posts, that is on the condition that reciprocity will be observed in this question.

You understand, Mr. President, that no country can assume unilateral commitments, and it would be wise to make them mutual. . . .

If you would give your representatives—McCloy, Stevenson and others—appropriate instructions on the question of UN posts in the Caribbean region and adjoining regions of the US—and our representatives have such instructions—and if they would come to an agreement then all this could be made public. Then there would be removed the difficulties connected with making a public announcement on the withdrawal of IL–28 planes and we would name then specific dates. These dates will be probably much closer than those which I name and maybe even closer than those which were named by you.

That is why we should make a final step in this direction. Then we would really cut the knot which was tied tightly enough and having cut it we would create normal relations between our countries to which our people aspire and which your people, we are sure of that, also want.

I will allow myself to express some other considerations and I believe you will not take offense and will not consider that I intrude too much into the sphere of [y]our internal affairs. Voting in the elections to the Senate, the House of Representatives and in gubernatorial elections which just took place has resulted in the defeat of your former rival[4] who was clearly preparing again for the next presidential elections. It is significant that as a result of the elections precisely those

_____

[4]See Document 12, footnote 2.

candidates were defeated who, if I may use such an expression, were making most frenzied bellicose speeches.

This indicates that the American people began to feel that if the arms race continues further, if a reasonable solution is not found and an understanding is not achieved between our countries then our peoples will feel still more strongly the threat of the dreadful catastrophe of a thermo-nuclear war.

Let us then not keep people of peace all over the world in suspense, let us give them joyous satisfaction. Having cut the knot in the Caribbean we would thereby immediately create better conditions and would reinforce people's hope for coping with other questions which are now awaiting their solution. Peoples expect wisdom from us, first of all from our two states. Of course our two states can not do everything, but all that depends on us in the sense of reaching an understanding will be of decisive importance. Needless to prove that other states would be also satisfied. And he who was especially displeased will have to agree after this understanding is reached that there is no other way of meeting the aspirations of all states, all peoples.

16. Message from President Kennedy to Chairman Khrushchev

JFK continues to seek Khrushchev's acceptance of his proposed method for removing the IL–28s: the Soviet leader should order their withdrawal, after which the president will announce the ending of the blockade. (The IL–28s would leave Cuba within thirty days of Khrushchev's order.)

Washington, November 15, 1962.

I am glad to learn of your assurance of agreement that the IL–28s should be withdrawn.[1] All that remains is to reach understanding on the timing.

Let me review the undertakings in my letter of October twenty-seventh and your letter of October twenty-eighth.[2] You agreed to remove the weapons systems we described as offensive and with suitable safeguards to halt the further introduction of such weapons into Cuba. On our side, we undertook to agree to remove the quarantine measures in effect and to give assurances against an invasion of Cuba. There were two conditions attached to our undertaking. The first was that the weapons systems would be removed "under appropriate United Nations observation and supervision," and, second, that there would be established "adequate arrangements through the United Nations to ensure the carrying out and continuation of these commitments."

[1] See Document 15.
[2] See Chapter 4, Documents 29 and 33.

I cannot agree with your statement that you have fulfilled your commitments and that we have not fulfilled ours. Let us recall what, in fact, has occurred. You have removed a certain number of missiles from Cuba—not under United Nations supervision—but you did cooperate in arrangements which enabled us to be reasonably sure that forty-two missiles were in fact taken out of Cuba. There has been no United Nations verification that other missiles were not left behind and, in fact, there have been many reports of their being concealed in caves and elsewhere, and we have no way of satisfying those who are concerned about these reports. The IL–28's are still in Cuba and are of deep concern to the people of our entire Hemisphere. Thus, three major parts of the undertakings on your side—the removal of the IL–28's, the arrangements for verification, and safeguards against introduction—have not yet been carried out.

We suppose that part of the trouble here may be in Cuba. The Secretary General of the United Nations was not allowed to make arrangements for the experts he took with him to Cuba to verify removal of the offensive weapons,[3] the Cuban Government did not agree to international Red Cross inspection at ports; they have refused the Secretary General's suggestion that the Latin American Ambassadors in Havana undertake this verification; they have rejected a further suggestion of the Secretary General concerning the use of various non-aligned Chiefs of Mission in Havana for this purpose. It is difficult for me to understand why the Cubans are so resistant to the series of reasonable proposals that have been made to them by U Thant unless, for reasons of their own, they are determined to see the crisis prolonged and worsened. We both have means of influencing the Cuban Government and I do not believe that we can allow that Government to frustrate the clear understandings our two governments have reached in the interests of peace.

In these circumstances we have so far been patient and careful, as we have been, indeed, at every stage. As you know from your own reports, we have always applied the quarantine with care and with regard for the position of others, and in recent days we have relied on the oral assurances of the masters of your ships and other ships. Moreover I myself held back orders for more forceful action right to the limit of possibility during the week of October 27th and 28th. But we cannot make progress from here—or avoid a return of danger to this situation—if your side now should fall into the mistake of claiming that it has met all its commitments, and refusing to help with the real business of carrying out our purpose of untying the Cuban knot.

What, in those circumstances, should be done? We are entitled to insist on removal of the IL–28's and on safeguards against reintroduction of offensive weapons before we lift the quarantine or give assurances of any sort. But we are interested in making rapid progress, step-by-step, and that is why we have proposed an arrangement more favorable from your standpoint: that as soon as you give the order for the removal of the IL–28's and their men and equipment, to be completed within thirty days, (and I am glad you say the length of time is not the real problem) we will announce the lifting of the quarantine. That is more

[3]See Document 3, footnote 2.

than we agreed to on October twenty-seventh and twenty-eighth, but we wish to end this crisis promptly.

Beyond that, we are quite willing to instruct our negotiators in New York[4] to work closely with yours in order to reach agreement on other matters affecting this problem. We believe, again, that these matters should follow the removal of offensive weapons systems, but just as we have been able to discuss other matters while a number of missiles were leaving, we believe the urgently needed talks can and should go forward while the bombers are leaving. We do not insist that everything wait its exact turn—but only that the essential first steps be clearly going forward.

But what is most urgent, after we can agree that offensive weapons are leaving, and after the quarantine is lifted, is to make some real progress on continuing observations and verification. It will be essential to have such arrangements—and this again is clear in the letters of October 27 and 28—before our assurances can be more formally stated. Our undertaking on this point remains firm and clear, and we want nothing better than to be able to give our assurances, just as we said we would, when the necessary conditions exist.

In the absence of any arrangements under the United Nations or otherwise for international verification or safeguards, we have of course been obliged to rely upon our own resources for surveillance of the situation in Cuba, although this course is unsatisfactory. Just today we learned of new threats by Castro against this necessary surveillance.[5] I should make it very clear that if there is any interference with this surveillance, we shall have to take the necessary action in reply, and it is for just this reason that it is so urgent to obtain better safeguards.

We note with interest that in your last message the arrangement of observation and verification is enlarged from Cuba to include certain other areas. This is a substantial change from the terms of our exchange of messages, and as we see it any such wider arrangements would necessarily require careful discussion. For example, if we move outside Cuba to observe what is happening in other countries which have been involved in the recent tensions, there might have to be observation posts at the appropriate ports in the Soviet Union from which weapons could be shipped to Cuba, as well as in appropriate places in the United States. This is a matter which deserves close study and it may offer a chance of real progress in the long run, but for the immediate future it seems to us better to work within the framework of our understanding of October 27 and 28.

We also think that the Brazilian proposal for a verified Denuclearized Zone in Latin America[6] could, with the cooperation of Cuba and if acceptable to the other Latin American countries, in the long run offer an acceptable means for a broader approach. However, the immediate problem is, I repeat, the carrying out of our understanding with regard to verification that offensive weapons have in

---

[4]Namely, John McCloy and Adlai Stevenson.

[5]Presumably a reference to the fact that on November 15 Cuban fighter aircraft were detected using low-level flight tactics in the Havana vicinity.

[6]On November 15 various Latin American countries, including Brazil, presented a revised version of this plan to the First Committee of the UN.

fact been removed from Cuba and the establishing of safeguards against their reintroduction pending the coming into effect of longer-term arrangements. Even apart from our understanding, given the history of this matter, I am sure, Mr. Chairman, that you can understand that this is a real necessity if we are to move to the settlement of other matters.

But the first step is to get the [IL–28] bombers started out, and the quarantine lifted—for both are sources of tension. Meanwhile discussion can continue on other aspects of the problem.

17. Memorandum from Chairman of the JCS Taylor (on behalf of the Joint Chiefs) to President Kennedy

The Joint Chiefs assure the president that the contingency plans to attack Cuba are up to date, and, by his instruction, the forces earmarked for an invasion of Cuba have been enlarged.

Washington, November 16, 1962.

SUBJECT

Status of Readiness for the Cuban Operation

1. The Joint Chiefs of Staff are glad to report that our Armed Forces are in an optimum posture to execute CINCLANT OPLANS 312–62 (Air Attack in Cuba) and 316–62 (Invasion of Cuba). We are not only ready to take any action you may order in Cuba, we are also in an excellent condition world-wide to counter any Soviet military response to such action. Our status of readiness includes:

a. SAC is maintaining 1/8 airborne alert and has implemented its force dispersal plan. . . .

b. Continental Air Defense Command interceptor forces have occupied their wartime dispersal bases and are partially deployed at increased alert (about 1/3). Special defensive measures have been taken to protect the Southeast, with particular attention to Florida.

c. Air forces involved in CINCLANT OPLAN 312–62 in daylight hours can respond for selective attack in graduated increments from two to twelve hours, according to the application of force desired.

d. Amphibious and assault forces are at a high state of readiness, providing a seven-day reaction capability for CINCLANT OPLAN 316–62 following the air strike (CINCLANT OPLAN 312–62), with accelerated introduction of follow-on forces.

e. All naval units are in a high state of readiness.

2. In response to your request,[1] we have studied the need for augmentation of forces for CINCLANT OPLAN 316–62 and have concluded that while the forces originally included in the plan are probably adequate, it would be prudent to earmark additional forces as a ready reserve for the operation. Accordingly, we are planning to earmark the 5th Infantry Division, at approximately 20,000 strength including supporting forces, and a combat command (strength 6,800) of the 2nd Armored Division for possible commitment as reserve forces for CINCLANT OPLAN 316–62. . . . The 5th MEB (Marine Expeditionary Brigade), at approximately 9,000 strength, has transited the Panama Canal, is in the Caribbean and has been added to the assault force. . . .

18. Message from Chairman Khrushchev to President Kennedy[1]

On November 19 Robert Kennedy informed Georgi Bolshakov, a leading Washington-based KGB official, that the United States would resume low-level aircraft reconnaissance of the Cuban island if Khrushchev did not remove the IL–28 bombers; and that the president needed a response to this ultimatum before his press conference, scheduled for the following evening. Also on November 19, Fidel Castro informed U Thant that Cuba would not oppose the Soviet withdrawal of the IL–28s from the island. The next day Khrushchev was therefore able to dispatch a message to JFK agreeing to withdraw the IL–28s.

Moscow, November 20, 1962.

I have studied attentively your considerations which were forwarded through our Ambassador in Washington in the evening of November 15.[2] I wish first of all to express satisfaction with regard to your statement that the United States is also interested in the achievement of a rapid progress in untying the Cuban knot. This is our great desire too. It is good that you have confirmed once again that the U.S. commitment to give assurance of non-invasion of Cuba, which was agreed upon in the exchange of messages on October 27 and 28 remains firm and clear. I fully share also the thought expressed by you about the necessity to act with caution, to take into consideration the position of others. Now when we speak of eliminating the remnants of the crisis this is as important as at any of its past stages.

---

[1]Presumably a reference to Document 10.
[1]Dobrynin handed Bobby Kennedy this message from Khrushchev at a November 20 meeting.
[2]See Document 16.

I always believed and believe now that both of us are guided by the realization of the immense responsibility for the peaceful settlement of the crisis over Cuba being completed. The basis for such settlement already exists: the sides have achieved an agreement and have taken upon themselves certain obligations. It is precisely where we proceed from.

What have we agreed upon? In brief our agreement has come to the following.

The Soviet Union removes from Cuba rocket weapons which you called offensive and gives a possibility to ascertain this. The United States of America promptly removes the quarantine and gives assurances that there will be no invasion of Cuba, not only by the US but also by other countries of the Western Hemisphere. This is the essence of our agreement.

Later on you raised the question of removal of IL–28 planes from Cuba. I think you could not feel the precariousness of that request. Now, of course, there may appear those who would wish to rummage in the wordings and to interpret them in different ways. But you and we do know well what kind of weapons they were that set the forest on fire, they were missiles. It was not accidental, indeed, that in our and your message of October 27 and 28 there was not a single mention of bomber planes and specifically of IL–28's. At the same time those messages have direct reference to rocket weapons.

By the way, you yourself refer not to direct obligations of the sides but to the understanding implied by the American side in the expression "offensive weapons" mentioned in the messages and in this connection you recall your TV address of October 22[3] and your proclamation of October 23. But you will agree, Mr. President, that messages that fix the subject of agreement and unilateral statements of the US Government are two different things indeed.

I informed you that the IL–28 planes are twelve years old and by their combat characteristics they at present cannot be classified as offensive types of weapons. In spite of all this, we regarded [y]our request with understanding. We took into consideration that you made certain statements and therefore the question of removal of IL–28 planes assumed for you as President a certain significance and probably created certain difficulties. We grant it. Since you might really have your difficulties in this question we moved in your direction having informed you of our consent to remove these planes from Cuba. What is the situation now if to summarize it in short and to speak of the main?

We have dismantled and removed from Cuba all the medium range ballistic missiles to the last with nuclear warheads for them. All the nuclear weapons have been taken away from Cuba. The Soviet personnel who were servicing the rocket installations have also been withdrawn. We have stated it to your representatives at the negotiations in New York too.

The US Government was afforded the possibility to ascertain the fact that all 42 missiles that were in Cuba have really been removed.

Moreover, we expressed our readiness to remove also the IL–28 planes from Cuba. I inform you that we intend to remove them within a month term and

[3]See Chapter 4, Document 14.

may be even sooner since the term for the removal of these planes is not a matter of principle for us. We are prepared to remove simultaneously with the IL–28 planes all the Soviet personnel connected with the servicing of these planes.

What can be said in connection with the commitments of the American side? Proper consideration through the UN of the commitment not to invade Cuba—and it is the main commitment of your side—so far is being delayed. The quarantine has not been lifted as yet. Permit me to express the hope that with receipt of this communication of mine you will issue instructions to the effect that the quarantine be lifted immediately with the withdrawal of your naval and other military units from the Caribbean area. . . .

19. Summary Record of ExComm Meeting

ExComm officials learn of Khrushchev's decision to remove the IL–28s. And JFK decides that the American no-invasion pledge regarding Cuba should be made only informally.

Washington, November 20, 1962, 3:30 p.m.

Khrushchev's reply[1] was read to the group, the President not having yet arrived.

A statement to be made by the President at his 6:00 PM press conference was discussed and approved.[2] The following decisions were reached:

a. The quarantine is to be lifted immediately and a proclamation revoking it is to be prepared.

b. U.S. naval forces in the Caribbean will remain there for the time being and carry out normal exercises. Ships in the area will not be removed because it is normal for some to be always on station in the Caribbean. Latin American ships which are in the quarantine force will be asked to stay and participate in exercises.

c. Secretary McNamara recommended, and the President agreed, that there would be no low-level reconnaissance missions flown tomorrow.

d. High-level flights averaging not more than one a day will continue intermittently because of the importance of knowing that the IL–28 bombers are actually being removed.

Two other actions are to be taken without public notice:

a. The SAC air alert will be terminated and all other military forces will be put on a reduced alert basis.

b. TAC planes concentrated along the coast will be deployed inland.

[1]See Document 18.
[2]See Document 20.

Secretary McNamara recommended that within forty-eight hours we announce that the air reserves called up for the Cuban [missile] crisis would be released before Christmas. . . .

The President [who arrived at 4 p.m.] asked where the question of our no-invasion assurance stands. In the light of what Khrushchev has agreed to do, if he does not get our assurances he will have very little. We should keep the assurances informal and not follow up with a formal document in the UN.

Alexis Johnson returned to the meeting to report that ABC reporter John Scali had been given the substance of Khrushchev's reply by a Russian source.[3] There followed a discussion of whether we should insist on shipside inspection of the IL–28 bomber removal. No clear decision was reached, some of the group believing we should insist on the shipside inspection and others saying this was not necessary.

There was further discussion of the no-invasion assurances. The Attorney General expressed his opposition to giving the assurance informally. We would be giving away a bargaining counter because Khrushchev is not insisting on having formal assurances. The President restated his view that Khrushchev would be in a difficult position if he gave us something and got nothing in return. We do not want to convey to him that we are going back on what he considers our bargain.

An instruction to McCloy and Stevenson[4] is to be drafted which says that we will make no formal no-invasion assurance and explained why we declined to do so.[5]

20. President Kennedy's News Conference

Khrushchev's message of November 20 enables the president to announce to the press that the quarantine around Cuba will be lifted as the IL–28 issue has been resolved. On the question of whether the American commitment not to invade Cuba is absolute, JFK is equivocal.

November 20, 1962.

[This press conference took place in the State Department Auditorium at 6 p.m.]

THE PRESIDENT.

. . . I have today been informed by Chairman Khrushchev that all of the IL–28 bombers now in Cuba will be withdrawn in 30 days. He also agrees that

---

[3]KGB officer Feklisov had met with Scali at Aldo's Restaurant in the early afternoon of November 20.

[4]These instructions were issued the following day.

[5]McGeorge Bundy produced this memorandum.

these planes can be observed and counted as they leave. Inasmuch as this goes a long way towards reducing the danger which faced this hemisphere 4 weeks ago, I have this afternoon instructed the Secretary of Defense to lift our naval quarantine.

In view of this action, I want to take this opportunity to bring the American people up to date on the Cuban crisis and to review the progress made thus far in fulfilling the understandings between Soviet Chairman Khrushchev and myself as set forth in our letters of October 27 and 28. Chairman Khrushchev, it will be recalled, agreed to remove from Cuba all weapons systems capable of offensive use, to halt the further introduction of such weapons into Cuba, and to permit appropriate United Nations observation and supervision to insure the carrying out and continuation of these commitments. We on our part agreed that once these adequate arrangements for verification had been established we would remove our naval quarantine and give assurances against an invasion of Cuba.

The evidence to date indicates that all known offensive missile sites in Cuba have been dismantled. The missiles and their associated equipment have been loaded on Soviet ships. And our inspection at sea of these departing ships has confirmed that the number of missiles reported by the Soviet Union as having been brought into Cuba, which closely corresponded to our own information, has now been removed. In addition, the Soviet Government has stated that all nuclear weapons have been withdrawn from Cuba and no offensive weapons will be reintroduced.

Nevertheless, important parts of the understanding of October 27th and 28th remain to be carried out. The Cuban Government has not yet permitted the United Nations to verify whether all offensive weapons have been removed, and no lasting safeguards have yet been established against the future introduction of offensive weapons back into Cuba.

Consequently, if the Western Hemisphere is to continue to be protected against offensive weapons, this Government has no choice but to pursue its own means of checking on military activities in Cuba. The importance of our continued vigilance is underlined by our identification in recent days of a number of Soviet ground combat units in Cuba, although we are informed that these and other Soviet units were associated with the protection of offensive weapons systems, and will also be withdrawn in due course.

I repeat, we would like nothing better than adequate international arrangements for the task of inspection and verification in Cuba, and we are prepared to continue our efforts to achieve such arrangements. Until that is done, difficult problems remain. As for our part, if all offensive weapons systems are removed from Cuba and kept out of the hemisphere in the future, under adequate verification and safeguards, and if Cuba is not used for the export of aggressive Communist purposes, there will be peace in the Caribbean. And as I said in September, "we shall neither initiate nor permit aggression in this hemisphere."[1]

We will not, of course, abandon the political, economic, and other efforts of

---

[1]From his statement at the press conference on September 13. See Chapter 3, Document 12.

this hemisphere to halt subversion from Cuba nor our purpose and hope that the Cuban people shall some day be truly free. But these policies are very different from any intent to launch a military invasion of the island.

In short, the record of recent weeks shows real progress and we are hopeful that further progress can be made. The completion of the commitment on both sides and the achievement of a peaceful solution to the Cuban crisis might well open the door to the solution of other outstanding problems.

May I add this final thought in this week of Thanksgiving: there is much for which we can be grateful as we look back to where we stood only 4 weeks ago — the unity of this hemisphere, the support of our allies, and the calm determination of the American people. These qualities may be tested many more times in this decade, but we have increased reason to be confident that those qualities will continue to serve the cause of freedom with distinction in the years to come. . . .

Q. Mr. President, with respect to your no-invasion pledge, there has been considerable discussion and speculation in the press as to the exact scope of this pledge. I believe that Chairman Khrushchev, in his letter of the 28th, made the assumption, or the implication, or the statement, that no attack would be made on Castro, not only by the United States, but any other country in the Western Hemisphere. It appeared to be an implication that possibly you would be willing to guarantee Castro against any and all enemies anywhere. Now I realize that in your letter there was nothing of that sort and you've touched on this today, but I'm wondering if you can be a bit more specific on the scope of your no-invasion pledge.

THE PRESIDENT. I think that today's statement describes very clearly what the policy is of the Government in regard to no-invasion. I think if you re-read the statement you will see the position of the Government on that matter.

Q. Mr. President, in speaking of "adequate verification," does this mean that we insist upon onsite inspection? Would we be satisfied with anything less than actual, on-the-spot inspection in Cuba?

THE PRESIDENT. Well, we have thought that to provide adequate inspection, it should be onsite. As you know, Mr. Castro has not agreed to that, so we have had to use our own resources to implement the decision of the Organization of American States that the hemisphere should continue to keep itself informed about the development of weapons systems in Cuba. . . .

Q. Mr. President, another question on Cuba. Is it your position, sir, that you will issue a formal no-invasion pledge only after satisfactory arrangements have been made for verification and after adequate arrangements have been made to make sure that such weapons are not reintroduced once more?

THE PRESIDENT. Quite obviously, as I said in my statements, serious problems remain as to verification and reassurance, and, therefore, this matter of our negotiations really are not—have not been completed and until they're completed, of course, I suppose we're not going to be fully satisfied that there will be peace in the Caribbean.

In regard to my feelings about what remains to be done, and on the matter of invasion, I think my statement is the best expression of our views.

Q. Mr. President, what would we accept as a guarantee, as a safeguard against reintroduction? Can that be achieved by anything short of continuous aerial reconnaissance?

THE PRESIDENT. Well, I think that what we would like to have is the kind of inspection on the ground which would make any other means of obtaining information unnecessary.

Q. A continuing inspection after the settlement—

THE PRESIDENT. Inspection which would provide us with assurances that there are not on the island weapons capable of offensive action against the United States or neighboring countries and that they will not be reintroduced. Obviously, that is our goal. If we do not achieve that goal, then we have to use other resources to assure ourselves that weapons are not there, or that they're not being reintroduced. . . .

Q. Sir, would you please clear up for us our relationship with the United Nations? If we wanted to invade Cuba, if we wanted to take unilateral action in any way, could we do so without the approval of the United Nations?

THE PRESIDENT. Well, I don't think a question—you have to really give me a much more detailed hypothetical question before I could consider answering it, and even under those conditions it might not be wise. Obviously, the United States—let's use a hypothetical case, which is always better—the United States has the means as a sovereign power to defend itself. And of course exercises that power, has in the past, and would in the future. We would hope to exercise it in a way consistent with our treaty obligations, including the United Nations Charter. But we, of course, keep to ourselves and hold to ourselves under the United States Constitution and under the laws of international law, the right to defend our security. On our own, if necessary—though we, as I say, hope to always move in concert with our allies, but on our own if that situation was necessary to protect our survival or integrity or other vital interests. . . .

21. Summary of ExComm Meeting

JFK tells his advisers he does not wish to give Khrushchev (and Castro) an ironclad guarantee against a U.S. invasion of Cuba.

Washington, November 21, 1962.

. . . Three draft instructions,[1] one written by McCloy, another by Stevenson, and a third by the State Department, were discussed. The State draft was largely a restatement of the President's press conference statement.[2] It made the point that we cannot ignore the necessity of ensuring the peace and security of the

---

[1] These draft instructions were for a U.S. declaration to be made at the UN on the question of an American no-invasion pledge regarding Cuba.

[2] On November 20. See Document 20.

hemisphere. We must satisfy ourselves that no offensive weapons remain in Cuba. The burden is on Cuba, not the USSR, to ensure that we can do this. The State [Department] draft was described as an offering document.

Mr. Ball said that McCloy's view is that we got from the Russians more than we expected. Therefore, we should not put so much stress on ground inspection[3] now that if we don't get it it is a defeat for us.

The President agreed that we could abandon insistence on ground inspection, but he felt that the proposed no-invasion assurances were too hard. He said our objective is to preserve our right to invade Cuba in the event of civil war, if there were guerrilla activities in other Latin American countries or if offensive weapons were reintroduced into Cuba. We do not want to build up Castro by means of a no-invasion guarantee. The pertinent sentence in the declaration which we would make to the UN Security Council was revised.[4]

The President left the meeting after approving an interim reply[5] to the most recent message from Khrushchev.[6] . . .

22. Message from President Kennedy to Chairman Khrushchev

Kennedy confirms for Khrushchev what he had stated at his press conference the previous day—that the blockade will end as the IL–28s are being withdrawn. He also touches on the issue of a U.S. no-invasion pledge.

Washington, November 21, 1962.

DEAR MR. CHAIRMAN: I have been glad to get your letter of November 20,[1] which arrived in good time yesterday. As you will have seen, I was able to announce the lifting of our quarantine promptly at my press conference, on the basis of your welcome assurance that the IL–28 bombers will be removed within a month.

I am now instructing our negotiators in New York[2] to move ahead promptly with proposals for a solution of the remaining elements in the Cuban problem. I do not wish to confuse the discussion by trying to state our present position in detail in this message, but I do want you to know that I continue to believe that

[3]The idea behind ground inspection was that it would prove that all the missiles had been withdrawn from Cuba.
[4]For this draft declaration as sent to U.S. officials at the UN, see Document 205 in Department of State, *Foreign Relations of the United States, 1961–1963*, XI (Washington, D.C., 1996), 517–519.
[5]See Document 22.
[6]See Document 18. Bromley Smith produced this memorandum.
[1]See Document 18.
[2]Namely, Stevenson and McCloy.

it is important to settle this matter promptly and on reasonable terms, so that we may move on to other issues. I regret that you have been unable to persuade Mr. Castro to accept a suitable form of inspection or verification in Cuba, and that in consequence we must continue to rely upon our own means of information. But, as I said yesterday,[3] there need be no fear of any invasion of Cuba while matters take their present favorable course.

23. Memorandum of Conversation Between First Deputy Chairman of the Soviet Council of Ministers Anastas I. Mikoyan and Attorney General Kennedy

One positive consequence of the missile crisis was a heightened desire on the part of the superpowers to make the cold war safer. The 1963 Nuclear Test Ban Treaty would be one sign of this enlarged Soviet-American commitment to conciliation. A meeting between Bobby Kennedy and one of Khrushchev's closest aides conveys a sense of this mutual superpower interest in improved relations.

November 30, 1962.

[. . .] On the evening of 30 November, A. I. Mikoyan was present at a dinner in honor of the American Secretary of the Interior [Stewart] Udall. The guests included R. Kennedy, Under Secretary of State [George] Ball, the chairman of the President's Council of Economic Advisors [Walter] Heller, the chairman of the Board of Directors of the "New York Times" [Orville] Dryfoos, and the Soviet Ambassador Dobrynin.

All the American guests were with their wives, except for Robert Kennedy who came with his eldest daughter, age 13. He has seven children in all. He said that his wife, together with the other six [children], who had the flu, had gone to Florida to bring them up to [good] condition.

Before dinner, <u>Robert Kennedy</u>, after conversations of a protocol-like nature in the presence of all, asked A. I. Mikoyan to step into another room. . . .

Then he [Robert Kennedy] touched on the major questions for which they had left the company—the significance of yesterday's conversations with President Kennedy[1] and the need for contacts between Khrushchev and Kennedy and mutual actions.

The President, <u>said R. Kennedy</u>, considers yesterday's conversation extremely useful, promoting further mutual comprehension between our governments and

[3]At his November 20 press conference. See Document 20.
[1]On November 29 JFK and Mikoyan had met for more than three hours.

their heads. In this respect, this meeting can be characterized as definite progress. Such is the opinion of the president himself.

What is most important now?, continued R. Kennedy. The most important, even more important than the fates of my children and your grandchildren, although they, of course, are the nearest and dearest to us, is the question of mutual understanding between Chairman Khrushchev and President Kennedy. Indeed, it now decides the fate of the world. One must admit that in the course of the recent crisis, their personal relations and mutual trust underwent serious trials, as a result of which, frankly speaking, damage was sustained. Therefore, it is very important to do everything to restore fully the trust on which so much depends. We ourselves understand the need for this, for we must look ahead. We, concluded R. Kennedy, sincerely hope that the development of our relations can follow a happier course than in the past.

A. I. Mikoyan replied to R. Kennedy that he fully agrees with the idea of the importance for preserving peace and for the basic improvement of relations between our countries of good personal relations between N. S. Khrushchev and President Kennedy, their mutual understanding and trust of one another. As one of N. S. Khrushchev's comrades-in-arms, said A. I. Mikoyan, I can assure you that exactly these thoughts define his approach to his relations with the USA president. N. S. Khrushchev values the personal quality of these relations. The Soviet government renders its due to the self-possession exhibited by the president in the most dangerous moment, when the world stood at the edge of thermonuclear war, but by mutual concessions and compromises, succeeded in averting this war.

Moscow, continued A. I. Mikoyan, noticed the positive role you, the president's brother, played during the confidential negotiations between the president and the head of the Soviet state. Of course, we understand, that you did this, as did we, in the interests of one's own country, one's own people. It was important, however, that you understood correctly, in the critical moment, what those interests were. Let us now complete the outlined resolution to the Cuban question, without complicating it with trivial formal cavils or even worse, some deviation from the agreement on the final settlement of this question. Indeed, if one speaks the truth, there's not much left to do; it is only necessary to put in writing or to finalize, without excessive procrastination that which the American side obligated itself to do during the exchange of messages between N. S. Khrushchev and the president.[2]

R. Kennedy noted that he agreed that little of essence remained to be done— indeed, "it's 90 percent done," although there are still difficulties that must be overcome. But he, R. Kennedy, did not intend to analyze these difficulties. They were the subject of detailed discussion in New York.[3] He only wanted to emphasize briefly that with which he began: the importance of further developing mutual understanding between the president and N. S. Khrushchev. This will

---

[2]Namely, the American no-invasion pledge contained in Kennedy's October 27 message to Khrushchev.

[3]McCloy, Stevenson, and Kuznetsov participated in this discussion.

determine to a large extent the success and solution of other questions that still await settlement.

A. I. Mikoyan agreed with this. . . .

In concluding the conversation, R. Kennedy asked [Mikoyan] to give greetings to N. S. Khrushchev. In his turn A. I. Mikoyan sent greetings to the president.

Robert Kennedy showed interest in visiting the Soviet Union and expressed this desire.

A. I. Mikoyan said that this was a good idea and completely realizable. If the decrease in tension between [our] countries continues further and the political atmosphere warms up, then this trip would not only be interesting but useful for him. . . .[4]

24. Message from Chairman Khrushchev to President Kennedy

Beginning on December 3, the Soviet IL–28 bombers were removed from Cuba. With this matter out of the way, the salient issue left over from the missile crisis, especially from Moscow's point of view, was the need to register in documents with the United Nations the Russian and American pledges made in the settlement. In correspondence with JFK, Khrushchev makes clear that he is particularly eager to see Kennedy's promise not to invade Cuba highlighted in this way. He also discusses the use of confidential channels of communication between the Soviet and American governments.

Moscow, December 11, 1962.

DEAR MR. PRESIDENT, It would seem that you and we have come now to a final stage in the elimination of tension around Cuba. Our relations are already entering now their formal course since all those means[1] placed by us on the Cuban territory which you considered offensive are withdrawn and you ascertained that to which effect a statement was already made by your side.[2]

That is good. We appreciate that you just as we approached not dogmatically the solution of the question of eliminating the tension which evolved and this enabled us under existing conditions to find also a more flexible form of verification of the withdrawal of the above mentioned means.[3] Understanding and

---

[4]Ambassador Dobrynin and Third Secretary at the Soviet Embassy Igor D. Bubnov transcribed this conversation between Bobby Kennedy and Mikoyan.

[1]Weapons, in other words.

[2]Presumably a reference to JFK's November 20 press conference. See Document 20.

[3]In other words, there had not been UN verification, as originally intended, but U.S. intelligence had been allowed by the Russians to count the offensive weapons on Soviet ships heading back to the Soviet Union.

flexibility displayed by you in this matter are highly appreciated by us though our criticism of American imperialism remains in force because that conflict was indeed created by the policy of the United States with regard to Cuba.

More resolute steps should be taken now to move towards finalizing the elimination of this tension, i.e. you on your part should clearly confirm at the U.N. as you did at your [November 20] press conference and in your messages to me the pledge of non-invasion of Cuba by the United States and your allies. . . .

I believe that you already had an opportunity to familiarize yourself with the text proposed by us[4] of a brief declaration of the Soviet Government in which the Soviet Union's main commitments resulting from the exchange of messages between us are formulated. We proceed from the assumption that an analogous brief declaration should be made by the U.S. Government and that the main U.S. commitments resulting from the exchange of messages[5] will also be fixed in it. Have a look, Mr. President, at this proposal submitted by us through your representatives in New York.

But notwithstanding what the agreement on the concrete texts of our declarations at this concluding stage will be, anyway the basic goal has been achieved and tension removed. I will tell you frankly that we have removed our means from Cuba relying on your assurance that the United States and its allies will not invade Cuba. . . .

Within a short period of time we and you have lived through a rather acute crisis. The acuteness of it was that we and you were already prepared to fight and this would lead to a thermonuclear war. Yes, to a thermonuclear world war with all its dreadful consequences. We took it into account and, being convinced that mankind would never forgive the statesmen who would not exhaust all possibilities to prevent catastrophe, agreed to a compromise although we understood— and we state it now—that your claims had no grounds whatsoever, had no legal basis and represented a manifestation of sheer arbitrariness in international affairs. We agreed to a compromise because our main purpose was to extend a helping hand to the Cuban people in order to exclude the possibility of invasion of Cuba so that Cuba could exist and develop as a free sovereign state. This is our main purpose today, it remains to be our main purpose for tomorrow and we did not and do not pursue any other purposes.

Therefore, Mr. President, everything—the stability in this area and not only in this area but in the entire world—depends on how you will now fulfill the commitments taken by you. Furthermore, it will be now a sort of litmus paper, an indicator whether it is possible to trust if similar difficulties arise in other geographical areas. I think you will agree that if our arrangement for settling the Cuban crisis fails it will undermine a possibility for manoeuvre which you and we would resort to for elimination of danger, a possibility for compromise in the future if similar difficulties arise in other areas of the world, and they really can

---

[4]In this draft declaration, presented by the Russians on December 6 during the ongoing negotiations in New York, the Soviet government stated that offensive weapons had been withdrawn from Cuba and would not be deployed again on the island; and called for the continuation of negotiations aimed at stabilizing the situation in the Caribbean.

[5]A reference to those sent between Kennedy and Khrushchev on October 27 and 28.

arise. We attach great significance to all this, and subsequent development will depend on you as President and on the U.S. Government.

We believe that the guarantees for non-invasion of Cuba given by you will be maintained and not only in the period of your stay in the White House, that, to use an expression, goes without saying. We believe that you will be able to receive a mandate at the next election too, that is that you will be the U.S. President for six years, which would appeal to us. At our times, six years in world politics is a long period of time and during that period we could create good conditions for peaceful coexistence on earth and this would be highly appreciated by the peoples of our countries as well as by all other peoples.

Therefore, Mr. President, I would like to express a wish that you follow the right way, as we do, in appraising the situation. Now it is of special importance to provide for the possibility of an exchange of opinion through confidential channels which you and I have set up and which we use.[6] But the confidential nature of our personal relations will depend on whether you fulfill—as we did—the commitments taken by you and give instructions to your representatives in New York to formalize these commitments in appropriate documents. This is needed in order that all the peoples be sure that tension in the Caribbean is a matter of yesterday and that now normal conditions have been really created in the world. And for this it is necessary to fix the assumed commitments in the documents of both sides and register them with the United Nations. . . .

I would like to express to you my disapproval of certain things. We read now various articles by your columnists and correspondents and we are concerned that in those articles they are widely commenting on the confidential exchange of opinion and it is being done by the people who as it would seem have no relation to confidential channels set up between us. Judging by the contents of these articles it is clear that their authors are well informed and we get an impression that this is not a result of an accidental leak of the confidential information but a result of benevolence for those people into whose hands gets the information they make public. This evidently is done for the purpose of informing the public in a one-sided way.

Frankly speaking, if we use the confidential communications this way, it will be far from facilitating confidence in those channels. You yourself realize that if your side begins to act in the way that our exchange of opinion by way of confidential channels will leak through fingers these channels will cease to be of use and may even cause harm. But this is up to you. If you consider that those channels have outlived themselves and are of no use any longer, then we also will draw appropriate conclusions in this respect. I tell you this straightforwardly and I would like to know your opinion on this matter. I have been denouncing American imperialism. But on the other hand I consider it useful for us to continue to maintain the possibility of confidential exchange of opinion because a minimum of personal trust is necessary for leading statesmen of both countries and this corresponds to the interests of our countries and peoples, to the interests of peace all over the world.

[6]A reference presumably to the Bolshakov and perhaps also the Dobrynin secret channel to Robert Kennedy. See also Document 25, footnote 6.

Let us, Mr. President, eliminate promptly the consequences of the Cuban crisis and get down to solving other questions, and we have them in number.[7]. . .

Please, excuse me for my straightforwardness and frankness but I believe as before that a frank and straightforward exchange of opinion is needed to avoid the worst.

Please, convey to your wife and your whole family wishes of good health from myself, my wife and my entire family.

25. Message from President Kennedy to Chairman Khrushchev

JFK replies to Khrushchev, saying that a U.S. no-invasion pledge regarding Cuba can be registered with the UN only if proper verification of the removal of all the missiles from Cuba takes place (a condition that could not be met, as Castro would not allow inspectors on Cuban soil), if Cuba committed no acts of aggression in the Western Hemisphere, and if no nuclear weapons were redeployed on the island.

Washington, December 14, 1962.

DEAR MR. CHAIRMAN: I was glad to have your message of December 11[1] and to know that you believe, as we do, that we have come to the final stage of the Cuban affair between us, the settlement of which will have significance for our future relations and for our ability to overcome other difficulties. I wish to thank you for your expression of appreciation of the understanding and flexibility we have tried to display.

I have followed with close attention the negotiations on the final settlement of the Cuban question between your representative, Mr. Kuznetsov, and our representatives, Ambassador Stevenson and Mr. McCloy, in New York. In these negotiations we have tried to understand your position and I am glad to note that Mr. Kuznetsov has also shown effort to understand our problems. It is clearly in the interest of both sides that we reach agreement on how finally to dispose of the Cuban crisis. To this end, Ambassador Stevenson and Mr. McCloy presented on Wednesday a new draft of a joint statement which by now has certainly reached you.[2] I wish to assure you that it is our purpose to end this affair as simply and clearly as possible.

You refer to the importance of my statements on an invasion of Cuba and of

[7]There follows at this point in the text a section on the test-ban issue and the German question.
[1]See Document 24.
[2]For this statement draft, see Document 243 in Department of State, *Foreign Relations of the United States, 1961–1963*, XI, 611–613.

our intention to fulfill them, so that no doubts are sown from the very start. I have already stated my position publicly in my press conference on November 20th,[3] and I am glad that this statement appears to have your understanding; we have never wanted to be driven by the acts of others into war in Cuba. The other side of the coin, however, is that we do need to have adequate assurances that all offensive weapons are removed from Cuba and are not reintroduced, and that Cuba itself commits no aggressive acts against any of the nations of the Western Hemisphere. As I understand you, you feel confident that Cuba will not in fact engage in such aggressive acts, and of course I already have your own assurance about the offensive weapons. So I myself should suppose that you could accept our position—but it is probably better to leave final discussion of these matters to our representatives in New York. I quite agree with you that the larger part of the crisis has now been ended and we should not permit others to stand in the way of promptly settling the rest without further acrimony.

With regard to your reference to the confidential channels set up between us, I can assure you that I value them. I have not concealed from you that it was a serious disappointment to me that dangerously misleading information should have come through these channels before the recent crisis.[4] You may also wish to know that by an accident or misunderstanding one of your diplomats appears to have used a representative of a private television network as a channel to us.[5] This is always unwise in our country, where the members of the press often insist on printing at some later time what they may learn privately.

Because our systems are so different, you may not be fully familiar with the practices of the American press. The competition for news in this country is fierce. A number of the competitors are not great admirers of my Administration, and perhaps an even larger number are not wholly friendly to yours. Here in Washington we have 1200 reporters accredited to the White House alone, and thousands more in other assignments. Not one of them is accountable to this government for what he reports. It would be a great mistake to think that what appears in newspapers and magazines necessarily has anything to do with the policy and purpose of this government. I am glad to say that I have some friends among newspapermen, but no spokesmen.

But let me emphasize again that we do indeed value these confidential channels. I entirely share your view that some trust is necessary for leading statesmen of our two countries; I believe that it is important to build the area of trust wherever possible. I shall of course continue to hold and to express my convictions about the relative merits of our systems of government, and I will not be surprised if you do the same.

In particular, we have been very glad to have opportunities for private exchanges with and through Mr. Bolshakov, and I am sorry to learn that he is re-

[3]See Document 20.

[4]Presumably a reference to Bolshakov's dealings with Robert Kennedy, and also to Dobrynin's statements in meetings with various American officials in early September that no offensive weapons were being sent to Cuba.

[5]JFK was referring to the secret dialogue between KGB agent Feklisov and American correspondent Scali, and specifically the leak to Scali, apparently by the Russians, of Khrushchev's November 20 message to JFK.

turning to Moscow.[6] It is our impression that he has made a real effort to improve communications and understanding between our two governments, and we shall miss him very much.

I appreciate your writing me so frankly, and in return I have tried to be as straightforward, for I agree with you that only through such frank exchanges can we better understand our respective points of view. Partly for this reason I refrained in my last press conference from commenting on certain aspects of your speech before the Supreme Soviet[7] with which you realize, of course, we could not agree.

We also are hopeful that once the Cuban crisis is behind us, we shall be able to tackle the other problems confronting us and to find the path to their solution.[8]. . .

Thank you for your expressions of good wishes to me and my family, and let me in turn send you and your wife and family our personal good wishes for the coming year.

26. Television and Radio Interview of President Kennedy

With 1962 drawing to a close, JFK reflects in an interview with the press on the dangers of the missile crisis. He gives the impression of a man deeply affected by the experience.

December 17, 1962.[1]

. . . THE PRESIDENT. I think, looking back on Cuba,[2] what is of concern is the fact that both governments were so far out of contact, really. I don't think that we expected that he [Khrushchev] would put the missiles in Cuba, because it would have seemed such an imprudent action for him to take, as it was later proved. Now, he obviously must have thought that he could do it in secret and that the United States would accept it. So that he did not judge our intentions accurately.

Well, now, if you look at the history of this century, where World War I really came through a series of misjudgments of the intentions of others, certainly

[6]Moscow had recalled Bolshakov, who had transmitted many messages between Khrushchev and John Kennedy via Robert Kennedy, after the American press reported that he had played a role in deceiving the Kennedy administration about the missiles in Cuba before the onset of the crisis.
[7]On December 12.
[8]There follows at this point in the text two paragraphs on the German question and the test ban.
[1]This interview was recorded on December 16 at the White House and broadcast on television on December 17.
[2]JFK meant the missile crisis, specifically.

World War II, where Hitler thought that he could seize Poland, that the British might not fight, and if they fought, after the defeat of Poland they might not continue to fight, Korea, where obviously the North Koreans did not think we were going to come in, and Korea, when we did not think the Chinese were going to come in, when you look at all those misjudgments which brought on war, and then you see the Soviet Union and the United States so far separated in their beliefs, we believing in a world of independent sovereign and different diverse nations, they believing in a monolithic Communist world, and you put the nuclear equation into that struggle, that is what makes this, as I said before, such a dangerous time, and that we must proceed with firmness and also with the best information we can get, and also with care. There is nothing—one mistake can make this whole thing blow up. So that—one major mistake either by Mr. Khrushchev or by us here—so that is why it is much easier to make speeches about some of the things which we ought to be doing, but I think that anybody who looks at the fatality lists on atomic weapons, and realizes that the Communists have a completely twisted view of the United States, and that we don't comprehend them, that is what makes life in the sixties hazardous. . . .

27. Letter from UN Ambassador Stevenson and Soviet First Deputy Minister of Foreign Affairs Kuznetsov to UN Secretary General U Thant

Adlai Stevenson and Vasily Kuznetsov, both of whom had been centrally involved in December in the effort to achieve closure on the missile crisis by producing a joint declaration on superpower commitments on Cuba, inform the UN secretary general in effect that they have been unable to accomplish this. Accordingly they ask U Thant to remove the Cuban issue from the Security Council agenda. The process of trying to tie up the loose ends of the missile crisis was finally at an end.

January 7, 1963.

On behalf of the Governments of the United States of America and the Soviet Union, we desire to express to you our appreciation for your efforts in assisting our Governments to avert the serious threat to the peace which recently arose in the Caribbean area.

While it has not been possible for our Governments to resolve all the problems that have arisen in connexion with this affair, they believe that, in view of the degree of understanding reached between them on the settlement of the crisis and the extent of progress in the implementation of this understanding, it is not necessary for this item to occupy further the attention of the Security Council at this time.

The Governments of the United States of America and of the Soviet Union express the hope that the actions taken to avert the threat of war in connexion with this crisis will lead toward the adjustment of other differences between them and the general easing of tensions that could cause a further threat of war.

PART 6

1963: Old Tactics, New Approaches

JOHN KENNEDY, it can be argued, changed as president during the final year of his life. The Cuban missile crisis appears to have sobered him, increasing his determination to make the cold war safer. Examples of this new resolve came in the summer of 1963 with his famous speech at American University, noteworthy for its conciliatory attitude toward the Soviet Union, and his signing of the Test Ban Treaty, which limited nuclear testing. A more progressive phase in his civil rights policies in 1963, with the introduction in Congress of a sweeping bill designed to end segregation, can be viewed as the domestic counterpart to this more accommodating thrust in his foreign policy.

The documents in this chapter can be examined to determine whether JFK's Cuban policies support the notion that he became an increasingly mature leader. Not all of them do, by any means. In 1963 Cuba was no longer the central focus of Kennedy's foreign policy. Vietnam came to assume a priority for U.S. policymakers that it retained over the course of the next decade. But when JFK and his advisers did turn their attention to Castro, their attitude was strikingly and troublingly reminiscent of their pre–missile crisis outlook: they remained determined to use covert means to undermine Castro's position. In June 1963 JFK gave the go-ahead for a CIA plan to carry out sabotage and other hostile activities against Cuba. It was a sort of condensed version of Operation Mongoose. Some of the documents in this chapter demonstrate that Russian officials soon learned of the resumption of covert U.S. pressure on Cuba, making this issue a bone of contention between the superpowers in the fall of 1963.

In contrast to this continuing effort to harass Castro, however, the Kennedy administration pursued another clandestine strategy in the fall of 1963, this one aimed at generating a dialogue with the Cuban leader. William Attwood, a U.S. official at the United Nations, was centrally involved in this enterprise, and he kept senior administration officials abreast of his efforts. Had Kennedy not been assassinated, this initiative may conceivably have brought about an accommodation with Castro.

Robert Kennedy, such a conspicuous figure on Cuban matters in 1961–1962, was less prominent in 1963 in shaping administration policy toward Castro. But his role remained significant.

1. Memorandum of a White House Conversation Between President Kennedy and First Deputy Minister of Foreign Affairs Kuznetsov

In a conversation with a senior Soviet official, JFK calls for the removal of Russian troops still in Cuba, and is asked to make good on his promise not to invade the island.

Washington, January 9, 1963, 5 p.m.

Kuznetsov thanked the President for receiving him, saying that he considered this an honor, particularly in view of how busy the President is. . . .

The President said that he thought Kuznetsov knew from his talks with Mc-Cloy and Stevenson of the particular sensitivity in the United States to anything involving Cuba. This is a delicate nerve in the United States stretching back to the beginning of our country. On the other hand, the President said, he was anxious to maintain good relations with the Soviet Union. He had noted before that these two most powerful countries have no national interests which bring them into collision. The President had spent a good deal of time defending this viewpoint prior to the Cuban crisis. Now that the matter had quieted down he saw no reason why the United States and the U.S.S.R. should be involved again in the same way. He asked Kuznetsov to explain to his principals American sensitivity over Cuba. The fact that there are 15 to 17,000 Soviet troops still in Cuba causes difficulties for the United States Government and for those in the United States who seek to maintain good relations with the U.S.S.R. The President said the Soviet Government could understand how the United States felt about this if they could imagine a similar situation in Finland. He was hopeful that Soviet policies toward Cuba, including the personnel and armaments there, would lead to a further relaxation of the situation. As to the question of the Bay of Pigs prisoners,[1] the President said he had put them on the beach and he felt responsible for

[1]In Miami on December 29, JFK addressed those Cubans who had participated in the Bay of Pigs invasion and had just been released by Castro. He told them that he looked forward to a change of government in Havana. Earlier in this meeting, Kuznetsov had spoken critically of Kennedy's remarks in Miami.

them. He had not said in his address to them that the United States would invade Cuba, though he had expressed the hope for a change in the situation there. All the U.S. forces which had been mobilized during the crisis were back in their camps. If the Soviet Union can comprehend the sensitivity and difficult nature of the problems the United States faces in the Caribbean, this can lead to a solution of other problems.

In reply, Kuznetsov said that the Soviet Government will fulfill all of the obligations it undertook with the exchange of letters between Khrushchev and the President. As for the Soviet military personnel in Cuba, it seemed to him that all the agreements in the exchange of letters had been carried out. This problem had been dealt with in the course of the exchange and there was a clear understanding on both sides concerning this matter. The Soviet Government will abide by all its agreements so there is nothing new in this problem.

The President noted that Khrushchev had given a clear commitment to withdraw all military personnel connected with the missile sites in Cuba and all others "in time." He recognized that the latter was not the same kind of commitment since no time was specified. Nevertheless, he wanted to mention this matter which occupied attention in the United States.

Kuznetsov reiterated that he thought that there was no misunderstanding on this point.

Referring to the President's comparison of the Cuban situation with Finland, Kuznetsov noted that there were many U.S. military bases, armed with deadly weapons and occupied by troops, around the U.S.S.R. However, he had no instructions on this point and said that the U.S.S.R. is not raising the question at this time.

The President replied that the U.S. had not introduced a new major base in any country such as Finland. A thermonuclear base there would have created a new situation. He repeated that Cuba was a matter of great sensitivity to the American people and again asked Kuznetsov to communicate this to his Government. Good relations between our two countries, the President said, will be made easier if the Soviet Government understands this.

Kuznetsov reverted to the question of the President's reception of the Cuban brigade in Florida.[2] He said this had created the opinion in Moscow that this brigade will be maintained, that others will be created and that then there would be a fresh invasion of Cuba.

The President replied that this was not going to happen. In a backgrounder which he had given in Florida he had said that the United States had no intention of invading Cuba and noted that our position remained that which he had set forth in his press conference of November 20.[3] He said there would be no third hand invasion of Cuba. Nevertheless, it would be easier for the United States if there were a reduction of the Soviet military presence in Cuba. The President noted that Castro makes many more speeches than the President does and in them calls for revolution in Latin America. However, Castro was of no concern to the United States. The relations between the United States and the

[2]Another reference to JFK's December 29 address. See the preceding note.
[3]See Chapter 5, Document 20.

U.S.S.R. are more important and the President was anxious to lessen areas of disagreement between the two countries.

Kuznetsov replied that while the results of the New York negotiations were not as great as they might have been,[4] the situation was better now than it had been at the end of October. The immediate threat had been averted. However, normalization of relations required that something else should be done. No one can agree that a situation is normal when a great power threatens a small one, and officially expresses a desire to strangle and overthrow the government of the smaller one. Thus, some problems remain and further normalization of the situation depends on the United States Government. . . .

The President reiterated that the United States was not concerned with Cuba but with the Soviet military presence there. He noted a number of speeches which Castro and Che Guevara had made during the last two months calling for armed struggle in Latin America, saying that small bands of guerrillas would act as a catalyst in the process of taking power from the hands of the Yankee imperialists and insisting that this must be done in a large number of Latin American countries. He read a quotation from an interview by Che Guevara on November 23.

Kuznetsov replied that he was not at all sure the quotes which the President had made from the Cuban speeches were exact. It seemed to him that the Cubans had far more reasons to fear and worry than the United States. Ever since the beginning of the 1959 revolution, Cuba had been under various undermining pressures. The Cuban Government and Castro had made quite clear their willingness to negotiate with the United States concerning all points awaiting solution. The United States could respond to these Cuban proposals in order to normalize relations. He noted that the New York talks had been between the United States and the U.S.S.R. but that the problem had been made more difficult by the fact that they had been talking about another country.[5]

2. Notes of President Kennedy's Remarks at a National Security Council Meeting

JFK tells his foreign policy advisers that the future use of force against Cuba cannot be ruled out.

Washington, January 22, 1963.

I will start by reviewing areas of policy which will be before us in the com-

---

[4]Kuznetsov had been negotiating with Adlai Stevenson and John McCloy in New York since the end of the missile crisis.

[5]American official John C. Guthrie drafted this memorandum.

ing months and indicate the general attitude which I have toward them and to emphasize where we might put our emphasis in the next few months. . . .

Would like to say a word first about Cuba.

The indications are that the importance of timing is of paramount importance in reaching judgments—both by the USSR and the US. Our big problem is to protect our interests and prevent a nuclear war. It was a very close thing whether we would engage in a quarantine or an air strike.[1] In looking back, it was really that it presented us with an immediate crisis and the USSR had to make their judgment and come to a decision to act in twelve hours. In looking back over that four or five day period, we all changed our views somewhat, or at least appreciated the advantages and disadvantages of alternate courses of action. That is what we should do in any other struggle with the Soviet Union—and I believe we will be in one in the future. We should have sufficient time to consider the alternatives. You could see that the Russians had a good deal of debate in a 48 hour period. If they had only to act in an hour or two, their actions would have been spasmodic and might have resulted in nuclear war. It is important that we have time to study their reaction. We should continue our policy even though we do not get Europe to go along with us.

The time will probably come when we will have to act again on Cuba. Cuba might be our response in some future situation—the same way the Russians have used Berlin. We may decide that Cuba might be a more satisfactory response than a nuclear response. We must be ready—although this might not come. We should be prepared to move on Cuba if it should be in our national interest. The planning by the US, by the Military, in the direction of our effort should be advanced always keeping Cuba in mind in the coming months and to be ready to move with all possible speed. We can use Cuba to limit their actions just as they have had Berlin to limit our actions.[2]

3. Memorandum from Gordon Chase of the National Security Council Staff to the President's Special Assistant for National Security Affairs McGeorge Bundy

Although Operation Mongoose was formally ended in early 1963, the idea of supporting an anti-Castro revolt was not altogether abandoned, as this administration response to news of a possible uprising in Cuba makes clear.

[1]JFK was obviously discussing here the first week of the missile crisis.
[2]An unidentified CIA official produced this memorandum.

Washington, February 18, 1963.

SUBJECT

Report of a Possible Revolt in Cuba on February 20th[1]

The discussion at [the] State [Department] this afternoon brought out the following points regarding the possibility of a revolt in Cuba on February 20th.

1. Both State and CIA doubt the reliability of the report. CIA noted, however, that if such a thing were about to happen, the report of it would come in just this way.

2. One of the tough questions—what size and type of revolt is worthwhile to support? Do you determine this by the number of people involved? The geographic area it covers? etc. The revolt should have a potential political appeal to a large cross section of Cuban people. For example, a revolt by a number of disgruntled farmers would not meet this criterion.

3. There was some discussion of a possible outline of action. First, there could be a deniable airdrop of supplies by CIA while the U.S. military arm began to wind up. This could be followed by a limited airstrike within about twenty-four hours and a full island air-strike within seventy-two hours. It would take a maximum of eighteen days to mount a full invasion force. Between the full airstrike and the invasion, things could be going on—e.g. special forces dropped in Cuba. A diversionary action should be initiated quickly so that Castro cannot concentrate his forces on the insurgents, leaving us no one to liberate.

4. The presence of Russian troops, of course, presents a very sticky problem. One of the first targets would be the SAM sites and inevitably Russians would be killed. The effect of this on Khrushchev would have to be weighed.

Perhaps we could tell Khrushchev what we are going to do and advise him to take all Russians off the SAM sites and move them to restricted areas. In this regard we could risk a flight or two over the SAM sites to test whether he has followed our advice.

If the prospects for the removal of the Russian troops in the near future look very good, we may want to dampen the revolt for now—broadcasts by Cuban exiles that Castro is setting a trap.

5. The present Department of Defense off-the-cuff estimate of fighting in Cuba is that there would be four or five days of heavy fighting and another thirty days of less severe fighting. There might or might not be prolonged guerrilla activity. If the campaign is short and sweet, there probably will be less guerrilla fighting afterwards.

6. It was noted that the invasion would violate the Havana Treaty (can respond to calls for help only by recognized governments).[2]

---

[1] On February 18 the State Department's Bureau of Intelligence and Research reported the possibility of minor uprisings in Cuba but cast doubt on the likelihood of a large-scale anti-Castro revolt.
[2] The Havana Convention on Duties and Rights of States in the Event of Civil Strife (1928).

4. Memorandum for the Record Drafted by Chairman of the JCS Taylor

Contingency planning for an attack on Cuba, an important feature of the Kennedy administration's covert approach toward Castro before the missile crisis, continues in 1963, with JFK's active involvement.

Washington, February 28, 1963.

SUBJECT

Meeting of the Joint Chiefs of Staff with the President on 28 February 1963

All the Chiefs were present at the above meeting which lasted from 5:30 p.m. to 6:45 p.m. The following subjects were the principal topics of discussion.

a. *The Cuba Invasion Plan.*

(1) The Chiefs discussed the time-space factors in the implementation of CINCLANT Operation Plan 312 and 316.[1] . . . The President was shown why it would take approximately 18 days from decision to D-Day from present troop and ship dispositions. In order to reduce this time to something like 7 days, considerable prepositioning would be required in order to get Army/Marine units to the East Coast and to assemble the necessary cargo shipping. The Chiefs expressed the view that it was unlikely that a period of tension would not precede a decision to invade Cuba which would allow ample time for preparatory measures; hence, it was undesirable to make permanent changes of station of Army and Marine units which would upset the present disposition of strategic reserve forces.

(2) The President expressed particular interest in the possibility of getting some troops quickly into Cuba in the event of a general uprising. He was told that only the airborne troops could arrive with little delay, that the first Marine elements would require about 7 days before landing. He asked the Chiefs to develop specific plans in anticipation of the need for this kind of quick reaction.[2] . . .

[1]These were U.S. contingency plans for an attack on Cuba, developed before the missile crisis.
[2]Maxwell Taylor drafted this memorandum on March 1.

5. Memorandum from Gordon Chase of the National Security Council Staff to the President's Special Assistant for National Security Affairs McGeorge Bundy

A variety of covert schemes to pressure Castro (and Soviet troops in Cuba) are devised.

Washington, April 3, 1963.

SUBJECT

Cuba Coordinating Committee—Covert Operations in Cuba

Attached is an agenda[1] which was discussed at a meeting of the Cottrell Committee[2] on April 1. The meeting was attended by Secretary Vance, Joe Califano, Dick Helms, Dez FitzGerald, and Bob Hurwitch.

1. *Balloon Operations Over Havana*—The plan is well under way. Assuming the winds are right, CIA proposes to release balloons containing 300,000 to 500,000 leaflets on May Day[3] (before daylight). The balloons will not be visible by radar or by the naked eye. The leaflets will (1) attack Castro's henchmen, and (2) contain cartoons illustrating sabotage techniques.

The decision on the balloons is scheduled for another review during the week preceding May Day.

2. *Training of CIA-Sponsored Cuban Exiles on Military Reservations*—CIA and the Army are now working on this one to find appropriate installations.

3. *Russian Language Programs*—The Committee decided in favor of instituting three programs (Radio Liberty, Radio Caribe, and an intrusion program). . . .

In approving the three programs for Special Group consideration, the Committee recognized that they will probably be of marginal value only; however, they will cost us very little, financial or otherwise.

4. *Sabotage of Cuban Shipping (19 ships)*—The Committee discussed three forms of sabotage—limpets,[4] incendiaries in the cargoes, and abrasives in the machinery.

The Committee decided against limpets. . . . Unfortunately, there is no certain way of controlling a limpet; it could sink a ship and the sinking could be billed as a U.S. submarine attack. Secretary Vance came down hard against sinkings.

---

[1] The agenda (not included here) enumerates the six items mentioned in this memorandum.

[2] An interdepartmental committee, chaired by Sterling J. Cottrell, was set up in early 1963 to coordinate the administration's overt and covert Cuban policies.

[3] A holiday in honor of workers.

[4] Literally a limpet is a marine mollusk which adheres to rocks.

The Committee will recommend to the Special Group the incendiaries which would be timed to go off in international waters and the abrasives in the machinery. While the propaganda boost might be nil, they are easier to effect than limpets and could really hurt Castro.

The Committee gave CIA the option of using either its own Cubans or of using DRE as a cut-out.

5. *Redirection of Cuban Exile Group Operations* — The Committee discussed this one briefly—i.e. what is an acceptable target? Dick Helms pointed out that although these groups may start out to get a non-Soviet target, once you let them go, you can never really be sure what they will do. Bob Hurwitch seemed to favor the approach that attacks and sabotage should appear to come from inside rather than from outside Cuba.

The Committee came to no decision on this one. More thinking is needed.

6. *Propaganda Inside Cuba to Attack Soviet Troops* — While Secretary Vance expressed some concern about the possibility that this would lead to a conflagration between the Cubans and the Soviets (what would we do), the Committee decided in favor of this course of action. While the results will probably not be startling for our side, the costs and risks are small. (I'm not sure a conflagration would be such a bad thing for us, even if it did occur. How much chance would these 5,000 combat troops have against the huge and well-equipped Cuban army? I don't think the Russians would dare try to impose their will by force; they would have to grin and bear it.)

Comment:

1. In considering specifics of a covert program, I think we should keep in the back of our minds the possibility that we may want to turn our policy around sometime in the future. This does not necessarily mean that we would rule out covert operations—rather, we would probably want to direct them towards splitting the Cuba/Soviet tie (e.g. a "Russki Go Home" campaign) instead of forcing Castro to embrace the Soviets more tightly (e.g. inactivation of Cuban shipping which would lead to further Cuban dependence on Bloc shipping). In this regard, we may wish to consider carefully the gains and risks involved in directing more violent efforts against selected Russian targets within Cuba. I have a feeling that the risks are not as great as they seem.

2. Assuming we continue our present policy or consider a turnaround policy very far down the road, I like an active covert program. It seems to me that a good sabotage program is one of the few tools we can use to really hurt Castro economically. Our present policy of isolating Cuba from the Free World is not going to bust Castro. Instead, I suspect that the Cuban economy is at its low right now. With no effective U.S. covert intervention, it will probably grow healthier from here on as the Cuban economy moves from the difficult transition stage between economic dependence on the West and economic dependence on the Bloc.

6. Memorandum from Attorney General Kennedy to President Kennedy

Resuming their clandestine dialogue, Robert Kennedy and Ambassador Dobrynin clash bitterly over Cuba.

Washington, April 3, 1963.

Mr. Markov of the Russian Embassy[1] called this morning and said that the Russian Ambassador [Dobrynin] wished to come by and see me. I arranged for him to come in at 3:30 p.m.

We exchanged some pleasantries. He told me that Norman Cousins had asked to see Khrushchev and he had arranged it.[2] What was Cousins' relationship to the President? Then, as is his custom, he handed me a so-called "talking paper." This document was particularly long—approximately 25 pages. It was ostensibly to me from the Ambassador but in fact it was from Khrushchev to the President.

The paper made five or six major points, among which were the following:

... Another point that was made was a sharp and bitter criticism about the raids that had taken place against Russian ships.[3] These were piratical acts and the United States must take responsibility for them. It isn't possible to believe that if we really wanted to stop these raids that we could not do so. They were glad to hear of the steps that are being taken lately but in the last analysis the specific acts, namely, the arrests that we made would be the criteria by which they would judge our sincerity. The Soviet Union questions whether in fact we wish to end these attacks for our criticism of them has been not that they were wrong but that they were ineffective. The clear implication was that if the raids had been effective they would have had our approval.

Further, our efforts to isolate Cuba, to build a virtual wall around it, was a barbaric act. Our actions to stifle Cuba's commerce and to create economic difficulties and isolate her from her neighbors in Latin America were completely unwarranted. The support given to counter-revolutionaries and the statements to the barbaric mercenaries in Miami by the President were also bitterly criticized.

The document also stated that the President should understand the continued pressure on the Soviet Union for the withdrawal of troops from Cuba was not going to be effective. The Soviet Union does not respond to pressure. As a matter of fact, they had already withdrawn twice as many troops as the largest number that had appeared in the newspapers here in the United States. However, he said that he was going to refuse to give the actual number that had been withdrawn because then public statements would be issued that they had been

---

[1]Petr I. Markov, attaché at the Soviet embassy.

[2]Cousins, editor of the *Saturday Review*, discussed the nuclear test-ban issue with Khrushchev on April 12.

[3]On March 26 anti-Castro group L-66 sunk the *Baku*, a Russian vessel, at the Cuban harbor of Caibarien, only a week after another Soviet ship had been attacked in a Cuban port.

withdrawn because of pressure by the United States and "trumpets would have been blown" by us.

This letter took note of the criticism of the fact that the Russian SAM sites remained within Cuba. The author of the letter wanted us to know that those ground-air missiles were going to stay in Cuba for the protection of the Cuban people.

The overflights [of Cuba by American reconnaissance planes] that were taking place were deeply resented by the Soviet Union and by Cuba. He then went on to say clearly and distinctly that these U–2 planes would be shot down and that this had better be clearly understood in the United States. The U–2 plane that Eisenhower sent over the Soviet Union was shot down[4] and they had better understand the same thing would be done in those flights over Cuba.

The document then returned to the theme that we were treating the Soviet Union as inferiors. The United States was interested only in making profits from munitions, building up their efforts to dominate the world through counter-revolutionary activity. We were run by capitalists and we should understand that we could not push the Soviet Union around. He also expressed deep concern about the deployment of the Polaris submarines in the Mediterranean, replacing the Jupiter missiles in Turkey and Italy.[5]

At the end of the document it said that Mr. Khrushchev had felt in the past that this confidential exchange had been helpful but he said it had not been used lately because of the provocative statements that had been made by representatives of the United States Government which were offensive to the Soviet Union. However, if President Kennedy wanted to reopen this area of contact he would be glad to accept it. He also said that as far as a meeting between Khrushchev and President Kennedy he thought that that might be helpful. This was, however, left in rather enigmatic terms.

After I read the document I returned it to Dobrynin. I pointed out to him that I had met with him frequently and that he had never talked like this before. He said that was correct. I asked what was the explanation for this document and he said that I should understand that it came from the Soviet Union. I said it demonstrated a complete lack of understanding of the United States and President Kennedy and that I thought it was so insulting and rude to the President and to the United States that I would neither accept it nor transmit its message. I said if they had a message of that kind to deliver it should be delivered formally through the State Department and not through me. I said that during our conversations in the past we attempted to work out matters on a mutually satisfactory basis. I said we might disagree but I never insulted or offended him or his country or Mr. Khrushchev. I said I felt that was the only basis for any kind of relationship. I said I thought this kind of document did not further that effort or our mutual interests and I repeated that if they intended to transmit that kind of message that it should be done through the State Department. He said he could understand my position. He was obviously embarrassed.

[4]A reference to the episode involving Francis Gary Powers in May 1960.
[5]Just before the removal of all the Jupiter missiles from Turkey, the first Polaris submarine was deployed in the Mediterranean on April 1.

7. Memorandum from Secretary of the Army's Special Assistant Joseph A. Califano to Secretary of the Army Cyrus R. Vance

JFK decides which of the covert operations proposed to him (see Document 5) will be carried out.

Washington, April 9, 1963.

SUBJECT

Presidential Action on Special Group Items Concerning Cuba

1. The President rejected the balloon item on the recommendation of Ed Murrow.

2. The President approved the propaganda item (inciting Cubans to harass, attack and sabotage Soviet military personnel in Cuba) provided every precaution is taken to prevent attribution.

3. The President approved the sabotage of cargoes on Cuban ships and the crippling of ships (through sand in the gears, etc.).

4. With respect to Russian language broadcasts, the President (a) rejected such broadcasts by exile groups over Radio Caribe in the Dominican Republic, (b) rejected black intrusion on Radio Moscow Russian language broadcasts, and (c) withheld a decision on the use of such broadcasts on Radio Liberty from North Carolina, pending consultation with Llewellyn Thompson.

5. Pursuant to Special Group approval of the use of DoD facilities to support training of CIA agents, General Rosson and I met with CIA representatives yesterday and agreed to provide certain weapons training on a military reservation, under such circumstances that the trainees would not know they were being trained by military personnel and would not know they were on a military reservation. Such training will probably commence within the next several days. Parachute jump training under comparable circumstances will commence at a later date but within the next few weeks.

6. We have also agreed with CIA that we would spot about 20 inductees now in training at Fort Jackson whom we consider to have the necessary characteristics for CIA operations inside Cuba. These personnel, along with those given jump training under 5 above, would also be used in advance of the introduction of Special Forces, should there be a decision to invade Cuba.

8. Message from President Kennedy to Chairman Khrushchev

JFK urges Khrushchev to order further Russian troop withdrawals from Cuba. But he also adopts a conciliatory tone, assuring the Soviet leader that he has no intention of invading Cuba.

Washington, April 11, 1963.

DEAR MR. CHAIRMAN: It has been some time since I have written you directly, and I think it may be helpful to have some exchange of views in this private channel.[1] As we have both earlier agreed, it is of great importance that we should try to understand each other clearly, so that we can avoid unnecessary dangers or obstacles to progress in the effort for peaceful agreements.[2] . . .

Although together we found workable arrangements for ending the very dangerous crisis which was created when strategic weapons were introduced into Cuba last year, I am sure we can agree that the situation in that island is not yet satisfactory or reassuring to those who care for the peace of the Caribbean. Although the recent withdrawal of a number of your forces has been an important contribution to the reduction of tension, the continued presence of Soviet forces in Cuba can never be regarded with equanimity by the people of this Hemisphere and therefore further withdrawals of such forces can only be helpful.

Meanwhile, we on our side have been endeavoring to reduce tension in this area in a number of ways. For example, the fundamental justification of our practice of peaceful observation of Cuba[3] is precisely that it is necessary to prevent further increase in tension and a repetition of the dangers of last fall. Without such peaceful observation in 1962, this Hemisphere would have been confronted with intolerable danger, and the people of the Hemisphere could not now accept a situation in which they were without adequate information on the situation in Cuba. It is for this reason that this peaceful observation must continue, and that any interference with it from Cuba would necessarily evoke whatever response was necessary to retain it.

We are also aware of the tension unduly created by recent private attacks on your ships in Caribbean waters,[4] and we are taking action to halt those attacks which are in violation of our laws, and obtaining the support of the British Government in preventing the use of their Caribbean islands for this purpose. The efforts of this Government to reduce tensions have, as you know, aroused much

[1]U.S. Ambassador-at-Large Llewellyn Thompson delivered this message to Dobrynin on April 11.

[2]There follows at this point in the text a section on the nuclear test-ban treaty and the proliferation of nuclear arms.

[3]A reference to American aircraft reconnaissance over Cuba.

[4]See Document 6, footnote 3.

criticism from certain quarters in this country.[5] But neither such criticism nor the opposition of any sector of our society will be allowed to determine the policies of this Government. In particular, I have neither the intention nor the desire to invade Cuba; I consider that it is for the Cuban people themselves to decide their destiny. I am determined to continue with policies which will contribute to peace in the Caribbean.[6]...

There are other issues and problems before us, but perhaps I have said enough to give you a sense of my own current thinking on these matters. Let me now also offer the suggestion that it might be helpful if some time in May I should send a senior personal representative to discuss these and other matters informally with you. The object would not be formal negotiations, but a fully frank, informal exchange of views, arranged in such a way as to receive as little attention as possible. If this thought is appealing to you, please let me know your views on the most convenient time.

In closing, I want again to send my warm personal wishes to you and all your family. These are difficult and dangerous times in which we live, and both you and I have grave responsibilities to our families and to all of mankind. The pressures from those who have a less patient and peaceful outlook are very great—but I assure you of my own determination to work at all times to strengthen world peace.

9. Memorandum of a Meeting with President Kennedy Prepared by CIA Director McCone

JFK and his CIA director discuss the right tack to take with Castro.

Palm Beach, Florida, April 15, 1963, 5:30 p.m.[1]

SUBJECT

Meeting with the President—5:30—15 Apr 1963

... I raised the question of the possibility of working on Castro with the objective of disenchanting him with his Soviet relations causing him to break relations with Khrushchev, to effect the removal of Soviet troops from Cuba, reorient his policies with respect to Latin America, and establish in Cuba government satisfactory to the rest of the Hemisphere. I explained to the President that the Cuban problem must be solved in one of two ways; either the manner outlined

---

[5]Presumably a reference to hawks in the Republican party.
[6]There follows at this point in the text a section on Laos.
[1]McCone drafted this memorandum on April 16.

above or alternatively, by bringing consistent pressure of every possible nature on Khrushchev to force his withdrawal from Cuba, and then to bring about the downfall of Castro by means which could be developed after the removal of the Soviets [sic] troops (but not before) and thereafter establish a satisfactory government in Cuba. I stated to the President that we were studying both courses of action and I had not made up my mind concerning the feasibility of either plan. The President thought both approaches should be carefully examined and suggested the possibility of pursuing both courses at the same time. In any event it was decided that we should keep the Donovan channel open.[2] I advised the President that Donovan has to return to Havana at the end of the week and that I will see him privately prior to his departure.

. . . The President and I talked at some length concerning sabotage in Cuba. I expressed grave doubts and pointed out the hazards from his standpoint in view of the stand-down of the hit-and-run exile operations, the danger of attribution, etc. The President seemed to question whether active sabotage was good unless it was of a type that could "come from within Cuba." I said this was very difficult and that the initial operations conceived were from the sea. I said I thought a program should be engaged in only if it was an essential building block in an agreed program to remove the Soviets from Cuba and to take care of Castro. . . .

10. Memorandum from Coordinator of Cuban Affairs Sterling J. Cottrell to the Special Group

Sterling Cottrell, installed in early 1963 as the coordinator of administration policy toward Cuba, reviews current covert actions against Castro and poses the question whether these actions should be intensified.

Washington, April 18, 1963.

SUBJECT

Proposed New Covert Policy and Program Towards Cuba

A. The following guidelines are being used in our present covert policy towards Cuba:

1. Producing comprehensive intelligence related to our basic policy objectives. (No offensive weapons reintroduced into Cuba, removal of Soviet forces, no aggressive Cuban military action, reducing subversion in the hemisphere, di-

---

[2]James B. Donovan, a New York lawyer, had been negotiating with Castro over the release of some Americans, including CIA officials, from prisons in Cuba.

vorcing Castro from USSR, replacing present regime, maximizing cost to USSR, political isolation of Cuba and preparing for military contingencies.)

2. Intensifying covert collection of intelligence within Cuba, especially within the regime.

3. Supporting the efforts of certain Cuban exiles, who are associated with the original aims of the 26 of July Movement[1] and who believe that the Castro regime can be overthrown from within in order that they may: a) cause a split in the leadership of the regime at the national or provincial levels; and b) create a political base of popular opposition to the regime; and c) secure intelligence.

4. The use of [a] variety of propaganda media to stimulate passive resistance and low-risk, simple, sabotage actions by the populace of Cuba.

5. The placing of incendiary devices and/or explosives with suitable time delay within the hull or cargo to disable or sink Cuban vessels and/or damage their cargos while on the high seas.

6. Introducing abrasives or other damaging materials into the propulsion, communication and other systems of the ship to inactivate the ship.

B. The questions now to be decided are:

1. Should the U.S. move beyond the above policy to a program of sabotage, harassment and resistance activities?

2. What kind of effective action can be taken?

3. What capabilities do we possess?

4. What repercussions can we expect?

C. With respect to (1.) above, the following considerations apply:

1. U.S. policy statements have consistently reiterated the view that the liberation of Cuba is primarily a function of the Cuban people themselves.

2. The absence of continued harassment against the regime inside Cuba will consolidate its control and indicate the success of Castro in imposing Communism upon the Cuban people.

3. The absence of U.S. assistance inside Cuba to those who desire the overthrow of the Communist regime will deny an important asset.

4. The U.S. effort to assist the fighters for freedom inside Cuba will involve expense and risk of lives to those Cubans who are trained for this purpose.

5. The risk of U.S. involvement through confessions of captured personnel is a continuing one. However, world opinion in the event of such exposure is not likely to be severely damaging to the U.S. position.

D. With respect to (2.) (3.) and (4.) above, the following additional proposals are submitted for consideration. . . .

1. *The placing of explosive devices with suitable time delays on the outside of ships either in Cuban or non-Cuban ports.*

Considerations: UDT teams can be ready by June for attack in July on a once monthly basis. This measure would place increased strain on Cuban shipping and demoralize Cuban crews. Soviet reaction is likely in form of propaganda and UN démarche. Retaliation in kind or forceful reactions are probably unlikely.

---

[1]A reference to the original effort to spark a revolution in Cuba when Castro and his cohorts tried to seize the Moncada military barracks in 1953.

2. *Surface attacks by maritime assets firing on Cuban ships in Cuban waters. When the maritime asset cannot reach the target, shore based attacks on shipping in port or passing the offshore keys will be undertaken.*

Considerations: Attack craft from the sea would be manned by Cubans. Shore based attacks by paramilitary trained Cubans firing on ships with recoilless rifles, rocket launchers or 20mm cannon. First sea attack in May and once monthly thereafter. First shore based attack in June. These operations would disrupt coastal commerce. US would probably be blamed. Cuban reprisal measures possible. Soviets likely allege US culpability. Probably no direct Soviet counter-action outside Cuba. Soviets would probably supply additional hardware to Cubans but caution against too aggressive Cuban response.

3. *Externally mounted hit and run attacks against land targets. Examples: molasses tanker, petroleum storage dumps, naval refueling base, refineries, power plants.*

Considerations: Operations conducted by Cubans with paramilitary training. High possibilities of complex operations going awry. First attack in April with one per month thereafter. Effects would be increased exile morale, some economic disruption. Repercussions would include charges of U.S. sponsorship, and increased Cuban security force activities. Soviet reaction likely to be propaganda-political moves and support to Cuban patrol activity but caution to avoid escalation.

4. *Support of Internal Resistance Elements, providing matériel and personnel to permit them to undertake a variety of sabotage and harassment operations.*

Considerations: The internal elements being supported will attack targets of their own choosing in their own manner. They will be targets of opportunity in line with their capabilities. Effect could be cumulative and snow-balling. The matériel will be introduced by maritime infiltration, diplomatic channels and concealment in open mail. Indigenous materials will be used and instructions provided. Initial sabotage results within 30 days. This program could produce major economic damage, lift morale and keep resistance alive. Repercussions would involve increased security measures. Soviet reaction largely propaganda and supplies.

Attachment

SUBJECT

A Covert Harassment/Sabotage Program against Cuba

1. This paper presents a covert Harassment/Sabotage program targeted against Cuba; included are those sabotage plans which have previously been approved as well as new proposals. While this program will cause a certain amount of economic damage, it will in no sense critically injure the economy or cause the overthrow of Castro. It may, however, create a situation which will delay the consolidation and stabilization of Castro's revolution and may cause some of his 26 July followers to doubt Castro's ability successfully to create a new Cuba.

Losses in men and equipment with the attendant adverse publicity must be expected. Even without such losses, U.S. attribution will be claimed.

When the policy and guidelines of the overall sabotage program are established, it will be possible progressively to develop up to a limit additional covert assets and support capabilities. However, materially to increase the pace of operations, a period of four to six months is required. Ultimate limiting factors are weather, length of "dark-of-the-moon" period each month and appropriate targets. A source of additional agent personnel is from Cuban personnel trained by the U.S. Military Forces under the recent programs, but released to civilian status. . . .

11. Summary Record of a Meeting of the Standing Group of the National Security Council

Robert Kennedy and other American officials look at ways to step up the pressure on Castro.

Washington, April 23, 1963, 5 p.m.

The basis of the discussion was a memorandum prepared by Mr. Bundy entitled "A Sketch of the Cuba Alternatives."[1]

Secretary McNamara stated that before the group discussed substance, it should consider whether the present policy we are following would produce a major change in Cuba. He expressed his firm view that Castro's position over the short term would improve if we took no actions other than those now under way or projected. He made clear his belief that the elimination of the Castro regime was a requirement and that, if others agreed our present policy would not result in its downfall, we should develop a program for approval which would produce changes acceptable to us. The program should aim at creating such a situation of dissidence within Cuba as to allow the U.S. to use force in support of anti-Castro forces without leading to retaliation by the USSR on the West.

Mr. McCone summarized information leading him to believe that Castro's position in Cuba would be stronger a year or two years from now than it is at present. He expressed his belief that present policy would not cause a major change in Cuba and that the Russians could provide sufficient aid and technical assistance to permit the Cuban economy to remain about where it is now or slightly improve.

Assistant Secretary Martin did not fully agree with the views of the Secretary

[1]This memorandum by McGeorge Bundy has not been included.

of Defense or Mr. McCone with respect to the effect of existing policy on the Castro regime. He cited evidence to indicate that present measures are crippling the Cuban economy, leading to shortages, lack of spare parts, and even sufficient food to permit full rations for Cuban militia. Mr. Martin saw no possibility of getting Castro to defect from the USSR. He said there was no way to finance Cuba during the transition period until Castro, by his deeds, had proved that he had broken his ties with the USSR. He said, for example, Congress would never approve the sugar quota for Cuba early enough to avoid a collapse of the Cuban economy cut loose from the USSR and not yet aided by the U.S. Furthermore, he said Castro was the kind of a man who might make promises and not keep them, i.e. he did not stay bought. The possibility of persuading Castro to leave Cuba was not feasible because Castro was a true revolutionary who could not be induced to give up his revolution.

The Attorney General proposed three studies:

a. A list of measures we would take following contingencies such as the death of Castro or the shooting down of a U–2.

b. A program with the objective of overthrowing Castro in eighteen months.

c. A program to cause as much trouble as we can for Communist Cuba during the next eighteen months.

Under Secretary Ball stated the view that we should not look at Cuba from the point of view of Cuba alone. He said the Cuban problem was a part of our relations with the USSR and with our global battle against Communist aggression. He urged that our policy toward Cuba always be kept in this perspective. The withdrawal of Soviet forces from Cuba and the disappearance of the Soviet presence in Cuba was of major importance to us.

USIA Director Murrow stated his view that we need promptly a statement of what we would think was an acceptable post-Castro Cuba.

Secretary Dillon raised certain questions as to what kind of a Cuba we could live with if it were no longer run by Castro or tied to Moscow. He said that American companies had written off their expropriated sugar properties in Cuba but the question remained as to who would own these properties in the event Castro and Communism disappeared in Cuba.

There was a discussion on what we would do for a non-Communist Cuba and what we could do to get Castro to defect from the USSR. There appeared to be some differing views as to whether economic measures we can take would wreck the Cuban economy or whether the only result would be to raise the cost to the USSR of maintaining Cuba.

Mr. Sorensen listed the seven objectives raised at the meeting as follows:

a. Improve our present course of action by doing some things that we are not now doing.

b. Agree on military responses which we should make to contingencies, such as the shooting down of a U–2 plane.

c. Develop a program to get rid of Castro.

d. Measures to disrupt the economy of Cuba.

e. A program to induce Soviet withdrawal.

f. The detachment of Cuba from Moscow.

g. A program of support for dissident elements in Cuba.

Overriding all these points would be a statement of our views as to the kind of a regime we would want to see in Cuba post-Castro.[2]

12. Memorandum from President Kennedy to Secretary of Defense McNamara

JFK continues to press for the development of contingency plans to attack Cuba.

Washington, April 29, 1963.

Are we keeping our Cuban contingency invasion plans up to date? I notice that there have been a number of new judgments on the amount of equipment that the Cubans have. I thought last October the number of troops we planned to have available was rather limited and the success of the operation was dependent upon, in large measure, our two airborne divisions getting in and controlling the two airfields. It seems to me that we should strengthen our contingency plans on this operation.

13. Extract of a Message from Chairman Khrushchev to President Kennedy

In response to JFK's message of April 11 (see Document 8), Khrushchev maintains that the number of Soviet troops still in Cuba is insignificant, and that U.S. reconnaissance flights over the island are unacceptable.

April 29, 1963.[1]

Already for a protracted period, in the exchange of opinions between us no matter in what channels they took place, one and the same question has inevitably arisen—concerning the situation around Cuba. To a considerable degree this is understandable if one considers how we passed through a most

---

[2]Bromley Smith produced this memorandum.
[1]The message was received on this date via a private communication channel.

dangerous crisis in the fall of last year. But it is impossible not to recognize also that tension around Cuba decreases too slowly and at times rises anew not unlike the way the mercury jumps in the thermometers of the present spring.

And of course when one thinks about where the abnormalities are coming from which are making the atmosphere in the region of the Caribbean Sea ever more feverish, one comes to the conclusion that a one-sided approach can least of all help the situation.

If one allows that in the Western Hemisphere uneasiness is evoked by the presence in Cuba of a certain small number of Soviet troops which are helping Cubans to master the weapons delivered by the Soviet Union for the purpose of strengthening the defense capabilities of Cuba, then how much more uneasiness should be evoked in the countries of Europe, Asia and Africa by the hundreds of thousands of American troops in the Eastern Hemisphere? It is sufficient to make such a comparison in order that things can be seen in proper perspective. At our meeting in Vienna we seemed to have agreed to proceed from the fact that the forces of our states were equal. Well, then, if our forces are equal, then there should also be equal possibilities. Why does the United States forget about this?

You know that we have withdrawn from Cuba a significant part of our military personnel. I can tell you that we have withdrawn several times more people than has been stated in the American press. How this matter will develop in the future depends on a number of circumstances and in the first place on the pace at which the atmosphere in the region of the Caribbean Sea will be normalized, and whether, as could be expected, the reasons which occasioned the necessity for assistance to the Cubans by Soviet military specialists and instructors will disappear.

I would like to express the thought of how important it is in evaluating what is happening around Cuba that one rise above one-sided understandings and base his judgments on the respective estimate of the situation of the interested parties. From your point of view, as set forth in your message,[2] the reconnaissance flights of American aircraft over Cuba are only "peaceful observation." But if one were to characterize these flights objectively, without even considering the point of view, understandable to everyone, of the country over which they are being carried out, then they cannot be described other than as an unrestrained intrusion into the air space of a sovereign government and as a flagrant violation of the elementary norms of international law and the principles of the UN Charter, to which are affixed the signatures of both the USA and Cuba. It is natural that no state prizing its sovereignty, no government solicitous of the interest and dignity of its people, can tolerate such flights.

Perhaps it is desired that we recognize the right of the USA to violate the Charter of the United Nations and international norms? But this we cannot do and will not do.

We have honestly carried out the obligations we assumed in the settlement of the crisis in the region of the Caribbean Sea, and withdrew from Cuba even more than we promised to withdraw. There are no grounds for you to doubt the

[2]See Document 8.

readiness of the Soviet Union to carry out firmly in the future as well the agreement which was reached between us. Why then are reconnaissance flights by American aircraft over Cuba necessary? What are they looking for there when there is not a single thing, seen in the light of the agreement reached, which could cause concern? Trampling on sovereignty in this way can lead to quite serious consequences for us if it is not stopped in time.

And can one pass over in silence or recognize as in accordance with the principles of the UN Charter the continuing efforts to strangle the economy of Cuba? I shall not address myself to this in more detail although of course I could find many words with which to characterize these actions, even from a purely humanitarian point of view.

The Soviet Union gives due credit to the measures which have recently been undertaken by the USA, as well as by England, in connection with the attacks which have taken place on Soviet vessels near the Cuban coast.[3] We of course do not underestimate the significance of these measures and hope that they will be sufficiently effective to preclude the possibility of a repetition of armed raids against Cuba.

I read with a feeling of satisfaction that passage of your message in which you confirm that you have neither the intention nor the desire to invade Cuba and where you recognize that it is up to the Cuban people to determine their fate. That is a good statement. We have always stressed that, like any other people, the Cuban people possess the inalienable right to determine their own fate as they see fit.

14. Memorandum from Secretary of Defense McNamara to President Kennedy

McNamara informs JFK of progress in improving military contingency plans for Cuba.

Washington, May 7, 1963.

SUBJECT

Contingency Plans for Cuba (U)

1. In response to your inquiry, dated 29 April 1963,[1] I wish to assure you that our contingency plans for invasion of Cuba have been and are being maintained

---

[3]Presumably a reference to the attacks mentioned in Document 6, footnote 3.
[1]See Document 12.

up to date. A revision of CINCLANT's basic invasion plan for Cuba was reviewed and approved by the Joint Chiefs of Staff on 26 February 1963.

2. Intelligence reports received since last October do indicate the assignment of additional matériel to the Cuban armed forces. Responsible commanders are being kept fully informed of the changing intelligence picture and our plans are continually updated to insure that the U.S. forces and equipment and their planned employment reflect the latest information available. For example, the order in which U.S. forces and their supporting equipment are committed is being restudied in the light of the estimated increases in Castro's T–34 medium tanks and self-propelled anti-tank guns.

3. The most significant change in the basic invasion plan since last October has resulted from our increasing capability to introduce larger numbers of troops and heavy equipment into the objective area early in the operation. This capability is being achieved by the reactivation of 11 LST's, which will materially expedite the delivery of combat forces and equipment. In the longer term, programmed acquisition of additional C–130 aircraft into the air lift force will expedite the delivery of airborne and airlanded forces during the initial assault. Through these measures the weight of our early attacks will be increased and the probability of their success further enhanced. . . .

15. Paper Prepared by the Central Intelligence Agency for the Standing Group of the National Security Council

The momentum that had been gathering in the Kennedy administration in the spring of 1963 in favor of greater covert pressure on Cuba culminates in this CIA plan of action.

Washington, June 8, 1963.

SUBJECT

Proposed Covert Policy and Integrated Program of Action towards Cuba

I. Introduction

1. Submitted herewith is a covert program for Cuba within CIA's capabilities. Some parts of the program have already been approved and are being implemented. Being closely inter-related, the total cumulative impact of the courses of action set forth in this program is dependent upon the simultaneous coordinated execution of the individual courses of action.

2. This program is based on the assumption that current U.S. policy does not

contemplate outright military intervention in Cuba or a provocation which can be used as a pretext for an invasion of Cuba by United States military forces. It is further assumed that U.S. policy calls for the exertion of maximum pressure by all means available to the U.S. Government, short of military intervention, to prevent the pacification of the population and the consolidation of the Castro/Communist regime. The ultimate objective of this policy would be to encourage dissident elements in the military and other power centers of the regime to bring about the eventual liquidation of the Castro/Communist entourage and the elimination of the Soviet presence from Cuba.

3. While the effect of a program of maximum pressure is unpredictable, it is suggested that a sustained intensive effort undertaken now to prevent the consolidation of the Castro/Communist regime may in the future present the United States with opportunities and options not now foreseeable. The consequences of a policy of allowing Castro to "stew in his own juice," however, are foreseeable. According to current estimates, barring Castro's death or a decisive change in the U.S. posture or Soviet policy towards Cuba, the Castro regime is likely to be more firmly established a year hence, despite possible economic setbacks. The mere passage of time tends to favor Castro as the population and elite groups in Cuba become accustomed to the idea that he is here to stay and as his regime gains in administrative experience and the security organs become more efficient. Over the long run, the existence of an organized party apparatus as well as a stable governmental machinery could reduce the indispensability of Castro's personal leadership. Thus, if left to chance, the U.S. must be prepared to accept for the indefinite future a Communist regime in Cuba closely tied to and a significant component of the Soviet world power structure.

4. Within the context of the policy assumptions and estimate of the situation in Cuba outlined above, CIA submits a program consisting of the following interdependent courses of action:

A. Covert collection of intelligence, both for U.S. strategic requirements as well as for operational requirements.

B. Propaganda actions to stimulate low-risk simple sabotage and other forms of active and passive resistance.

C. Exploitation and stimulation of disaffection in the Cuban military and other power centers.

D. Economic denial actions on an increased basis.

E. General sabotage and harassment.

F. Support of autonomous anti-Castro Cuban groups to supplement and assist in the execution of the above courses of action.

5. A vital feature of the foregoing program to exert maximum pressure on the Castro/Communist regime is the dependence of the impact of each course of action on the simultaneous and effective execution of the other courses of action. Thus, intelligence information is needed to permit the planning and mounting of operations against economic denial and sabotage targets. Covert propaganda actions are designed to produce a psychological climate in Cuba conducive to the accomplishment of the other courses of action in the integrated covert program. Only after the effects of economic denial and sabotage actions are deeply

felt by the populace and the elite groups can one hope to convert disaffection in the armed forces and other power centers of the regime into militant revolt against the Castro/Communist entourage. It is also at this point where CIA-controlled and autonomous activist elements in the Cuban exile community can begin to assume genuine resistance proportions. As a consequence of this interrelated and continuous process, it is reasonable to expect a considerable increase in the volume and quality of the intelligence product on the basis of which additional and increasingly more effective operations can be mounted. Unless all the components of this program are executed in tandem, the individual courses of action are almost certain to be of marginal value, even in terms of achieving relatively limited policy objectives. This is clearly a case where the whole is greater than the sum of its parts.

II. Discussion of Components of an Integrated Program

6. In amplification of the courses of action listed in paragraph 4 above, the following additional description and terms of reference are offered:

A. *Covert collection of intelligence, both for U.S. strategic requirements as well as for operational requirements.*

Covert collection of intelligence continues to be a major CIA mission. Without detracting from our strategic intelligence efforts, emphasis is being given to increasing the volume and quality of intelligence needed for planning and mounting the operations contemplated in the integrated program described in this paper, particularly for defections and penetrations and for economic denial and sabotage actions against vulnerable sectors of the Cuban economy.

B. *Propaganda actions to stimulate low-risk simple sabotage and other forms of active and passive resistance.*

In accordance with a previously approved psychological program in support of U.S. policy on Cuba, CIA-controlled radio programs and other propaganda media directed at Cuba encourage low-risk simple sabotage and other forms of active and passive resistance. These media also seek to stimulate and exacerbate tensions within the regime and between Cuba and the Soviet Bloc, taking advantage of Sino-Soviet tensions. All of these propaganda operations are calculated to create a psychological atmosphere within Cuba which will facilitate the accomplishment of the other courses of action within the integrated covert action program.

C. *Exploitation and stimulation of disaffection in the Cuban military and other power centers.*

We are undertaking an intensive probing effort to identify, seek out and establish channels of communication with disaffected and potentially dissident non-Communist elements in the power centers of the regime, particularly in the armed forces hierarchy. The objective is to promote the fragmentation of the regime and possibly lead to an internal coup which would dislodge Castro and his entourage, and make it possible to eliminate the Cuban Communists from positions of power and force the withdrawal of the Soviet military presence and the termination of its economic aid. Several promising operations are already underway.

D. Economic denial actions.

Overt official U.S. economic sanctions in conjunction with covert economic denial operations . . . is [sic] causing a marked adverse effect on the Cuban economy. For maximum impact on the Cuban economy this effort must be coordinated with sabotage operations. We propose to continue and intensify economic denial operations which would be greatly enhanced by an inter-agency committee with a charter enabling it to call upon member agencies for rapid action.

E. General sabotage and harassment.

Sabotage in this program is both an economic weapon and a stimulus to resistance. As an economic weapon, it is a supplement to and therefore must be coordinated with the economic denial effort. As a stimulus to resistance, there must be visible and dramatic evidence of sabotage to serve as a symbol of growing popular defiance of the Castro regime.

These operations will be conducted either by externally held assets[1] now available or by existing internal assets or those to be developed. Assets trained and controlled by CIA will be used as will selected autonomous exile groups. Initially, the emphasis will be on the use of externally held assets with a shift to internal assets as soon as operationally feasible.

The types of sabotage considered appropriate for this program are:

(1) Simple low-risk sabotage on a large scale stimulated by propaganda media (approved and being implemented).

(2) Sabotage of Cuban ships outside Cuban waters (approved and being implemented).

(3) Externally mounted hit-and-run attacks against appropriately selected targets.

(4) Support of internal resistance elements, providing matériel and personnel to permit them to undertake a variety of sabotage and harassment operations.

It must be recognized that no single act of sabotage by itself can materially affect the economy or stimulate significant resistance. However, it is our opinion that a well-planned series of sabotage efforts, properly executed, would in time produce the effect we seek. Each action will have its dangers: there will be failures with consequent loss of life and charges of attribution to the United States resulting in criticism at home and abroad. None of these expected consequences should cause us to change our course if the program as outlined can be expected to be successful.

Annex A is an elaboration of a proposed sabotage and harassment program against Cuba.

F. Support of autonomous anti-Castro Cuban groups to supplement and assist in the execution of the above courses of action.

In the past, CIA has utilized only fully controlled and disciplined agent assets as a safeguard against unilateral and irresponsible action by Cuban exiles intent upon the liberation of their country. If sabotage and resistance activities are to be undertaken on a larger scale, it will be necessary to accept the risks involved in utilizing autonomous Cuban exile groups and individuals who will not nec-

---

[1]Presumably a reference to Cuban emigrés.

essarily be responsive to our guidance. CIA proposes the following "rules of engagement" to govern the conduct of these autonomous operations:

(1) It is the keystone of autonomous operations that they will be executed exclusively by Cuban nationals motivated by the conviction that the overthrow of the Castro/Communist regime must be accomplished by Cubans, both inside and outside Cuba acting in consonance.

(2) The effort will probably cost many Cuban lives. If this cost in lives becomes unacceptable to the U.S. conscience, autonomous operations can be effectively halted by the withdrawal of U.S. support; but once halted, it cannot be resumed.

(3) All autonomous operations will be mounted outside the territory of the United States.

(4) The United States Government must be prepared to deny publicly any participation in these acts no matter how loud or even how accurate may be the reports of U.S. complicity.

(5) The United States presence and direct participation in the operation would be kept to an absolute minimum. Before entering into an operational relationship with a group, the U.S. representative will make it clear that his Government has no intention of intervening militarily, except to counter intervention by the Soviets. An experienced CIA officer would be assigned to work with the group in a liaison capacity. He would provide general advice as requested as well as funds and necessary material support. He may be expected to influence but not control the conduct of operations.

(6) These operations would not be undertaken within a fixed time schedule.

III. Recommendation

7. Policy authority already exists for courses of action described in paragraph 6 A–D. In order that full advantage can be taken of an integrated covert action program, the Standing Group is requested to approve courses of action outlined in paragraph 6 E and F within the terms of reference and rules of engagement therein.[2]

Annex A

SUBJECT

Sabotage/Harassment Program

The broad target categories against which the sabotage/harassment operations would be mounted and a preliminary evaluation of their effect, can be summarized as follows:

A. *Electric Power*
Disruption of any of the existing power grids which might be effected by damage to or destruction of the generating facilities or of the critical sub-stations in the distribution network, would significantly weaken the existing economic

---

[2]On June 18 the NSC Standing Group endorsed the course of action outlined in this paper, passing it to President Kennedy the next day for final approval (see Document 16).

and social structure, particularly in view of the fact that in many areas the power now available is not adequate to meet the demands of industrial and public consumers. Smaller acts of sabotage/harassment by the populace such as throwing chains over high tension lines to short them out, would also exacerbate the current power shortage, and the cumulative effect of all such actions could cause a prolonged breakdown of the power system as there is already a shortage of spare parts and replacement matériels.

B. Petroleum, Oil and Lubricants (POL)

Damage to or destruction of POL production and/or storage facilities would seriously affect almost all aspects of the Cuban economy. The electric power industry depends almost entirely upon POL as fuel for the generating plants and the sugar industry depends upon POL powered processing and transportation facilities as does all intra-province transportation. Production and storage facilities are susceptible to external attacks by heavy weapons or by more subtle methods if internal assets having an appropriate degree of accessibility can be developed. The loss of refining facilities could be offset by increased [Communist] Bloc shipments of refined products but such a shift would require a period of readjustment during which there would be a heavy strain on the Cuban economy. An additional burden on the Bloc refining capacity would also exist until Cuba's refining capacity is restored.

C. Transportation

Damage to or destruction of railway and/or highway rolling stock or the destruction of key bridges would lead to breakdowns in the regional economies which to a large degree are dependent on the distribution of imported products. The processing and export of the vitally important sugar crop is also entirely dependent on transportation. It is not anticipated that we could achieve that degree of disruption which would cause a collapse of the economy or social structure, but even a minor degree of disruption will adversely affect the standard of living and the output of the economy, both of which are key factors in the stability of the regime. The type of operations envisioned in this category would range from fairly sophisticated attacks by external or internal assets against the rolling stock, key bridges and repair facilities to simple low risk acts by the populace such as the derailing of rail transportation or placing tire puncturing material on highways.

D. Production Processing and Manufacturing Facilities

While the Cuban economy primarily depends on imports for indigenous consumption and even though the sugar crop is by far the most important item in Cuban exports, there are still a number of other facilities such as the nickel complex at Nicaro, cement plants, distilleries, and the myriad industries associated with the provision of food, clothing and shelter, which are worthwhile targets in that stopping or lessening their output will weaken the economy and breed discontent against the regime. These targets are particularly susceptible to attack by external or internal assets in that due to their profusion and their relatively low strategic importance they are not well guarded or otherwise secured against attack.

The selection of specific targets within the above categories and the determination of timing and tactics will be predicated upon detailed analysis of the following factors:

1. The extent to which the target can be physically damaged.
2. The resultant effect upon the Cuban economy.
3. The cost or effort required if additional burdens are placed on Bloc support.
4. The psychological effect on the Cuban population.
5. Anticipated adverse reactions.
6. Operational capabilities and limitations of CIA assets.

16. Memorandum for the Record

JFK approves a new program of sabotage operations and other covert actions against Cuba—the CIA plan of June 8 (see the preceding document).

Washington, June 19, 1963.

SUBJECT

Meeting at the White House concerning Proposed Covert Policy and Integrated Program of Action towards Cuba

PRESENT

Higher Authority [JFK]
Secretary McNamara
Under Secretary Harriman
Mr. McCone
Mr. McGeorge Bundy
Mr. Thomas Parrott
Mr. Desmond FitzGerald
Air Force Vice Chief of Staff, General W. F. McKee

1. The program as recommended by the Standing Group of the NSC[1] was presented briefly to Higher Authority who showed a particular interest in proposed external sabotage operations. He was shown charts indicating typical targets for this program and a discussion of the advantages and disadvantages ensued. It was well recognized that there would be failures and a considerable noise level. . . . Mr. Bundy described the integrated nature of the program presented and made the point that, having made the decision to go ahead, we be prepared to take the consequences of flaps and criticisms for a sufficient period

[1]See Document 15, including footnote 2.

to give the program a real chance. Mr. Harriman stated that the program would be "reviewed weekly" by the Special Group.[2] (It is believed that an arrangement can be made with Mr. Bundy for less detailed control by the Special Group than was indicated by Mr. Harriman.)

2. Higher Authority asked how soon we could get into action with the external sabotage program and was told that we should be able to conduct our first operation in the dark-of-the-moon period in July although he was informed that we would prefer to start the program with some caution selecting softer targets to begin with. Higher Authority said this was a matter for our judgement. Although at one stage in the discussion Higher Authority said that we should move ahead with the program "this summer" it is believed that Mr. Bundy will be able to convince him that this is not a sufficiently long trial period to demonstrate what the program can do.[3]

17. Memorandum of Conversation

In a secret message to JFK, Khrushchev makes clear that he is aware of the recent resumption of sabotage by the United States against Cuba. He also warns Kennedy that the Soviet Union will respond if Cuba is attacked.

Washington, September 10, 1963.

SUBJECT

United States Actions in Cuba

PARTICIPANTS

Ambassador Anatoliy F. Dobrynin, USSR
Llewellyn E. Thompson, Ambassador-at-Large, Department of State

Ambassador Dobrynin said he had a personal message for the President, and he considered it so confidential, that he had not had it typed but would read from his handwritten notes.

He said that the Soviet Government considered that things had recently taken a turn for the better in the international situation and in relations between the Soviet Union and the United States. With the signing of the Test Ban Treaty[1] and the exchange of views with Secretary Rusk,[2] there had developed a relax-

---

[2]It was customary for the National Security Council Special Group to oversee covert operations.
[3]CIA official Desmond FitzGerald prepared this memorandum.
[1]An agreement limiting nuclear testing, signed in Moscow on August 5, 1963, by Rusk, Gromyko, and British Foreign Secretary Lord Home.
[2]Presumably a reference to Rusk's talks with Khrushchev and other Soviet officials in August 1963.

ation of tension and the prerequisite for the settlement of other questions had been established. This could lead to a real turning point, and the end of the cold war. The Soviet Union took satisfaction from the willingness of the United States to look for the solution of other international problems. If both countries were determined to accomplish this, it was important that nothing be done contrary to this intention. The Soviets wished to tell the President, frankly, what was of concern to them. There were certain facts which did not fit in with the situation and these were the provocative actions against Cuba, which had increased in recent weeks. Unknown planes had shelled industrial establishments and there had been landings of saboteurs on the Cuban coast. These actions had been intensified after the conclusion of the nuclear Test Ban treaty. It had been stated that the United States had nothing to do with these actions, but no one could believe this. When the United States took a position against the attacks on Soviet ships in Cuban waters,[3] these attacks had stopped. This action had been understood by the Soviet Union as a measure showing the good intentions of the United States. How then could these recent actions be interpreted? If such attacks continued—and they could only be taken from the United States proper or from countries allied with the United States and with the knowledge and connivance of the United States—this could only lead to a new crisis.

The Soviet Union did not want a new crisis to emerge. Both sides had expressed their satisfaction over the elimination of the last crisis, which had been resolved after each side had undertaken certain commitments. The President had said that these commitments should be carried out. The Soviets agreed with this. They believed that for the future of our relations, it was important that effective measures be taken to stop the piratic attacks against Cuba. The Soviet Union had undertaken certain commitments in respect to the protection of the independence of Cuba which were aimed exclusively at preventing Cuba from becoming a victim of aggression, and the Soviet Union would certainly fulfill its commitments if aggression were unleashed against Cuba.

The Soviet Union hoped for understanding of the motives that prompted them to convey to the President, personally from N. S. Khrushchev, this assessment of the effect of the activation lately of provocative actions against Cuba.[4]

18. Memorandum of Conversation Prepared by Ambassador-at-Large Llewellyn E. Thompson

Responding to Khrushchev's September 10 message, JFK tries to change the subject from sabotage against Cuba to Cuban subversion in Latin America.

[3]Probably a reference to the matter addressed in Document 6, footnote 3.
[4]Llewellyn Thompson drafted this memorandum.

Washington, September 13, 1963.

SUBJECT

Cuba

PARTICIPANTS

Ambassador Anatoliy F. Dobrynin, USSR
Llewellyn E. Thompson, Ambassador-at-Large, Department of State

I made the oral statement which is attached hereto. . . .

The Ambassador [Dobrynin] said he hoped that Mr. Khrushchev's motives in raising this question were understood. He said that the Chairman believed it was to our mutual interest to reduce tension in the Caribbean and to avoid a crisis over the Cuban problem.

I said I was sure that the President did understand, and thought that our position was clear from the statement which I had just made to him.

Attachment

ORAL STATEMENT

The President wished Mr. Khrushchev to know that he shares his view that the signing of the Test Ban Treaty[1] and the recent exchange of views with the Soviet Government is encouraging, and he hopes it will be possible to proceed to the solution of other problems. The President is hopeful that the Test Ban Treaty will be approved by the United States Senate in the course of next week.[2]

With respect to the Cuban situation, the President also agrees that the emergence of a new crisis would be in the interest neither of the Soviet Union nor of the United States, and can assure him that the United States will faithfully carry out its commitments.

With respect to any air attacks on Cuba, it can be stated categorically that not only was the United States not involved in any way in such attacks, but has been making every effort to prevent them. It is possible, but not likely, that a light private aircraft could take off from one of the large number of private fields in the southeastern portion of the United States. No such illegal flights have been detected by the means available to us. The President has directed, however, that the measures already taken be reviewed to see what further steps could be taken.

In keeping with the March 30, 1963 declaration by the Departments of State and Justice concerning hit and run attacks by Cuban exile groups against targets in Cuba, the law enforcement agencies are taking vigorous measures to assure that the pertinent laws of the United States are observed.

Apparently it is assumed that the United States exercises control over the policies and actions of the other sovereign, independent states of this Hemisphere. This assumption betrays a fundamental misunderstanding of the relationship between the United States and the other American Republics. The

---

[1]See Document 17, footnote 1.
[2]The Senate did ratify the treaty in September, by a vote of 80 to 19.

history of inter-American relations makes abundantly clear that the American Governments will not tolerate interference with their foreign or domestic affairs. The states of this Hemisphere jealously defend the principle of juridical equality of states and reject any insinuation that difference of size and power in any way modifies this fundamental rule governing their relations.

The United States could, of course, consult with any government in this Hemisphere from whose territory we have information indicating that flights were originating against Cuba, but, in all candor, we must point out that such consultation would be greatly complicated by the increasing sense of outrage among the governments of this Hemisphere about Cuba's deliberate stimulation and support of subversive activities throughout the Hemisphere in direct violation of international norms. This is not simply a matter of speeches or words by Castro, as has sometimes been indicated. Clear evidence of Cuban involvement in this form of aggression is to be found in the fact that:

a) The Cuban Government is recruiting Latin Americans, sending them to Cuba for training in guerrilla tactics and returning them to their countries to engage in terroristic activities. A case in point are the Cuban-trained Peruvians captured on May 14 and 15, 1963, at Puerto Maldonado as they attempted clandestinely to enter Peru from Bolivia.

b) The Cuban Government is furnishing funds to revolutionary groups seeking the overthrow of governments by force and violence. By way of illustration, in May 1963, two leading members of the Ecuadorean Communist Party, Jose Maria Roura and Alejandro Roman were seized as they were returning to Ecuador. They were carrying over $30,000 which they confessed had been given them by Chinese and Cuban sources.

c) The Cuban leaders continue to exhort revolutionaries in Latin American countries to resort to sabotage, terrorism and guerrilla action. Premier Castro returned to this theme in his July twenty-sixth address when he called on activists in Venezuela and other countries to "open the breach" and begin fighting. Major Ernesto Guevara, in an article published in the September issue of *Cuba Socialista*, strongly advocates guerrilla warfare as the surest road to power in Latin America. Information available to us shows a direct connection between terroristic activities in Venezuela and the Castro regime. In addition to being guilty of such aggression against other American Republics by promoting these and other activities, the Cuban Government recently embarked on a most risky venture of direct violation of the territory and territorial waters of another country in this Hemisphere using units of its armed forces. On August 14, 1963, a Cuban helicopter and two patrol boats furnished by the Soviet Union forcibly removed from Cay Anguila, one of the islands of the Bahamas group, nineteen persons who had sought refuge on the island. This incident led to a vigorous protest by the British Government on August 21, 1963, requesting an apology and return of the persons taken prisoners.

In sum, it is not the United States, but the behavior of the Castro regime that is to blame for the difficulties in the Caribbean area.

19. Memorandum of Conversation at the White House

In a meeting with the Soviet foreign minister, JFK again learns of Moscow's cognizance of the sabotage being carried out against Cuba. Kennedy and Gromyko also discuss the final withdrawal of all Soviet military personnel from the Caribbean island.

Washington, October 10, 1963, 4 p.m.

SUBJECT

Cuba

PARTICIPANTS

US
The President
The Secretary [Rusk]
Ambassador Thompson
Assistant Secretary Tyler
Mr. Akalovsky

USSR
Foreign Minister Gromyko
Deputy Foreign Minister Semenov
Ambassador Dobrynin
Mr. Sukhodrev, Foreign Ministry

Mr. Gromyko recalled the President's remark about Soviet personnel in Cuba and said that, as Mr. Khrushchev had told Mr. Harriman,[1] there were now no Soviet troops in Cuba. The Soviet personnel now in Cuba were specialists training the Cubans in the use of arms supplied by the USSR. When this limited task was accomplished these would be withdrawn. As to what had been done in Cuba so far, there was no need to repeat that now because the President was informed on this matter. The Soviet Government was acting in Cuba on the basis of the understanding the President and Mr. Khrushchev had reached in their correspondence.[2]

The President asked how many Soviet military specialists would remain in Cuba in, say, six months.

Mr. Gromyko said that he was unable to answer this question. He preferred not to speak in terms of dates but he wished to ask the President to understand that the USSR had in Cuba only military specialists with a limited mission.

The President commented that it would be helpful if, when the specialists

[1]This was presumably during Harriman's talks in Moscow in July 1963 regarding the nuclear test-ban treaty.
[2]Namely, their correspondence at the end of the missile crisis.

were completely withdrawn, Mr. Khrushchev were to consider making a statement to that effect.

Mr. Gromyko said he would inform Mr. Khrushchev about this. However he suggested that the President take into account the difficulty of mentioning specific dates. So if Mr. Khrushchev did not mention any dates, this did not mean that specialists would stay forever.

The President said this might be so, but perhaps Mr. Khrushchev could make such a statement to one of the visiting newsmen in terms of an accomplished fact.

Mr. Gromyko said that he did not think there was any need to remind the President that Cuba was being subjected to constant pressure and provocation on the part of some forces which engaged even in such things as sending planes with bombs. The President probably knew better than he, Gromyko, who those forces were. The Soviet Government was convinced that if the US Government and the President personally wished to stop these activities, they would cease immediately.

The President said we believed we had stopped harassment by planes and had given warning, although perhaps if someone was close enough he could still fly in and drop a bomb. In any event, he did not see any benefit to the US from harassment. This would not unseat Castro and serve no useful purpose.

Mr. Gromyko commented that those air raids must be originating somewhere. If they originated outside the US, they could be stopped too, because the USSR had a high opinion of US influence in Latin America.

The President said we were not sure that the planes came from Latin America. Of two recent flights over Cuba, one has perhaps come from Central America, and some plane may have come even from Florida. We tried to stop the planes, but there were many fields in Florida, light planes were used and it was very difficult to keep them under control.

The Secretary [Rusk] recalled his remarks to Mr. Gromyko about activities in the other direction,[3] noting this made it more difficult for us to deal with this situation. He also observed that the Chinese may be involved in this matter.

Mr. Gromyko asserted that the USSR had no information about such activities. If the US regarded speeches by Castro or other Cuban leaders as subversive, then Soviet speeches about capitalism and US speeches about communism were also subversive. In any event, the USSR had no information about any subversive activities from Cuba.[4] . . .

[3]A reference to Cuban subversion in Latin America.
[4]Akalovsky drafted this memorandum.

20. Memorandum from U.S. Delegate at the UN William Attwood to Gordon Chase of the National Security Council Staff

By the autumn of 1963 the Kennedy administration was pursuing a two-track policy toward Castro. While sabotage activities against Cuba continued, an effort was under way to develop a secret dialogue with Castro, with a view to achieving some sort of accommodation between Havana and Washington. UN official William Attwood, formerly an editor of Look *magazine, was a key figure in this diplomatic endeavor. Here he recounts his role in the period from August through early November 1963.*

New York, November 8, 1963.

Following is a chronology of events leading up to Castro's invitation on October 31, to receive a U.S. official for talks in Cuba:

Soon after joining the U.S. Mission to the U.N. on August 26, I met Seydou Diallo, the Guinea Ambassador to Havana, whom I had known well in Conakry.[1] He went out of his way to tell me that Castro was isolated from contact with neutralist diplomats by his "Communist entourage" because it was known he was unhappy with Cuba's satellite status and looking for a way out. He, Diallo, had finally been able to see Castro alone once and was convinced he was personally receptive to changing courses and getting Cuba on the road to non-alignment. Diallo added that the exile raids [on Cuba] were an obstacle since they strengthened the hand of the hard-liners both with Castro and the public.

In the first week of September, I also read ABC correspondent, Lisa Howard's article, "Castro's Overture,"[2] based on her conversation with Castro last April. This article stressed Castro's expressed desire for reaching an accommodation with the United States and his willingness to make substantial concessions to this end.[3] On September 12, I talked with Miss Howard, whom I have known for some years, and she echoed Ambassador Diallo's opinion that there was a rift between Castro and the Guevara-Hart-Alveida group[4] on the question of Cuba's future course.

On September 12, I discussed this with Under Secretary Harriman in Washington. He suggested I prepare a memo and we arranged to meet in New York the following week.

On September 18, I wrote a memorandum based on these talks and on corroborating information I had heard in Conakry. In it I suggested that discreet

---

[1]Attwood had been U.S. ambassador to Guinea from March 1961 to May 1963.

[2]In *War/Peace Report*, September 1963.

[3]Cuban officials had expressed an interest in improved relations with the United States on several occasions. See Mark J. White, *The Cuban Missile Crisis* (New York, 1996), pp. 51–53.

[4]A reference to various senior Cuban political figures.

contact might be established with the Cubans at the United Nations to find out whether Castro in fact wanted to talk, and on our terms. I showed this memo to Ambassador Stevenson, who felt the matter was worth exploring quietly and who indicated he might discuss it with the President.

On September 19, I met Harriman in New York. After reading my memo, he suggested I also discuss it with the Attorney-General [Robert Kennedy] because of the political implications of the Cuban issue.

On September 20, I made an appointment with the Attorney-General in Washington. Meanwhile, Stevenson obtained the President's approval for me to make discreet contact with Dr. Lechuga, Cuba's chief delegate at the United Nations.

On September 23, I met Dr. Lechuga at Miss Howard's apartment. She has been on good terms with Lechuga since her visit with Castro and invited him for a drink to met [sic] some friends who had also been to Cuba. I was just one of those friends. In the course of our conversation, which started with recollections of my own talks with Castro in 1959, I mentioned having read Miss Howard's article. Lechuga hinted that Castro was indeed in a mood to talk, especially with someone he had met before. He thought there was a good chance that I might be invited to Cuba if I wished to resume our 1959 talk. I told him that in my present position, I would need official authorization to make such a trip, and did not know if it would be forthcoming. However, I said an exchange of views might well be useful and that I would find out and let him know.

On September 24, I saw the Attorney-General in Washington, gave him my September 18 memo, and reported my meeting with Lechuga. He said he would pass the memo on to Mr. McGeorge Bundy; meanwhile, he thought that it would be difficult for me to visit Cuba without it being known and risking the accusation that we were trying to make a deal with Castro. He wondered if it might be possible to meet Castro—if that's what he wanted—in another country, such as Mexico, or at the United Nations. Meanwhile, he agreed it would be useful to maintain contact with Lechuga. I said I would so inform Lechuga and wait to hear from him or Bundy.

Back in New York, I informed Stevenson of my talk with Lechuga and the Attorney-General.

On September 27, I ran into Lechuga at the United Nations, where he was doing a television interview in the lobby with Miss Howard. I told him that I had discussed our talk in Washington, and that it was felt that my accepting an invitation to go to Cuba would be difficult under present circumstances, especially in view of my official status. I added, however, that if Castro or a personal emissary had something to tell us, we were prepared to meet him and listen wherever else would be convenient. Lechuga said he would so inform Havana. Meanwhile, he forewarned me that he would be making a "hard" anti-U.S. speech in the United Nations on October 7. I remarked that it wouldn't help reduce tensions; he replied he couldn't help making it because of the "blockade."[5]

On October 7, in his reply to Lechuga's tough speech, Stevenson suggested

[5]Perhaps a reference to the American economic embargo on Cuba, imposed in February 1962.

that if Castro wanted peace with his neighbors, he need only do three things— stop being a Soviet stooge, stop trying to subvert other nations, and start carrying out the promises of his revolution regarding constitutional rights.

On October 18, at dinner at the home of Mrs. Eugene Meyer, I talked with Mr. C. A. Doxiades, a noted Greek architect and town-planner, who had just returned from an architects' congress in Havana, where he had talked alone to both Castro and Guevara, among others. He sought me out, as a government official, to say he was convinced Castro would welcome a normalization of relations with the United States if he could do so without losing too much face. He also said that Guevara and the other communists were opposed to any deal, and regarded Castro as dangerously unreliable; and that they would get rid of Castro if they thought they could carry on without him and retain his popular support.

On October 20, Miss Howard asked me if she might call Major Rene Vallejo, a Cuban surgeon who is also Castro's current right-hand man and confidant. She said Vallejo helped her see Castro and made it plain to her he opposed the Guevara group. They became friends and have talked on the phone several times since the interview. Miss Howard's purpose in calling him now was that she thought any message from Lechuga would not get past the foreign office, and she wanted to make certain, through Vallejo, that Castro knew there was a U.S. official available if he wanted to talk. I told her to go ahead, so long as she referred to my talk with Lechuga and made it quite plain we were not soliciting a meeting but only expressing our willingness to listen to anything they had to say. She then called Vallejo at his home. He was out and she left word for him to call her back.

On October 21, Gordon Chase called me from the White House in connection with my September 18 memo. I brought him up to date and said the ball was in their court.

On October 23, Vallejo called Miss Howard at her New York apartment. She was out of town; he left word with the maid that he would call again.

On October 28, I ran into Lechuga in the U.N. Delegates Lounge. He told me that Havana did not think sending someone to the United Nations for talks would be "useful at this time." But he hoped he and I might have some informal chats from time to time. I said it was up to him and he could call me if he felt like it. He wrote down my extension.

On October 29, Vallejo again called Miss Howard at home. He assured her, in response to her question, that Castro still felt as he did in April about improving relations with us. As to his going to the United Nations or elsewhere for such a talk, Vallejo said it was impossible for Castro to leave the country at the present time. But he said he would relay her message to Castro (that there was now a U.S. official authorized to listen to him), and would call her back soon.

On October 31, Vallejo called Miss Howard, apologizing for the delay and saying he had been out of town with Castro and "could not get to a phone from which I could call you." He said Castro would very much like to talk to the U.S. official anytime and appreciated the importance of discretion to all concerned. Castro would therefore be willing to send a plane to Mexico to pick up the official and fly him to a private airport near Veradero where Castro would talk to him alone. The plane would fly him back immediately after the talk. In this way there would be no risk of identification at Havana airport. Miss Howard said she doubted if a U.S. official could come to Cuba but perhaps he, Vallejo, could come and see the official at the U.N. or in Mexico, as Castro's personal spokesman. Vallejo replied that Castro wanted to do the talking himself but did not completely rule out this situation if there was no other way of engaging a dialogue. It was agreed Miss Howard would relay the invitation to me and call Vallejo back as soon as possible with our reply. At this point she identified me as the U.S. official. Vallejo asked for the spelling, and recalled having met me in 1959 (I do not remember him). Miss Howard got the impression that Lechuga's previous message to Havana had not reached Vallejo or Castro.

On November 1, Miss Howard reported the Vallejo call to me and I repeated it to Chase on November 4.

On November 5, I met with Bundy and Chase at the White House and informed them of the foregoing. The next day, Chase called and asked me to put it in writing.

21. Memorandum for the Record

CIA Director McCone presents an update on the situation in Cuba, and JFK and his advisers evaluate their sabotage program.

Washington, November 12, 1963, 10:30 a.m.

SUBJECT

Meeting on Policy Relating to Cuba — 10:30 a.m. — 12 Nov 63

IN ATTENDANCE

The President, Secty. McNamara, Secty. Rusk, Secty. Gilpatric, Attorney General [Robert Kennedy], Secty. Vance, General Taylor, Mr. Bundy, Secty. Johnson, Mr. McCone, Mr. Helms, Mr. FitzGerald, Mr. Shackley

McCone opened the meeting with a brief résumé of conditions in Cuba along these lines:

1. Cuba still belongs to Castro though his grip is weakening.

2. The military remain essentially loyal to Castro with some evidences of dissension and dissidents which are being exploited by CIA.

3. The internal security forces and apparatus are effective and show evidence of increasing efficiency.

4. The economy is bad and is deteriorating, causing increasing hardships to the civilian population. . . .

5. The Soviets are continuing a gradual withdrawal. No organized Soviet units appear in Cuba although they apparently provide principal manning for the SAMs. There are recent evidences of considerable rotation with between 1,000 and 2,000 new arrivals, but in balance there is a decrease.

6. Training of Cubans continues on all Soviet equipment including the SAMs. It is not clear whether the SAMs will be turned over to full Cuban control; however it is clear the Cubans will supply the majority of the operating personnel.

7. The only equipment which has been withdrawn has been the advanced C-band radar for the SAMs and certain communication equipment. No military equipment has been withdrawn. There have been some recent new arrivals of military equipment, particularly between 25 and 50 tanks.

McCone then stated that the program which had been followed for the last several months, having been approved about the first of June,[1] was integrated and interdependent one part on the other and therefore should be considered as a comprehensive program and not a number of independent actions.

FitzGerald then made a presentation.[2]

With respect to sabotage, McCone stated that no one event will particularly affect the economy. However a continuous program will have its effects on the economy and it will encourage internal sabotage by dissident people within Cuba. There have been 109 events since April which were probably internally-inspired sabotage.

The President then raised the question of the sabotage program; whether it was worthwhile and whether it would accomplish our purpose.

Secretary Rusk then spoke at considerable length, the thrust of his remarks being opposed to sabotage. He stated we should concentrate on obtaining information as to what Castro is doing with respect to other countries, particularly sending arms to Latin American countries. Rusk said we must replace Castro; we must accomplish a reduction in Soviet troops, however sabotage might result in an increase in troops. Rusk had no problem with infiltration of black teams; furthermore internal sabotage gave him no problem and the more of this, the better. In addition he strongly supported our economic efforts. However he opposed the hit-and-run sabotage tactics as being unproductive, complicating our relationships with the Soviets and also with our friends and indicated a connection between our sabotage activities and the autobahn problem.[3]

McCone observed that infiltration was difficult, internal sabotage was extremely difficult to stimulate but that external hit-and-run sabotage had the effect of automatically stimulating internal sabotage.

McNamara could see no connection between the Cuban operations and the Berlin autobahn incidents. He saw many advantages to going ahead which he advocated but ordered a careful watch.

[1]This was the sabotage program approved by JFK on June 19, 1963. See Documents 15 and 16.

[2]FitzGerald's presentation was a progress report on the six-point covert program proposed by the CIA on June 8 and endorsed by JFK eleven days later. See Documents 15 and 16.

[3]In early November the Russians had harassed traffic en route to Berlin, detaining a British and American convoy for nearly two days before allowing it to proceed down the Autobahn.

The President asked questions concerning the immediate operations, and the next one on the schedule was approved.[4] . . .

22. Memorandum for the Record Prepared by the President's Special Assistant for National Security Affairs McGeorge Bundy

A memorandum by his national security adviser indicates that JFK was interested in generating a dialogue with Castro via intermediaries, though he did not want the talks to commence in Cuba.

Washington, November 12, 1963.

I talked this afternoon with William Attwood and told him that at the President's instruction I was conveying this message orally and not by cable. I told him that the President hoped he would get in touch with Vallejo to report that it did not seem practicable to us at this stage to send an American official to Cuba and that we would prefer to begin with a visit by Vallejo to the U.S. where Attwood would be glad to see him and to listen to any messages he might bring from Castro. In particular, we would be interested in knowing whether there was any prospect of important modification in those parts of Castro's policy which are flatly unacceptable to us: namely, the three points in Ambassador Stevenson's recent speech[1] of which the central elements are (1) submission to external Communist influence, and (2) a determined campaign of subversion directed at the rest of the Hemisphere. Reversals of these policies may or may not be sufficient to produce a change in the policy of the United States, but they are certainly necessary, and without an indication of readiness to move in these directions, it is hard for us to see what could be accomplished by a visit to Cuba.

I left it to Attwood how much of this he would convey in the initial message to Vallejo, and I also gave him discretion as to how this message was to be transmitted, with the proviso that it must be clear at all times that we were not supplicants in this matter and that the initiative for exploratory conversations was coming from the Cubans. Attwood indicated to me that he expected Lisa Howard to telephone Vallejo and then probably to get on the line himself to handle the conversation along the lines stated above. Attwood will report the results of this communication and in the event that an arrangement is made for Vallejo to come to New York Attwood will come to Washington to concert a position for his use in this conversation.

[4]McCone produced this memorandum.
[1]Delivered October 7.

23. Memorandum from Gordon Chase of the National Security Council Staff to the President's Special Assistant for National Security Affairs McGeorge Bundy

On the day of John Kennedy's assassination in Dallas, William Attwood records the developments that had taken place during the final days of the Kennedy presidency regarding the attempt to hold private discussions with Cuban officials. What might be called the Attwood initiative raises the question whether relations between Washington and Havana would have improved had JFK not been assassinated.

Washington, November 25, 1963.

SUBJECT

Cuba—Bill Attwood

1. Attached is an unsolicited chronology from Bill Attwood which describes the activities of the Cuba–Attwood tie-line from November 11 to the present. Apparently, the memo was dispatched on November 22, but because of the recent events,[1] did not reach us until today.

Attachment

Memorandum From William Attwood to Gordon Chase of the National Security Council Staff

New York, November 22, 1963.

Following is an addition to my memorandum to you dated November 8, 1963:[2]

On November 11, Vallejo called Miss Howard again to reiterate their appreciation of the need for security and to say that Castro would go along with any arrangements we might want to make. He specifically suggested that a Cuban plane could come to Key West and pick up the emissary; alternatively they would agree to have him come in a U.S. plane which could land at one of several "secret airfields" near Havana. He emphasized that only Castro and himself would be present at the talks and that no one else—he specifically mentioned Guevara—would be involved. Vallejo also reiterated Castro's desire for this talk and hoped to hear our answer soon.

On November 12, Bundy called me and I reported Vallejo's message. He said this did not affect the White House decision that a preliminary talk with Vallejo

[1]Namely, the assassination of JFK in Dallas on November 22.
[2]See Document 20.

at the United Nations should be held in order to find out what Castro wanted to talk about—particularly if he was seriously interested in discussing the points cited in Stevenson's October 7 speech.[3] Bundy suggested I transmit our decision to Vallejo, stressing the fact that, since we are responding to their invitation and are not soliciting a meeting, we would like to know more about what is on Castro's mind before committing ourselves to further talks in Cuba.

On November 13, I went to Miss Howard's apartment and called Vallejo at home. There was no answer. She then sent a telegram asking that he call her at his convenience.

On November 14, Vallejo called her. She gave him my message—that we would want to talk to him here at the United Nations before accepting an invitation to go to Cuba. She said that, if he wished to confirm or discuss this further with the U.S. official, he could call him (Vallejo) at home on the evening of November 18. Vallejo said he would be there to receive the call. Meanwhile, he did not exclude the possibility of his coming to the United Nations and said he would discuss it with Castro.

On November 18, Miss Howard reached Vallejo at home and passed the phone to me. I told him Miss Howard had kept me informed of her talks with him and that I assumed he knew of our interest in hearing what Castro had in mind. Vallejo said he did, and reiterated the invitation to Cuba, stressing the fact that security could be guaranteed. I replied that we felt a preliminary meeting was essential to make sure there was something useful to talk about, and asked if he was able to come to New York. Vallejo said he could not come "at this time." However, if that's how we felt, he said that "we" would send instructions to Lechuga to propose and discuss with me "an agenda" for a later meeting with Castro. I said I would await Lechuga's call. Vallejo's manner was extremely cordial and he called me "Sir" throughout the conversation.

On November 19, I called Chase, and reported the conversation.

---

[3] If Castro wanted peaceful relations with his neighbors, Stevenson had asserted, he needed to cut ties with Moscow, end his subversive activities in Latin America, and provide basic constitutional rights for his people.

Index

Acheson, Dean G., 174, 184, 185
Act of Bogota, 22
Adenauer, Konrad, 175, 270–271
Akalovsky, Alexander A., 59
Alliance for Progress, 53, 64, 67, 68
Anderson, George W., 159, 197
Argentina, 67–68
Attwood, William, 302, 337–340, 342–344

Ball, George W.: during missile crisis, 165, 173, 179, 184, 191, 193, 217, 229, 230, 234n. 235; after missile crisis, 290, 320
Barnes, C. Tracy, 16–17, 54–55, 65, 69
Batista, Fulgencio, 25, 34, 60, 61, 117
Bay of Pigs operation, 89, 100, 182; air strikes during, 26, 28–29, 30, 31; assessed by John Kennedy, 30–31, 182, 223–224; CIA during, 4, 9, 16, 17–18, 19, 20–21, 25, 28–29, 33, 39–40; compared to Operation Mongoose, 71, 108; consequences of, 45, 65, 88, 95; John Kennedy during, 4–5, 7, 9, 10, 13, 16–17, 19–21, 22, 26, 28–29, 30–31, 33, 34–35, 37–38, 44, 50; Robert Kennedy during, 30, 33, 35–36, 37–38, 43–44; opposition to, 9, 13, 16n, 19–20, 22–24, 25. *See also*

Covert operations; Operation Mongoose.
Bell, David, 19
Berle, Adolf A., 19, 25
Berlin, 7, 58, 152, 160; as potential Soviet target, 39, 120, 140, 142, 144, 162, 173, 175, 177, 179, 191, 196, 197, 199, 200, 202, 206, 212–213, 235, 257, 306, 341
Bissell, Richard M.: during Bay of Pigs operation, 21, 26, 28, 29; during Bay of Pigs aftermath, 54–55, 65; during Operation Mongoose, 74, 98
Board of National Estimates, 136–138, 142
Bohlen, Charles E., 173–174, 175, 178, 188
Bolshakov, Georgi, 283, 295n, 297, 298n
Bowles, Chester, 22–24, 37, 43–44, 49–50
Brazil, 68, 218–219, 281
Bundy, McGeorge, 9, 306, 309, 330–331; during Bay of Pigs operation, 16–17, 28, 116; and dialogue with Castro, 338, 340, 342–344; during missile crisis, 169, 172, 178, 184, 185, 186, 189, 190, 192, 219, 220, 230–231, 233, 244; during Operation Mongoose, 135, 140, 157, 166n, 171
Bundy, William P., 21

A NOTE ON THE AUTHOR

Mark J. White is Lecturer in American History at Queen Mary and Westfield College, University of London. He was born in Holbrook, England, and studied at the University of Nottingham, the University of Wisconsin, Milwaukee, and Rutgers University, where he received a Ph.D. in history. He has written widely on American foreign policy and is the author of *Missiles in Cuba* and *The Cuban Missile Crisis*, and editor of *Kennedy: The New Frontier Revisited*.